# Pro ODP .NET for Oracle Database 11g

**Edmund Zehoo**

**Apress®**

**Pro ODP .NET for Oracle Database 11g**

Copyright © 2010 by Edmund Zehoo

ISBN-13 (pbk): 978-1-4302-2820-2

ISBN-13 (electronic): 978-1-4302-2821-9

Printed and bound in the United States of America 9 8 7 6 5 4 3 2 1

President and Publisher: Paul Manning
Lead Editor: Jonathan Gennick
Technical Reviewer: Stephanie Lim
Editorial Board: Clay Andres, Steve Anglin, Mark Beckner, Ewan Buckingham, Gary Cornell, Jonathan Gennick, Jonathan Hassell, Michelle Lowman, Matthew Moodie, Duncan Parkes, Jeffrey Pepper, Frank Pohlmann, Douglas Pundick, Ben Renow-Clarke, Dominic Shakeshaft, Matt Wade, Tom Welsh
Coordinating Editor: Anita Castro
Copy Editor: Heather Lang
Compositor: Bytheway Publishing Services
Indexer: Toma Mulligan
Artist: April Milne
Cover Designer: Anna Ishchenko

Distributed to the book trade worldwide by Springer-Verlag New York, Inc., 233 Spring Street, 6th Floor, New York, NY 10013. Phone 1-800-SPRINGER, fax 201-348-4505, e-mail orders-ny@springer-sbm.com, or visit www.springeronline.com.

For information on translations, please e-mail rights@apress.com, or visit www.apress.com.

Apress and friends of ED books may be purchased in bulk for academic, corporate, or promotional use. eBook versions and licenses are also available for most titles. For more information, reference our Special Bulk Sales–eBook Licensing web page at www.apress.com/info/bulksales.

The source code for this book is available to readers at http://www.apress.com. You will need to answer questions pertaining to this book in order to successfully download the code.

*To my family,*
*for you are truly all I have.*

# Contents at a Glance

# Contents

# About the Author

 **Edmund Tan Zehoo** is the Chief Technical Officer of an e-forms and workflows solution vendor based in Singapore. He took the role of lead architect in the design of several workflow products, one of the most popular being the Quickflows product. He has also spent the last eight years building performance critical .NET e-forms and workflows solutions hosted on top of Oracle databases for large companies and governmental institutions in Singapore.

Edmund is a frequent speaker at various workflow conferences held in Singapore and Malaysia, and continually preaches about the synergistic power of using Oracle with the .NET framework. During his free time he can often be found engaging in his favourite pastime exploring the innerworkings of the brain and mind, with the ultimate goal of writing intelligent software to emulate the behavior of the mind. He is also an avid believer in the Technological Singularity.

# About the Technical Reviewer

**Stephanie Lim** is an accomplished .NET developer who has worked on major Oracle database projects in Indonesia, Singapore and Malaysia. She is well versed with ODP.NET and can often be found programming on her laptop in her free time. When not programming, she enjoys making handcrafts and a good bed-time novel. She also somehow manages to find time for her Schnoodle "Sticky" after work.

# Acknowledgments

This book is the result of the combined efforts of a team of wonderful people I've had the pleasure of working with. I'll start with a special word of thanks to my editor Jonathan Gennick - thanks for giving this author halfway around the world a chance. Your encouraging remarks and insightful edits constantly remind me that authoring a book can indeed be so much fun.

My heartfelt gratitude also goes out to Anita Castro for her timekeeping and the always cheerful e-mails, Heather Lang for making me sound so much better in print, Dominic Shakeshaft and the Apress editorial board for giving me a shot at this book, and all the other Apress team members who've contributed to this book.

I also thank my good friend Greg Yap for his code contributions and his scrutinizing eye on my every sentence in the book, and also Hui Shen for her great (and sometimes tough) reviews.

Last and definitely not least, I have a small but fiercely-loving family that I would like to individually thank - my mom and late dad for being the greatest parents one could ever hope for, my late godmother for instilling the bookworm in me, my brother and sister for their silly jokes and the two persons who've suffered most during this project – my wife and daughter who've had to put up without a husband and father for 8 months – thank you for being the understanding family I knew you'd be.

# CHAPTER 1

■■■

# Introduction to Oracle .NET Connectivity

The release of Oracle Database 11g, and more recently, revision R2 offers up a trove of advanced Oracle database functionality ranging from features like database change notifications to performance boosts like query result caching. As new features are added, the functionality you could achieve with the database increased manifold, but what you, as a .NET developer, could do using Microsoft's ADO.NET and OLEDB.NET technologies were still quite limited. Without native access to the database, NET developers could not tap onto many of these Oracle-specific features that would otherwise allow them to fine-tune data access performance. To many, it was like being in a racecar stuck in first gear.

Fortunately, both Microsoft and Oracle have released providers that enable .NET developers to write applications that are more tightly integrated with the Oracle database. Microsoft released the .NET Managed Provider for Oracle, and Oracle released the Oracle Data Provider for .NET (ODP.NET). These data providers were different from the rest in that they communicated directly with the native Oracle Call Interface (OCI) application programmer interface (API) and exposed a larger set of the native functionality in Oracle.

---

■ **Note**: The OCI is Oracle's native interface—the most direct method to talk to an Oracle database. Calls made via other interfaces such as JDBC, ADO.NET, and even ODP.NET all translate into OCI calls. Even Oracle's own management tools ultimately depend on the OCI. Thus, the OCI can be relied on to expose all possible functionality in Oracle.

---

With Microsoft's .NET Managed Provider for Oracle recently deprecated, .NET developers are now turning to ODP.NET, the managed provider from Oracle that offers exceptional performance and yet exposes all the advanced Oracle functionality you need to create compelling applications.

This first chapter aims to introduce to you the ODP.NET library. It also takes a look at Oracle connectivity in general (from managed and unmanaged code) using the other data access methods available and provides an overview of how they measure up to each other in terms of performance. You will learn the following:

- A breakdown of the Oracle suite of products
- The main differences between Oracle 11g and SQL Server 2008

- The various managed and unmanaged providers used to connect to an Oracle database and how they differ architecturally and in terms of performance

# Making the Transition from SQL Server to Oracle

If you're one of those moving from Microsoft SQL Server to Oracle, you're probably curious about what their differences are and what those would mean to you as a .NET developer. Although there are still some major feature differences between the latest versions of these two databases, the recently released Microsoft SQL Server 2008 has been a large step toward achieving the range of functionality available in Oracle 11g. For instance, Microsoft has introduced Transparent Data Encryption (a technology that encrypts the database without requiring any additional code to be written) with SQL Server 2008, a feature that also exists in Oracle 11g.

The biggest change in moving to Oracle would be the SQL dialect that is used to query the database. Oracle uses its own dialect called PL/SQL, and at times, that can be drastically different from T-SQL in SQL Server. Even in its simplest form, there are still many tiny SQL differences to watch out for when writing SQL statements and stored procedures on Oracle. For instance, Oracle uses the double quotation mark to handle whitespace in table column names while SQL Server uses the square brackets. Listing 1-1 shows the difference. The PL/SQL language itself would fill up an entire book on its own and will not be covered in this book. To maximize your usage of ODP.NET, it is recommended to at least familiarize yourself with the basics of PL/SQL.

*Listing 1-1. SQL Syntax Difference Between SQL Server and Oracle*

**SQL SERVER**
```
SELECT [Full Price] FROM [Global Products]
```

**ORACLE**
```
SELECT "Full Price" FROM "Global Products"
```

Another difference to note is that Oracle provides numerous advanced data types and cursors that can boost query performances if used correctly. For instance, Oracle provides the **LOB** data types that perform faster than the standard **LONG** data types used for storing large objects. We will cover more ground on accessing these data types via ODP.NET in the later chapters of this book.

There are, of course, many other differences between these two databases from a database administrator's point of view, but we will only account for the major differences that affect .NET development. This list is briefly summarized in Table 1-1.

*Table 1-1. Major Differences Between Oracle and SQL Server*

| Oracle | Microsoft SQL Server |
|---|---|
| Supports most known platforms including Windows-based platforms and AIX-based and HP-UX–based systems | Supports only Windows-based platforms |
| Provides the PL/SQL language, which is more powerful than T-SQL. For example, PL/SQL | Provides the T-SQL language |

| supports the usage of arrays (called associative arrays), nested tables as well as Java methods in its declaration | |
| Enables the developer to control the client result cache (an area of client-side memory allocated to cache query results to fine-tune performance | No equivalent functionality available |
| Provides push database change notifications that can raise events directly in .NET code | No equivalent functionality available |
| Supports the use of **REF** cursors that allow the developer to reference a result set directly in memory, thereby optimizing data retrieval | No equivalent functionality available |
| Supports collection data types such as **VARRAY** tables and nested data tables as column data types | No equivalent functionality available |
| Message queuing is achieved at the database level through Oracle Advanced Queuing | The closest equivalent is Microsoft Messaging Queue Server (MSMQ), which is an entirely different product and not implemented at the database level. |

# Introducing Oracle Connectivity

The Oracle database has seen many revisions since its inception and has grown into a fairly complicated (but powerful) database product. There are at least five different ways to access the database from unmanaged code and another six ways to access it from managed code!

In my conversations with developers starting out in Oracle development, the most frequent question I hear is, "Which data access provider yields the best performance?" My take on this question has always been that you should look not just at performance alone but also the accessible feature set of the database. You also need to consider how generic your data tier code needs to be in your application, because some providers, like the Oracle Objects for OLE (OO4O) provider, do not use ADO/ADO.NET but instead use a proprietary set of classes to access the database. In short, it all depends on what you need for your project.

As an example, if you needed to receive Oracle database change notifications in your project, you would be better off using ODP.NET instead of OLEDB.NET. And if your legacy Visual Basic 6 (VB6) project only ever needed to use Oracle but had to run at the fastest speed possible, OO4O would be a good choice.

With all the different terminology and providers from both Microsoft and Oracle, it's easy to confuse the various providers available, or worse, choose the wrong one in your project only to realize its limitations midway during development.

The following sections list all the data providers (managed and unmanaged) available to you and explain their performance and feature set differences. They also explain how these data providers are architecturally arranged in the data access stack.

■ **Note** There are also popular third-party data providers offered by other companies such as dotConnect for Oracle; we will not focus on these third party providers in this book.

# Accessing Oracle from Unmanaged Code

Before the advent of the .NET platform, programmers would use the Microsoft Active Data Objects (ADO) libraries to connect to the database. Microsoft ADO is part of the Microsoft Data Access Components (MDAC) package and allows developers to connect to Oracle databases through either Object Linking and Embedding, Database (OLEDB) or Open Database Connectivity (ODBC).

OLEDB is faster than ODBC because there are fewer layers in between the OLEDB provider and the native Oracle Call Interface (OCI) API. To use ODBC, the ADO application would have to use an OLEDB-to-ODBC bridge to translate OLEDB requests into ODBC requests. This contributes to a performance detriment when using ODBC with ADO. In fact, using OLEDB for data access yields a more stable environment compared to ODBC for the same reason.

There is also a third option that produces the fastest performance for data access—the Oracle Objects for OLE (OO4O) library, which is a suite of Component Object Model (COM) components that allows native access to an Oracle database without the use of ADO. The three data access methods can be visually summarized as shown in Figure 1-1.

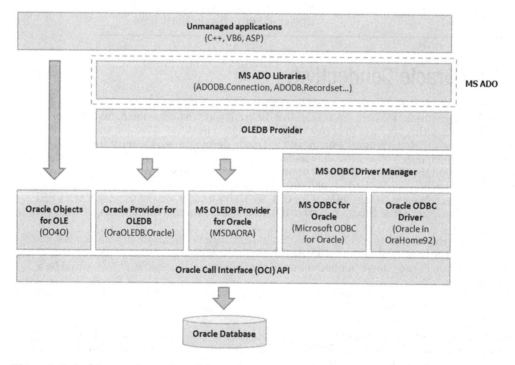

*Figure 1-1. Architectural overview of the various providers available to unmanaged code*

# Using OLEDB in Unmanaged Code

OLEDB is an open standard developed by Microsoft that is basically a generic set of COM interfaces that define data access to a variety of data sources. The concept of OLEDB is straightforward: the provider implements these COM interfaces and provides, for example, the functionality of retrieving data into a table, which is then returned to the consumer.

There are numerous OLEDB providers out there; typically, most databases would have an OLEDB driver written specifically for it so that developers can gain access to them. For instance, Oracle provides the Oracle provider for OLEDB driver to access Oracle databases, and Microsoft provides the Microsoft SQL Server provider to access Microsoft SQL Server databases.

OLEDB technology is versatile enough in that it is able to retrieve data from even nondatabase data sources as long as an OLEDB provider is written for it. An example of this is the Microsoft Jet OLEDB provider, which is able to retrieve and store data from a Microsoft Excel file using OLEDB.

## Oracle Provider for OLEDB

The Oracle Provider for OLEDB (OraOLEDB) is Oracle's de facto standard OLEDB provider for the Oracle database. Compared to the Microsoft OLEDB provider for Oracle (at the same level), it provides reasonably higher performance because certain features of the OraOLEDB provider are exposed to the developer. For instance, OraOLEDB supports returning more than one rowset from a stored procedure. When used correctly, this feature can significantly reduce the number of data fetches required and lead to better performance.

OraOLEDB also supports some Oracle-specific features, such as those in Oracle's grid feature set. It also supports Oracle-specific data types such as the **LOB** data types, binding **NCHAR** parameters with SQL statements, and enhanced failover capability.

A connection to an Oracle database can be easily established with OraOLEDB using a connection string that looks something like that in Listing 1-2.

*Listing 1-2. Data Retrieval Code Sample in Visual Basic using OraOLEDB and ADO*

```
strConn = "Provider=OraOLEDB.Oracle;Data Source=TEST;User Id=edzehoo;Password=admin123;"
Set OraConnection = CreateObject("ADODB.Connection")
OraConnection.Open(strConn)
Set OraResultset = Server.CreateObject("ADODB.Recordset")
OraResultset.Open "SELECT Price FROM Products", OraConnection

Do While(OraResultset.EOF = false)
        Msgbox OraResultset.Fields("Price")
        OraResultset.MoveNext
Loop
OraResultset.Close()
OraConnection.Close()
```

The OraOLEDB provider continues to receive sustained support from Oracle and has gone through many releases. At the time of this writing, the latest version of OraOLEDB released is version 11.1.0.6.20.

■ **Note** There is also a 64-bit version of the Oracle Provider for OLEDB (OraOLEDB), which natively supports 64-bit Windows (x64 and Itanium) available to OLEDB developers.

## MS OLEDB Provider for Oracle

The Microsoft OLEDB Provider for Oracle (MSDAORA) is Microsoft's architectural equivalent of the OraOLEDB provider. It only supports Oracle database versions up to 7*i*, with limited support for version 8*i*.

■ **Note** MSDAORA has been deprecated because it uses OCI version 7.0, which is no longer supported by Oracle.

# Using ODBC in Unmanaged Code

ODBC is a standard data access protocol created by Microsoft that allows users to connect to various relational or nonrelational data sources in heterogeneous systems. ODBC consists of two components: the ODBC client (which is any application that uses ODBC to access a data source) and the ODBC driver (similar to the concept of an OLEDB provider, the ODBC driver is an ODBC implementation of a specific data source).

The ODBC client sends commands (based on the ODBC protocol) to the desired ODBC driver, which then translates these commands into underlying calls that the database can understand. This translation is done by the ODBC driver on the client side before the command is sent to the database server.

## Oracle ODBC Driver

The Oracle ODBC driver underperforms the Oracle provider for OLEDB. As explained earlier, the ODBC driver has to additionally translate requests to the native query language of the database. This translation incurs a performance overhead on all ODBC requests, leading to reduced overall performance compared to OLEDB.

You can utilize an ODBC driver by defining it in the connection string and letting ADO do the rest. The code in Listing 1-3 demonstrates how this can be done.

*Listing 1-3. Data Retrieval Code Sample in Visual Basic Using the Oracle ODBC Driver and ADO*

```
strConn = "Driver={Oracle in OraHome92};Dbq=TEST_TNS;Uid=edzehoo;Pwd=admin123;"
Set OraConnection = CreateObject("ADODB.Connection")
OraConnection.Open(strConn)
Set OraResultset = Server.CreateObject("ADODB.Recordset")
OraResultset.Open "SELECT Price FROM Products", OraConnection
```

```
Do While(OraResultset.EOF = false)
        Msgbox OraResultset.Fields("Price")
        OraResultset.MoveNext
Loop
OraResultset.Close()
OraConnection.Close()
```

## Microsoft ODBC for Oracle

Microsoft ODBC for Oracle is an ODBC implementation for access to Oracle databases. Like the Microsoft OLE DB provider for Oracle, it only supports Oracle database versions up to 7x, with limited support for Oracle 8x. It uses a connection string that looks like the following sample:

```
Driver={Microsoft ODBC for Oracle};Server=TEST;Uid=edzehoo;Pwd=admin123;
```

---

■ **Note** Microsoft ODBC for Oracle has also been deprecated due to its dependency on the OCI version 7.0.

---

# Using OO4O in Unmanaged Code

OO4O is a library of COM components that provide data access to Oracle databases. It is a native driver that entirely bypasses the ADO, OLEDB, and ODBC stack. Because of this, OO4O has its own set of proprietary methods to access the database. Consider the sample code in Listing 1-4 that connects to an Oracle database using OO4O.

*Listing 1-4. Data Retrieval Code Sample in Visual Basic Using OO4O*

```
Set OraSession = CreateObject("OracleInProcServer.XOraSession")
Set OraDatabase = OraSession.DbOpenDatabase("TEST", "edzehoo/admin123", O&)
Set OraDynaset = OraDatabase.DbCreateDynaset("SELECT Price FROM Products", O&)

Do While(OraDynaset.EOF = false)
        Msgbox OraDynaset.Fields("Price")
        OraDynaset.MoveNext
Loop
OraDynaset.Close()
OraSession.Close()
```

OO4O also provides the fastest performance of all the methods used to access the database from unmanaged code. This is due to OO4O being a purely native driver. OO4O also supports a large range of Oracle-specific functionality, of which the major ones follow:

- Transparent Oracle grid support
- Support for advanced Oracle data types such as **REF** cursors, **LOB**s, and nested tables
- Support for Advanced Queuing (AQ) feature (Oracle's message queuing facility)

- Support for database events (for example, receiving notifications when someone inserts a record in a table)
- XML support

OO4O has also seen new releases for each major Oracle database version and continues to be a part of the Oracle Data Access Components (ODAC) product family. It currently stands at version 11.1.0.6.20 as of the time of writing.

# Accessing Oracle from Managed Code

There are a number of ways for managed .NET code to connect to Oracle. In managed code, users can still connect to the database using the unmanaged OLEDB or ODBC providers. This interoperability is achieved through the OLEDB.NET and ODBC.NET data access bridges provided by Microsoft. Microsoft provides the ADO.NET libraries, which provide a programming interface for developers to access OLEDB.NET and ODBC.NET data sources.

The ODP.NET provider from Oracle, which is the focus of this book, offers yet another way for managed code to connect to Oracle. In the following sections, we take a look at how these various providers work.

## Using OLEDB.NET in Managed Code

OLEDB.NET is simply a data access bridge to OLEDB. It provides interoperability between the managed .NET layer and the unmanaged COM OLEDB providers. The underlying providers used are same as the ones used by unmanaged code (OraOLEDB.Oracle and MSDAORA). Figure 1-2 illustrates the architecture.

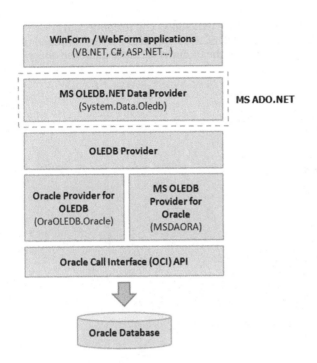

*Figure 1-2. Architectural overview of the OLEDB.NET provider*

The snippet of code in Listing 1-5 connects to an Oracle database via OLEDB.NET and retrieves some data. It gives a good example of how to use OLEDB.NET.

*Listing 1-5. Data Retrieval Code Sample in VB.NET Using OLEDB.NET*

```
strConn = "Provider=OraOLEDB.Oracle;Data Source=TEST;User Id=edzehoo;Password=admin123;"
OraConnection = New OleDb.OleDbConnection(strConn)
OraConnection.Open()
OraCommand = New OleDb.OleDbCommand("SELECT Price FROM Products", OraConnection)
OraReader = OraCommand.ExecuteReader()
Do While OraReader.Read
        MsgBox(OraReader.GetInt32(OraReader.GetOrdinal("Price")))
Loop
OraReader.Close()
OraConnection.Close()
```

## Using ODBC.NET in Managed Code

Like OLEDB.NET, ODBC.NET is also a data access bridge to its unmanaged COM equivalent (that is, ODBC). Figure 1-3 shows the architecture.

In managed code, .NET provides the **System.Data.Odbc** namespace that allows you to connect to an ODBC driver directly without going through OLEDB. However, ODBC.NET still runs slower compared to OLEDB.NET for the same reason; it needs to translate requests to the underlying native database query language.

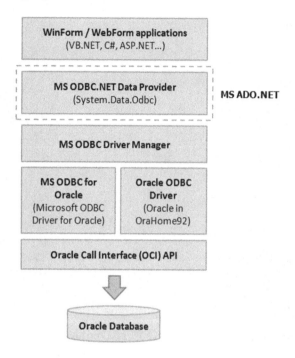

***Figure 1-3.*** *Architectural overview of the ODBC.NET provider*

The snippet of code in Listing 1-6 gives an example of using ODBC.NET. The code connects to an ODBC data source and retrieves some data from the Oracle database.

*Listing 1-6. Data Retrieval Code Sample in VB.NET Using ODBC.NET*

```
strConn = "Driver={Oracle in OraHome92};Dbq=TEST_TNS;Uid=edzehoo;Pwd=admin123;"
OraConnection = New Odbc.OdbcConnection(strConn)
OraConnection.Open()
OraCommand = New Odbc.OdbcCommand("SELECT Price FROM Products", OraConnection)
OraReader = OraCommand.ExecuteReader()
Do While OraReader.Read
        MsgBox(OraReader.GetInt32(OraReader.GetOrdinal("Price")))
Loop
OraReader.Close()
OraConnection.Close()
```

## Using the Microsoft .NET Managed Provider for Oracle

The Microsoft.NET Managed Provider for Oracle is a provider built by Microsoft on top of the OCI API. It sits in the call stack as shown in Figure 1-4. It is the closest equivalent to Oracle's ODP.NET provider.

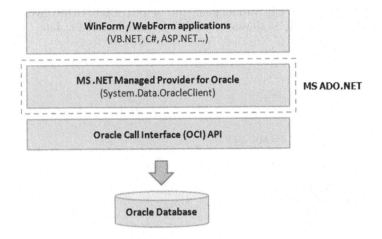

*Figure 1-4. Architectural overview of the Microsoft .NET Managed Provider for Oracle*

---

■ **Note** The Microsoft ADO.NET team has deprecated the Microsoft .NET Managed Provider for Oracle as of June 2009. The provider will still be available in .NET Framework 4 to support backward compatibility but will be labeled as deprecated.

---

# Introducing ODP.NET

The Oracle Data Provider for .NET (ODP.NET) developed by Oracle is the preferred way to connect to an Oracle database from managed code. It works with ADO.NET to provide fast and efficient access to the database. Among all the other managed providers, it is also one of the most powerful in terms of performance and Oracle feature set accessibility.

Unlike ODBC.NET and OLEDB.NET, ODP.NET does not depend on any data access bridge. It bypasses the OLEDB and ODBC layers entirely and, in doing so, is not limited by the generic interfaces required of ODBC or OLEDB-compliant providers. ODP.NET therefore has the advantage (over the other providers) of being able to natively access advanced Oracle database functionality such as XML databases, **REF** cursors and Real Application Clusters (running a single database across a cluster of servers).

11

# Understanding the ODP.NET Architecture

ODP.NET calls the OCI directly. As mentioned earlier, the OCI is a low-level API that allows the provider to access native Oracle functionality. It also provides a set of methods to control the execution of SQL statements in the Oracle database engine.

The fact that ODP.NET accesses the OCI layer directly without going through OLEDB or ODBC gives it a performance edge over the other providers. Figure 1-5 shows how ODP.NET is laid out in the data access stack.

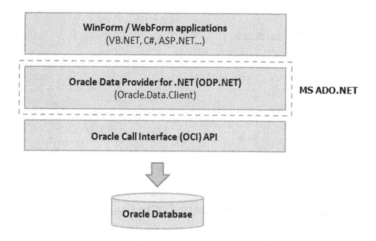

*Figure 1-5. Architectural overview of the ODP.NET provider*

# Understanding the ODP.NET Classes

ODP.NET uses the namespace **Oracle.Data.Client**. It inherits from the ADO.NET base classes and therefore provides a set of data access classes, methods, and properties familiar to the .NET/SQL Server developer. There is very little difference between code used to access Oracle via ODP.NET and code used to access Microsoft SQL Server via the .NET Framework Data Provider for SQL Server. For instance, consider the comparison of classes between these two providers as shown in Table 1-2.

*Table 1-2. A Comparison of Classes in Oracle.DataAccess.Client and System.Data.SqlClient*

| Oracle.DataAccess.Client | System.Data.SqlClient |
|---|---|
| OracleConnection | SqlConnection |
| OracleCommand | SqlCommand |
| OracleCommandBuilder | SqlCommandBuilder |
| OracleParameter | SqlParameter |

| | |
|---|---|
| OracleDataAdapter | SqlDataAdapter |
| OracleDataReader | SqlDataReader |
| OracleDependency | SqlDependency |
| OracleError | SqlError |
| OracleException | SqlException |
| OracleTransaction | SqlTransaction |

The **OracleConnection** class, for example, provides the developer a set of methods to connect to the Oracle database. The **OracleCommand** class allows the developer to set up an SQL statement or stored procedure to execute. Finally, the **OracleDataAdapter** class allows ODP.NET to fill an ADO.NET dataset object with data.

## Accessing Data using ODP.NET

Accessing data in ODP.NET is straightforward process. The code snippet in Listing 1-7 shows how this can be done.

*Listing 1-7. Data Retrieval Code Sample in VB.NET Using ODP.NET*

```
strConn = "Data Source=TEST;User Id=edzehoo;Password=admin123;"
OraConnection = New OracleConnection(strConn)
OraConnection.Open()
OraCommand = New OracleCommand("SELECT Price FROM Products", OraConnection)
OraReader = OraCommand.ExecuteReader()
Do While OraReader.Read
        MsgBox(OraReader.GetInt32(OraReader.GetOrdinal("Price")))
Loop
OraReader.Close()
OraConnection.Close()
```

## Using ODP.NET in ASP.NET Projects

The ASP.NET language supports the use of various providers (not to be confused with database providers) to supply common web application functionality. For example, ASP.NET ships with a default membership provider, which uses an SQL Server-based database to globally store and register web application users. Another example is the default session state provider, which uses a SQL Server–based database to store session state data.

Fortunately for us, the ASP.NET language also supports the use of custom providers, which allow developers to create their own custom ASP.NET providers to store and handle web data. Through custom providers, developers can, for instance, create a custom session state provider that stores and retrieves session state data to and from an entirely different data source such as MySQL or even a flat file.

The latest release of ODP.NET features a suite of ASP.NET providers specifically created for the Oracle database, collectively referred to as the Oracle Providers for ASP.NET. Table 1-3 lists the various ASP.NET providers and describes what they do.

**Table 1-3.** *The Oracle Providers for ASP.NET*

| Provider Name | Description |
| --- | --- |
| Oracle Membership | This membership provider provides functionality to manage (create, edit, and delete) users, retrieve users, verify login credentials, reset passwords, and handle other user-management–related tasks. |
| Oracle Role | This role provider implements the functionality of managing (creating, editing, and deleting) roles, retrieving roles, checking the list of users in a role, and handling other role-management–related tasks. |
| Oracle Profile | This provider enables the ASP.NET application to store and retrieve individual user profile information to and from an Oracle database. |
| Oracle Site Map | This provider retrieves site map information from an Oracle database and builds a tree of SiteMapNode objects. It also implements the functions that allow the ASP.NET application to find and retrieve nodes from this tree. |
| Oracle Session State | This provider allows the ASP.NET application to store and retrieve session state to and from an Oracle database. |
| Oracle Web Event | This provider processes ASP.NET health events and stores them in the Oracle database. |
| Oracle Web Parts Personalization | Web Parts is a Microsoft technology that enables the end user to modify the content and layout of web pages directly in the browser. This sort of personalization data is usually stored in a database. The Oracle Web Parts Personalization provider allows |

|  | the ASP.NET application to store and retrieve personalization data to and from the Oracle database. |
|---|---|
| Oracle Cache Dependency | This provider automatically invalidates cache data created by the ASP.NET application when there are changes in the underlying Oracle database. This provider helps improve ASP.NET application performance by keeping database data in the cache as long as possible and performing a fetch only when the data has been invalidated. |

## Considering ODP.NET Performance

ODP.NET provides superior performance over the other providers, because it is native to the .NET Framework and data does not have to travel through additional layers between the application and the Oracle database. In ODBC.NET, for example, performance costs are incurred when ODBC data types have to be mapped to Oracle data types and vice versa. We talked about this performance advantage earlier.

ODP.NET also supports a myriad of features that can be used to tune performance, such as connection pooling, the ability to control the fetch size, statement caching (with bind variables), associative arrays, parameter array binding, and so on, most of which are not accessible through OLEDB.NET and ODBC.NET.

ODP.NET also supports manipulation of native Oracle data types such as **LOB**s and **REF** cursors, both of which can lead to better performance.

You will explore all of these performance optimization techniques in detail in Chapter 12.

---

■ **Note**  Beginning version 10.2.0.3, ODP.NET provides support for 64-bit .NET applications on both the Windows x64 and Windows Itanium operating systems. ODP.NET also provides native 64-bit versions of the data access drivers on both platforms.

---

# Introducing the Oracle Suite of Products

Throughout this book, you will be using these three product suites from Oracle:

- Oracle Database 11g Release 2 (R2)
- Oracle Data Access Components (ODAC) 11g
- Oracle Developer Tools (ODT.NET) for Visual Studio

It's a good idea to know what you're installing in your machine, so let's take a brief look, in Table 1-4, at the various components in Oracle's product portfolio that are relevant to this book.

*Table 1-4. A Breakdown of the Oracle Suite of Products*

| Product Name | Description |
|---|---|
| Oracle Database 11*g* R2 | This is the main Oracle 11g Database Management System (DBMS). It contains the Oracle database engine and a set of administrative tools. |
| Oracle Data Access Components (ODAC) 11*g* | The ODAC suite contains all the Oracle data access providers, including ODP.NET. |
| Oracle Providers for ASP.NET | The Oracle providers for ASP.NET include the eight ASP.NET providers in Listing 1-2. |
| Oracle Data Provider for .NET 2.0 | This is the ODP.NET provider for the .NET 2.0 framework. |
| Oracle Data Provider for .NET 1.x | This is the ODP.NET provider for the .NET 1.x framework. |
| Oracle Database Extensions for .NET 2.0 | Oracle Database Extensions allow developers to create, run, and deploy stored procedures written in the .NET 2.x framework. |
| Oracle Database Extensions for .NET 1.x | This performs the same functionality as the preceding product, but for the .NET 1.x framework. |
| Oracle Provider for OLEDB | This is the OraOLEDB.Oracle provider for Oracle 11g. |
| Oracle Objects for OLE | This is the OO4O provider for Oracle 11g. |
| Oracle ODBC Driver | This is the OraHome 92 driver for Oracle 11g. |
| Oracle Services for Microsoft Transaction Server | This component provides strong integration between the Oracle database and Microsoft Transaction Server to provide distributed transaction support |
| Oracle SQL*Plus | Oracle SQL*Plus is a command-line PL/SQL tool that allows you to run SQL queries against the Oracle database. |

| | |
|---|---|
| Oracle Instant Client | The Oracle Instant Client is a redistributable package that contains the minimal set of files required to run your applications without having to install the full Oracle client. |
| Oracle Developer Tools (ODT.NET) for Visual Studio | The ODT.NET for Visual Studio is a Microsoft Visual Studio 2003/2005/2008 add-in that provides a set of powerful tools to the .NET developer, such as an integrated PL/SQL debugger and an AQ designer. ODT.NET will be covered in further detail in Chapters 14 and 15 of this book. |

# Summary

In this chapter, we've taken a look at the various technologies available that allow you to access data in Oracle 11*g*. The following are the Object Linking and Embedding, Database (OLEDB) and Open Database Connectivity (ODBC) providers accessible to both managed and unmanaged applications:

- Oracle Provider for OLEDB (OraOLEDB.Oracle)
- MS OLEDB Provider for Oracle (MSDAORA)
- MS ODBC For Oracle
- Oracle ODBC Driver

Unmanaged applications can utilize ADO to access these providers, while managed applications can utilize ADO.NET.

Unmanaged applications can optionally use Oracle Objects for OLE (OO4O), the best-performing unmanaged provider for data access. The equivalent for managed applications is the Oracle Data Provider (ODP.NET).

In the next chapter, we will take an in-depth look at the features provided in each major release of ODP.NET. I will also walk you through the installation of the core Oracle components necessary for you to get started on writing your first ODP.NET application!

**C H A P T E R 2**

■ ■ ■

# ODP.NET: A Functional Overview

You can almost always tell the maturity of a product by looking at the number of iterations it has undergone. A serious product offering usually receives consistent product updates and enhancements throughout its lifespan. ODP.NET is one such product, having had a steady number of releases (roughly ten iterations) since its inception. This chapter aims to provide you an overview of the new features in each of the three major versions of ODP.NET (versions 9, 10, and 11) and how they can help you write .NET applications that work better with the Oracle database. At the end of this chapter, I will also walk you through the process of installing the Oracle database server as well as the other components required for you to start writing ODP.NET applications.

If you're reading this book, chances are you're either a seasoned Oracle developer moving to the .NET platform or a .NET programmer phasing from Microsoft SQL Server to the Oracle world. Regardless of which camp you fall into, this chapter will give you an in-depth view of some of the underlying concepts in the Oracle database. In this chapter, you will learn about the following:

- The new features and enhancements in each major release of ODP.NET
- How these features and enhancements can be applied to real world scenarios
- How to install Oracle Database 11*g*, ODAC.NET, ODT.NET, and Oracle providers for ASP.NET

## Exploring Oracle Features Accessible in ODP.NET Version 9

The first major release for ODP.NET was version 9. It was developed to work specifically with the Oracle 9*i* client.

---

■ **Note** The ODP.NET version you should use depends on the version of the Oracle client, not the version of the Oracle database server. For example, you should use ODP.NET version 10 with the Oracle 10*i* Client and ODP.NET version 11 with the Oracle 11*g* client. Additionally, since you can connect the Oracle 9*i* Client to an 8*i* database server, you can also technically use ODP.NET version 9 on an 8*i* database server.

---

The introduction of ODP.NET gave .NET developers the ability to communicate with Oracle directly through the OCI, a native C API for the Oracle database. The following sections describe key features supported by this version of ODP.NET.

# Manipulating XML

As data become increasingly complex and semistructured, there is a growing requirement among a wide range of industries to store and access it natively in a semistructured format.

---

■ **Note** Semistructured data is a type of structured data that does not conform to the relational (tuple and column) structure of a database but uses tags or markers to semantically organize information. HTML is an example of semistructured data. HTML tags impart organization to the data; they describe links, images, tables, subtables, and so on.

---

Developers have always tried to represent hierarchically structured data in relational databases by defining relationships among master and child tables, but such relationships become impractical when data relationships reach a certain complexity.

Take a car manufacturer for example. Any particular unit of car manufactured will consist of an engine, which may be composed of multiple engine cylinders, and each cylinder, in turn, may be composed of pistons, spark plugs, valves, crankshafts, and so on. Trying to represent these relationships in a relational database can be messy and imposes on the developer extra effort to maintain these relationships in the database and its code. There is thus a need to represent this data in a better way.

XML fits this requirement perfectly—it is able to provide a model to define content and metadata of any complexity. Under the stewardship of the W3C, XML, a vendor-neutral format has also since become the de facto standard for information interchange among businesses. As a result, developers are always on the lookout for ways to reduce their development cycles by manipulating and storing XML data directly in the database.

Oracle has provided XML support for years, since the release of Oracle 9*i*. It provides high-performance native XML storage and retrieval capability in the database and supports XML standards like XQuery, XSLT, and so on. ODP.NET exposes all this functionality to the .NET developer through a set of XML-specific classes.

# Manipulating LOBs

As you probably know, the Oracle database supports structured data (relational data that can be structurally stored in rows in a table). You've then read that Oracle can also provide support for semistructured data through Oracle's native XML data types. We now come to the last type of data that can be stored in the Oracle database—unstructured data.

Unstructured data is simply data with no specific structure. Binary files, images, and so on are good examples of unstructured data, or flat binary data.

The Large Object (**LOB**) data type in Oracle allows you to store unstructured data up to 4GB in size in each **LOB** field. The **LOB** data types in Oracle are analogous to the **BINARY** and **TEXT** data types in Microsoft SQL Server. There are a few different types of **LOB**s to handle the different types of unstructured data:

- **BLOB**: Stores binary data
- **CLOB**: Stores character data
- **NCLOB**: Stores multibyte character data
- **BFILE**: Stores binary data in an external file

ODP.NET provides a special set of classes for you to manipulate **LOB** objects in the Oracle database. The **OracleBLOB** class, for example, contains methods that allow you to read, write, and erase data from a **BLOB** object. Through this same class, you can also fine-tune the performance of read and write operations by manipulating the size of the internal data buffer used.

---

■ **Note** The **LONG** data type has traditionally been used to store large objects but has been deprecated since release 10*g*. Its replacement is the **LOB** data types listed previously.

---

**LOB**s are commonly used in applications to store file attachments. For example, the oncology department in a hospital might store large resolution x-ray image scans of their patients using **BLOB** fields in the database.

## Using PL/SQL Associative Array Binding

A PL/SQL associative array, known as index-by tables in earlier Oracle releases, allows you to define an array object in PL/SQL (the dialect of SQL used in Oracle) that is indexable using string values. It can be roughly thought of as similar to a VB.NET collection object or a hash table object. Consider the associative array sample (written in PL/SQL) in Listing 2-1.

*Listing 2-1. Associative Array Example in PL/SQL*

```
DECLARE
  TYPE state_type IS TABLE OF VARCHAR2(50)
    INDEX BY VARCHAR2(5);
  state_type state;
BEGIN
  state('NY') := 'New York';
  state('PA') := 'Pennsylvania';
  state('FL') := 'Florida';
  state('AK') := 'Alaska';

  --Here we can reference an associative array item via its index string
  DBMS_OUTPUT.PUT_LINE('The full name of the state of NY is:' || state('NY'));
END;
```

ODP.NET allows you to bind an associative array to the **OracleParameter** class. This lets you create an array of integers in your .NET code, for example, and pass it to a PL/SQL stored procedure as an associative array input parameter (via the **OracleParameter** class). You can also do the same thing with an array of dates, characters, or other data types.

PL/SQL associative array binding can be particularly useful: you can pass large arrays of indexable objects directly into a PL/SQL function without the need to marshal or serialize the data! For instance, an organization might have a PL/SQL function that needs to look up currency conversion rates by country codes. You could easily write a routine to retrieve the latest exchange rates from the Internet, save them into an array, and pass this entire array into the PL/SQL function as an associative array. The

PL/SQL function will then be able to directly reference the currency conversion rate using the associative array as a lookup list.

## Supporting Active Data Objects (ADO.NET) 2.0

ODP.NET has embraced the ADO.NET specification from Microsoft, providing an extensive set of classes that are familiar to the .NET developer. Let's take a look at some of the basic ADO.NET features supported by ODP.NET in the table in Table 2-1.

**Table 2-1.** *ADO.NET Features Supported by ODP.NET*

| ADO.NET Feature | Description |
| --- | --- |
| Base classes | ODP.NET supports all the basic ADO.NET classes such as the `DataAdapter`, `DataReader`, `Connection`, `Command`, and `Parameter` classes. The ODP.NET classes are correspondingly named `OracleDataAdapter`, `OracleDataReader`, `OracleConnection`, `OracleCommand`, and `OracleParameter`. |
| Transactions | ODP.NET supports both local and distributed transactions. It can also additionally support promotable transactions (covered in the later parts of this chapter). |
| Schema discovery | ODP.NET supports the `GetSchema` method and is able to retrieve an extensive set of database metadata. |
| Connection string building | ODP.NET provides the `OracleConnectionStringBuilder` class to assist you in constructing connection strings. |

# Accessing Oracle Features from ODP.NET Version 10

The next few releases of ODP.NET under version 10 provided support for important technologies such as Oracle's Real Application Clusters (RAC) framework. The version 10 releases also provided numerous performance improvements such as statement caching and connection pooling optimizations for RAC. The following sections highlight some of these improvements.

# Supporting Oracle Grids

What is grid computing? Simply put, grid computing uses the combined processing power of multiple computer resources to process a particular task. In similar vein, an Oracle grid is simply a database that runs on top of two or more servers. Grid functionality is implemented in Oracle via RAC. Figure 2-1 shows how RAC looks architecturally.

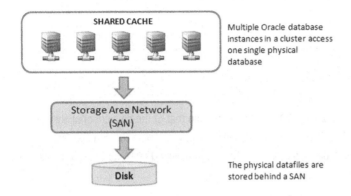

*Figure 2-1. Architecture of an Oracle grid*

In RAC, the Oracle instance (the memory structures and services that allow access to the data) is decoupled from the physical database itself. Each instance runs in a separate server, and data access load is balanced across the servers in a cluster.

Grid computing can benefit you in a few ways. First, it can provide high availability (HA) capabilities; if one server in the grid fails, another takes over instantly. A second advantage is increased overall performance. The Oracle grid is also easily scalable. Increasing processing power and database performance is a matter of adding more machines to the grid.

ODP.NET takes advantage of grid support transparently; it does not require you to write any special code in your application to take advantage of its benefits.

# Supporting Multiple Oracle Homes

"Oracle home" refers to the environment that hosts the Oracle software. The term may be used to refer to the path where the Oracle database is installed, registry entries, program groups associated with the path, and other services that might be running from this home.

Oracle supports multiple Oracle homes, which means that you can run different versions of the same product concurrently. For example, you can install Oracle Database 9*i* and Oracle Database 10*g* in different homes on the same computer. The benefit of being able to do this is that you could test your applications for compatibility against new releases of Oracle products on the same machine.

Through the Home Selector installed together with the database, you can also change the primary Oracle home, and correspondingly, the Oracle client version that your applications use.

ODP.NET supports the use of multiple product homes; it can be installed in multiple Oracle homes. The only requirement is that the ODP.NET version must match the Oracle database version it is intended for.

## Using Floating Point Data Types

Developers traditionally used the **NUMBER** (or **DECIMAL**) data types to store floating point numbers. The release of Oracle Database 10*g* introduced two new floating point data types:

- **BINARY_FLOAT**
- **BINARY_DOUBLE**

The **BINARY_FLOAT** and **BINARY_DOUBLE** data types are different in that they use machine arithmetic; the computation work is passed directly to the operating system. These two data types are thus extremely efficient for heavy computation involving floating point numbers and use less storage space compared to the conventional **NUMBER** data type.

---

■ **Tip** The performance for **BINARY_FLOAT** and **BINARY_DOUBLE** is higher than that of the conventional **NUMBER** data type. In a test script running one million iterations of an add operation between two **BINARY_FLOAT** values against the same operation for **NUMBER** values, I found that addition between **BINARY_FLOAT** variables was twice as fast as the ones between **NUMBER** variables.

---

## Using Statement Caching

Statement caching is another Oracle Database 10*g* feature; with it, you can cache repeatedly used SQL statements. When you use statement caching, Oracle does not have to reparse your SQL statements, which means it can save time by not having to re-create the server objects every time it runs the same SQL.

You can control statement caching behavior by changing the statement cache size via ODP.NET. For instance, specifying a statement cache size of 10 means that Oracle will attempt to cache ten SQL statements.

### How statement caching works under the hood

Before you try to understand how statement caching works, it might be a good idea to first understand the memory structures used by Oracle. Oracle uses a memory structure called the System Global Area (SGA), sometimes alternatively referred to as the Shared Global Area. The SGA is a shared memory area that holds data and control information used by a single database instance. All users connected to the same database instance share the same data held in the SGA.

The most important structure in the SGA is the shared pool, a memory area composed mostly of caches. One such type of cache is the shared SQL area (which holds the reusable execution plans for each SQL statement). Each time the Oracle server encounters a new SQL statement, it sets up a new shared SQL area (allocated from the shared pool). When you pass the same SQL statement to the server a second time, the server parses it, and then checks if the execution plan already existed in the cache. If it does, the plan is reused, thus reducing the overhead of having to recreate the execution plan.

Keep in mind that the server still needs to parse every SQL statement that it receives, even if two are exactly the same. Statement caching aims to further remove this workload from the server by caching the SQL statements at the client side. When your code passes the same SQL statement to ODP.NET a second time, what is sent to the server is not the full SQL, but rather a hash value. This hash value represents a direct index to the cache entry stored at the server-side shared pool.

This essentially reduces network traffic (from not having to send the same SQL statements across the network repeatedly) and shifts the workload of SQL statement parsing from the database server to the client.

It is, of course, not a good idea to cache every single SQL statement that you execute. The best performance gains come from caching statements that you know are going to be executed repeatedly. To get a feel of the performance benefits of statement caching, let's consider the following SQL statement:

```
SELECT empID FROM Employees WHERE Status=:1
```

If we run 1,000 iterations of the preceding SQL code with statement caching turned on and another time with statement caching turned off, we get these performance statistics:

```
Without Statement Caching : 0.7314417 total seconds

With Statement Caching : 0.4133213 total seconds
```

As you can see, using statement caching on highly repetitive code can lead to significant performance boosts and should be considered whenever possible.

# Supporting Command Cancellation and Timeout

ODP.NET supports command cancellation and timeout features. These allow you to cancel an executing command on a running connection and to set a timeout period for an executing command to automatically terminate respectively.

The command automatic timeout feature could be used to limit the resource consumption of specific SQL queries. For example, if your application allowed end users to build and run their own queries, you could use this feature to prevent users from (accidentally or intentionally) executing long-running queries that hog database resources in a shared environment.

The command cancellation feature could find its use in gracefully terminating running queries. Consider, for instance, a scenario where the administrator has to shut down the database service for maintenance. In some cases stopping the web server may not immediately stop all running queries at the database, and stopping the database service directly would raise ugly exceptions to the end user. Instead, the application could be made to iterate through a collection of command objects and to run the cancel command on each object to effectively halt all running queries.

## Retrieving Parameters Programmatically

The **DeriveParameters** method in the **OracleCommandBuilder** class is a useful ODP.NET function that lets you programmatically retrieve the set of parameters for a given stored procedure or function at run time. It populates the **Parameter** collection of an **OracleCommand** object representing the stored procedure or function.

This method can be put to good use, however, in applications where you need to dynamically call stored procedures or functions that are not known during design time.

## Supporting .NET Stored Procedures

Microsoft SQL Server's tight integration with the .NET Common Language Runtime (CLR) allowed .NET developers to write stored procedures in a managed language of their choice such as VB.NET or C#. These stored procedures (called .NET stored procedures) are .NET classes that can be written in Visual Studio, compiled into an assembly, and registered and loaded into Microsoft SQL Server. An application could then invoke these stored procedures as if they were any other stored procedure.

Oracle Database Extensions for .NET, a new feature in Oracle Database 10g allows this same functionality to be used with an Oracle database. In other words, you could write a .NET stored procedure in a managed language of your choice and load it into the Oracle database for use.

This feature is especially useful for Oracle newcomers who wish to use stored procedures without getting into the large learning curve required to learn PL/SQL. They would be able to create stored procedures from the comfort zone of their favorite .NET language.

---

■ **Note** It must be noted, however, that there are certain feature limitations in using Oracle with .NET stored procedures. For instance, .NET stored procedures do not support the use of local nor distributed transactions. If you need to utilize transactions in your stored procedure, you would have to create one using PL/SQL.

---

## Using Client Identifiers

Web applications would typically use a single database account to service all the users of the application. For instance, a web application would use the same connection string for all users:

```
Data Source=ORCL;User Id=webUser;Password=admin123;
```

In a setup like this, there is usually no way to distinguish between each user at the database level. There is little accountability; all database actions are performed under the same user account. Any audit trail facility would have to be implemented at the application level in your code. Furthermore, there is little separation of data between different users at the database level.

Oracle allows you to preserve user identity in database sessions by letting you specify a client identifier each time you open a database connection. The **OracleConnection** class in ODP.NET provides a **ClientID** property that allows you to use any string that you wish (it can be an employee ID, Social Security number, IP address, or username) to distinguish between different users in the same database session. Let's consider a scenario illustrating how this property can be used.

Edmund is a user in a web sales force application. He does not have a corresponding account in the database however. When Edmund logs on to this sales force application, it uses a general database account to transact with the Oracle database. The sales force application sets the **ClientID** property of all **OracleConnection** objects used to **'EDMUND'**. When another user, Greg logs in to the application, it does the same thing; it sets the **ClientID** property of all **OracleConnection** objects used to **'GREG'**. If we've enabled auditing on the tables in this database, Oracle will automatically tag all generated audit trail records with this **ClientID** value. We could then retrieve the audit trail records for **EDMUND** (or **GREG**) using the SQL **SELECT** in Listing 2-2.

*Listing 2-2. Retrieving Audit Trails Using the Client Identifier*

```
SELECT * FROM dba_audit_object
WHERE username = 'webUser'
AND client_id = 'EDMUND'
AND OBJ_NAME = 'SalesData'
```

# Using Database Change Notifications

Database change notification is an interesting feature released with Oracle Database 10*g* Release 2. The basic concept is that a .NET application can keep watch over a database object (for instance, a table) and be automatically notified whenever any change occurs on that table.

You might wonder how change notifications compare to database triggers. They are different in that database triggers usually run within the confines of the database. Change notifications bubble events all the way up to your .NET code, allowing you to do much more when something happens in the database.

Database change notifications can also be regarded as push (as opposed to pull) technology; your application does not have to continually poll the database for changes. ODP.NET alerts your code instantly the moment they occur.

There are many uses of such a feature. Think of a jobs tray in the BugBusters pest control company for example. A call center operator receives a house call to rid an area of rats and will create a new job via the pest control support system, which ends up creating a job record in the database. Using change notifications, all technicians can be instantly alerted the moment a new job is created instead of having to continually poll the database every minute for the latest list of jobs.

Another example of how database notifications could be used to refresh the display of a flight information display terminal follows in Figure 2-2. The master flight database could be configured in such a way that it would broadcast notifications to all flight information display terminals the moment any database change was detected. This way, the display terminals need only refresh its display when it receives this notification, instead of repeatedly polling the database for the latest changes. There are tremendous performance cost savings in such deployments too—imagine 100 flight information display terminals (a fairly reasonable number for any airport) all polling the same database for changes every 5 seconds. This would put an unnecessarily large processing load on the database. Database notifications solve problems like these elegantly by employing a push rather than pull approach to data access.

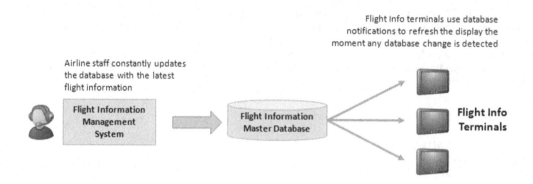

**Figure 2-2.** *Flight Information Display Application Example*

There are many other interesting ways to utilize change notifications. You could use them to create audit logs when data is changed or to send out e-mail alerts when specific changes are detected. ODP.NET allows you to tap on the power of this functionality from .NET code.

## Managing Connection Pools

Connection pooling allows Oracle connections to be retrieved from a cached pool of connections and to be returned to this pool after use. Connection pooling leads to a reduced overhead when opening connections.

When your application opens a connection to Oracle for the first time, it is a relatively costly operation in terms of performance. In web applications, for instance, where each page request opens a new connection, this could lead to a significant impact on performance. Connection pooling addresses this cost by keeping these connections cached in the pool and reusing them the next time your application attempts to open a new connection with the same settings.

Connection pool behavior can be modified by specifying certain settings (such as the minimum and maximum size of the pool or whether pooling is disabled or enabled) in the connection string used to connect to the database. ODP.NET takes this a step further by allowing you to explicitly clear the connection pool of connections using these two functions:

- `ClearPool:` Clears all connections from a connection pool
- `ClearAllPools:` Clears all connections from all connection pools in an application domain

There are times when a connection pool can become corrupt due to, for instance, the database service restarting from a power outage or from other reasons. Your application would receive an exception when it attempts to connect to the database. These two functions come in handy during such scenarios, allowing you to clear the connection pool and reconnect again.

## Optimizing Connection Pools for RAC

As mentioned earlier, Oracle RAC technology allows a single Oracle database to be distributed across a cluster of servers. This increases the scalability and performance of the database as a whole, allowing the administrator to simply add more servers when needed to boost the performance of the database.

The behavior of ODP.NET's connection pooling features is tightly coupled with RAC technology as well. ODP.NET is able to optimize connection pooling in a RAC environment by balancing connection requests across multiple Oracle RAC instances (that is, connection load balancing). When an RAC instance fails, the connection objects on that RAC instance are also automatically removed from the connection pool, freeing up resources that are no longer used. These features can be enabled or disabled by the developer through connection string parameters.

## Using a REF Cursor as an IN/OUT Parameter

A **REF** cursor is a type of cursor in Oracle that allows you to directly reference any result set kept in memory. A **REF** cursor is extremely fast, as it is really a pointer to a direct location in random access memory (RAM). When you retrieve data using a **REF** cursor, you are directly retrieving that data from memory. Because it is a pointer, it is also efficient to pass **REF** cursors around. When you pass a **REF** cursor between functions, you are simply passing a reference, not the entire result set.

**REF** cursors can be used as an input or output parameter in an Oracle stored procedure. For instance, ODP.NET allows you to retrieve a **REF** cursor output from a PL/SQL stored procedure into an **OracleParameter** object. You can then pass this same **REF** cursor as an input parameter into another PL/SQL stored procedure.

## Using 64-bit ODP.NET

With this release, a 64-bit version of ODP.NET that supports Windows x64 (AMD64/Intel EM64T) and 64-bit Windows for Intel Itanium was made available as well. It natively supports the 64-bit version of the .NET Framework. The 64-bit version of ODP.NET naturally provides better performance and scalability over its 32-bit counterpart.

## Controlling the FetchSize Property

The **OracleDataReader** class in ODP.NET has a property called **FetchSize**, which is the amount of memory (in bytes) that can be used by the **OracleDataReader** object to fetch data from the database. Setting the **FetchSize** value determines the number of rows that are returned from the query with each roundtrip to the database.

You can improve the performance of your application by increasing the **FetchSize** property to ensure that more data is returned with each round-trip to the server. This is especially useful when dealing with large amounts of data. The default **FetchSize** in ODP.NET is 64KB. Using another property, the **RowSize** property (which holds the size of each row returned, in bytes), you can easily determine the **FetchSize** value for a specific number of rows:

```
FetchSize = (NumberOfRows) * RowSize
```

A larger **FetchSize** value means that a larger memory buffer is used to store the retrieved data, so it is usually advisable to find a reasonable balance between the desired number of round-trips to the server and the size of the data retrieved in each round-trip.

## Configuring ODP.NET

In previous versions, ODP.NET supports the configuration of its settings via either the connection string or through the ODP.NET classes. With version 10 of ODP.NET, developers can additionally configure ODP.NET settings via .NET configuration files such as the **web.config** and **machine.config** files. With so many different ways to configure ODP.NET settings, Figure 2-3 shows how this affects settings precedence.

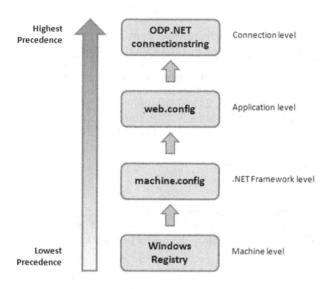

*Figure 2-3. ODP.NET configuration settings precedence*

As you can see from Figure 2-3, you can configure ODP.NET at four different levels, and the precedence is such that settings configured at the connection level overrides settings configured at the **web.config** level, and so on. Some of the settings that can be configured include the **FetchSize** (covered earlier), maximum statement cache size, thread pool maximum size, and so on. The next chapter will cover more of these settings in detail.

The ability to configure settings at many levels allows an application to fall back to a set of default settings when none are specified. For instance, a server in an organization might need to satisfy an organization's internal quality of service benchmark by having its maximum statement cache size set to a value of 100 at the machine level. If you forget to explicitly set this maximum statement cache size in the connection string, the statement cache size used will still fall back to the machine-level setting of 100.

# Accessing Oracle Features from ODP.NET Version 11

The next few releases under ODP.NET major version 11 open up a host of Oracle database 10*g* and 11*g* functionality to the .NET developer. It provides support for features like Advanced Queuing (AQ)– a messaging framework based on the Oracle database, high availability (HA) event notifications, promotable transactions, and other enhancements. The following section describes these features in detail.

## Enhancing Performance

The release of ODP.NET version 11 provided two additional performance enhancements that were transparent to the developer (requiring no code change):

- Improved parameter context caching
- Efficient retrieval of small-sized **LOB** files

Parameter context caching improved performance for applications that executed the same SQL statement repeatedly. Retrieval of small-sized **LOB** files also performed better due to fewer round-trips required to the server with this release.

## Deploying ODP.NET Using xcopy

The **xcopy** command is a handy command line tool that ships with Microsoft Windows. It allows users to copy entire folders and subfolders (recursively) from one location to another. ODP.NET supports using this tool to deploy ODP.NET to a large number of computers during production.

---

■ **Note**  The ODP.NET package that is tailored for **xcopy** has a smaller footprint than the one installed through the Oracle Universal Installer, because **xcopy** does not install ODP.NET documentation and code samples.

---

It is not difficult to see how this feature can benefit large deployments. In a deployment consisting of 50 servers, for example, the systems administrator does not have to run the Oracle Universal Installer (and the wizard after that) 50 times to install the ODP.NET client on each machine. The installation could be done centrally from a single server by copying the files required directly into the target machines over the network using **xcopy**.

## Supporting Oracle User Defined Types (UDTs)

Oracle supports UDTs, allowing users to create their own custom data types for use in PL/SQL. Listing 2-3 shows a sample UDT consisting of multiple columns.

*Listing 2-3. A Sample UDT*

```
CREATE OR REPLACE TYPE ADDRESSTYPE AS OBJECT (
STREET VARCHAR2 (50),
CITY VARCHAR2 (50),
STATE VARCHAR2 (2),
ZIPCODE VARCHAR2(9));
```

Through a set of special classes, ODP.NET provides the ability to represent Oracle UDTs as custom data types in .NET applications. There are generally two types of UDTs:

- Object types (Oracle objects)
- Collection types (**VARRAY**s or nested tables)

Both types are supported by ODP.NET. Oracle objects map into .NET classes and collection types map to .NET arrays.

## Performing Bulk Copy Operations

Let's say your boss drops 2TB of raw data on your lap one morning and tells you to process and get all of that data loaded into Oracle. What's the fastest way to do it? Oracle provides a command line tool called Oracle SQL*Loader that is able to load large amounts of data from a variety of formats (such as CSV, multiple-line records, and even images) into the database in bulk. In ODP.NET, the **OracleBulkCopy** class allows you to achieve something similar programmatically.

The Oracle SQL* Loader tool and ODP.NET's **OracleBulkCopy** class can load data into Oracle at very high speeds, because they are essentially direct path loaders (as opposed to conventional path loaders). A conventional path loader loads data into the database using SQL **INSERT** statements, whereas a direct path loader does not use SQL but loads data directly into the Oracle data files. A direct path loader achieves better performance, because it bypasses the logic and processing required for SQL. A bulk copy does not have to compete with other users and processes for database resources as well, so it can usually load data into the database at near disk-write speeds.

There are, of course, some limitations with bulk copy that would favor the use of a conventional path loader instead in certain cases. For instance, bulk copy does not support the use of UDT columns. In most cases, however, bulk copy can be exceptionally useful during data migration and business scenarios where you have a large feed of data that you need to load frequently into the database. It is not hard to imagine a scenario that might depend heavily on this feature.

Take the telecommunications industry for example. Major telecommunication service providers usually have large subscriber bases numbering in the millions. When a subscriber makes a phone call, powerful telecommunication servers generate a corresponding call detail record. These records are usually spat out in raw binary format. With millions of phone calls everyday, it is not surprising to find 100-GB files containing millions of call detail records generated on a daily basis.

These organizations use call accounting software to import the data into a database so that they can be used to generate meaningful reports such as weekly call volume, average call duration, and so on. In such a scenario, ODP.NET bulk copy's exceptional performance would ensure that newly generated call detail records are pushed into the database in the shortest time possible.

## Using Windows Authenticated User Connections Pooling

The Oracle database supports using Windows login credentials for database authentication. This is a form of integrated windows authentication that does not require your code to explicitly pass in any user ID or password to the database. Connection pooling is also enabled for windows authenticated connections.

# Publishing Connection Pool Performance Counters

The Oracle database can publish a set of performance counters for the connection pool to the Windows Performance Monitoring (**Perfmon**) tool. ODP.NET allows you to enable or disable individual performance counters. Table 2-2 shows some of the various performance counters available.

*Table 2-2. Performance Counters in Oracle*

| Performance Counter | Description |
| --- | --- |
| HardConnectsPerSecond | Total number of new database sessions established each second |
| HardDisconnectsPerSecond | Total number of database sessions closed each second |
| SoftConnectsPerSecond | Total number of cached connections retrieved from the connection pool |
| SoftDisconnectsPerSecond | Total number of cached connections released into the connection pool |
| NumberOfActiveConnectionPools | Total number of active connection pools |
| NumberOfInactiveConnectionPools | Total number of inactive connection pools |
| NumberOfActiveConnections | Total number of connections in use |
| NumberOfFreeConnections | Total number of connections available across all connection pools |
| NumberOfPooledConnections | Total number of pooled active (open) connections |
| NumberOfNonPooledConnections | Total number of nonpooled active (open) connections |
| NumberOfReclaimedConnections | Total number of connections internally disposed of by the garbage collector |
| NumberOfStasisConnections | Total number of connections that have been closed by the user but are in stasis (that is, awaiting release back into the connection pool) |

The screenshot in Figure 2-4 shows how you can add the ODP.NET performance counters for display in Microsoft Window's **Perfmon** utility.

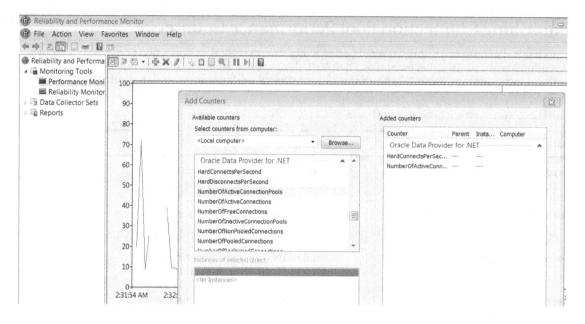

***Figure 2-4.*** *Adding ODP.NET performance counters to Perfmon*

## Supporting Self-Tuning for Applications

ODP.NET has the capability of dynamically adjusting the statement cache size on its own to improve application performance. It dynamically monitors queries and collects statistics based on run time sampling and uses this information to determine an optimal value for the statement cache size. When self-tuning is enabled, this automatically determined statement cache size overwrites any other statement cache size setting.

## Using Oracle Streaming AQ

AQ is a powerful message queuing mechanism implemented on top of the database, as illustrated in Figure 2-5. At the mention of message queuing, the Microsoft Messaging Queue Server (MSMQ) might have instantly popped into your mind. MSMQ is different from AQ in that it is a separate service on its own that stores messages as files. The AQ service on the other hand is powered on top of a database.

AQ uses the Oracle database to represent message queues. An application can place or remove a message to and from a queue (called enqueue and dequeue respectively). Messages are stored in a queue on the database and can be received by other applications that subscribe to the queue. Through this method, data messages can be passed from one application to another using the database as an intermediary form of storage.

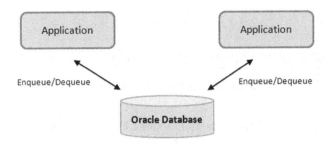

***Figure 2-5.*** *Communicating between two applications using AQ*

Queues allow communication between applications sitting on different machines to take place. ODP.NET allows your code to take advantage of this message queuing facility to communicate with remote applications.

Needless to say, there are numerous ways this technology can be used. To give you an idea of the benefits of using AQ in your applications, consider the following scenarios:

- Communication between heterogeneous applications: How does a background service communicate with an ASP.NET application, for example? Previously, you had to resort to pipes or Windows sockets to pass data between processes that execute in different application pools or even different machines. AQ provides an easy and reliable solution to bridge this gap.

- Guarantee of message receipt even if applications are offline: When an application sends a message to a queue, and the receiving application is offline, the message will be kept in the queue until the next time the receiving application logs on.

- Near real-time communication between different applications: You could technically build an instant chat program that works on top of AQ. The chat client could send a message to a queue whenever you type in a friendly message to your friend. The receiving chat client subscribes to this queue so that when a message arrives, the chat client code is immediately alerted via a callback function. The friendly message can then be retrieved and displayed.

- Improving user interface responsiveness: Messaging applications are usually asynchronous (nonblocking). For instance, an ASP.NET application can submit a job order to a queue for processing; it does not have to wait for the order to be processed before allowing the user to proceed.

## Supporting Promotable Local Transactions

A transaction is a series of SQL statements that must be executed as a batch. If either one of these statements fail, a rollback is usually performed. A transaction follows the all-or-nothing rule. Consider the SQL statements in Listing 2-4 for instance. These three statements execute as a batch. If any of them fails, none of these records are committed to the database.

*Listing 2-4. A Sample Local Transaction*

```
INSERT INTO Customer(CustID,Name) VALUES('IHC01','IHEARTCLIPPIES INC');
INSERT INTO Addresses(CustID, Address) VALUES('IHC01', '3 Fifth Ave, 10020, NY');
INSERT INTO Contacts(CustID, ContactPerson) VALUES ('IHC01','Stephanie L. HS');
COMMIT;
```

There are two types of transactions—local and distributed. Local transactions, like the example in Listing 2-4, all run within the same database. Distributed transactions, however, can run across multiple databases distributed across multiple machines. Consider the distributed transaction shown in Listing 2-5.

*Listing 2-5. A Sample Distributed Transaction*

```
INSERT INTO Jobs@hq.com(JobID,JobName) VALUES('J01','New Hair clips series');
INSERT INTO Announcements@abc.com(Description) VALUES('New hair clips arriving Dec 09');
INSERT INTO Products@acme.com(ProdID,Price) VALUES ('HClips01', '3.40');
COMMIT;
```

The three tables exist in three different databases set up in the configuration shown in Figure 2-6.

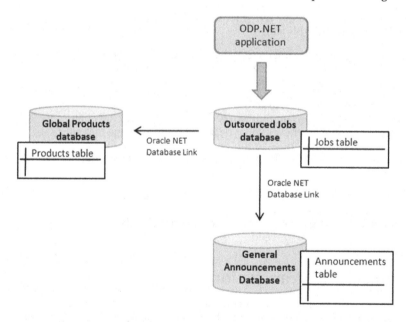

***Figure 2-6.*** *Example of a distributed transaction*

During development, it is sometimes difficult to know whether a transaction will be local or distributed as this depends on the way the databases are deployed in production. Developers would try to remain prudent by assuming that all the transactions are distributed and then design their applications with this in mind. As a result, the application uses more resources than necessary.

Promotable local transactions help avert this problem by assuming all transactions are local. It automatically promotes a local transaction to a distributed one only when more than one database participates in a transaction.

## Using ODP.NET Security Enhancements

The .NET CLR provides its own layer of security called Code Access Security (CAS). It serves as a sort of gatekeeper to control which resources a particular piece of executing code can have access to. This process is depicted in the diagram in Figure 2-7.

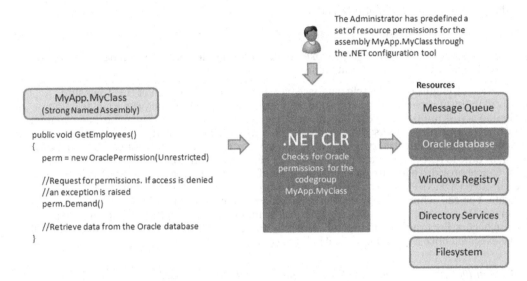

*Figure 2-7. The Code Access Security framework and OraclePermission*

Through the .NET configuration tool, an administrator can define a set of resource permissions for any managed assembly. This set of permissions defines whether an assembly is allowed to access system resources such as the filesystem (**FileIOPermission**), Windows registry (**RegistryPermission**), directory services (**DirectoryServicesPermission**), and so on. ODP.NET provides the **OraclePermission** class that lets your code request for permissions from CAS in the same manner when attempting to access an Oracle database.

Organizations use CAS as an added layer of security on top of the security model provided by standard database authentication. For instance, an organization might have just deployed a payroll application that uses a single database account to connect to the database:

```
Data Source=ORCL;User Id=payrollUser;Password=admin123;
```

This use of a single login can be potentially dangerous; anyone who is aware of the username and password used by this payroll application could create an application in Visual Studio and connect to the database over the network using the same particulars. That user would then gain access to all the underlying tables in the database. CAS can help prevent this because it only allows access to the Oracle database if the exact executing assembly was already granted permission to do so by the .NET administrator.

## Running Callbacks for HA Event Notifications

Most organizations need to run their databases 24 hours a day and 7 days a week with as much resistance to failure as possible. Database downtime of even a few minutes can be disastrous to organizations like banks or stock exchanges. The database and the application must therefore work in tandem to

- Ensure maximum availability of service

- Reduce the impact of data loss in the event of failure

- Immediately and automatically invoke organization-defined protocols in the event of failure or recovery from failure

One of the key strengths of the Oracle database has always been in the area of HA. To ensure maximum availability of service, Oracle grid support (implemented via RAC) allowed a single database to be distributed across multiple servers. This means that if one machine goes down, the load can then be shared with the remaining servers; data availability as a whole is not impacted.

In the case of data loss due to server failure, for example, you could rewind your database back to a certain point in time to recover your data (using Oracle Flashback technology).

Finally, Oracle provides a feature called HA event notifications. This feature allows Oracle to notify your code (through ODP.NET) when a database service, host or instance has gone down or when it is available again. You can achieve this by registering a callback function with ODP.NET.

You can use HA event notifications to automatically run organization-defined protocols whenever a service failure occurs. For example, an organization may design the series of steps shown in Listing 2-6 that must be executed once a database service failure occurs.

*Listing 2-6. A Sample Protocol in an Organization When the Database Service Fails*

```
1.Alert the system administrator by e-mail
2.Automatically shut down all webservers in North American offices
3.Send an SMS (Short Messaging Service) message to the database administrator
4.Automatically log the event with the organization's internal IT Audit software
5.Attempt an automatic restart of the database service for a maximum of three tries.
```

Through ODP.NET's HA event notifications, you can write code to make your applications more responsive to database-related disasters.

## Starting Up and Shutting Down Databases

In ODP.NET 11*g*, you can start up or shut down a database instance using the **OracleDatabase** class (assuming you have database administrator privileges). For instance, an organization with highly sensitive information might, for security reasons, write an application to automatically shut down a database instance entirely upon detecting suspicious user activity or intrusion attempts.

# Getting Started

Now that you have a feel of the sort of functionality you have access to using ODP.NET, let's take a look at the Oracle software that you need installed on your development machine before you can write an ODP.NET application. I assume, in the following subsections, that you have already installed Microsoft Visual Studio 2005/2008 and .NET Framework (Version 2.0.50727 or higher).

## Installing Oracle Database 11g

The Oracle Universal Installer provides a step-by-step wizard to make installation of the Oracle database a breeze. You can download the latest Oracle Database 11g installer from the Oracle website at this location:

`http://www.oracle.com/technology/software/products/database/index.html`

After downloading the package, run the Universal installer by running the Setup application. You can choose between two different installation methods: basic and advanced.

The basic installation allows you to select the base and home location of the Oracle database as well as the database version (standard or enterprise) to install. It also allows you to automatically create a starter database; you can specify a database name of your own and the password you wish to use for the system master accounts. The advanced installation allows you to set different passwords for the system accounts as well as other globalization settings.

Let's select Basic Installation, as illustrated in Figure 2-8. You can change the global database name if you wish, but the rest of the samples in this book will use the **NEWDB** name. Choose a database password that you can remember.

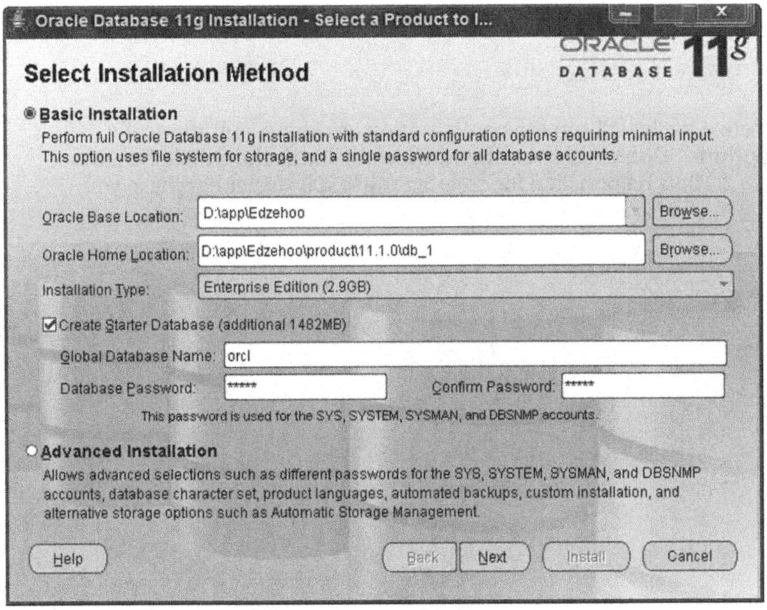

*Figure 2-8.* Selecting Oracle Database 11g installation type

After Oracle gathers the necessary information it needs from your PC, it will provide a brief summary of the installation. You can begin the installation by clicking the Install button in the summary screen shown in Figure 2-9.

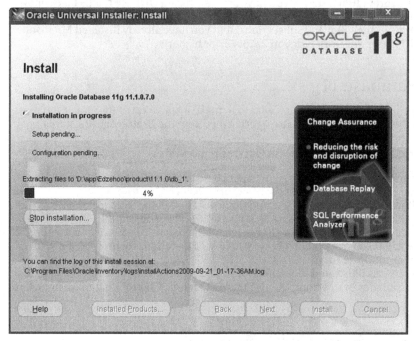

***Figure 2-9.*** *Installation progress screen*

After the installation is complete, Oracle will run the configuration assistants automatically (depending on your installation options). One of these configuration assistants, the Oracle Database Configuration Assistant (see Figure 2-10) is responsible for creating the NEWDB starter database you specified earlier.

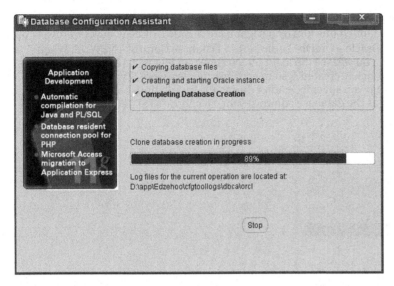

**Figure 2-10.** *The Database Configuration Assistant*

After the automated installation has completed, you will see the End of Installation screen shown in Figure 2-11.

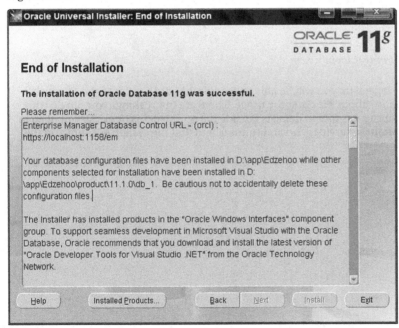

**Figure 2-11.** *End of Oracle Database 11g installation*

41

Do take note that this installation comes with a web-based Enterprise Manager tool, located at **http://localhost:1158/em**. You can launch this tool by navigating to this URL directly in your browser or by going to Start → All Programs → Oracle – OraDb11g_home1 → Database Control – NEWDB. When you launch the Enterprise Manager, you will see the login screen shown in Figure 2-12.

You can try logging in with your newly created system account and password. Type **SYSTEM** as the username, and type the password that you specified earlier during the installation. For the Connect As field, you probably want to connect as the database administrator, so choose SYSDBA from the drop-down list.

*Figure 2-12. Oracle Enterprise Manager login screen*

Once you have successfully logged in, you will be able to see a dashboard similar to the screenshot in Figure 2-13 with general statistics about the database usage. There are many things you can do with the Enterprise Manager, but covering this tool in detail is outside the scope of this book. All you need to know at this point is that your database service is up and running and that the system account and the password you've created works.

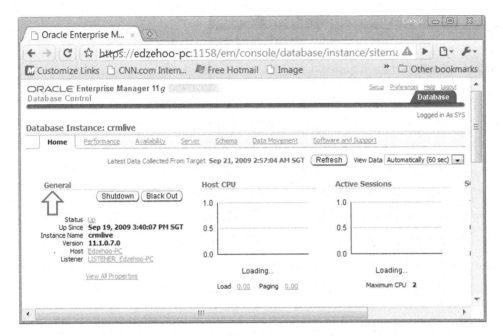

*Figure 2-13. Oracle Enterprise Manager home page*

# Installing ODAC.NET

You are now ready to install the suite that contains the ODP.NET provider —the Oracle Data Access Components for .NET (ODAC.NET) package. You can download the installation files from the following URL:

`http://www.oracle.com/technology/software/tech/windows/odpnet/index.html`

---

■ **Note** This installation package includes the ODAC.NET components as well as ODT.NET, covered in Chapters 14 and 15 of this book.

---

The first screen in the universal installer (shown in Figure 2-14) allows you to install ODAC.NET for the Oracle client or server. The first option is meant to be installed on client machines accessing the Oracle database, while the second option is meant to be installed on the server hosting the Oracle database.

In a .NET Winforms application scenario for instance, you might have installed the Oracle database on a server. For each client machine that needs to access the database over the network, you would need to install ODAC for Oracle Client. ODAC for Oracle Client not only installs the ODP.NET libraries necessary but also the Oracle client software necessary for access to the Oracle database. It can therefore be used for installation on a clean machine.

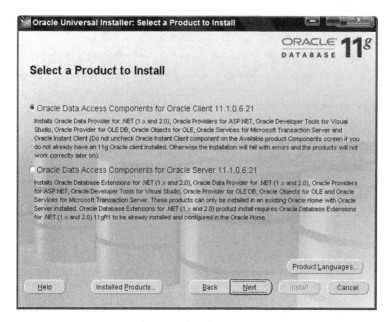

*Figure 2-14. Selecting the ODAC.NET product to install*

In the next screen (shown in Figure 2-15), you can select the install location for the ODAC.NET software. You can use the default settings provided.

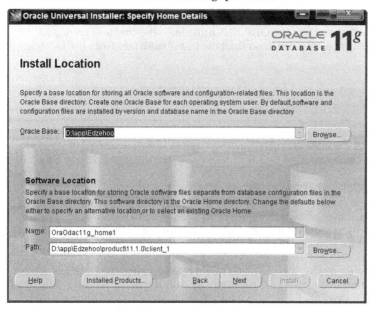

*Figure 2-15. Specifying installation folders*

The next screen (shown in Figure 2-16) allows you to select or deselect the list of ODAC.NET components to install. Ensure that all the components are selected before proceeding.

*Figure 2-16. Selecting the list of products to install*

Follow through the remaining screens by clicking the Next button. You may also be requested to specify a port number to use for the Oracle Microsoft Transaction Server (MTS) Recovery service (as shown in Figure 2-17). You can use the default port number specified.

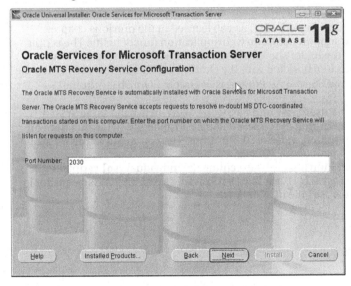

*Figure 2-17. Configuring Oracle Services for Microsoft Transaction Server*

At the end of the installation you will see a screen similar to the screenshot shown in Figure 2-18. The ODAC setup wizard will remind you to manually run the Oracle providers for ASP.NET SQL scripts.

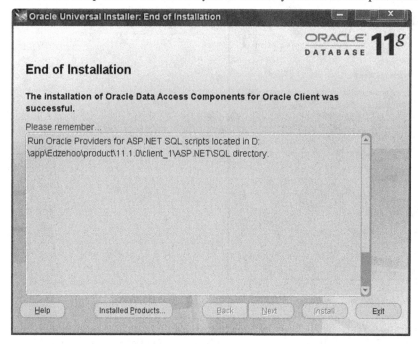

*Figure 2-18. End of ODAC.NET installation*

You're almost there! The Oracle providers for ASP.NET, as you learned in the previous chapter, provides a bunch of ASP.NET providers to support common web application functionality. The scripts for these ASP.NET providers are placed in the folder shown at the End of Installation screen. To run these scripts, you need to use the SQL*Plus tool bundled with the Oracle installation. You can launch the SQL*Plus tool from the Windows start menu: Start → All Programs → Oracle – OraDb11g_home1 → Application Development → SQLPlus.

You will immediately be prompted for a username and password. You can use the same **SYSTEM** username and password you created earlier during the Oracle database installation to log in. After you have successfully logged in, you will be presented with the **SQL>** prompt. The command to run a **.sql** file is an alias character (**@**) followed by the full path of the SQL file.

You can install each ASP.NET provider individually by executing the individual **.sql** script files in the same folder, or all in one go using the **InstallAllOracleASPNetProviders.sql** file. The screenshot in Figure 2-19 shows how you can execute this **.sql** file in SQL*Plus.

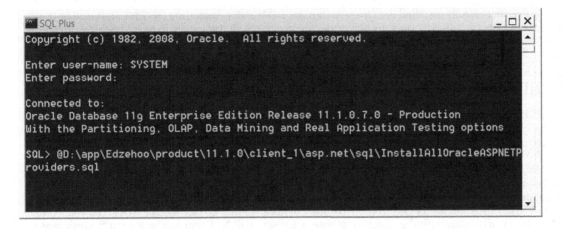

*Figure 2-19. Running the InstallAllOracleASPNetProviders.sql script using SQL\*Plus*

After executing this command a stream of text output will be displayed. A message showing "PL/SQL procedure successfully completed" will be displayed at the end of this output if the scripts executed successfully (as shown in Figure 2-20).

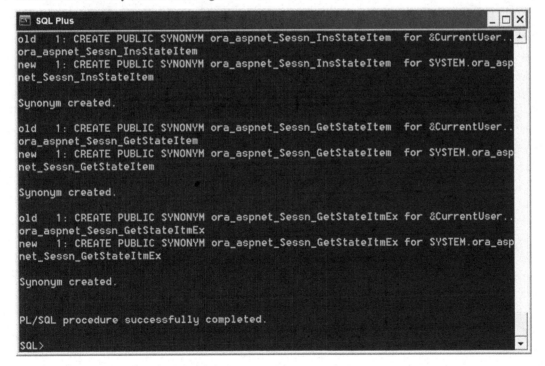

*Figure 2-20. Script executed successfully screen*

You've successfully installed the Oracle database, ODAC.NET (including ODT.NET) as well as the Oracle providers for ASP.NET on your machine. You now have all the tools you need to start writing ODP.NET applications.

## Summary

In this chapter, you've taken a look at some of the features in the Oracle database that you can access through ODP.NET. Most importantly, ODP.NET's support for the basic ADO.NET classes means that you can access the Oracle database using code familiar to you.

The Oracle database is a large software suite that extends far beyond the capabilities of a simple RDBMS. In this chapter, you've seen how each major release of ODP.NET attempts to keep up with the new technology features introduced with each new release of the Oracle database. Since ODP.NET is an Oracle product, it is also expected to enjoy sustained support in the Oracle database releases to come.

ODP.NET provides a very comprehensive suite of libraries that go beyond the ADO.NET stack and is designed to work tightly with the Oracle database. Through ODP.NET you will be able to tap on a larger subset of Oracle database functionality in your .NET applications to interact better with the database.

■ ■ ■

# CHAPTER 3

# Connecting to Oracle with ODP.NET

You now have all the basic software set up to write your first ODP.NET application. In this chapter, you will explore the different ways to connect to an Oracle database using ODP.NET and the various connection parameters you can use to control ODP.NET behavior. Specifically, we will explore the following:

- How Transparent Network Substrate (TNS) works

- How you can build connection strings dynamically instead of hard-wiring them into your code

- How to utilize Oracle's transparent application failover feature to build robust applications that continue to work even when database connections drop midway in your code

## Connecting via TNS

Let's start this chapter by putting you right where the action is. In this section, you will write your first ODP.NET application, a simple application to connect and disconnect from an Oracle database.

Start by creating a new C# Windows Forms Visual Studio project. You will need to add the `Oracle.DataAccess` reference shown in Figure 3-1 to your project.

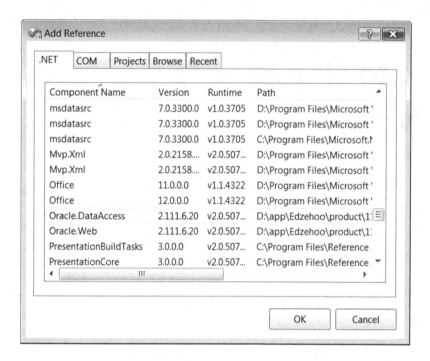

***Figure 3-1.*** *Adding a reference to the Oracle.DataAccess (ODP.NET) library*

You will also need to import the **Oracle.DataAccess.Client** namespace into your form. You can do that using the following code:

```
using Oracle.DataAccess.Client;
```

Drag a button control to the main form in your project, and name it **btnConnectNow**. In the **Click** event handler of this button, write the code shown in Listing 3-1.

*Listing 3-1. Connecting to the Oracle Database Via TNS*

```
public void btnConnectNow_Click(System.Object sender, System.EventArgs e)
{
        OracleConnection conn = new OracleConnection();
        conn.ConnectionString = "Data Source=NEWDB;User ID=SYSTEM;Password=admin";
        try
        {
                conn.Open();
                conn.Close();
                MessageBox.Show("Connection successful!");
        }
        catch (Exception ex)
        {
```

```
            MessageBox.Show(ex.ToString(), "Error connecting to Oracle");
    }
}
```

Let's take a closer look at what you've just written. The **OracleConnection** class is the ODP.NET class used to establish a connection to the database. The connection string you've written is the standard vanilla one and consists of three parts:

- **Data Source**: The net service name of the database; in this case, **NEWDB**, the starter database that was created during your installation of the Oracle database in this example

- **User ID**: A valid database username

- **Password**: A valid database password

If you run this code and click the button you've just created, you get the "Connection successful!" message shown in Figure 3-2 (assuming you have installed the Oracle database correctly and set the correct connection string). Congratulations, you have just written your first ODP.NET application!

*Figure 3-2. Connecting to the Oracle database via TNS*

The code you've written here connects to the Oracle database via what is called Transparent Network Substrate (TNS). Let's consider this scenario: Your Oracle database service could possibly be sitting on a computer server at **hq.sales.a_very_long_name.com**, listening on a particular port number. Instead of cramming all this information into the connection string, you could organize it in a file, stick a shorter label on it, and use that label to refer to it in your connection string. This is precisely what TNS does. This label is called the net service name and was what you've used earlier for the **Data Source** attribute in your connection string.

# Understanding the TNSNames.ora file

The solution in Listing 3-1 depends on a special file in your Oracle installation. This file is commonly referred to as the **TNSNames.ora** file and is located in the following folder:

```
<OraHome>\Network\Admin
```

You can edit it by hand using the Microsoft Notepad program. Inside this file, you might see one or more blocks of configuration data that look like that in Listing 3-2.

*Listing 3-2. Format of a TNS Descriptor*

```
<Net Service Name>=
(DESCRIPTION =
        (ADDRESS_LIST =
                (ADDRESS = (PROTOCOL = TCP)(Host = <hostname>)(Port = <port>))
        )
        (CONNECT_DATA =
                (SERVICE_NAME = <sid>)
        )
)
```

The following lists the components of this descriptor:

- *Net service name*: This is the net service name is the label you wish to use for the descriptor, and it is the name that you will refer to in the data source attribute of your connection strings.

- *Host name*: This is the name of the machine hosting the Oracle database service, and could be, for example, your `hq.sales.a_very_long_name.com string.`

- *Port*: This is the port number that your Oracle database service is listening on.

- *SID*: This is the global database name of your database. In your case it would be `NEWDB`.

There is probably an entry in your `TNSNames.ora` file for the `NEWDB` database; the Oracle Universal Installer created this entry for you when it generated the `NEWDB` starter database, and it was how you could connect to the database using TNS earlier.

You can add more descriptors of your own manually. Alternatively, especially if you are not in the mood to carefully count parentheses, you can use the GUI-based Oracle Net Configuration Assistant to add a new descriptor to the `TNSNames.ora` file.

# Connecting in Other Ways

You can use other settings and methods to connect to Oracle using ODP.NET. Most of these connection methods and settings are specified through the connection string. Let's take a look at the other different ways to connect to Oracle in the following subsections.

## Connecting Without TNSNames.ora

You can choose to connect to the Oracle database without referring to a net service name in the `TNSNames.ora` file. In such a case, you can define an entire descriptor in the connection string (in the same format as the descriptors in the **TNSNames.ora** file). Let's take a closer look at the format of this descriptor in Listing 3-3.

*Listing 3-3. Connecting to the Database Without TNSNames.ora*

```
public void btnConnectNow_Click(System.Object sender, System.EventArgs e)
{
        OracleConnection conn = new OracleConnection();
        conn.ConnectionString = "Data Source = " +
                        "(DESCRIPTION = " +
                        "       (ADDRESS_LIST = " +
                        "               (ADDRESS = (PROTOCOL = TCP)" +
                        "                       (HOST = 127.0.0.1) " +
                        "                       (PORT = 1521) " +
                        "               )" +
                        "       )" +
                        "       (CONNECT_DATA = " +
                        "               (SERVICE_NAME = NEWDB)" +
                        "       )" +
                        ");" +
                        "User Id=SYSTEM;" +
                        "password=admin;"
        try
        {
                conn.Open();
                conn.Close();
                MessageBox.Show("Connection successful!");
        }
        catch (Exception ex)
        {
                MessageBox.Show(ex.ToString(), "Error connecting to Oracle");
        }
}
```

The only difference between this inline descriptor and a descriptor in the **TNSNames.ora** file is that you don't need to define a net service name in the connection string. This method of connecting to the Oracle database is useful if you want to dynamically generate the details of a descriptor. For example, if the port number, host address, and service name of the database change frequently in your organization, you might want to consider generating this type of connection string dynamically.

## Connecting via EZConnect

Another way to connect to the Oracle database without any frills is to use the EZConnect method. This method also lets the developer set the host name, port number, and service name all in one go. Unlike the inline-descriptor method in the previous section, EZConnect is specific to TCP/IP connections. It gives you a programmer-friendly way to specify host, port, and service name.

Listing 3-4 provides an example of the EZConnect syntax.

53

*Listing 3-4. Connecting to the Database Via EZConnect*

```
public void btnConnectNow_Click(System.Object sender, System.EventArgs e)
{
        OracleConnection conn = new OracleConnection();
        conn.ConnectionString = "Data Source=EDZEHOO-PC:1521/NEWDB;
                                 User ID=SYSTEM;Password=admin";
        try
        {
                conn.Open();
                conn.Close();
                MessageBox.Show("Connection successful!");
        }
        catch (Exception ex)
        {
                MessageBox.Show(ex.ToString(), "Error connecting to Oracle");
        }
}
```

■ **Tip**    If you need to use Oracle advanced features such as connection pooling, external procedure calls, and so on, these require additional connection parameters; EZConnect is not advisable in such a case.

# Learning the ODP.NET Connection Parameters

You can tap on a rich host of Oracle functionality, such as connection pooling, integrated Windows authentication, and statement caching, by specifying additional parameters in the connection string. In the following sections, we take a look at some of these parameters.

## Connecting with Connection Pooling Activated

As you've read in the previous chapter, opening a new database connection is a costly operation in terms of performance. Connection pooling allows database connections to be cached for reuse. When a new connection is requested, ODP.NET retrieves a connection from a cache, and when it is closed, the connection is not physically closed but merely returned to the cache.

You can control connection pooling behavior in ODP.NET by manipulating six different attributes in the connection string. Let's take a look at the source code used to do this. Listing 3-5 shows an example of connecting to a database service that implements connection pooling. The code is a modification of that shown earlier in Listing 3-1.

*Listing 3-5. Connecting to Oracle with Connection Pooling Activated*

```
public void btnConnectNow_Click(System.Object sender, System.EventArgs e)
{
        OracleConnection conn = new OracleConnection();
        conn.ConnectionString = "Data Source=NEWDB;
                                User ID=SYSTEM;
                                Password=admin;
                                Min Pool Size=10;
                                Max Pool Size=100;
                                Connection Lifetime=120;
                                Connection Timeout=60;
                                Incr Pool Size=3;
                                Decr Pool Size=1;"
        try
        {
                conn.Open();
                conn.Close();
                MessageBox.Show("Connection successful!");
        }
        catch (Exception ex)
        {
                MessageBox.Show(ex.ToString(), "Error connecting to Oracle");
        }
}
```

The six connection string attributes used are explained in Table 3-1.

*Table 3-1. Connection Pool Attributes*

| Connection Pool Attribute | Description |
| --- | --- |
| Min Pool Size | This attribute defines the minimum number of connections that must be kept in the pool. When the connection pool is first created, it will attempt to open and cache this number of connections in the pool even if no connection request was received. |
| Max Pool Size | This attribute defines the maximum number of connections that can be kept in the pool. |
| Connection Lifetime | This attribute defines the maximum duration (in seconds) that a connection can stay cached in the pool. It is enforced after you close the connection from your application. |
| | You can see why this attribute is important in the following scenario: John has a cluster composed of two database servers running with connection pooling |

turned on. Load balancing works perfectly, but both servers are overworked. John decides to add a third server to ease the load, but he finds that the third server experiences no workload at all.

What has happened is that without the **Connection Lifetime** attribute, all connections will remain cached in the pool, and no new connections will ever need to be created. The third server will not experience any load, as the same physical connections that were opened earlier (by the first and second servers) are retrieved from the cached pool.

The **Connection Lifetime** attribute ensures that connections don't stay too long in the cache and that they are recycled after a period of time.

| | |
|---|---|
| **Connection Timeout** | This is the amount of time (in seconds) that each connection request is given to connect to the database before it raises a time-out exception. |
| **Incr Pool Size** | This attribute defines the number of new connections to create whenever more connections are needed in the connection pool. For instance, if there are zero connections in the connection pool, and you've defined **Incr Pool Size=2**, the moment your application requests a new connection, the connection pool will internally open and cache two new database connections. |
| **Decr Pool Size** | The connection pooling service will attempt to close cached connections that are not in use for longer than 3 minutes. This attribute defines the maximum number of connections that can be closed at one go. |

Connection pooling is enabled by default in ODP.NET, and I recommend that you keep it enabled for performance gains. Take note, however, that it is possible for the connection pool to get corrupted at times and for many reasons. For example, consider the following scenario: The network connection between your application and the database server might have dropped momentarily, and on resumption of service, you try to reconnect to the database. You will find that any attempt to use the connection object will result in an exception, because Oracle's connection pooling feature is unaware that a connection has gone bad and will keep handing you the same bad connection.

In such cases, you might wish to clear the connection pool. Fortunately, ODP.NET allows you to clear the connection pool quite easily using the static **ClearAllPools** method. To try this, drag a new button to your form, and name it **btnClearPool**. In the **Click** event of this button, write the code shown in Listing 3-6 below to clear all connection pools.

*Listing 3-6. Clearing All Connection Pools*

```
public void btnClearPool_Click(System.Object sender, System.EventArgs e)
{
        try
        {
                OracleConnection.ClearAllPools();
                MessageBox.Show("Connection pools cleared!");
        }
        catch (Exception ex)
        {
                MessageBox.Show(ex.ToString(), "Error clearing connection pools");
        }
}
```

■ **Tip**    You can also completely disable connection pooling if you wish by setting `Pooling=false` in the connection string.

## Connecting via Integrated Windows Authentication

ODP.NET supports integrated Windows authentication, which allows an application to use the host machine's Windows logon credentials to log in to the database. The main benefit in using integrated Windows authentication is that you do not have to store any passwords in the connection string.

However, take note that Windows authentication may require additional effort on the part of the Oracle database administrator to ensure that all the necessary Windows users have been granted access to the database.

You can tell ODP.NET to use integrated Windows authentication by specifying the slash character (/) for the **User ID** attribute in the connection string. The code to do this is shown in Listing 3-7.

*Listing 3-7. Connecting Using Integrated Windows Authentication*

```
public void btnConnectNow_Click(System.Object sender, System.EventArgs e)
{
        OracleConnection conn = new OracleConnection();
        conn.ConnectionString = "Data Source=NEWDB;User ID=/;";
        try
        {
                conn.Open();
                conn.Close();
                MessageBox.Show("Connection successful!");
        }
        catch (Exception ex)
        {
                MessageBox.Show(ex.ToString(), "Error connecting to Oracle");
        }
}
```

For the preceding code to run, you will first need to grant your Windows logon account access to the Oracle database. You can find out what your Windows logon account is from your .NET application using the **My.User.Name** property. Take note that Oracle will append a system authentication prefix to your Windows logon account. This prefix differs from system to system. You can find out what this prefix is on your system by running the following command in SQL*Plus:

```
SQL>show parameter os_authent_prefix
```

After appending this prefix, your Windows logon account should look something like this:

```
OPS$ACME\Edzehoo
```

You can now create this user in the database and grant it connect privileges in SQL*Plus:

```
SQL>CREATE USER "OPS$ACME\Edzehoo" IDENTIFIED EXTERNALLY
SQL>GRANT CONNECT TO "OPS$ACME\Edzehoo"
```

---

≡ **Tip**    If you don't wish to use the SQL*Plus command line tool, you can also create the user using the Oracle Administration Assistant for Windows.

---

## Connecting with Special Privileges

There is also an option that allows you to connect to the database using either one of these special roles:

- **SYSOPER**: Database operator
- **SYSDBA**: Database administrator

The **SYSOPER** and **SYSDBA** roles grant the connection privilege to execute the special tasks shown in Table 3-2.

**Table 3-2.** *A Brief Comparison of SYSOPER and SYSDBA Privileges*

| Privileges | SYSOPER | SYSDBA |
|---|---|---|
| Start up and shut down the database. | Yes | Yes |
| Create an SPFile. | Yes | Yes |
| Create a database. | No | Yes |
| Alter the database. | Yes | Yes |
| Mount and dismount the database. | Yes | Yes |

| | | |
|---|---|---|
| Backup and restore a database. | Yes | Yes |
| Perform archive log failure recovery. | Yes | Yes |
| Includes the **RESTRICTED SESSION** privilege. | Yes | Yes |
| Allows the user account to login as the **SYS** user. | No | Yes |
| Perform operational tasks. | Yes | Yes |
| View user-generated data. | No | Yes |

You can use the **DBA Privilege** attribute to specify which of these two roles to use for a connection. The code snippet in Listing 3-8 shows how this can be achieved.

*Listing 3-8. Connecting with Special Privileges*

```
public void btnConnectNow_Click(System.Object sender, System.EventArgs e)
{
        OracleConnection conn = new OracleConnection();
        conn.ConnectionString = "User Id=SYSTEM;Password=admin;" +
                                "DBA Privilege=SYSDBA;Data Source=NEWDB;";
        try
        {
                conn.Open();
                conn.Close();
                MessageBox.Show("Connection successful!");
        }
        catch (Exception ex)
        {
                MessageBox.Show(ex.ToString(), "Error connecting to Oracle");
        }
}
```

# Using Other Connection String Attributes

There are other connection strings attributes, of course, that you can use in combination with the ones covered previously. Table 3-3 provides a list of common connection attributes for ODP.NET release 11.1.0.7.20.

*Table 3-3. Connection String Attributes*

| Attribute Name | Description |
|---|---|
| Enlist | Enlist allows you to decide whether or not a connection should participate in a distributed transaction. |
| HA Events | This setting, if set to **true**, enables high availability (HA) event notifications to be received on the connection. |
| Load Balancing | This feature activates load balancing of connection requests in an RAC cluster. |
| Promotable Transaction | This setting disables and enables promotable transactions on the connection. |
| Proxy User Id | This represents the username of a proxy user. |
| Proxy Password | This represents the password of a proxy user. |
| Self Tuning | This setting enables ODP.NET to self-tune performance by automatically adjusting the statement cache size. |
| Statement Cache Purge | If this attribute is set to **true**, ODP.NET purges the statement cache when the connection is released back into the pool. |
| Statement Cache Size | If set to a value more than 0, this setting enables statement caching; it represents the number of statements that will be cached. |
| Validate Connection | This enables or disables validation of connections retrieved from the pool. |

# Checking Whether ODP.NET Is Installed

In some cases, it may be a good idea to programmatically check if ODP.NET is installed on your machine. You can do so by iterating through the `DataTable` object retrieved from the `System.Data.Common.DBProviderFactories.GetFactoryClasses` function, which provides a full list of database providers registered on your PC. The code to do this is shown in Listing 3-9.

*Listing 3-9. Checking If the ODP.NET Provider Exists*

```
private bool ODPExists()
{
        DataTable _table = System.Data.Common.DbProviderFactories.GetFactoryClasses();
        for (_counter = 0; _counter <= _table.Rows.Count - 1; _counter++)
        {
                if (Strings.StrComp(_table.Rows.Item(_counter).Item("Name"),
                        "Oracle Data Provider for .NET", CompareMethod.Text) == 0)
                {
                        return true;
                }
        }
        return false;
}
```

# Dynamically Building an ODP.NET Connection String

ODP.NET provides the `OracleConnectionStringBuilder` class for you to build a connection string from constituent parts instead of hard-wiring it as a whole string. This can be useful if you want to store the different parts of a connection string separately in your application. For example, you might want to store the **UserID** and **Password** in different locations from the data source name.

## Using the OracleConnectionStringBuilder Class

You can use the `OracleConnectionStringBuilder` class to build a connection string. Let's take a look at how you can rewrite the connection string (with connection pooling activated) earlier with `OracleConnectionStringBuilder` in Listing 3-10.

*Listing 3-10. Building a Connection String Using OracleConnectionStringBuilder*

```
private string BuildConnectionString(string TNSName, string UserID, string
Password)
{
    OracleConnectionStringBuilder _conn = new OracleConnectionStringBuilder();
    {
        _conn.DataSource = TNSName;
        _conn.DecrPoolSize = 5;
        _conn.IncrPoolSize = 10;
        _conn.Pooling = true;
        _conn.MaxPoolSize = 100;
        _conn.MinPoolSize = 5;
        _conn.ConnectionLifeTime = 120
        _conn.ConnectionTimeout = 60
        _conn.UserID = UserID;
        _conn.Password = Password;
```

```
    }
    return _conn.ConnectionString;
}
```

## Retrieving Available Oracle Data Sources

Now that you can build a connection string from its pieces, it would be quite useful if could retrieve a list of Oracle data sources registered on a machine. By doing so, users could choose which data source they wanted to connect to from a drop-down list, for instance. The code snippet in Listing 3-11 shows how this can be done.

*Listing 3-11. Displaying the List of Oracle Data Sources Registered on the PC*

```
using System.Data.Common;
.
.
.
DbProviderFactory _ftry;
_ftry=DbProviderFactories.GetFactory("Oracle.DataAccess.Client");
DbDataSourceEnumerator _datasourceEnum = _ftry.CreateDataSourceEnumerator;
DataTable _datasources = _datasourceEnum.GetDataSources;
for (_counter = 0; _counter <= _datasources.Rows.Count - 1; _counter++)
{
        MessageBox.Show(_datasources.Rows(_counter).Item("ServiceName"),"Service name");
}
```

Using the **System.Data.Common.DbProviderFactories.GetFactory** function, you can retrieve the provider factory for ODP.NET and iterate through the data sources available using a **DbDataSourceEnumerator** object. The **ServiceName** field of the data table returned gives you the service name of the Oracle data source. You can plug this value directly into the **Data Source** property of your connection strings.

# Understanding Transparent Application Failover

How do developers handle connection failures midway in their applications? If you've never considered this likelihood during development, it's probably a good time to do so. Connection drops can and *do* happen, especially in large deployments. For example, a system that has run out of memory might cause live connections to fail unexpectedly. Consider the code in Listing 3-12, which runs an SQL **SELECT** query against a database and iterates through its results

*Listing 3-12. Sample .NET Code Demonstrating the Possibility of Connection Drops*

```
public void btnDoSomething(System.Object sender, System.EventArgs e)
{
        .
        .
        .
        conn.Open();
        OracleCommand cmd= new OracleCommand('SELECT * FROM Employees',conn);
        OracleDataReader rows = cmd.ExecuteReader(CommandBehavior.CloseConnection)
        if (rows.HasRows())
        {
                rows.Read();
                txtName.text = rows("EmployeeName");
        }
        conn.Close();
}
```

It is possible for the live and open connection (**conn**) to fail midway while iterating through the **rows** object. You could still protect your application from an ugly death by wrapping the whole block of code within a try-catch block, but your end-users would likely still get a cryptic error message like "Sorry— unexpected error occurred while retrieving the list of employees. Please refresh the page." They would be left guessing what had happened.

It can be sometimes difficult or even impractical to remember to wrap every single block of code that uses an Oracle connection object within a try-catch statement. So how do you protect yourself from a live connection dropping midway in your code?

Fortunately for us, Oracle provides a feature called transparent application failover (TAF) that addresses this problem transparently without requiring any change in your code. TAF is an HA feature in Oracle that does two basic tasks:

- Automatically reconnect to the database if a connection fails (preserving the identical set of connection settings used in the original connection).

- Notify your .NET code (via function callbacks) whenever a failover occurs.

These tasks allow your application to carry on running with a newly established connection (that is identical) if an existing one drops. This would be transparent to you, as the .NET developer, and to your end users; it would be as if the connection had never dropped.

## Enabling TAF in Your Application

Let's see how you can enable TAF in your applications. TAF has to be enabled in the TNS descriptor. You must include a **FAILOVER_MODE** parameter in the **CONNECT_DATA** section of your connection descriptor. Open the **TNSNames.ora** file for editing in the Windows Notepad program, and add the highlighted section in Listing 3-13 to your TNS descriptor.

*Listing 3-13. Sample TNS Descriptor with TAF Enabled to Retry a Connection*

```
NEWDB=
(DESCRIPTION=
        (ADDRESS=
                (PROTOCOL=tcp)
                (HOST=127.0.0.1)
                (PORT=1521)
        )
        (CONNECT_DATA=
                (SERVICE_NAME=NEWDB)
                (FAILOVER_MODE=
                        (TYPE=select)
                        (METHOD=basic)
                        (RETRIES=20)
                        (DELAY=15)
                )
        )
)
```

Let's take a look at what these settings mean. Table 3-4 describes the various attributes of the `FAILOVER_MODE` parameter.

*Table 3-4. Attributes in the FAILOVER_MODE Parameter*

| Attribute Name | Description |
| --- | --- |
| METHOD | This attribute defines how the TAF functionality is implemented. There are two options: **basic**, in which connections are not actually created until a failover occurs, and **preconnect**, in which a connection is preestablished and used when a failover occurs. |
| BACKUP | This is the net service name of the connection to use as the backup connection. This is used when you use the **preconnect** method to preestablish backup connections. |
| TYPE | This attribute defines the type of failover. There are three types of failover: **session**, **select**, and **none**. When **session** is used and a connection drops, a new session is established; cursors opened before the failover will not be able to continue fetching data after the failover. With **select**, cursors opened before the failover will still be able to continue fetching data after the failover. **none** means that no failover functionality is used; this is the default setting. |

| RETRIES | This is the number connect attempts after a failover. The default is five retry attempts. |
| --- | --- |
| DELAY | This is the delay (in seconds) between each connect attempt. The default is one second. |

There are some things that TAF can restore when a new connection is established and some that it can't. The following briefly lists a few features that are supported and unsupported by TAF:

- TAF cannot preserve active transactions after a failover. Any noncommited transaction will be rolled back during the failover.

- TAF can automatically reestablish an identical connection or another designated connection when a failover occurs

- After a failover, TAF enables applications to automatically refetch rows from a cursor that was opened before a failover (using the select type in the FAILOVER_MODE parameter).

- Server-side program variables (in PL/SQL) cannot be recovered after a failover.

- TAF can preserve user sessions; it automatically logs the users in to the new connection using the same user login details in place before the failover.

- Distributed transactions are not supported when TAF is enabled.

# Using TAF Callbacks

As mentioned earlier, TAF also allows your .NET to be notified via function callbacks when a failover occurs. Listing 3-13 shows how you could implement this in your code.

*Listing 3-13. Registering a Custom TAF Callback Function*

```
public void RegisterTAFHandler()
{
        OracleConnection con = new OracleConnection();
        con.ConnectionString = "User Id=SYSTEM;Password=admin;Data Source=NEWDB;";
        con.Open();
        con.Failover += new OracleFailoverEventHandler(OnFailover);
        .
        .
        .
}

public FailoverReturnCode OnFailOver(object sender, OracleFailoverEventArgs eventArgs)
{
        switch (eventArgs.FailoverEvent)
        {
                case FailoverEvent.Begin:
                {
```

```
                    MessageBox.Show("Failover has just begun", "Notice");
                    break;
            }
            case FailoverEvent.Abort:
            {
                    MessageBox.Show("Failover has been aborted", "Notice");
                    break;
            }
            case FailoverEvent.End:
            {
                    MessageBox.Show("Failover has ended", "Service will resume");
                    break;
            }
            case FailoverEvent.Reauth:
            {
                    MessageBox.Show("User has been reauthenticated", "Notice");
                    break;
            }
            case FailoverEvent.Error:
            {
                    MessageBox.Show("Failover has encountered an error", "Error");
                    return FailoverReturnCode.Retry;
            }
            default:
            {
                    MessageBox.Show("Bad failover event", "Error");
                    break;
            }
    }
    return FailoverReturnCode.Success;
}
```

---

■ **Tip**    To test the code in Listing 3-13, it is helpful to know how you can artificially induce a connection drop midway through your code. You can do this by issuing a database restart command in SQL*Plus. After you've connected to the database and registered the TAF callback function, open SQL*Plus in a separate window, log in as the SYSDBA and type **startup force** at the SQL> prompt. This will force a database restart. After you've done this, continue to run your application; you will find that it is able to continue running from where it left off without having to reestablish a new connection.

---

As failovers may cause brief delays in your application, it is usually a good idea to at least let your users know that the database connection has dropped and that the application is attempting to reconnect. TAF callbacks allow your application to take appropriate action (such as displaying user-friendly messages to your end users) at different stages of the failover.

Even if you do not plan to display such messages to your end users, you can still use TAF callbacks to capture and log useful information such as connection failure frequency in your application.

# Summary

In this chapter, you've taken a look at some of the various ways you can use to connect to an Oracle database via ODP.NET:

- TNS connections

- Connections without using **TNSNames.ora**

- Oracle's EZConnect

You've also seen how you can use various connection string parameters to implement connection pooling, integrated Windows authentication, and connections with special privileges. Last, we covered the basic groundwork on TAF and its limitations and how you can ultimately enable it in your application.

In the next chapter, you will take a step further and write code to transact with the Oracle database.

# CHAPTER 4

■ ■ ■

# Retrieving and Manipulating Data with ODP.NET

I was once told during a technical workshop filled with geeky programmers that "an enterprise application is only as strong as its data tier." The programmers loved catchy phrases like that. I'm not sure how true that rings, but I can definitely agree with the most of them that if you don't know your database well enough, you're going to build underperforming routines that the remaining 70 percent of your application will unfortunately be based on.

A robust data tier goes a long way, and understanding the features and limits of what you can or cannot do with ODP.NET is important. This chapter aims to lay the basic groundwork of the types of data retrieval and manipulation possible through ODP.NET. In this chapter, you will also work with the various basic data types available in the Oracle database, such as the

- Standard Oracle data types (**VARCHAR2, NUMBER**, etc.)

- **LOB**s and **BFILE**s

- **RAW** data types

You will also try your hand at writing applications that use the **OracleDataReader**, **OracleDataAdapter**, **OracleCommand**, **OracleCommandBuilder**, and **OracleException** classes to execute SQL queries and to iterate through their result sets. In addition, you will learn how to update disconnected datasets and have your changes propagated to the Oracle database.

Before we begin, it's probably a good idea to have an overview of the different data types available in Oracle.

## Understanding ODP.NET Data Types

Oracle supports quite an extensive set of native data types, and ODP.NET is able to provide support for these data types through a set of classes in the **Oracle.DataAccess.Types** namespace. For example, the **OracleString** class in ODP.NET provides methods to manipulate the **CHAR, NCHAR, VARCHAR2, NVARCHAR2**, and **LONG** native data types. Let's take a look at the various data types in Table 4-1.

***Table 4-1.*** *ODP.NET Data Types*

| Oracle Native Data Type | ODP.NET Type | Description |
| --- | --- | --- |
| **Text Data Types** | | |
| CHAR | OracleString | This data type stores fixed-length character data up to a maximum of 2000 bytes. This data type is ideal for storing short fixed-length text such as ID values. |
| NCHAR | OracleString | This data type is the Unicode equivalent of the **CHAR** data type. |
| VARCHAR2 | OracleString | This data type stores variable length characters up to a maximum of 4000 bytes. It is ideal for storage of textual data that vary in length, such as remarks or the name of a person. |
| NVARCHAR2 | OracleString | This data type is the Unicode equivalent of the **VARCHAR2** data type. |
| **Numerical Data Types** | | |
| NUMBER | OracleDecimal | This flexible data type stores a number with a specified precision and scale. It is ideal for storage of general numbers, quantities, or prices. |
| BINARY_DOUBLE | OracleDecimal | This new data type in Oracle 11*g* offers better performance and storage efficiency compared to the **NUMBER** data type. However, its accuracy is lower than the **NUMBER** data type. It is hence ideal for storage of numbers where accuracy does not matter as much as performance of computation. |
| BINARY_FLOAT | OracleDecimal | This is the same as the **BINARY_DOUBLE** data type. |

## Date and Time Data Types

| DATE | OracleDate | This data type stores date values. |
|------|-----------|-----------------------------------|
| INTERVAL DAY TO SECOND | OracleIntervalDS | This data type stores a time interval measured from days to seconds. This can be used to store a value such as "3 days, 2 hours, 10 minutes, and 10 seconds." |
| INTERVAL YEAR TO MONTH | OracleIntervalYM | This data type stores a time interval measured in years and months. This can be used to store a value such as "4 years, 7 months." |
| TIMESTAMP | OracleTimeStamp | This data type captures a standard timestamp (without the time zone). |
| TIMESTAMP WITH LOCAL TIME ZONE | OracleTimeStampLTZ | This data type extends the standard **TIMESTAMP** to store a timestamp in the local time zone. |
| TIMESTAMP WITH TIME ZONE | OracleTimeStampTZ | This data type extends the standard **TIMESTAMP** to allow you to store a timestamp together with a time zone. |

## Large Objects

| BLOB | OracleBLOB | This is the binary large object type (with a maximum size of 4GB). It is ideal for storage of large files such as images, video, or audio. |
|------|-----------|-----------------------------------|
| CLOB | OracleCLOB | This is the character large object type (with a maximum size of 4GB), and it is ideal for storage of large amounts of text. |
| NCLOB | OracleCLOB | This is the Unicode equivalent of the **CLOB** data type. |
| BFILE | OracleBFILE | This data type holds a reference to a file stored externally outside the database. This is ideal if you want to store documents outside the database in the filesystem but wish |

| | | to maintain a link to that document. |
|---|---|---|
| LONG | OracleString | This data type has been deprecated. Its replacement is the **CLOB** data type. |
| LONG RAW | OracleBinary | This data type has been deprecated. Its replacement is the **BLOB** data type. |
| RAW | OracleBinary | This is a binary data type of a specified length. It is ideal for storage of **GUID** values and small amounts of binary data. For larger amounts of binary data, the **BLOB** data type is usually preferred. |

## PL/SQL Types

| | | |
|---|---|---|
| BINARY_INTEGER | OracleString | This data type is used in PL/SQL to store signed integers. Its performance is lower than that of **PLS_INTEGER**. |
| PLS_INTEGER | OracleDecimal | This data type is identical to the **BINARY_INTEGER** data type but performs faster. |
| REF_CURSOR | OracleRefCursor | This data type is a cursor data type that represents a result set in Oracle. **REF** cursors are usually used to obtain high performance access to result set data in memory. |

## Miscellaneous Types

| | | |
|---|---|---|
| ROWID | OracleString | This data type is a binary value that is unique only within a particular table. It is typically used as a record identifier. |
| UROWID | OracleString | This data type came after the **ROWID** data type, and is a universal row identifier. It can universally identify rows in an index organized tables (IOTs) and even non-Oracle tables. |

| REF | OracleRef | A **REF** data type is usually declared in the following manner: **REF object_type.** It represents a pointer to that specific object type. |
|---|---|---|
| XMLType | OracleXmlType | This data type stores XML-formatted data natively and is ideal for storage of semistructured data. |

# Creating a Sample Table

In the previous chapter, you accessed Oracle using the **SYSTEM** account, which is probably not a good idea in a production environment. You should, therefore, create a new user account to run the samples in this chapter. There are a few different ways for you to do this:

- Using the web-based Oracle Enterprise Manager tool

- Using the desktop-based Oracle SQL Developer tool

- Using the command-line SQL*Plus tool

You can use any one of these three tools to create the user account and sample tables necessary for the code examples throughout this book. The Oracle Enterprise Manager and Oracle SQL Developer tools both provide a visual interface for you to manage your database objects. These tools also allow you to run custom SQL queries to insert, update, or delete data from the database objects you have created.

If you prefer to create a new account by hand using Data Definition Language (DDL) statements, you can use the SQL*Plus command-line tool. You've had your first look at using SQL*Plus in Chapter 2. Let's create a new user account using SQL*Plus.

Launch SQL*Plus from the Start → All Programs → Oracle - OraDb11g_home1 →Application Development → SQL Plus menu, and log in to the tool using the **SYSTEM** account you used earlier. After doing so, type in the DDL code in Listing 4-1 at the **SQL>** prompt.

*Listing 4-1. Creating a User*

```
CREATE USER "EDZEHOO" PROFILE "DEFAULT" IDENTIFIED BY "PASS123"
DEFAULT TABLESPACE "EXAMPLE" ACCOUNT UNLOCK
QUOTA UNLIMITED ON "EXAMPLE";
GRANT "CONNECT" TO "EDZEHOO";
GRANT ALTER ANY TABLE TO "EDZEHOO";
GRANT CREATE ANY TABLE TO "EDZEHOO";
```

■ **Tip** You can press the Enter key each time to type on a new line in SQL*Plus. The SQL statement as a whole isn't executed until you end a line with the semicolon (;) character.

These DDL statements will create a new user account (**EDZEHOO**) with the password (**PASS123**) and assign this user rights to create unlimited objects on the **EXAMPLE** table space. These statements also grant this user account basic rights to connect to the database, as well as the ability to issue **CREATE TABLE** and **ALTER TABLE** SQL commands. Figure 4-1 shows a screenshot of the output from running these statements.

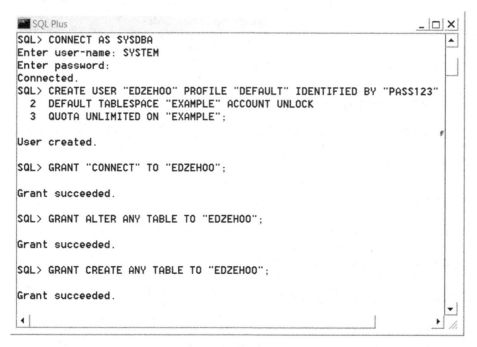

```
SQL Plus                                                    _ □ X
SQL> CONNECT AS SYSDBA                                          ▲
Enter user-name: SYSTEM
Enter password:
Connected.
SQL> CREATE USER "EDZEHOO" PROFILE "DEFAULT" IDENTIFIED BY "PASS123"
  2   DEFAULT TABLESPACE "EXAMPLE" ACCOUNT UNLOCK
  3   QUOTA UNLIMITED ON "EXAMPLE";

User created.

SQL> GRANT "CONNECT" TO "EDZEHOO";

Grant succeeded.

SQL> GRANT ALTER ANY TABLE TO "EDZEHOO";

Grant succeeded.

SQL> GRANT CREATE ANY TABLE TO "EDZEHOO";

Grant succeeded.
                                                               ▼
◄                                                         ►  //
```

***Figure 4-1.*** *Creating the user in SQL\*Plus*

You can try logging in with this new user account to create the sample table needed for this chapter. Issue a **CONNECT** command at the **SQL>** prompt, and log in using your new account details. After logging in, issue the SQL command in Listing 4-2 to create the **Products** table.

*Listing 4-2. Creating the Example Table*

```
CREATE TABLE "EDZEHOO"."PRODUCTS" (
"ID" VARCHAR2(10) NOT NULL,
"NAME" VARCHAR2(255),
"PRICE" NUMBER(10, 2),
"REMARKS" VARCHAR2(4000),
CONSTRAINT "PRIMKEY" PRIMARY KEY ("ID") VALIDATE);
```

You should see the output shown in Figure 4-2.

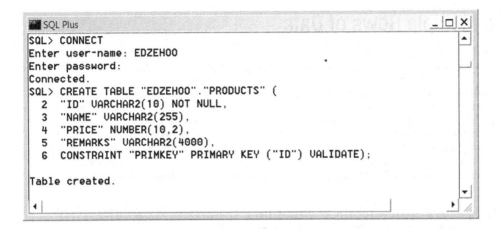

*Figure 4-2. Creating the Products table*

Now that you have created a table, you will need to key in some sample data. Execute the SQL
**INSERT** statements shown in Listing 4-3.

*Listing 4-3. Inserting Some Data into the Products Table*

```
INSERT INTO PRODUCTS(ID, NAME, PRICE, REMARKS) VALUES('E1', 'Engine', 3000, 'Stan↵
dard car engine');
INSERT INTO PRODUCTS(ID, NAME, PRICE, REMARKS) VALUES('W1', 'Windshield', 500, 'Q↵
uality windshields');
INSERT INTO PRODUCTS(ID, NAME, PRICE, REMARKS) VALUES('R1', 'Rear Lights', 200.50↵
, 'Standard rear lights');
```

To confirm that your data has been added successfully to the table, you can run a simple SQL **SELECT**
statement to retrieve the products you've created. See Figure 4-3 for an example.

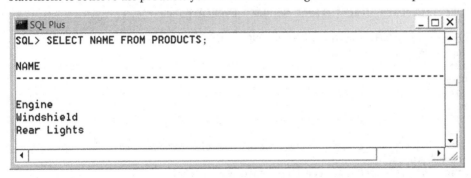

*Figure 4-3. Viewing data in the Products table*

You're now ready to start writing an ODP.NET application to read data from this table!

# Retrieving Multiple Rows of Data

One of the simplest (and most efficient) ways to read data from a table is to use a **DataReader**. A **DataReader** is an ADO.NET class that provides you a read-only and forward-only data stream reader to retrieve rows from a database. Since the class is read only, you can only use the **DataReader** to retrieve data from the database. You won't be able to use it for insert, update, or delete operations.

The **DataReader** keeps only one record in memory at a time and allows you to iterate forward through the records in the result set. You cannot iterate through the result set backward.

ODP.NET provides **DataReader** functionality in the form of the **OracleDataReader** class. Let's take a look at how you can retrieve the three rows of data you've keyed in earlier in the **Products** database. To execute an SQL statement, you need to first create an **OracleCommand** object. You can obtain an **OracleCommand** object by calling the **CreateCommand()** method in the **OracleConnection** object, for example:

```
string connstring="Data Source=localhost/NEWDB;User Id=EDZEHOO;Password=PASS123;";
OracleConnection _connObj = new OracleConnection(_connstring);
_connObj.Open ();
OracleCommand _cmdObj = _connObj.CreateCommand ();
```

To retrieve data into an **OracleDataReader** object, write the following code.

```
OracleDataReader _rdrObj;
_cmdObj.CommandText = "SELECT * FROM Products";
_rdrObj = _cmdObj.ExecuteReader();
```

We can use the **HasRows** property to check if there are any rows in the execution results. If there are, we loop through each record in the result set by calling **Read()** repeatedly. Each time you call **Read()**, the **DataReader** will attempt to fetch the next record. As long as there are more rows to fetch, the **Read()** method will always return true. After it fetches the last record, the **Read()** function will return false. Listing 4-4 puts everything together into a working example that returns data from the **Products** table.

*Listing 4-4. Retrieving Data Via the OracleDataReader Interface*

```
private void btnRetrieveData_Click(object sender, EventArgs e)
{
        string _connstring = "Data Source=localhost/NEWDB;User
                Id=EDZEHOO;Password=PASS123;";
        string _ID;
        string _name;
        decimal _price;
        string _remarks;
        try
        {
                OracleConnection _connObj = new OracleConnection(_connstring);
                _connObj.Open();
                OracleCommand _cmdObj = _connObj.CreateCommand ();
                _cmdObj.CommandText = "SELECT * FROM Products";
                OracleDataReader _rdrObj = _cmdObj.ExecuteReader();
                if (_rdrObj.HasRows)
                {
```

```
            while (_rdrObj.Read())
            {
                    _ID = _rdrObj.GetString(_rdrObj.GetOrdinal ("ID"));
                    _name = _rdrObj.GetString(_rdrObj.GetOrdinal ("Name"));
                    _price = _rdrObj.GetDecimal (_rdrObj.GetOrdinal ("Price"));
                    _remarks = _rdrObj.GetString(_rdrObj.GetOrdinal
                            ("Remarks"));
                    MessageBox.Show("ID: " + _ID + "\nName: " + _name +
                            "\nPrice: " + _price + "\nRemarks: " +
                            _remarks,"Products");
            };
        };
        _connObj.Close();
        _connObj.Dispose();
        _connObj = null;
    }
    catch (Exception ex)
    {
            MessageBox.Show(ex.ToString());
    }
}
```

As you can see from Listing 4-4, you can retrieve typed data from each column by calling the appropriate **GetXXXXX** method (**GetString**, **GetDecimal**, **GetDate**, **GetInt32**, and so on). You will need to specify the index of the column you wish to retrieve. If you would rather refer to a column by its name, you can use the **OracleDataReader**'s **GetOrdinal()** method to get the column index for a particular column name.

To try this code snippet, create a form, and place a button on the form. In the click event of this button, write the code shown in Listing 4-4. Run this form, and click the button. You will see a summary of the data for each of the records you've created earlier displayed in a pop-up window (as shown in Figure 4-4).

*Figure 4-4. Displaying data retrieved using the OracleDataReader*

# Retrieving a Single Value

If you've developed any database-driven application before, you've definitely attempted at one time or another to retrieve a single value from the database. For example, you could be using an SQL statement like the following to retrieve the **COUNT** or **SUM** of the data in a particular field:

```
SELECT COUNT(*) AS TotalRecords FROM Products
SELECT SUM(Price) AS TotalPrice FROM Products
```

If you know in advance that your SQL query is going to return only a single result (a single row or column), you can consider using the **OracleCommand.ExecuteScalar** method instead of the **ExecuteReader** method to retrieve the data. The **ExecuteScalar** method returns only a single result from the SQL statement. The type of the object returned depends on the Oracle data type of the return field. Listing 4-5 shows how you can retrieve a value using **ExecuteScalar**.

*Listing 4-5. Retrieving the Count from the Products Table*

```
public void GetProductCount()
{
        string _connstring = "Data Source=localhost/NEWDB;User
            Id=EDZEHOO;Password=PASS123;";
        decimal _totalRecords;
        try
        {
                OracleConnection _connObj = new OracleConnection(_connstring);
                _connObj.Open();
                OracleCommand _cmdObj = _connObj.CreateCommand();
                _cmdObj.CommandText = "SELECT COUNT(*) AS TotalRecords FROM Products";
                _totalRecords = (decimal)_cmdObj.ExecuteScalar();
                MessageBox.Show("Total records:" + _totalRecords);
                _connObj.Close();
                _connObj.Dispose();
                _connObj = null;
        }
        catch (Exception ex)
        {
                MessageBox.Show(ex.ToString());
        }
}
```

Running the code sample in Listing 4-5 yields the result shown in figure 4-5.

**Figure 4-5.** *Displaying total count of Products*

# Handling NULL Values in ODP.NET

**NULL** values are an inevitable evil in database programming. Developers tend to forget to handle **NULL** values and end up seeing the error message shown in Figure 4-6 all too often.

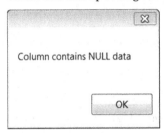

**Figure 4-6.** *NULL data exception*

To check for **NULL** values in **OracleDataReader** results, you can use the **IsDBNull()** method. The code in Listing 4-6 shows how **NULL** checking can be implemented to prevent your code from raising an ugly exception.

*Listing 4-6. Checking for NULL Values*

```
if (_rdrObj.HasRows)
{
        if (_rdrObj.Read())
        {
                if (_rdrObj.IsDBNull(_rdrObj.GetOrdinal("Name"))==false)
                        {txtName.Text = _rdrObj.GetString(_rdrObj.GetOrdinal("Name"));}

                if (_rdrObj.IsDBNull(_rdrObj.GetOrdinal("Remarks")) == false)
                        {txtRemarks.Text = rdrObj.GetString(_rdrObj.GetOrdinal("Remarks"));}

                if (_rdrObj.IsDBNull(_rdrObj.GetOrdinal("Price")) == false)
                        {numPrice.Value = _rdrObj.GetDecimal(_rdrObj.GetOrdinal("Price"));}
        }
}
```

# Retrieving Data into a Dataset

If you need to retrieve data and keep it in memory for subsequent update, you need to use a **DataAdapter.** The **DataAdapter** allows data to be retrieved into a **DataSet** object. A **DataSet** object is a placeholder in memory used to hold retrieved records. The **DataAdapter** handles all exchange of data between the **DataSet** and the database, including the writing of changes in the **DataSet** back to the database. To populate a **DataSet** with data, the **DataAdapter** provides the **Fill()** method.

The **OracleDataAdapter** class is a **DataAdapter** optimized for the Oracle database. Let's take a look at how you can use **OracleDataAdapter** to fill a dataset with data from the **Products** table and subsequently display the data in a **DataGridView** control.

To begin, you'll first need to create a form in your project. Drag a **DataGridView** control onto your form and add a button with the caption "Fill grid" to the top of the form. In the click event of this button, write the code shown in Listing 4-7.

*Listing 4-7. Retrieving Data Using the OracleDataAdapter*

```
private DataSet  ds=null;
private void btnFillGrid_Click(object sender, EventArgs e)
{
        string _connstring = "Data Source=localhost/NEWDB;User
                Id=EDZEHOO;Password=PASS123;";
        string _sql;
        try
        {
                OracleConnection _connObj = new OracleConnection(_connstring);
                _ds = new DataSet();
                _connObj.Open();
                _sql = "SELECT * FROM Products";
                OracleDataAdapter _adapterObj = new OracleDataAdapter(_sql, _connObj);
                _adapterObj.Fill(_ds);
                _connObj.Close();
                _connObj.Dispose();
                _connObj = null;
                dataGridView1.DataSource = _ds.Tables[0];
        }
        catch (Exception ex)
        {
                MessageBox.Show(ex.ToString());
        }
}
```

Run the form that you've just created, and click the "Fill grid" button. You will see the data from your **Products** table in the DataGridView control, as shown in Figure 4-7.

*Figure 4-7. Displaying data retrieved through the OracleDataAdapter*

# Using Parameterized Queries

If you have built a database-driven search feature before, you would most definitely have encountered cases where user input is used to build the filters for a particular SQL statement. For instance, you might let the user pull out the full details for a product by specifying the ID of the product. You might then build a **SELECT** statement as follows:

```
SELECT * FROM Products WHERE ID='" + txtID.text + "'"
```

Instead of dynamically building the SQL string yourself, you could choose to use bind variables. Bind variables allow you to create parameterized queries that are easier to maintain in code. The following is an example of a bind variable being used in an SQL statement:

```
SELECT * FROM Products WHERE ID=:IDValue
```

Since bind variables force you to strongly define your SQL parameters, they also allow you to avoid common security pitfalls such as SQL injection attacks, which you will read more about in Chapter 11 of this book. When you use bind variables in your SQL, you must define where the actual data for these variables come from. You must create a corresponding parameter object for each bind variable that you use in your SQL, for example:

```
OracleParameter _idParam = _cmdObj.CreateParameter();
_idParam.ParameterName = "IDValue";
_idParam.OracleDbType = OracleDbType.Varchar2;
_idParam.Value = txtID.Text;
_cmdObj.Parameters.Add(_idParam);
```

Let's take a look at an example of bind variables in action. Create a new form and add the text boxes, numeric boxes, labels, and buttons shown in Figure 4-8 to the form. The user is meant to type in the ID of the product in the ID box and click "Retrieve data" to retrieve the full details of the product. The full details of the product will be displayed in the Name, Price, and Remarks boxes.

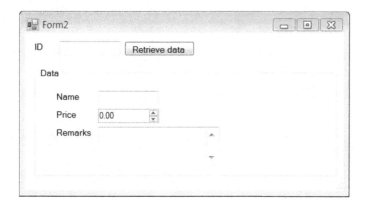

*Figure 4-8. Designing the sample form used to demonstrate bind variables*

In the click event of the "Retrieve data" button, write the code in Listing 4-8. Take note that the code to create and add a new parameter to the **OracleCommand** object is highlighted in bold.

*Listing 4-8. Using Bind Variables*

```
private void btnRetrieveData_Click(object sender, EventArgs e)
{
        string _connstring = "Data Source=localhost/NEWDB;User
                Id=EDZEHOO;Password=PASS123;";
        string _sql;
        OracleDataReader _rdrObj;
        try
        {
                OracleConnection _connObj = new OracleConnection(_connstring);
                DataSet _ds = new DataSet();
                _connObj.Open();
                _sql = "SELECT * FROM Products WHERE ID=:IDValue";
                OracleCommand _cmdObj = new OracleCommand(_sql, _connObj);
                OracleParameter _idParam = _cmdObj.CreateParameter();
                _idParam.ParameterName = "IDValue";
                _idParam.OracleDbType = OracleDbType.Varchar2;
                _idParam.Value = txtID.Text;
                _cmdObj.Parameters.Add(_idParam);
                _rdrObj = _cmdObj.ExecuteReader();
                if (_rdrObj.HasRows)
                {
                    if (_rdrObj.Read())
                    {
                        txtName.Text = _rdrObj.GetString(_rdrObj.GetOrdinal("Name"));
                        txtRemarks.Text = _rdrObj.GetString(_rdrObj.GetOrdinal("Remarks"));
                        numPrice.Value = _rdrObj.GetDecimal(_rdrObj.GetOrdinal("Price"));
                    }
                }
```

```
            else
            {
                MessageBox.Show("A record with a matching ID was not found");
            }
            _connObj.Close();
            _connObj.Dispose();
            _connObj = null;
        }
        catch (Exception ex)
        {
                MessageBox.Show(ex.ToString());
        }
    }
}
```

To test this sample, run the application, type either **W1**, **E1**, or **R1** (the IDs of the products you created earlier) in the ID box, and click the "Retrieve data" button. The full details of the matching record will be displayed as shown in Figure 4-9.

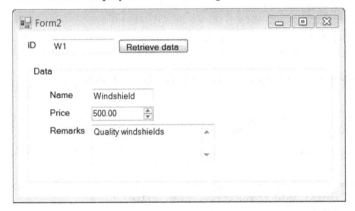

*Figure 4-9. Running the Bind Variables example*

---

■ **Tip** One of the most common reasons why developers use bind variables is performance. Bind variables help improve performance by allowing SQL statements with the same structure to be cached in a shared pool. We will cover more on bind variable performance in Chapter 12 of this book.

---

# Updating Data

You have written ODP.NET code to retrieve data so far; now, let's take a look in the other direction. You can update data in the Oracle database using two common methods:

- Executing a single SQL **UPDATE, INSERT,** or **DELETE** statement

- Committing dataset changes to the database through the **OracleDataAdapter** class

Let's take a look at both approaches in the sections to follow.

## Executing a Single INSERT, UPDATE, or DELETE Statement

If you are planning to format your own SQL statements and just need ODP.NET to execute them as they are, you can use the **ExecuteNonQuery()** method of the **OracleCommand** object. The **ExecuteNonQuery()** method allows you to run any statement that does not return a result. These statements include SQL **INSERT, UPDATE, DELETE, ALTER TABLE,** and even **CREATE TABLE** statements. Let's build a sample application to test this out. You will write some code to add a new record, update the record, and then finally delete the record. Create a new form, and place a button on the form. In the click event of this button, write the code in Listing 4-9.

*Listing 4-9. Executing SQL INSERT, UPDATE, and DELETE Statements*

```
private void btnRunStatements_Click(object sender, EventArgs e)
{
        string _connstring;
        _connstring = "Data Source=localhost/NEWDB;User Id=EDZEHOO;Password=PASS123;";
        int _recordsAffected;
        try
        {
                OracleConnection _connObj = new OracleConnection(_connstring);
                _connObj.Open();

                //Insert a new record
                OracleCommand _cmdObj = _connObj.CreateCommand();
                _cmdObj.CommandText = "INSERT INTO Products(ID, Name, Price)
                        VALUES(:ID,:Name,:Price)";
                _cmdObj.Parameters.Add (new OracleParameter ("ID","M1"));
                _cmdObj.Parameters.Add (new OracleParameter ("Name","Mudguards"));
                _cmdObj.Parameters.Add (new OracleParameter ("Price","250.50"));
                _recordsAffected=_cmdObj.ExecuteNonQuery();
                MessageBox.Show("Total records affected after insert:" + _recordsAffected);

                //Update an existing record
                _cmdObj.CommandText = "UPDATE Products SET Remarks=:Remarks WHERE ID=:ID";
                _cmdObj.Parameters.Clear();
                _cmdObj.Parameters.Add (new OracleParameter ("Remarks","Quality mud
                        guards"));
                _cmdObj.Parameters.Add(new OracleParameter("ID", "M1"));
                _recordsAffected=_cmdObj.ExecuteNonQuery();
                MessageBox.Show("Total records affected after update:" + _recordsAffected);

                //Delete an existing record
                _cmdObj.CommandText = "DELETE FROM Products WHERE ID=:ID";
                _cmdObj.Parameters.Clear();
```

```
                _cmdObj.Parameters.Add(new OracleParameter("ID", "M1"));
                _recordsAffected = _cmdObj.ExecuteNonQuery();
                MessageBox.Show("Total records affected after delete:" + _recordsAffected);

                _connObj.Close();
                _connObj.Dispose();
                _connObj = null;
        }
        catch (Exception ex)
        {
                MessageBox.Show(ex.ToString());
        }
}
```

If you now run the application, you will see the message box in Figure 4-10 appear three times, once for each of the insert, update, and delete operations. The record count of one indicates that each SQL statement executed successfully.

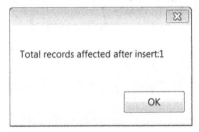

*Figure 4-10. Displaying the total number of affected records*

## Committing Dataset Changes to the Database

What if you've made changes to a dataset that was retrieved through the **OracleDataAdapter**? How do you get those changes in the dataset propagated back to the database? Fortunately, the **OracleDataAdapter** object is able to discover the changes you've made to the dataset and commit them to the database with a single method call.

Let's take a look at how this works. A dataset can contain multiple records and, at any time, can hold changes to more than one record. These changes can include altering a field value in an existing row, deleting existing rows, or maybe adding entirely new rows. Figure 4-11 illustrates such a situation.

To commit all the changes from a dataset to the database, the **DataAdapter** object must know how to handle each type of change. We must hence define the corresponding **UpdateCommand**, **InsertCommand**, and **DeleteCommand** objects for the DataAdapter object.

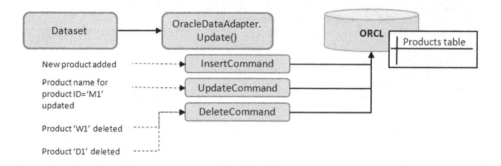

*Figure 4-11. How the Update() method of the OracleDataAdapter works*

After you have defined the **UpdateCommand**, **InsertCommand**, and **DeleteCommand** objects, you can pass the dataset containing the changes to the **OracleDataAdapter** object and call its **Update()** method. The **OracleDataAdapter** will then scan through each change in the dataset and use the appropriate **Command** object to commit changes accordingly to the database.

Let's begin by using the same form you created earlier in the first **OracleDataAdapter** example (in the "Retrieving Data Using OracleDataAdapter" section). If you recall, that example retrieves **Products** data into a **DataGridView** control. The **DataGridView** control supports in-grid editing by default, so it already allows the user to make changes to the dataset.

You will now need to add the functionality to commit these dataset changes to the database. Add a new button labeled "Save to database" on the same form. In the click event of the button, write the code from Listing 4-10.

*Listing 4-10. Saving Dataset Changes to the Database*

```
private void btnSaveToDatabase_Click(object sender, EventArgs e)
{
        string _connstring = "Data Source=localhost/NEWDB;User
                Id=EDZEHOO;Password=PASS123;";
        string _sql;
        try
        {
                OracleConnection _connObj = new OracleConnection(_connstring);
                _connObj.Open();
                OracleCommand _commandObj = _connObj.CreateCommand();
                OracleDataAdapter _adapterObj = new OracleDataAdapter(_commandObj);

                //Manually define the UPDATE command in the OracleDataAdapter
                _sql = "UPDATE Products SET Name=:Name, Price=:Price, Remarks=:Remarks WHERE
                        ID=:ID";
                _adapterObj.UpdateCommand = new OracleCommand(_sql, _connObj);
                _adapterObj.UpdateCommand.Parameters.Add (new OracleParameter("Name",
                        OracleDbType.Varchar2, 255, "Name"));
                _adapterObj.UpdateCommand.Parameters.Add (new OracleParameter("Price",
                        OracleDbType.Decimal, 10, "Price"));
```

```
                _adapterObj.UpdateCommand.Parameters.Add (new OracleParameter("Remarks",
                        OracleDbType.Varchar2, 4000, "Remarks"));
                _adapterObj.UpdateCommand.Parameters.Add (new OracleParameter("ID",
                        OracleDbType.Varchar2, 10, "ID"));

                //Manually define the INSERT command in the OracleDataAdapter
                _sql = "INSERT INTO Products(Name, Price, Remarks, ID) VALUES(:Name, :Price,
                        :Remarks, :ID)";
                _adapterObj.InsertCommand = new OracleCommand(_sql, _connObj);
                _adapterObj.InsertCommand.Parameters.Add(new OracleParameter("Name",
                        OracleDbType.Varchar2, 255, "Name"));
                _adapterObj.InsertCommand.Parameters.Add(new OracleParameter("Price",
                        OracleDbType.Decimal, 10, "Price"));
                _adapterObj.InsertCommand.Parameters.Add(new OracleParameter("Remarks",
                        OracleDbType.Varchar2, 4000, "Remarks"));
                _adapterObj.InsertCommand.Parameters.Add(new OracleParameter("ID",
                        OracleDbType.Varchar2, 10, "ID"));

                //Manually define the DELETE command in the OracleDataAdapter
                _sql = "DELETE FROM Products WHERE ID=:ID";
                _adapterObj.DeleteCommand = new OracleCommand(_sql, _connObj);
                _adapterObj.DeleteCommand.Parameters.Add(new OracleParameter("ID",
                        OracleDbType.Varchar2, 10, "ID"));

                //Now we pass in the dataset to the DataAdapter and request it
                //to commit the changes to the database (using the command objects above)
                _adapterObj.Update(_ds);
                _connObj.Close();
                _connObj.Dispose();
                _connObj = null;
                MessageBox.Show("Dataset committed!");
        }
        catch (Exception ex)
        {
                MessageBox.Show(ex.ToString());
        }
}
```

To test whether **DataSet** changes are saved, run the form, and click the "Fill grid" button to first fill the grid with data. After that, make as many changes as you wish to the data in the grid. Try a combination of changes: delete a row, insert a new one, and update an existing one. After you're done, click the "Save to database" button. You will see a "Dataset committed!" message, as shown in Figure 4-12. To test if the changes have really been saved to the database, you can try closing the form, reopening it, and clicking "Fill grid" again. You will find that the data with your latest changes will be displayed.

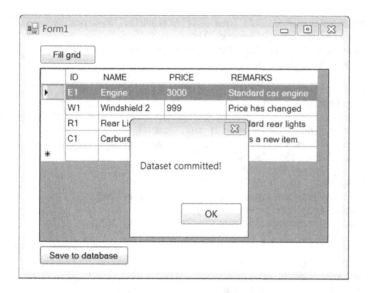

**Figure 4-12.** *Committing* **DataSet** *changes to the database*

## Generating Command Objects

In most cases when you're dealing with updates to a single table, it can be quite a hassle to define the **UpdateCommand**, **InsertCommand**, and **DeleteCommand** objects for each table you wish to update, especially if the table contains a large number of columns. Fortunately, ODP.NET provides the **OracleCommandBuilder** class that can help save your time by automatically generating the **UPDATE**, **INSERT**, and **DELETE** commands on its own whenever needed.

Using the same form you created earlier, add one more button next to the "Save to database" button. Label this button "Save to database – using CommandBuilder". In the click event of this button, write the code shown in Listing 4-11.

*Listing 4-11. Using the OracleCommandBuilder Class*

```
private void btnSaveButtonWithCommBuilder_Click(object sender, EventArgs e)
{
        string _connstring = "Data Source=localhost/NEWDB;User
            Id=EDZEHOO;Password=PASS123;";
        string _sql;
        try
        {
                OracleConnection _connObj = new OracleConnection(_connstring);
                _connObj.Open();
                _sql = "SELECT * FROM Products";
                OracleDataAdapter _adapterObj = new OracleDataAdapter(_sql, _connObj);
                OracleCommandBuilder _commBldrObj = new OracleCommandBuilder(_adapterObj);
```

```
            //We must specify the unique column in the dataset so that the
            //OracleCommandBuilder knows which field to use as the primary key when
            //generating the UpdateCommand and DeleteCommand objects
            _ds.Tables[0].Columns["ID"].Unique = true;

            _adapterObj.Update(_ds);
            _connObj.Close();
            _connObj.Dispose();
            _connObj = null;
            MessageBox.Show("Dataset committed!");
        }
        catch (Exception ex)
        {
            MessageBox.Show(ex.ToString());
        }
}
```

You can test this code the same way you tested the previous example. Instead of using the "Save to database" button, click the "Save to database – using CommandBuilder" button. You will see that you are able to remove, edit, and insert rows despite having created no corresponding command objects. As before, the message "Dataset committed!" indicates success; see Figure 4-13.

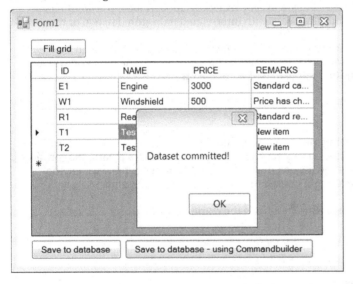

*Figure 4-13. Committing* DataSet *changes to the database with CommandBuilder*

Take note, however, that the **OracleCommandBuilder** works only with single table updates. If you have used table joins in your SQL, using the **OracleCommandBuilder** will not be a viable option. You would likely need to hand-code your own command objects.

Another reason to hand-code command objects is to achieve a greater degree of control over the SQL statements used for updating, inserting, and deleting. For instance, let's say you had another column called **Date Modified** in the **Products** table. Let's say each time you update an existing record in this table, you wanted to capture the current timestamp in the **Date Modified** field. If you use the **OracleCommandBuilder** object, this would not have been possible. You could, however, hand-code the **UpdateCommand** object like this:

```
_sql = "UPDATE Products SET Name=:Name, Price=:Price, Remarks=:Remarks,
DateModified=SYSDATE() WHERE ID=:ID";
_adapterObj.UpdateCommand = new OracleCommand(_sql, _connObj);
_adapterObj.UpdateCommand.Parameters.Add (new OracleParameter("Name",
        OracleDbType.Varchar2, 255, "Name"));
_adapterObj.UpdateCommand.Parameters.Add (new OracleParameter("Price",
        OracleDbType.Decimal, 10, "Price"));
_adapterObj.UpdateCommand.Parameters.Add (new OracleParameter("Remarks",
        OracleDbType.Varchar2, 4000, "Remarks"));
_adapterObj.UpdateCommand.Parameters.Add (new OracleParameter("ID",
        OracleDbType.Varchar2, 10, "ID"));
```

# Handling Master-Detail Relationships

Master-detail relationships between database tables are an inevitable part of database-driven application development. From expense claims to job order processing applications, you would have one way or another encountered applications that work with interrelated data stored in two or more tables.

In the next few sections, you will see how you can retrieve rows from multiple tables into a single dataset and then apply relationship constraints on these tables. Once you have done that, you will make changes to the data and have them committed to the database in one run.

## Creating a Second Table

Before you can run the sample code involving multiple tables, you'll need to create another table in the database—the **ProductComponents** table. This table stores the list of components for a particular product. The **Products** table you've created earlier is the master, and the **ProductComponents** table will be the detail. For example, the car engine product might consist of the spark plug, piston, and crankshaft components.

To create and populate the **ProductComponents** table, run the commands in Listing 4-12 using SQL*Plus.

*Listing 4-12. Creating and Populating a Components Table*

```
CREATE TABLE "EDZEHOO"."PRODUCTCOMPONENTS" (
"COMPONENTID" VARCHAR2(10) NOT NULL,
"PARENTPRODUCTID" VARCHAR2(10) NOT NULL,
"NAME" VARCHAR2(255),
"QUANTITY" NUMBER(10,2),
"REMARKS" VARCHAR2(4000),
CONSTRAINT "PRIMKEY2" PRIMARY KEY ("COMPONENTID") VALIDATE);
INSERT INTO PRODUCTCOMPONENTS(COMPONENTID, PARENTPRODUCTID, NAME, QUANTITY, REMARKS) VALUES
('C1','E1','SPARK PLUG', 1, 'The part that starts the engine');
```

```
INSERT INTO PRODUCTCOMPONENTS(COMPONENTID, PARENTPRODUCTID, NAME, QUANTITY, REMARKS) VALUES
('C2','E1','PISTON', 4, 'The part that makes the car move');
INSERT INTO PRODUCTCOMPONENTS(COMPONENTID, PARENTPRODUCTID, NAME, QUANTITY, REMARKS) VALUES
('C3','R1','LIGHT DIODES', 20, 'The part that makes the lamps blink');
```

Now that you have two tables, it's time to move on and look at some examples of querying and updating those tables.

## Retrieving from Multiple Tables

First, let's look at the problem of retrieving from multiple tables into a single **DataSet**. Consider a product details form for example. The data for such a form would most likely come from two different tables: the **Products** table (containing the product master information), and the **ProductComponents** table (containing the list of components of the product). Since both are displayed in the same page, it would definitely make sense to retrieve all the data in one single dataset.

We can do this by calling the **OracleDataAdapter.Fill()** method on the same dataset more than once. Let's take a look at the code to do this. The two **Fill()** method calls are highlighted in Listing 4-13.

*Listing 4-13. Filling a Dataset with Results from Multiple Tables*

```
private DataSet _ds=null;
private OracleCommand _productsCmdObj = null;
private OracleCommand _productComponentsCmdObj = null;
private OracleDataAdapter _productsAdpObj = null;
private OracleDataAdapter _productComponentsAdpObj = null;
private OracleConnection _connObj = null;

//In this example, we load the Product identified by the ID value of "E1"
string _productID = "E1";

private void LoadData()
{
        string _connstring = "Data Source=localhost/NEWDB;User
            Id=EDZEHOO;Password=PASS123;";
        string _sql;
        try
        {
            OracleConnection _connObj = new OracleConnection(_connstring);
            _connObj.Open();
            _ds = new DataSet();

            //Retrieve from the Products table
            _sql = "SELECT * FROM Products WHERE ID=:ID";
            _productsCmdObj = new OracleCommand(_sql, _connObj);
            _productsCmdObj.Parameters.Add(new OracleParameter("ID", _productID));
            _productsAdpObj = new OracleDataAdapter(_productsCmdObj);
            _productsAdpObj.Fill(_ds, "Products");

            //Retrieve from the ProductComponents table
            _sql = "SELECT * FROM ProductComponents WHERE
```

```
                    ParentProductID=:ParentProductID";
                _productComponentsCmdObj = new OracleCommand(_sql, _connObj);
                _productComponentsCmdObj.Parameters.Add(new
                        OracleParameter("ParentProductID", _productID));
                _productComponentsAdpObj = new OracleDataAdapter(_productComponentsCmdObj);
                _productComponentsAdpObj.Fill(_ds, "ProductComponents");
        }
        catch (Exception ex)
        {
                MessageBox.Show(ex.ToString());
        }
}
```

## Binding a .NET Form to Your Dataset

To test the **LoadData()** method you've created in Listing 4-13, you need to first design a new form
(named **frmProducts**) to display the data. Let's start with the form. Design a new form that looks like the
one shown in Figure 4-14. Use text boxes and numerical controls to display product master details and a
**DataGridView** control to display the list of components for the product.

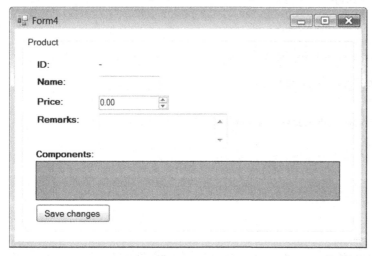

*Figure 4-14. Designing a sample form for the Data Binding example*

After you've designed the form, you'll need to bind the dataset to the form. Drag and drop a
**BindingSource** control to the form. Name this **BindingSource** control **bsProducts**. A **BindingSource**
control acts as an intermediary between the **DataSet** and the controls on the form. Let's take a look at the
code that does the binding. You can see it in Figure 4-14.

*Listing 4-14. Data Binding the Products Table to the Form Controls*

```
private void BindData()
{
        bsProducts.DataSource = _ds.Tables["Products"];
        txtName.DataBindings.Add(new Binding("Text",
                bsProducts, "Name", true));
        numPrice.DataBindings.Add(new Binding("Value",
                bsProducts, "Price", true));
        txtRemarks.DataBindings.Add(new Binding("Text",
                bsProducts, "Remarks", true));
        dgComponents.DataSource = _ds.Tables["ProductComponents"];
}
```

In the first line of code, you specify the **Products** table in your **_ds DataSet** as the data source for the **BindingSource** control. After that, you need to tell each control on the form where to bind its display property. Each control can (although not necessarily) bind to a different field in the **Products** table. As for the **dgComponents DataGridView** control, we simply pass in the entire **ProductComponents** table, and it will do the work of displaying the data.

To test this, add a form load event handler to your form, and call the two functions you've created so far like this:

```
private void frmProducts_Load(object sender, EventArgs e)
{
        LoadData();
        BindData();
}
```

You will be able to see the details of the **Engine** product show up when you load the form. You should see results as shown in Figure 4-15.

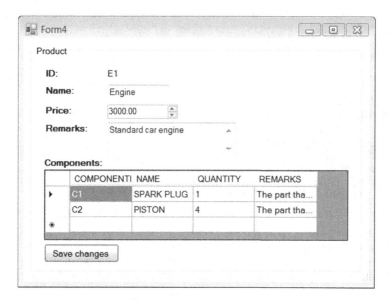

**Figure 4-15.** *Data binding in action*

## Committing Changes to Multiple Tables

To commit data from multiple tables to the database, you can use two separate **OracleDataAdapter** objects, one for each table. You can use the **OracleCommandBuilder** class you learned about earlier to generate the corresponding update, insert, and delete commands for each adapter. Using the form from the previous section, write the code in Listing 4-15.

*Listing 4-15. Updating Data from Multiple Tables*

```
private void SaveData(string productID)
{
        bsProducts.EndEdit();
try
{
        OracleCommandBuilder _commBldrObj = new OracleCommandBuilder(_productsAdpObj);
        OracleCommandBuilder _commBldrObj2 = new
                OracleCommandBuilder(_productComponentsAdpObj);

        //Designate each primary column as unique
        _ds.Tables["Products"].Columns["ID"].Unique = true;
        _ds.Tables["ProductComponents"].Columns["ComponentID"].Unique = true;

        //Now we pass in the dataset to the DataAdapter and request it
        //to commit the changes to the database (using the command objects above)
        _productsAdpObj.Update(_ds, "Products");
        _productComponentsAdpObj.Update(_ds, "ProductComponents");
```

```
                MessageBox.Show("Dataset committed!");
}
catch (Exception ex)
{
        MessageBox.Show(ex.ToString());
}
}
private void btnSave_Click(object sender, EventArgs e)
{
        SaveData(_productID);
}
```

You can test the save functionality by making changes to both the data in the **Components** grid and the **Products** master details at the same time and then clicking the Save button.

## Defining Table Relationships and Constraints in a DataSet

The ADO.NET dataset object allows you to specify relationships and constraints between two tables. This has the effect of making the **DataSet** check for constraints when you modify data in it. For example, if you've created a foreign key constraint on the **ProductComponents DataTable**, the **DataSet** will raise an exception every time you add a new row to the **ProductComponents DataTable** without specifying the **ParentProductID**.

Let's create a relationship between the **Products.ID** and **ProductComponents.ParentProductID** columns. You can represent a relationship using the **DataRelation** object, as shown in the **CreateRelationships** method in Listing 4-16. You should also place a call to this **CreateRelationships** function from inside the **Load event** of your **frmProducts** form.

*Listing 4-16. Defining Dataset Relationships and Contraints*

```
private void CreateRelationships()
{
        DataColumn _parentColumn = _ds.Tables["Products"].Columns["ID"];
        DataColumn _childColumn =
                _ds.Tables["ProductComponents"].Columns["ParentProductID"];
        DataRelation _dr = new DataRelation
                ("ProductRelation1",_parentColumn,_childColumn,true);
        _ds.Relations.Add(_dr);
        _dr.ChildKeyConstraint.DeleteRule = Rule.Cascade;
        _dr.ChildKeyConstraint.UpdateRule = Rule.Cascade;
        _ds.EnforceConstraints = true;
}private void frmProducts_Load(object sender, EventArgs e)
{
        LoadData();
        CreateRelationships();
        BindData();
}
```

You can see the effect that this code has by running the form. Try to add a new row to the **ProductComponents** table, and click the Save button without specifying a value for the **ParentProductID**. You will see an error message that looks like the one shown in Figure 4-16.

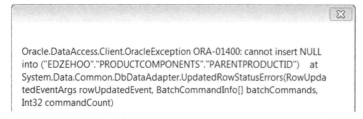

Oracle.DataAccess.Client.OracleException ORA-01400: cannot insert NULL into ("EDZEHOO"."PRODUCTCOMPONENTS"."PARENTPRODUCTID")    at System.Data.Common.DbDataAdapter.UpdatedRowStatusErrors(RowUpda tedEventArgs rowUpdatedEvent, BatchCommandInfo[] batchCommands, Int32 commandCount)

***Figure 4-16.*** *Dataset contraints in action*

You get the error in Figure 4-16 because the dataset is expecting the foreign key (**ParentProductID** ) to have been filled in. Since your users should not be expected to specify the foreign key, you can write code to automatically fill in this value whenever a new row is added to the Components grid. The following highlighted code shows what you need to change in your code to achieve this.

```
private void BindData()
{
        bsProducts.DataSource = _ds.Tables["Products"];
        txtName.DataBindings.Add(new Binding("Text", bsProducts, "Name", true));
        numPrice.DataBindings.Add(new Binding("Value", bsProducts, "Price", true));
        txtRemarks.DataBindings.Add(new Binding("Text", bsProducts, "Remarks", true));
        lblID.DataBindings.Add(new Binding("Text", bsProducts, "ID", true));
        dgComponents.DataSource = _ds.Tables["ProductComponents"];
        dgComponents.Columns["ParentProductID"].Visible = false;
        dgComponents.RowsAdded += new
                DataGridViewRowsAddedEventHandler(dgComponents_RowsAdded);
}

private void dgComponents_RowsAdded(object sender, DataGridViewRowsAddedEventArgs e)
{
        dgComponents.Rows[e.RowIndex - 1].Cells["ParentProductID"].Value = _productID;
}
```

If you run the program again, you will find that you can add a new row to the **Components** grid and save the changes without having to specify the **ParentProductID** this time.

# Manipulating LOBs and BFILEs

Large objects (**LOB**s) are special data types in Oracle that allow you to store large amounts of data (up to a maximum of about 4GB). They are commonly used to store binary data such as image, video, and audio files or large amounts of text. There are three types of **LOB**s:

- **BLOB**: Stores binary data up to 4GB

- **CLOB**: Stores text (characters) data up to 4 billion characters

- **NCLOB**: Stores double-byte text (characters) data up to 2 billion characters

The **BFILE** type is another data type used by Oracle to store files. It is different from a **BLOB** in that **BFILE**s are not stored in the database. The physical file is stored on the operating system while a reference to the file is stored in the **BFILE** column. In the next few sections, we will look at how we can manipulate these various large objects from ODP.NET.

To run the code samples in these sections, you need to first create the various **BLOB**, **CLOB**, **NCLOB**, and **BFILE** table columns. Let's create a new table to store these data types. To that end, execute Listing 4-17 using SQL*Plus.

*Listing 4-17. Creating a Large Object Table*

```
CREATE TABLE "EDZEHOO"."PRODUCTFILES" (
"PRODUCTID" VARCHAR2(10),
"FILEATTACHMENT" BLOB,
"FILEATTACHMENT2" BFILE,
"REMARKS" CLOB,
"REMARKSINJAPANESE" NCLOB
);
```

## Uploading BLOB Data

To upload a file to a **BLOB** field, you need to read all the data from the file into a byte array and then pass this byte array to an **OracleParameter** object, which will handle the rest. Let's take a look at how this is done. Create a new form with the layout shown in Figure 4-17. Add an **OpenFileDialog** control to the form so that you can browse for a file on your system and have the full path show up in the "File to upload" text box.

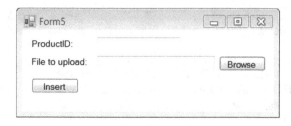

*Figure 4-17. Designing a sample form for the BLOB insert example*

In the click event of the Insert button, write the code from Listing 4-18. The highlighted code snippet shows how you can pass the byte array to a **BLOB** field using the **OracleParameter** class.

*Listing 4-18. Inserting BLOB Data*

```
using Oracle.DataAccess.Types;
private void btnInsert_Click(object sender, EventArgs e)
{
        //We first read the full contents of the file into a byte array
        byte[] _fileContents = System.IO.File.ReadAllBytes(txtFilepath.Text);
        string _connstring = "Data Source=localhost/NEWDB;User
                Id=EDZEHOO;Password=PASS123;";
        int _recordsAffected;
        try
        {
                OracleConnection _connObj = new OracleConnection(_connstring);
                _connObj.Open();
                OracleCommand _cmdObj = _connObj.CreateCommand();
                _cmdObj.CommandText = "INSERT INTO ProductFiles(ProductID, FileAttachment)
                        VALUES(:ProductID,:FileAttachment)";
                _cmdObj.Parameters.Add (new OracleParameter
                        ("ProductID",txtProductID.Text));
                OracleBlob _blob = new OracleBlob(_connObj);
                _blob.Write(_fileContents, 0, _fileContents.Length);
                _cmdObj.Parameters.Add(new OracleParameter ("FileAttachment",_blob));
                _recordsAffected = _cmdObj.ExecuteNonQuery();
                if (_recordsAffected == 1) { MessageBox.Show("File uploaded!"); }
                _connObj.Close();
                _connObj.Dispose();
                _connObj = null;
        }
        catch (Exception ex)
        {
                MessageBox.Show(ex.ToString());
        }
}
```

Try uploading an image file. You should see the "File uploaded!" message shown in Figure 4-18.

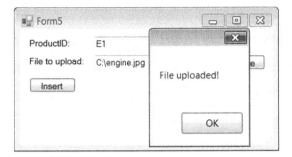

*Figure 4-18. Uploading data to a BLOB column*

## Retrieving BLOB Data

To retrieve **BLOB** data, you can use the **OracleBlob** class to retrieve the byte array for that data that you are after. Create a new form, and place a text box for the user to type in the Product ID as well as button next to it called "Get BLOB." Place an enlarged **PictureBox** control at the bottom. The idea is to let the user retrieve the file attachment (an image is assumed to be uploaded earlier) for the specified Product ID and to then display it in the picture box control. The code to do this is shown in Listing 4-19.

*Listing 4-19. Retrieving BLOB Data*

```
private void btnGetBLOB_Click(object sender, EventArgs e)
{
        //We first read the full contents of the file into a byte array
        string _connstring = "Data Source=localhost/NEWDB;User
                Id=EDZEHOO;Password=PASS123;";
        try
        {
                OracleConnection _connObj = new OracleConnection(_connstring);
                OracleDataReader _rdrObj;
                _connObj.Open();
                OracleCommand _cmdObj = _connObj.CreateCommand();
                _cmdObj.CommandText = "SELECT FileAttachment FROM ProductFiles WHERE
                        ProductID=:ProductID";
                _cmdObj.Parameters.Add(new OracleParameter("ProductID", txtProductID.Text));
                _rdrObj=_cmdObj.ExecuteReader();
                if (_rdrObj.HasRows)
                {
                    if (_rdrObj.Read())
                    {
                        OracleBlob _blobObj =
                                _rdrObj.GetOracleBlob(_rdrObj.GetOrdinal("FileAttachment"));
                        picProductImage.Image = Image.FromStream(new
                                System.IO.MemoryStream(_blobObj.Value));
                    }
                }
```

```
        else
        {
            MessageBox.Show("An item with the matching product ID was not found!");
        }
        _connObj.Close();
        _connObj.Dispose();
        _connObj = null;
    }
    catch (Exception ex)
    {
        MessageBox.Show(ex.ToString());
    }
}
```

Run the form that you've just created. Type the Product ID you specified earlier when you uploaded your file. When you click "Get BLOB," your file attachment will show in the **PictureBox** control. You should see something similar to Figure 4-19.

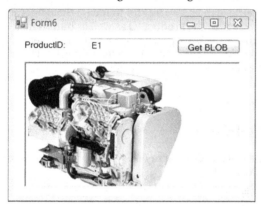

*Figure 4-19. Retrieving and displaying BLOB data*

# Inserting CLOB/NCLOB Data

**CLOB** and **NCLOB** data types are character-based data and are meant to store large amounts of text. You can insert **CLOB** and **NCLOB** data pretty much the same way as you did for the **BLOB** using the **OracleClob** class (which handles for both the **CLOB** and **NCLOB** data types). Let's take a look at the code in Listing 4-20.

*Listing 4-20. Inserting CLOB Data*

```
using Oracle.DataAccess.Types;
private void btnInsert_Click(object sender, EventArgs e)
{
        string _connstring = "Data Source=localhost/NEWDB;User
                Id=EDZEHOO;Password=PASS123;";
        int _recordsAffected;
```

```
try
{
        OracleConnection _connObj = new OracleConnection(_connstring);
        _connObj.Open();
        OracleCommand _cmdObj = _connObj.CreateCommand();
        _cmdObj.CommandText = "INSERT INTO ProductFiles(ProductID, Remarks)
                VALUES(:ProductID,:Remarks)";
        _cmdObj.Parameters.Add (new OracleParameter
                ("ProductID",txtProductID.Text));
        OracleClob _clobObj = new OracleClob(_connObj);
        _clobObj.Write(txtRemarks.Text.ToCharArray(), 0, txtRemarks.Text.Length);
        _cmdObj.Parameters.Add (new OracleParameter("Remarks", _clobObj));
        _recordsAffected = _cmdObj.ExecuteNonQuery();
        if (_recordsAffected == 1) { MessageBox.Show("CLOB saved!"); }
        _connObj.Close();
        _connObj.Dispose();
        _connObj = null;
}
catch (Exception ex)
{
        MessageBox.Show(ex.ToString());
}
}
```

For **NCLOB**s, you can use the same **OracleClob** class in the same manner. You will need to additionally specify the second (whether to enable caching) and third arguments (whether this is an **NCLOB**) in the constructor for the **OracleClob** class. The following code illustrates how this can be done (changes are highlighted in bold):

```
OracleClob _clobObj = new OracleClob(_connObj, true, true);
_clobObj.Write(txtRemarks.Text.ToCharArray(), 0, txtRemarks.Text.Length);
_cmdObj.Parameters.Add (new OracleParameter("RemarksInJapanese", _clobObj));
```

---

■ **Note**  The difference between a CLOB and an NCLOB is that a CLOB is meant to store single-byte data while an NCLOB is meant for double-byte data (for example, Unicode text)

---

## Retrieving CLOB/NCLOB Data

To retrieve data from a **CLOB** field, you can use the **GetOracleClob()** method of the **OracleClob** class. Listing 4-21 provides an example. The use of **OracleCLOB** is highlighted in the listing.

*Listing 4-21. Retrieving CLOB Data*

```
private void btnGetCLOB_Click(object sender, EventArgs e)
{
        //We first read the full contents of the file into a byte array
        string _connstring = "Data Source=localhost/NEWDB;User
               Id=EDZEHOO;Password=PASS123;";
        try
        {
                OracleConnection _connObj = new OracleConnection(_connstring);
                OracleDataReader _rdrObj;
                _connObj.Open();
                OracleCommand _cmdObj = _connObj.CreateCommand();
                _cmdObj.CommandText = "SELECT Remarks FROM ProductFiles WHERE
                        ProductID=:ProductID";
                _cmdObj.Parameters.Add(new OracleParameter("ProductID", txtProductID.Text));
                _rdrObj= _cmdObj.ExecuteReader();
                if (_rdrObj.HasRows)
                {
                    if (_rdrObj.Read())
                    {
                        OracleClob _clobObj =
                                _rdrObj.GetOracleClob(_rdrObj.GetOrdinal("Remarks"));
                        txtRemarks.text = _clobObj.Value
                    }
                }
                else
                {
                    MessageBox.Show("An item with the matching product ID was not found!");
                }
                _connObj.Close();
                _connObj.Dispose();
                _connObj = null;
        }
        catch (Exception ex)
        {
                MessageBox.Show(ex.ToString());
        }
}
```

## Creating BFILE Directory Mappings

As I mentioned earlier, **BFILE**s are basically references in Oracle to files that are stored externally in the operating system. You can define which folder these files are actually stored in. Oracle allows you to create logical directories that map to a specific folder on your machine. Your SQL statements refer to these folders not by path but by logical directory name. For example, you'll need to run the following statement in SQL*Plus:

```
CREATE OR REPLACE DIRECTORY "PRODUCTFILESFOLDER" AS 'C:\PRODUCTFILES';
```

---

■ **Note** Before you can run the preceding statement, the EDZEHOO user account must first be granted permissions to create directories. You can grant that permission from SQL*Plus by logging on with SYSDBA privileges and running the following statement: GRANT CREATE ANY DIRECTORY TO "EDZEHOO";.

---

Successfully executing a **CREATE DIRECTORY** statement will get you a "Directory created" message. The **CREATE DIRECTORY** statement in this section basically tells Oracle to map the logical directory name **ProductFilesFolder** to the folder **C:\ProductFiles**.

## Inserting BFILE Data

After creating a directory mapping, you can try your hand at inserting your first **BFILE** record. Oracle provides the **BFILENAME()** SQL function that can generate a special type of link (called a **BFILE** locator) when you pass in a logical directory name and the full name of the file. For example, the following SQL **INSERT** command attempts to insert the local file at **C:\ProductFiles\myfile.jpg** as a **BFILE** in the database:

```
INSERT INTO ProductFiles(FileAttachment2)
VALUES (BFILENAME('PRODUCTFILESFOLDER ', 'myfile.jpg '))
```

Take a look at the full code in Listing 4-22.

*Listing 4-22. Inserting BFILE Data*

```
private void btnInsert_Click(object sender, EventArgs e)
{
        //We first read the full contents of the file into a byte array
        string _connstring = "Data Source=localhost/NEWDB;User
                Id=EDZEHOO;Password=PASS123;";
        int _recordsAffected;
        try
        {
                OracleConnection _connObj = new OracleConnection(_connstring);
                _connObj.Open();
                OracleCommand _cmdObj = _connObj.CreateCommand();
                _cmdObj.CommandText = "INSERT INTO ProductFiles(ProductID, FileAttachment2)
                        VALUES(:ProductID,BFILENAME('PRODUCTFILESFOLDER',:FileName))";
                _cmdObj.Parameters.Add (new OracleParameter
                        ("ProductID",txtProductID.Text));
                _cmdObj.Parameters.Add(new OracleParameter("FileName",txtFilename.Text));
                _recordsAffected = _cmdObj.ExecuteNonQuery();
                if (_recordsAffected == 1) { MessageBox.Show("File uploaded!"); }
                _connObj.Close();
```

```
                _connObj.Dispose();
                _connObj = null;
        }
        catch (Exception ex)
        {
                MessageBox.Show(ex.ToString());
        }
}
```

## Retrieving BFILE Data

You can retrieve a **BFILE** using the **OracleBFile** class. The great thing about the **OracleBFile** class is that it returns you the actual file itself, not just a link or pointer to the file. Oracle does all the work of mapping the **BFILE** locator to the on-disk file and returning you the file. Let's take a look at the code in Listing 4-23.

*Listing 4-23. Retrieving BFILE Data*

```
private void btnGetBFile_Click(object sender, EventArgs e)
{
        //We first read the full contents of the file into a byte array
        string _connstring = "Data Source=localhost/NEWDB;User
                Id=EDZEHOO;Password=PASS123;";
        byte[] _fileContents;
        try
        {
                OracleConnection _connObj = new OracleConnection(_connstring);
                OracleDataReader _rdrObj;
                _connObj.Open();
                OracleCommand _cmdObj = _connObj.CreateCommand();
                _cmdObj.CommandText = "SELECT FileAttachment2 FROM ProductFiles WHERE
                        ProductID=:ProductID";
                _cmdObj.Parameters.Add(new OracleParameter("ProductID", txtProductID.Text));
                _rdrObj = _cmdObj.ExecuteReader();
                if (_rdrObj.HasRows)
                {
                        if (_rdrObj.Read())
                        {
                                OracleBFile _bfileObj = _rdrObj.GetOracleBFile
                                        (_rdrObj.GetOrdinal("FileAttachment2"));
                                if (_bfileObj.FileExists)
                                {
                                        _fileContents = _bfileObj.Value;

                                        //_fileContents now holds the array of bytes
                                        //representing the BFILE
                                        MessageBox.Show("The name of the file is: " +
                                                _bfileObj.FileName + "\nThe length of the
                                                file is :" + _bfileObj.Length);
```

```
                        }
                    }
            }
            else
            {
                MessageBox.Show("An item with the matching product ID was not found!");
            }
            _connObj.Close();
            _connObj.Dispose();
            _connObj = null;
        }
        catch (Exception ex)
        {
                MessageBox.Show(ex.ToString());
        }
}
```

---

■ **Tip**   Obviously one of the questions that might pop into your mind is when to use BFILEs and when to use BLOBs. The answer is simple: if you don't wish to bloat your database size, the BFILE is a better choice since it stores all files outside the database. On the other hand, if you prefer to keep all your files in the database for easier backup operations, it makes more sense to use BLOBs.

---

# Manipulating RAW Data Types

A globally unique identifier (GUID) is a 16-byte value that is guaranteed to be globally unique (it is generated through a complex algorithm involving your network MAC address) and can be easily generated in .NET with the **System.Guid.NewGuid()** method call. The fact that GUIDs are always guaranteed to be globally unique makes them suitable to be used internally as record identifiers. It is not uncommon to represent for example, user, customer, or invoice IDs as GUID values in the database.

Oracle does not provide a data type that can natively store GUID values. The Oracle **ROWID** and **UROWID** data types, although sounding conspicuously like GUID data types, do not resemble a GUID in any way: **ROWID**s store the address of a particular row in a table. The closest (and most efficient) match we have is the **RAW(16)** data type. The **RAW** data type is basically a binary data type of a configurable size. **RAW(16)** suits us well; it stores all 16 bytes required for a GUID value.

Let's try saving and loading a GUID from an Oracle table. Before you run the code sample below, create the table shown in Listing 4-24 via SQL*Plus.

*Listing 4-24. Creating a Table Holding Globally Unique Identifiers*

```
CREATE TABLE "EDZEHOO"."GUIDTEST" (
"GUID" RAW(16),
"NAME" VARCHAR2(255));
```

Listing 4-25 shows how you can insert in a GUID value into the **RAW** column in the table that you created in Listing 4-24. The code highlighted in bold saves the GUID into the **RAW** column using the **OracleParameter** class.

*Listing 4-25. Inserting a GUID into a RAW Column*

```
private void btnGenerate_Click(object sender, EventArgs e)
{
        string _connstring = "Data Source=localhost/NEWDB;User
                Id=EDZEHOO;Password=PASS123;";
        int _recordsAffected;
        try
        {
                OracleConnection _connObj = new OracleConnection(_connstring);
                _connObj.Open();
                //Insert a new record
                OracleCommand _cmdObj = _connObj.CreateCommand();
                _cmdObj.CommandText = "INSERT INTO GUIDTest(GUID, Name)
                        VALUES(:GUID,:Name)";
                OracleParameter _rawObj = new OracleParameter("GUID", OracleDbType.Raw);
                _rawObj.Value = System.Guid.NewGuid().ToByteArray();
                _cmdObj.Parameters.Add(_rawObj);
                _cmdObj.Parameters.Add(new OracleParameter("Name", "Test1"));
                _recordsAffected = _cmdObj.ExecuteNonQuery();
                MessageBox.Show("Total records affected after insert:" + _recordsAffected);
                _connObj.Close();
                _connObj.Dispose();
                _connObj = null;
        }
        catch (Exception ex)
        {
                MessageBox.Show(ex.ToString());
        }
}
```

You can run an SQL **SELECT** in SQL*PLUS to see how the GUID is stored internally in Oracle. In the screenshot shown in Figure 4-20, the GUID value is displayed in hexadecimal form.

*Figure 4-20. GUID displayed in hexadecimal format*

Retrieving a GUID value from a **RAW** column into a **System.Guid** class is relatively straightforward. The highlighted code in Listing 4-26 below shows how this can be rather easily achieved using the **OracleBinary** class.

*Listing 4-26. Retrieving a GUID from a RAW Column*

```
using Oracle.DataAccess.Types;
private void button1_Click(object sender, EventArgs e)
{
        string _connstring = "Data Source=localhost/NEWDB;User
                Id=EDZEHOO;Password=PASS123;";
        string _sql;
        OracleDataReader _rdrObj;
        try
        {
                OracleConnection _connObj = new OracleConnection(_connstring);
                DataSet _ds = new DataSet();
                _connObj.Open();
                _sql = "SELECT GUID FROM GUIDTest";
                OracleCommand _cmdObj = new OracleCommand(_sql, _connObj);
                _rdrObj = _cmdObj.ExecuteReader();
                if (_rdrObj.HasRows)
                {
                    if (_rdrObj.Read())
                    {
                        OracleBinary _binaryObj = _rdrObj.GetOracleBinary
                                (_rdrObj.GetOrdinal("GUID"));
                        System.Guid _GUIDObj = new System.Guid(_binaryObj.Value);
                        MessageBox.Show("The GUID retrieved is: " + _GUIDObj.ToString());
                    }
                }
                _connObj.Close();
                _connObj.Dispose();
                _connObj = null;
        }
        catch (Exception ex)
        {
```

```
                        MessageBox.Show(ex.ToString());
        }
}
```

Running the code sample in Listing 4-26 should yield the output shown in Figure 4-21.

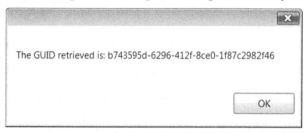

*Figure 4-21.* *GUID retrieved and displayed in a pop-up window*

# Creating Automatically Incrementing Columns

If you have ever programmed in Microsoft SQL Server or Microsoft Access before, you would be quite familiar with the concept of the Autonumber or Identity column type. These are numerical-based column types that increment automatically whenever you insert a new record into the table. At first glance, you might find that Oracle does not have an equivalent data type. That is true, but Oracle implements automatic numbers in its own way—through the use of sequences.

Sequences are objects in Oracle that can be used to generate running numbers. They must be created explicitly. Create a sequence using the following DDL via SQL*Plus (you may need to log in as the **SYSDBA** to create the sequence):

```
CREATE SEQUENCE "EDZEHOO"."PRODUCTIDSEQUENCE"
INCREMENT BY 1 MINVALUE 1 MAXVALUE 99999;
```

You can create incrementing or decrementing sequences by changing the Increment By, Minimum, and Maximum values. Create a new table as well so that you can try out the code sample in this section. Here is the table to create:

```
CREATE TABLE "EDZEHOO"."TESTPRODUCTS" (
"ID" NUMBER(10),
"NAME" VARCHAR2(255),
CONSTRAINT "PRIMKEY3" PRIMARY KEY ("ID") VALIDATE);
```

When you create a sequence, it is simply a stand-alone set of running numbers. To make any use of a sequence, you need to grab the value automatically generated by the sequence and include it in your SQL **INSERT** statements. The **NEXTVAL()** SQL function allows you to get the next running number from a specified sequence. The following illustrates how this can be done:

```
INSERT INTO TESTPRODUCTS(ID, NAME) VALUES
(PRODUCTIDSEQUENCE.NEXTVAL(), 'SHOCKABSORBERS');
```

Let's try this sample out. Log in as **EDZEHOO** again, and run the SQL statement preceding code three times consecutively. After that, run an SQL **SELECT** statement on the **TestProducts** table. You will find three records inserted, as shown in Figure 4-22, each with a different incrementing sequence number.

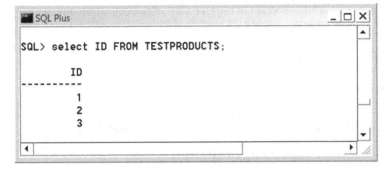

*Figure 4-22. Sequences inserted successfully into the TestProducts table*

# Executing DDL from ODP.NET

You can execute DDL statements such as **CREATE TABLE** and **ALTER TABLE** statements in ODP.NET through the **ExecuteNonQuery()** method. For example, the code in Listing 4-27 allows you to programmatically add a new column to the **Products** table.

*Listing 4-27. Adding a New Column to a Table Using the ALTER TABLE Command*

```
private void btnAddNewColumn_Click(object sender, EventArgs e)
{
        string _connstring = "Data Source=localhost/NEWDB;User
            Id=EDZEHOO;Password=PASS123;";
        try
        {
            OracleConnection _connObj = new OracleConnection(_connstring);
            _connObj.Open();
            OracleCommand _cmdObj = _connObj.CreateCommand();
            _cmdObj.CommandText = "ALTER TABLE PRODUCTS ADD (SPECIALREMARKS
                VARCHAR2(255))";
            _cmdObj.ExecuteNonQuery();
            MessageBox.Show("New column added!");
            _connObj.Close();
            _connObj.Dispose();
            _connObj = null;
        }
        catch (Exception ex)
        {
            MessageBox.Show(ex.ToString());
        }
}
```

# Discovering Schema in ODP.NET

Through ODP.NET's **GetSchema()** implementation, you can retrieve a rich set of information about the database. You can pass in the name of the desired collection to retrieve a list of the collection objects from the database. Take a look at the sample code in Listing 4-28.

*Listing 4-28. Retrieving Database Schema Information Using GetSchema()*

```
private void btnGetSchema_Click(object sender, EventArgs e)
{
        string _connstring;
        _connstring = "Data Source=localhost/NEWDB;User Id=EDZEHOO;Password=PASS123;";
        DataTable _dt = null;
        OracleConnection myconn = new OracleConnection(_connstring);
        myconn.Open();
        _dt = myconn.GetSchema("tables");
        dataGridView1.DataSource = _dt;
}
```

By passing in the collection name **"tables"**, you can retrieve the full set of tables in the Oracle database you're connected to. When displayed in a form, such a list might look like the one show in Figure 4-23.

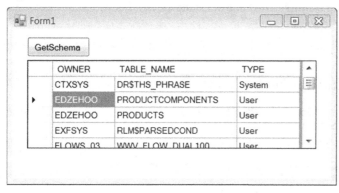

*Figure 4-23. Displaying schema information for the "tables" collection*

The list of common collection names you can use with **GetSchema()** is given in Table 4-2. There are other collections that you can retrieve, such as the list of stored procedures, indexes, or functions available in Oracle. You can see the full list of collections by calling **GetSchema (DbMetaDataCollectionNames.MetaDataCollections)**.

*Table 4-2. A List of Commonly Used Collection Names for GetSchema()*

| Collection Name | Description |
| --- | --- |
| `"Tables"` | A list of all tables in Oracle |
| `"Views"` | A list of all views in Oracle |
| `"Columns"` | A list of all table columns in Oracle |
| `"Users"` | A list of all users in Oracle |
| `System.Data.Common.DbMetaDataCollectionNames.MetaDataCollections` | Returns a list of all the names of the collections that can be obtained through `GetSchema()` |
| `System.Data.Common.DbMetaDataCollectionNames.Restrictions` | Returns a list of the restrictions (filters) that can be used with each collection type in **GetSchema** |
| `System.Data.Common.DbMetaDataCollectionNames.DatasourceInformation` | Returns information about the data source, such as the Oracle product version number, and so on |
| `System.Data.Common.DbMetaDataCollectionNames.DataTypes` | Returns a list of all the data types in Oracle and their column sizes |
| `System.Data.Common.DbMetaDataCollectionNames.ReservedWords` | Returns a list of all the reserved words in Oracle |

With most of these collections, you can further filter what you need to retrieve. For example, the **"Columns"** collection is pretty vast; it retrieves every single column of every single table available in Oracle, including the system tables. This wouldn't be very useful. Retrieving the columns for one specific table at a time would make much more sense. We can use restrictions to limit what you wish to retrieve with **GetSchema()**. For example, the **"Columns"** collection allows for three types of restrictions to be specified (in this order):

- *Restriction 0*: By owner name

- *Restriction 1*: By table name

- *Restriction 2*: By column name

If you wanted to retrieve metadata on all the columns in the table **PRODUCTS** created by the user **EDZEHOO**, you could write the code in Listing 4-29.

*Listing 4-29. Retrieving Metadata for All Columns in a Table*

```
private void btnGetSchema_Click(object sender, EventArgs e)
{
        string _connstring;
        _connstring = "Data Source=localhost/NEWDB;User Id=EDZEHOO;Password=PASS123;";
        DataTable _dt = null;
        OracleConnection myconn = new OracleConnection(_connstring);
        myconn.Open();

        string[] restrictions= new string[3];

        //Here we initialize all restrictions to null - take note that null is different
        //from "". To make sure a restriction is not used, set it to null
        for (int _counter = 0; _counter < 3; _counter++) { restrictions[_counter] = null; }
        restrictions[0] = "EDZEHOO";
        restrictions[1] = "PRODUCTS";
        _dt = myconn.GetSchema("columns",restrictions);
        dataGridView1.DataSource = _dt;
}
```

Running this code would yield results such as those in Figure 4-24.

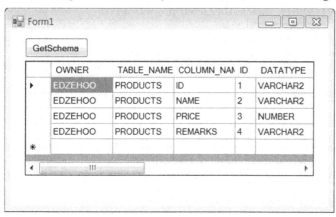

*Figure 4-24. Displaying column information for the "Products" table*

There are different sets of restrictions for different collections. You can see the full list of these restrictions by calling GetSchema (DbMetaDataCollectionNames.Restrictions).

# Handling ODP.NET Exceptions

The **OracleException** class in ODP.NET can provide error messages that are more detailed than the ones in the standard **Exception** class. For example, run the code in Listing 4-30.

*Listing 4-30. Error Handling Using the Standard Exception Class*

```
private void btnRunQuery_Click(object sender, EventArgs e)
{
        string _connstring = "Data Source=localhost/NEWDB;User
                Id=EDZEHOO;Password=PASS123;";
        string _sql;
        OracleDataReader _rdrObj;
        try
        {
                OracleConnection _connObj = new OracleConnection(_connstring);
                DataSet _ds = new DataSet();
                _connObj.Open();
                //Intentionally run an incorrect query
                _sql = "SELECT aaa FROM bbb WHERE ccc=ddd";
                OracleCommand _cmdObj = new OracleCommand(_sql, _connObj);
                _rdrObj = _cmdObj.ExecuteReader();
                _connObj.Close();
                _connObj.Dispose();
                _connObj = null;
        }
        catch (Exception ex)
        {
                MessageBox.Show(ex.Message.ToString());
        }
}
```

You will notice that the error message captured by the standard **Exception** object, and shown in Figure 4-25, shows limited information.

*Figure 4-25. Standard Exception error message*

Now, try changing the earlier code to use the **OracleException** class. You should end up with Listing 4-31 (the changes are highlighted in bold).

113

*Listing 4-31. Error Handling Using the OracleException Class*

```
private void btnRunQuery_Click(object sender, EventArgs e)
{
        string _connstring = "Data Source=localhost/NEWDB;User
                Id=EDZEHOO;Password=PASS123;";
        string _sql;
        OracleDataReader _rdrObj;
        try
        {
                OracleConnection _connObj = new OracleConnection(_connstring);
                DataSet _ds = new DataSet();
                _connObj.Open();
                //Intentionally run an incorrect query
                _sql = "SELECT aaa FROM bbb WHERE ccc=ddd";
                OracleCommand _cmdObj = new OracleCommand(_sql, _connObj);
                _rdrObj = _cmdObj.ExecuteReader();
                _connObj.Close();
                _connObj.Dispose();
                _connObj = null;
        }
        catch (OracleException ex)
        {
                MessageBox.Show("Oracle Error Number: " + ex.Number + "\nSource: " +
                        ex.Source + "\nData source: " + ex.DataSource + "\nProcedure: " +
                        ex.Procedure + "\nMessage: " + ex.Message + "\nInnerException: " +
                        ex.InnerException);
        }
}
```

If you run this code again, you will see the error message in Figure 4-26. That error message gives slightly more detail than the previous message in Figure 4-25.

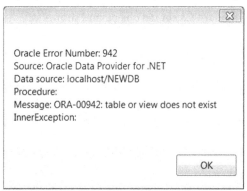

*Figure 4-26. Custom Exception error message using OracleException*

# Summary

In this chapter, you've taken a look at how to read and write different types of data to and from an Oracle database using ODP.NET. Specifically, you learned the following:

- The various data types available in ODP.NET and which Oracle native types they map to

- How to use the **OracleDataReader**, **OracleDataAdapter**, **OracleCommand**, and **OracleCommandBuilder** classes to read and write data in Oracle

- How to use the **OracleBLOB**, **OracleCLOB**, and **OracleBFILE** classes to manipulate large data types (such as file attachments and large amounts of text) in Oracle

- How to retrieve database schema information via ODP.NET

- How to trap and handle ODP.NET exceptions in your code

With the information from this chapter, you are now well equipped to start designing applications on top of the Oracle database, but we're just only getting started! You will discover throughout the next few chapters that there is more to ODP.NET than just basic data retrieval and manipulation.

In the next chapter, we will dive into the world of PL/SQL. You will learn how you can communicate effectively with PL/SQL stored procedures from within your .NET code.

# CHAPTER 5

∎ ∎ ∎

# Using PL/SQL and .NET CLR Stored Procedures with ODP.NET

Stored procedures remain one of the most common ways of separating the data tier from the logic tier of an application. They shield the developer from having to make changes to the code when the underlying database structure changes. And with stored procedures backed up by a powerful SQL dialect (PL/SQL), it isn't hard to see why many developers choose to stuff as much database logic as they can behind them.

In this chapter, we explore the different ways you can interact with PL/SQL code through ODP.NET. We will particularly look at how to accomplish the following:

- Executing PL/SQL stored functions, functions, and anonymous blocks

- Passing input data and retrieve output data from PL/SQL blocks via parameters

- Handling complex input/output parameters such as associative arrays, **VARRAYs**, nested tables, UDTs, **REF** cursors, and multiple **REF** cursors in your .NET code

- Creating and deploying a .NET CLR stored procedure

## Understanding the Basics of PL/SQL

PL/SQL is the dialect (and extension) of SQL in Oracle. You might know your dialect as T-SQL if you're a Microsoft SQL Server developer. PL/SQL provides a rich set of data types that allow you to retrieve and manipulate complex data types in an Oracle database. PL/SQL code can exist in three main forms:

- As a PL/SQL anonymous block

- As a PL/SQL stored procedure

- As a PL/SQL function

The anonymous block is the simplest form that PL/SQL code can exist in. An anonymous block is not stored in the Oracle database, and it requires no name. Executing anonymous PL/SQL blocks is thus a matter of directly tossing blocks of code (as strings) to ODP.NET for execution.

PL/SQL most commonly takes on the form of stored procedures. Stored procedures are named blocks of PL/SQL code that are stored in the database. A stored procedure can be executed by referencing its name in code.

Functions are similar to stored procedures except that they must return a value.

You can communicate with all three forms using ODP.NET's input and output parameters. We will look at these three forms in detail in the sections to follow.

# Working with Anonymous PL/SQL Blocks

An anonymous PL/SQL block is simply an unnamed block of PL/SQL code. This means that it does not have a header section. An anonymous PL/SQL block has the following characteristics:

- Can only be a procedure, not a function

- Has no name

- Is not stored in the database

The following is an example of an anonymous PL/SQL block:

```
BEGIN
      printLine('Hello World');
END;
```

You can pass data into an anonymous PL/SQL block and retrieve data in return through **IN**, **OUT** and **IN-OUT** Oracle parameters. We will explore how we can do this in the next few sections.

## Executing an Anonymous PL/SQL Block

An anonymous PL/SQL block can be treated like any other SQL statement. You can use the **ExecuteNonQuery** method of the **OracleCommand** object to execute the statement. Let's take a look at how you can do this. You can use the **Products** table you've created in the previous chapter to try your code sample. Create a new form, add a new button named **btnRunPLSQL** to the form, and write the code in Listing 5-1 into the click event of that button.

---

■ **Note**   Developers occasionally make the wrong assumption that the **OracleCommand.CommandType** parameter should be set to **StoredProcedure** for an anonymous PL/SQL block. This is incorrect. Anonymous PL/SQL blocks are really text statements; the parameter should be set to (the default value) **Text**.

---

*Listing 5-1. Inserting a New Record Via an Anonymous PL/SQL Block*

```
private void btnRunPLSQL_Click(object sender, EventArgs e)
{
      string _connstring = "Data Source=localhost/NEWDB;User
            Id=EDZEHOO;Password=PASS123;";
      try
      {
            OracleConnection _connObj = new OracleConnection(_connstring);
            _connObj.Open();
            OracleCommand _cmdObj = _connObj.CreateCommand();
            _cmdObj.CommandText =   "BEGIN" +
                              "      INSERT INTO Products(ID, NAME, PRICE," +
                              "      REMARKS) VALUES('B1', 'Brake Fluid'," +
```

```
                                    "          80.50, 'Inserted via PL/SQL');" +
                                "END;";
                _cmdObj.ExecuteNonQuery();
                MessageBox.Show("New row added!");
                _connObj.Close();
                _connObj.Dispose();
                _connObj = null;
            }
            catch (Exception ex)
            {
                MessageBox.Show(ex.ToString());
            }
        }
```

Try running this code sample! You should of course see the "New row added!" message. If you try running a **SELECT** query against the **Products** table, you should be able to see the newly inserted product (shown in Figure 5-1).

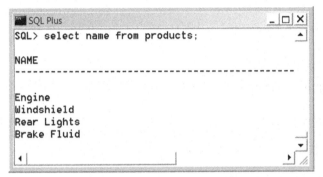

*Figure 5-1. Newly inserted product*

## Passing Data into an Anonymous Block

Now let's take a look at how we can pass input data into an anonymous PL/SQL block. Passing data into PL/SQL is very similar to executing a parameterized query. For example, your anonymous PL/SQL block could look like this:

```
BEGIN
        UPDATE Products SET Price=100 WHERE Name = :1
END;
```

You can pass in data by declaring **OracleParameter** objects and adding them to the **OracleCommand** object. Given the preceding example, you could declare an **OracleParameter** object in this fashion:

```
OracleParameter _paramObj = new OracleParameter();
_paramObj.ParameterName = ":1";
_paramObj.OracleDbType = OracleDbType.Varchar2;
_paramObj.Direction = ParameterDirection.Input;
_paramObj.Value = 'Engine';
```

119

When creating a parameter, you need to set the correct parameter name as well as the correct Oracle data type of the field. The **Direction** field can be set to any one of the following values:

- **ParameterDirection.Input** (also referred to as an **IN** parameter)
- **ParameterDirection.InputOutput** (also referred to as an **IN-OUT** parameter)
- **ParameterDirection.Output** (also referred to as an **OUT** parameter)
- **ParameterDirection.ReturnValue** (used with PL/SQL functions)

Let's build a sample that passes in user input from a form into an anonymous PL/SQL block. Create a form with the controls shown in Figure 5-2.

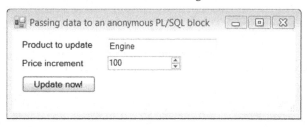

**Figure 5-2.** *Sample form to pass data to an anonymous block*

In the click event of the "Update now!' button, write the code from Listing 5-2.

*Listing 5-2. Updating a Record Via an Anonymous PL/SQL Block*

```
private void btnUpdateNow_Click(object sender, EventArgs e)
{
        string _connstring = "Data Source=localhost/NEWDB;User
                Id=EDZEHOO;Password=PASS123;";
        try
        {
                OracleConnection _connObj = new OracleConnection(_connstring);
                _connObj.Open();
                OracleCommand _cmdObj = _connObj.CreateCommand();
                _cmdObj.CommandText =    "BEGIN" +
                                "        UPDATE Products SET Price=Price + :1 " +
                                "        WHERE Name = :2;" +
                                "END;";
                OracleParameter _PriceParam = new OracleParameter();
                _PriceParam.ParameterName = ":1";
                _PriceParam.OracleDbType = OracleDbType.Int32;
                _PriceParam.Direction = ParameterDirection.Input;
                _PriceParam.Value = numPriceIncrement.Value;
                _cmdObj.Parameters.Add(_PriceParam);

                OracleParameter _NameParam = new OracleParameter();
                _NameParam.ParameterName = ":2";
                _NameParam.OracleDbType = OracleDbType.Varchar2;
```

```
            _NameParam.Direction = ParameterDirection.Input;
            _NameParam.Value = txtProductName.Text;
            _cmdObj.Parameters.Add(_NameParam);

            _cmdObj.ExecuteNonQuery();
            MessageBox.Show("Updating done!");

            _connObj.Close();
            _connObj.Dispose();
            _connObj = null;
    }
    catch (Exception ex)
    {
            MessageBox.Show(ex.ToString());
    }
}
```

Run the form, and specify the name of an existing product in the **Products** table in the first text box. Specify an increment value in the numeric control, and click the "Update Now!" button. Upon successful execution, run a **SELECT** statement in SQL*Plus to check the price of the product you've just updated. You should see it incremented by the amount you keyed in earlier.

# Returning Data from an Anonymous Block

Let's look at how we can pass data in the opposite direction now. To return data, we simply declare output parameters (that is, parameters with the **Direction** set to **ParameterDirection.Output**). In PL/SQL, the **INTO** keyword allows you to set the value of a parameter, as shown in the following example:

```
BEGIN
        SELECT COUNT(*) INTO :1 FROM Products;
END;
```

The **INTO :1** syntax allows you to return a value from an anonymous PL/SQL block. Let's try out this technique by writing some code to retrieve the total number of records in the **Products** table using an anonymous PL/SQL block.

Create a new form, and place a button named **btnRetrieveData** on the form. In the click event of this button, write the code shown in Listing 5-3.

*Listing 5-3. Returning Data Via an Anonymous PL/SQL Block*

```
private void btnRetrieveData_Click(object sender, EventArgs e)
{
        string _connstring = "Data Source=localhost/NEWDB;User
                Id=EDZEHOO;Password=PASS123;";
        try
        {
                OracleConnection _connObj = new OracleConnection(_connstring);
                _connObj.Open();
                OracleCommand _cmdObj = _connObj.CreateCommand();
                _cmdObj.CommandText = "BEGIN" +
```

121

```
                              "     SELECT COUNT(*) INTO :1 FROM Products;" +
                              "END;";
            OracleParameter _countParam = new OracleParameter();
            _countParam.ParameterName = ":1";
            _countParam.OracleDbType = OracleDbType.Int32;
            _countParam.Direction = ParameterDirection.Output;
            _cmdObj.Parameters.Add(_countParam);

            _cmdObj.ExecuteNonQuery();
            MessageBox.Show("Total number of records : " + _countParam.Value);

            _connObj.Close();
            _connObj.Dispose();
            _connObj = null;
        }
        catch (Exception ex)
        {
            MessageBox.Show(ex.ToString());
        }
}
```

If you run this code sample and click the "Retrieve Data" button, you will see the number of records show up in a pop-up message box, as shown in Figure 5-3.

*Figure 5-3. Retrieving the total number of records from an anonymous PL/SQL block*

---

■ **Note**   Take note that this method involving the keyword INTO is used to retrieve single field values such as the result of a SUM, COUNT, MAX, or MIN operation, or the value of a single field. To retrieve multiple rows of data, you need to use REF cursors or arrays (covered later).

---

# Working with PL/SQL Stored Procedures

The PL/SQL stored procedure can be said to be the equivalent of the standard T-SQL stored procedure in Microsoft SQL Server. A PL/SQL stored procedure can be distinguished from an anonymous PL/SQL block by the following characteristics:

- Is stored in the database

- Is declared with a header and a body section (and is therefore named)

Just like anonymous PL/SQL blocks, you can pass and retrieve data from PL/SQL stored procedures via **IN**, **OUT**, and **IN-OUT** parameters. Let's take a look at how this can be done in code.

## Executing a PL/SQL Stored Procedure

To execute a PL/SQL stored procedure, you simply need to pass the name of the stored procedure to the **OracleCommand** object, set its **CommandType** property to **StoredProcedure**, and then execute the statement using the **ExecuteNonQuery** method (as shown in the following example):

```
_cmdObj.CommandText = "name_of_stored_procedure";
_cmdObj.CommandType = CommandType.StoredProcedure;
_cmdObj.ExecuteNonQuery();
```

Let's try this out with a code sample. You can create the PL/SQL stored procedure in Oracle using SQL*Plus. Take note that you must first grant yourself privileges to create and alter stored procedures by running the following under the **SYSTEM** account:

```
GRANT CREATE ANY PROCEDURE TO "EDZEHOO";
GRANT ALTER ANY PROCEDURE TO "EDZEHOO";
```

Once you have done that, log in under your user account, and type the following stored procedure declaration in SQL*Plus. Add a slash (/) character as the last line to get SQL*Plus to create your stored procedure. (The code from **CREATE** to END gets sent to Oracle to create the procedure. The slash (/) character tells SQL*Plus that you are finished typing the procedure and to send the procedure to Oracle).

```
CREATE OR REPLACE PROCEDURE proc_InsertProduct IS
BEGIN
        INSERT INTO Products(ID, NAME, PRICE,REMARKS) VALUES('H1', 'Hydraulics',100.00,
        'Inserted via PL/SQL stored procedure');
END;
/
```

Now, let's look at the code you need to write to call this procedure. Create a new form and place a button named **btnCallStoredProc** on this form. Write the code from Listing 5-4 into the click event of this button.

*Listing 5-4. Inserting a New Record Via a PL/SQL Stored Procedure*

```
private void btnCallStoredProc_Click(object sender, EventArgs e)
{
        string _connstring = "Data Source=localhost/NEWDB;User
                Id=EDZEHOO;Password=PASS123;";
        try
        {
                OracleConnection _connObj = new OracleConnection(_connstring);
                _connObj.Open();
                OracleCommand _cmdObj = _connObj.CreateCommand();
                _cmdObj.CommandText = "proc_InsertProduct";
                _cmdObj.CommandType = CommandType.StoredProcedure;
                _cmdObj.ExecuteNonQuery();

                MessageBox.Show ("Product inserted");

                _connObj.Close();
                _connObj.Dispose();
                _connObj = null;
        }
        catch (Exception ex)
        {
                MessageBox.Show(ex.ToString());
        }
}
```

Run this form, and click the button. You will see the "Product Inserted" pop-up message. You can then check to make sure the new product was inserted by running a **SELECT** query on the **Products** table in SQL*Plus.

## Passing Data into a PL/SQL Stored Procedure

Let's take a look at how we can pass in data to a PL/SQL stored procedure. Create another stored procedure like the following:

```
CREATE OR REPLACE PROCEDURE proc_UpdateProduct
(
        decPrice IN DECIMAL,
        strProductName IN VARCHAR2
)
IS
BEGIN
        UPDATE Products SET Price=Price + decPrice WHERE Name=strProductName;
END;
```

---

■ **Note**  The **IN** keyword declares that the parameter is meant to hold input data passed in to the stored procedure.

---

Use the same form you've built earlier for the "Passing Data Into an Anonymous PL/SQL Block" sample. But now change the code for the click event of the **btnUpdateNow** button to that shown in Listing 5-5.

*Listing 5-5. Updating a Record Via a PL/SQL Stored Procedure*

```
private void btnUpdateNow_Click(object sender, EventArgs e)
{
        string _connstring = "Data Source=localhost/NEWDB;User
                Id=EDZEHOO;Password=PASS123;";
        try
        {
                OracleConnection _connObj = new OracleConnection(_connstring);
                _connObj.Open();
                OracleCommand _cmdObj = _connObj.CreateCommand();
                _cmdObj.CommandText = "proc_UpdateProduct";
                _cmdObj.CommandType = CommandType.StoredProcedure;

                OracleParameter _PriceParam = new OracleParameter();
                _PriceParam.ParameterName = "decPrice";
                _PriceParam.OracleDbType = OracleDbType.Decimal;
                _PriceParam.Direction = ParameterDirection.Input;
                _PriceParam.Value = numPriceIncrement.Value;
                _cmdObj.Parameters.Add(_PriceParam);

                OracleParameter _NameParam = new OracleParameter();
                _NameParam.ParameterName = "strProductName";
                _NameParam.OracleDbType = OracleDbType.Varchar2;
                _NameParam.Direction = ParameterDirection.Input;
                _NameParam.Value = txtProductName.Text;
                _cmdObj.Parameters.Add(_NameParam);
                _cmdObj.ExecuteNonQuery();

                MessageBox.Show ("Product updated");

                _connObj.Close();
                _connObj.Dispose();
                _connObj = null;
        }
        catch (Exception ex)
        {
                MessageBox.Show(ex.ToString());
        }
}
```

Notice that you can also refer to stored procedure parameters by name. This is in contrast to your use of identifiers, such as **:1** and **:2**, when passing data into an anonymous block. After running this example, you can query the **Products** table again via SQL*Plus to confirm that the changes were made to the table.

## Retrieving Data from a PL/SQL Stored Procedure

Now let's try to get the record count of the **Products** table via a stored procedure. Create the following stored procedure in the database.

```
CREATE OR REPLACE PROCEDURE proc_RetrieveCount
(
        intRecordCount OUT NUMBER
)
IS
BEGIN
        SELECT COUNT(*) INTO intRecordCount FROM Products;
END;
```

---

■ **Note** In this stored procedure, we have declared the parameter as an **OUT** parameter rather than an **IN** parameter. This means that the parameter will hold an output value.

---

Create a new form and place a button named **btnRetrieveCount** on the form. In the click event of this button, write the code from Listing 5-6.

*Listing 5-6. Retrieving the Record Count Via a PL/SQL Stored Procedure*

```
private void btnRetrieveCount_Click(object sender, EventArgs e)
{
        string _connstring = "Data Source=localhost/NEWDB;User
                Id=EDZEHOO;Password=PASS123;";
        try
        {
                OracleConnection _connObj = new OracleConnection(_connstring);
                _connObj.Open();
                OracleCommand _cmdObj = _connObj.CreateCommand();
                _cmdObj.CommandText = "proc_RetrieveCount";
                _cmdObj.CommandType = CommandType.StoredProcedure;

                OracleParameter _countParam = new OracleParameter();
                _countParam.ParameterName = "intRecordCount";
                _countParam.OracleDbType = OracleDbType.Int32;
                _countParam.Direction = ParameterDirection.Output;
                _cmdObj.Parameters.Add(_countParam);
```

```
                _cmdObj.ExecuteNonQuery();
                MessageBox.Show ("Total number of records : " + _countParam.Value );

                _connObj.Close();
                _connObj.Dispose();
                _connObj = null;
        }
        catch (Exception ex)
        {
                MessageBox.Show(ex.ToString());
        }
}
```

Take note that the **Direction** property of the Oracle parameter is set to **Output** instead of **Input**. If you run this code and click the "Retrieve Count" button, you will be able to see the total number of records show in a pop-up message box.

# Executing a PL/SQL Function

A PL/SQL function is similar to the PL/SQL stored procedure except that it will always return a value. PL/SQL functions can return values of any data type, including complex data types. Just in case you're wondering how a PL/SQL function looks, here's a sample one that returns the number of records in the **Products** table:

```
CREATE OR REPLACE FUNCTION func_RetrieveCount
RETURN NUMBER
IS
        intRecordCount NUMBER;
BEGIN
        SELECT COUNT(*) INTO intRecordCount FROM Products;
        RETURN intRecordCount;
END;
```

To call this PL/SQL function and read its return value, you will need to declare an **OracleParameter** that has the **ParameterDirection.ReturnValue** type instead of the **ParameterDirection.Output** type. Let's try this. Create a new form, and place a new button on the form. In the click event of the button, write the code in Listing 5-7.

*Listing 5-7. Retrieving the Record Count Via a PL/SQL Function*

```
private void btnRetrieveCount_Click(object sender, EventArgs e)
{
        string _connstring = "Data Source=localhost/NEWDB;User
                Id=EDZEHOO;Password=PASS123;";
        try
        {
                OracleConnection _connObj = new OracleConnection(_connstring);
                _connObj.Open();
                OracleCommand _cmdObj = _connObj.CreateCommand();
```

127

```
        _cmdObj.CommandText = "func_RetrieveCount";
        _cmdObj.CommandType = CommandType.StoredProcedure ;

        //Declare the return parameter
        OracleParameter _retValueParam = new OracleParameter();
        _retValueParam.ParameterName = "Any_name";
        _retValueParam.OracleDbType = OracleDbType.Int32;
        _retValueParam.Direction = ParameterDirection.ReturnValue;
        _cmdObj.Parameters.Add(_retValueParam);

        _cmdObj.ExecuteNonQuery();
        MessageBox.Show("The return value is :" + _retValueParam.Value.ToString());
        _connObj.Close();
        _connObj.Dispose();
        _connObj = null;
    }
    catch (Exception ex)
    {
        MessageBox.Show(ex.ToString());
    }
}
```

Run the form, and click the button. You should be able to see the number of records show up in a pop-up message box.

---

▪ **Tip**    Return values are usually used when a single value needs to be returned from a stored procedure. Output parameters are used instead when multiple values need to be returned. You can, however, have both output parameters and return values in the same PL/SQL function.

---

# Handling Special IN and OUT Data Types

There are many different data types that can be passed as **IN/OUT** parameters to and from stored procedures. In the sections earlier, you've seen examples on how to do this with simpler data types such as the **VARCHAR2** and **NUMBER** data types. In this section, we'll take an in-depth look at more complex types:

- Collection data types (associative arrays, **VARRAY**s, and nested tables)
- Reference data types (**REF** cursors and multiple **REF** cursors)
- Custom UDTs

## Using Associative Arrays

PL/SQL provides a data type called the associative array that allows you to use collections in your PL/SQL code. This data type behaves just like any collection would—you can loop through its elements, reference an item using an index or a key, and so on. An associative array can be thought of as the equivalent of a hash table in .NET. It can be declared in the following format:

```
TYPE <ArrayName> IS TABLE OF <Element Type> INDEX BY <Key Type>;
```

For example, you might need to have an array of numerical elements that can be iterated through using a numerical index. In such a case, you would declare the associative array as follows:

```
TYPE MyArray IS TABLE OF NUMBER INDEX BY BINARY_INTEGER;
```

---

■ **Tip** You can also index an associative array using strings. In such a case, you would declare the associative array as TYPE MyArray IS TABLE OF NUMBER INDEX BY VARCHAR2(255).

---

Let's take a look at an example of how associative arrays can be passed in or retrieved from a PL/SQL stored procedure.

## Passing Associative Arrays to PL/SQL Code

It would be great to be able to update the prices of multiple items in the **Products** table in one go. You can achieve this using two arrays: one to hold the names of the products you wanted to update and the other to hold the corresponding prices for each product in the first array. Let's create and declare a stored procedure to do this.

The first step is to declare the associative arrays in a PL/SQL package. You will also need to declare a sample stored procedure in the same package as well. You can do this by running the following script in SQL*Plus:

```
CREATE OR REPLACE PACKAGE ProductsPackage IS
        TYPE DecimalArray IS TABLE OF DECIMAL INDEX BY BINARY_INTEGER;
        TYPE StringArray IS TABLE OF VARCHAR2(255) INDEX BY BINARY_INTEGER;
        PROCEDURE proc_UpdateMultiplePrices(ProdPrices IN DecimalArray, ProdNames IN
                StringArray);
END ProductsPackage;
```

---

■ **Note** As you can see, the associative arrays are being passed as stored procedure arguments. You must hence declare these associative arrays first. We use a PL/SQL package in this example because it lets you wrap all these declarations in a tidy code block.

---

The next thing you will need to do is to create the stored procedure itself. In the **UpdateMultiplePrices** stored procedure, we will loop through the **ProdNames** array and run an SQL **UPDATE** statement to update the price for each product found (using the prices from the **ProdPrices** array). Run the following PL/SQL script in SQL*Plus as well:

```
CREATE OR REPLACE PACKAGE BODY ProductsPackage IS
        PROCEDURE proc_UpdateMultiplePrices(ProdPrices IN DecimalArray, ProdNames IN
                StringArray)
        IS
        BEGIN
                FOR i IN 1..ProdNames.LAST
                LOOP
                        UPDATE Products SET Price = Price + ProdPrices(i) WHERE Name = ↵
                                ProdNames(i);
                END LOOP;
        END;
END ProductsPackage;
```

Now that you've created the PL/SQL package and the stored procedure, you can easily refer to it using the following notation:

**<Package Name>.<Stored Procedure Name>**

To pass in an array created in C# or VB.NET to a PL/SQL stored procedure as an associative array, you can use the following code:

```
OracleParameter _priceParam = new OracleParameter();
_priceParam.ParameterName = "ProdPrices";
_priceParam.OracleDbType = OracleDbType.Decimal;
_priceParam.Direction = ParameterDirection.Input;

//Declare the parameter as a PL/SQL Associative array
_priceParam.CollectionType = OracleCollectionType.PLSQLAssociativeArray;

//Create the array
Decimal [] decArray= new Decimal[3];
decArray[0] = 100;
decArray[1] = 300;
decArray[2] = 500;

//Pass it to the parameter object
_priceParam.Value = decArray;
_cmdObj.Parameters.Add(_priceParam);
```

Let's take a look at the full code in Listing 5-8, where you will be passing two arrays (a decimal and string array) to the PL/SQL stored procedure. Create a new form, and place a button called **btnUpdateMultiplePrices** on the form. In the click event of this button, write the code shown in Listing 5-8.

*Listing 5-8. Updating Multiple Prices Using Associative Arrays*

```
private void btnUpdateMultiplePrices_Click(object sender, EventArgs e)
{
        String _connstring = "Data Source=localhost/NEWDB;User
                Id=EDZEHOO;Password=PASS123;";
        try
        {
```

```
OracleConnection _connObj = new OracleConnection(_connstring);
_connObj.Open();
OracleCommand _cmdObj = _connObj.CreateCommand();
_cmdObj.CommandText = "ProductsPackage.proc_UpdateMultiplePrices";
_cmdObj.CommandType = CommandType.StoredProcedure;

OracleParameter _priceParam = new OracleParameter();
_priceParam.ParameterName = "ProdPrices";
_priceParam.OracleDbType = OracleDbType.Decimal;
_priceParam.Direction = ParameterDirection.Input;
_priceParam.CollectionType = OracleCollectionType.PLSQLAssociativeArray;
Decimal [] decArray= new Decimal[3];
decArray[0] = 100;
decArray[1] = 300;
decArray[2] = 500;
_priceParam.Value = decArray;
_cmdObj.Parameters.Add(_priceParam);

OracleParameter _NameParam = new OracleParameter();
_NameParam.ParameterName = "ProdNames";
_NameParam.OracleDbType = OracleDbType.Varchar2;
_NameParam.Direction = ParameterDirection.Input;
_NameParam.CollectionType = OracleCollectionType.PLSQLAssociativeArray;
String[] stringArray = new String[3];
stringArray[0] = "Engine";
stringArray[1] = "Windshield";
stringArray[2] = "Rear Lights";
_NameParam.Value = stringArray;
_cmdObj.Parameters.Add(_NameParam);
_cmdObj.ExecuteNonQuery();

MessageBox.Show("All products updated!");

_connObj.Close();
_connObj.Dispose();
_connObj = null;
}
catch (Exception ex)
{
        MessageBox.Show(ex.ToString());
}
}
}
```

After running this code sample, you will find that the prices for the "Engine", "Windshield", and "Rear Lights" products have increased by the amounts specified in the **ProdPrices** array.

## Retrieving Associative Arrays from PL/SQL Code

There will definitely be occasions when you need to retrieve multiple rows of data from a stored procedure. You can use associative arrays for this purpose. In the following code sample, you will write a stored procedure to retrieve the names of all your products into an associative array. Title this procedure proc_GetAllProductNames.

Before you proceed, make the following changes (highlighted in bold) to the **ProductsPackage** you created earlier. Run the following scripts in SQL*Plus:

```
CREATE OR REPLACE PACKAGE ProductsPackage IS
        TYPE DecimalArray IS TABLE OF DECIMAL INDEX BY BINARY_INTEGER;
        TYPE StringArray IS TABLE OF VARCHAR2(255) INDEX BY BINARY_INTEGER;
        PROCEDURE proc_GetAllProductNames(ProdNames OUT StringArray);
END ProductsPackage;

CREATE OR REPLACE PACKAGE BODY ProductsPackage IS
        PROCEDURE proc_GetAllProductNames(ProdNames OUT StringArray)
        IS
        BEGIN
                SELECT Name BULK COLLECT INTO ProdNames FROM Products;
        END;
END ProductsPackage;
```

---

■ **Tip**    The BULK COLLECT INTO syntax tells Oracle to bulk bind the output from the multiple rows fetched by a query into a PL/SQL collection.

---

Create a new form, and place a new button named **btnGetAllProductNames** on the form. In the click event of this button, write the code from Listing 5-9.

*Listing 5-9. Retrieving Multiple Rows of Data Via Associative Arrays*

```
private void btnGetAllProductNames(object sender, EventArgs e)
{
        String _connstring = "Data Source=localhost/NEWDB;User
                Id=EDZEHOO;Password=PASS123;";
        try
        {
                OracleConnection _connObj = new OracleConnection(_connstring);
                _connObj.Open();
                OracleCommand _cmdObj = _connObj.CreateCommand();
                _cmdObj.CommandText = "ProductsPackage.proc_GetAllProductNames";
                _cmdObj.CommandType = CommandType.StoredProcedure;

                //Create an output parameter
                OracleParameter _NameParam = new OracleParameter();
                _NameParam.ParameterName = "ProdNames";
                _NameParam.OracleDbType = OracleDbType.Varchar2 ;
                _NameParam.Direction = ParameterDirection.Output;
                _NameParam.CollectionType = OracleCollectionType.PLSQLAssociativeArray;
```

```
//You must explicitly define the number of elements to return
_NameParam.Size = 10;

//Because you are retrieving an object with a variable size, you need to
//define the size of the string returned. This size must be specified for
//each element in the output result
int[] intArray= new int[10];
int _counter;
for (_counter = 0; _counter < 10; _counter++) {intArray[_counter] = 255;}
_NameParam.ArrayBindSize = intArray;

//Execute the stored procedure
_cmdObj.Parameters.Add(_NameParam);
_cmdObj.ExecuteNonQuery();

//For VARCHAR2 data types, an array of OracleString objects is returned
String _result="";
OracleString[] stringArray = (OracleString[])_NameParam.Value;
for (_counter = 0; _counter <= stringArray.GetUpperBound(0); _counter++)
{
    OracleString _outputString = stringArray[_counter];
    _result = _result + _outputString.Value + "\n";
}
MessageBox.Show("Product names are:\n" + _result);

_connObj.Close();
_connObj.Dispose();
_connObj = null;
}
catch (Exception ex)
{
        MessageBox.Show(ex.ToString());
}
}
```

If you run the code in Listing 5-9, you will see the list of products retrieved in a pop-up message box, as shown in Figure 5-4.

*Figure 5-4. Retrieving associative arrays*

133

■ **Note** When retrieving data from a stored procedure using an associative array, you must explicitly know the maximum **Size** of the output array in advance. Setting a value that is lower than the actual retrieved data would raise an exception.

## Using VARRAYs

The variable-size array (**VARRAY**) is another type of collection object that can be used in PL/SQL in addition to associative arrays (which you saw earlier). The **VARRAY** is an ordered set of elements and is quite similar to the associative array in that it is usually used if you know the size of the array that you need in advance.

■ **Tip** One difference between a **VARRAY** and an associative array is that it is defined, not declared. You've seen earlier that you can simply declare an associative array inside the body of a PL/SQL package. For **VARRAY**s, however, you must explicitly define them using the **CREATE OR REPLACE TYPE** statement.

Let's write a code sample to selectively delete records from the **Products** table by passing in a **VARRAY** containing a list of IDs of the products that you wish to delete. First, create the **VARRAY** object in SQL*Plus using the following statement:

```
CREATE OR REPLACE TYPE ProductVArray AS VARRAY(3000) OF VARCHAR2(10);
```

This creates a **VARRAY** that can contain a maximum of 3,000 elements of ten-character strings. Next, create the following stored procedure to loop through the array and delete the corresponding products:

```
CREATE OR REPLACE PROCEDURE proc_DeleteProducts(arrProduct IN ProductVArray) IS
BEGIN
        FOR i IN 1..arrProduct.LAST
        LOOP
                DELETE FROM Products WHERE ID = arrProduct(i);
        END LOOP;
END;
```

The **VARRAY** is also different from associative arrays in that it can be considered a custom data type. You cannot receive a **VARRAY** directly from the **OracleParameter.Value** property as you did earlier for associative arrays. To be able to use it in your code, you will need to create a .NET class that encapsulates this array. Listing 5-10 does that for you, creating the **ProductVArray** class referenced by the stored procedure. This class will also need to implement the **IOracleCustomType** interface so that it can be recognized by Oracle.

*Listing 5-10. The ProductVArray Class*

```
using System;
using System.Data;
using System.Collections;
using Oracle.DataAccess.Client;
using Oracle.DataAccess.Types;

public class ProductVArray : IOracleCustomType, INullable
{
        //You will need to define a local array to hold the VARRAY elements. The data
        //type must correspond to the type declared in the VARRAY. You've defined a VARRAY
        //of VARCHAR2(10) values, hence your local array will hold String objects.
        [OracleArrayMapping()]
        public String[] Array;

        //The status array is used to store the status of an array index - whether the
        //element at the index is a NULL value or not.
        private OracleUdtStatus[] m_statusArray;
        public OracleUdtStatus[] StatusArray
        {
                get
                {
                        return this.m_statusArray;
                }
                set
                {
                        this.m_statusArray = value;
                }
        }

        private bool m_bIsNull;

        public bool IsNull
        {
                get
                {
                        return m_bIsNull;
                }
        }

        public static ProductVArray Null
        {
                get
                {
                        ProductVArray obj = new ProductVArray();
                        obj.m_bIsNull = true;
                        return obj;
                }
        }
```

135

```
//The ToCustomObject method is required as part of the IOracleCustomType
//implementation. It maps the retrieved VARRAY to the local array.
public void ToCustomObject(OracleConnection con, IntPtr pUdt)
{
        object objectStatusArray = null;
        Array = (String[])OracleUdt.GetValue(con, pUdt, 0, out objectStatusArray);
        m_statusArray = (OracleUdtStatus[])objectStatusArray;
}

//The FromCustomObject method is the opposite equivalent. It maps a local array to a
//VARRAY
public void FromCustomObject(OracleConnection con, IntPtr pUdt)
{
        OracleUdt.SetValue(con, pUdt, 0, Array, m_statusArray);
}

public override string ToString()
{
        if (m_bIsNull)
                return "ProductVArray.Null";
        else
        {
                string rtnstr = String.Empty;
                if (m_statusArray[0] == OracleUdtStatus.Null)
                        rtnstr = "NULL";
                else
                        rtnstr = Array.GetValue(0).ToString();

                for (int i = 1; i < m_statusArray.Length; i++)
                {
                        if (m_statusArray[i] == OracleUdtStatus.Null)
                                rtnstr += "," + "NULL";
                        else
                                rtnstr += "," + Array.GetValue(i).ToString();
                }
                return "ProductVArray(" + rtnstr + ")";
        }
}
}
```

You will also need to create another class—the factory class for your **ProductVArray** class. You can create the class using the code in Listing 5-11.

*Listing 5-11. The ProductVArrayFactory Class*

```
[OracleCustomTypeMapping("EDZEHOO.PRODUCTVARRAY")]
public class ProductVArrayFactory : IOracleCustomTypeFactory, IOracleArrayTypeFactory
{
        public IOracleCustomType CreateObject()
        {
                return new ProductVArray();
```

```
        }
        public Array CreateArray(int numElems)
        {
                return new String[numElems];
        }

        public Array CreateStatusArray(int numElems)
        {
                return new OracleUdtStatus[numElems];
        }
}
```

You will now need to write the code to instantiate the **ProductVArray** class, initialize it to a set of values, and then pass it to the **proc_DeleteValues** stored procedure as a **VARRAY**. Create a new form and place a button named **btnDeleteProducts** on it. In the click event of the button, write the code from Listing 5-12.

*Listing 5-12. Deleting Products Via a VARRAY*

```
private void btnDeleteProducts_Click(object sender, EventArgs e)
{
        String _connstring = "Data Source=localhost/NEWDB;User
                Id=EDZEHOO;Password=PASS123;";
        try
        {
                OracleConnection _connObj = new OracleConnection(_connstring);
                _connObj.Open();
                OracleCommand _cmdObj = _connObj.CreateCommand();
                _cmdObj.CommandText = "proc_DeleteProducts";
                _cmdObj.CommandType = CommandType.StoredProcedure;

                //Instantiate the ProductVArray class and add two elements
                ProductVArray _products = new ProductVArray();
                _products.Array = new String[] { "E1", "C1" };

                //Create a UDT-based OracleParameter, and pass in the ProductVArray
                //object
                OracleParameter param = new OracleParameter();
                param.OracleDbType = OracleDbType.Object;
                param.Direction = ParameterDirection.Input;
                param.UdtTypeName = "EDZEHOO.PRODUCTVARRAY";
                param.Value = _products;
                _cmdObj.Parameters.Add(param);

                int _result = _cmdObj.ExecuteNonQuery();
                if (_result > 0)
                {
                    MessageBox.Show("Records deleted successfully");
                }
                else
                {
```

137

```
                    MessageBox.Show("No records deleted");
            }
            _connObj.Close();
            _connObj.Dispose();
            _connObj = null;
        }
        catch (Exception ex)
        {
                MessageBox.Show(ex.ToString());
        }
    }
}
```

If you try running the preceding code, you will find the Products with the IDs E1 and C1 deleted.

## Using Nested Tables

The nested table is the third type of collection object available to PL/SQL developers. It is basically a table that is embedded in another table. A nested table, unlike the other two collection types you've seen earlier, does not have a maximum size limit. It is hence commonly used when developers don't know in advance how big the collection needs to be.

A nested table has to be defined, not declared. The syntax to define a nested table is quite similar to that of the associative array. You will notice however that the INDEX BY part is not defined with nested tables, for example:

```
CREATE OR REPLACE TYPE ProductNestedTable AS TABLE OF VARCHAR2(10);
```

Let's try rewriting the VARRAY code example from the previous section using nested tables. First, define the nested table by running the statement above in SQL*Plus. After that, you will need to redefine the proc_DeleteProducts stored procedure. Run the following statement next:

```
CREATE OR REPLACE PROCEDURE proc_DeleteProducts(tblProduct IN ProductNestedTable) IS
BEGIN
        FOR i IN 1..tblProduct.LAST
        LOOP
                DELETE FROM Products WHERE ID = tblProduct(i);
        END LOOP;
END;
```

The next thing you need to do is to create a new factory class for the nested table type you've created. The following class will implement the IOracleArrayTypeFactory interface:

```
[OracleCustomTypeMappingAttribute("EDZEHOO.PRODUCTNESTEDTABLE")]
public class ProductNestedTableFactory : IOracleArrayTypeFactory
{
        public Array CreateArray(int numElems)
        {
                return new String[numElems];
        }

        public Array CreateStatusArray(int numElems)
        {
                return new OracleUdtStatus[numElems];
```

138

```
        }
}
```

You must now write code to create the string array, fill it with data, and then pass the array on to your stored procedure as a nested table type. Create a new form, and place a button on it. In the click event of this form, write the code from Listing 5-13.

*Listing 5-13. Deleting Products Via a Nested Table*

```csharp
private void btnDeleteProducts_Click(object sender, EventArgs e)
{
        String _connString = "Data Source=localhost/NEWDB;User
                Id=EDZEHOO;Password=PASS123;";
        try
        {
                OracleConnection _connObj = new OracleConnection(_connString);
                _connObj.Open();

                OracleCommand _cmdObj = _connObj.CreateCommand();
                _cmdObj.CommandText = "proc_DeleteProducts";
                _cmdObj.CommandType = CommandType.StoredProcedure;

                // Create a string array and populate it with the IDs of the Products you
                //wish to delete
                String[] _productsTable = new String[] { "R1", "W1" };

                //Create a parameter object and pass in the string array
                OracleParameter _productTblParam = new OracleParameter();
                _productTblParam.OracleDbType = OracleDbType.Array;
                _productTblParam.Direction = ParameterDirection.Input;
                _productTblParam.UdtTypeName = "EDZEHOO.PRODUCTNESTEDTABLE";
                _productTblParam.Value = _productsTable;
                _cmdObj.Parameters.Add(_productTblParam);

                int _result = _cmdObj.ExecuteNonQuery();
                if (_result > 0)
                {
                    MessageBox.Show("Records deleted successfully");
                }
                else
                {
                    MessageBox.Show("No records deleted");
                }
                _connObj.Close();
                _connObj.Dispose();
                _connObj = null;
        }
        catch (OracleException ex)
        {
                MessageBox.Show(ex.ToString());
```

```
        }
}
```

Try running this code sample and clicking the button. You will find the products with the IDs **R1** and **W1** deleted.

## Using REF Cursors

A **REF** cursor is a pointer to a result set generated on the server from a query. **REF** cursors can be used, for example, when you need to run a query in one stored procedure and have the results processed by another stored procedure. Because it is essentially a pointer to a result set in memory, what is passed around is the reference or pointer, not the actual result set itself.

What is important to note is that a **REF** cursor points to a result set existing in server memory, not client memory. When a **REF** cursor-generating query executes on the server, initially only the pointer, not the actual data, is returned to the client. Data are only returned to the client when they are requested. This may mean additional roundtrips to the server but is better in terms of performance in cases where you do not immediately need to use the data after running a query.

---

▪ **Caution** Another indirect implication of accessing a **REF** cursor is that (unlike a **DataSet**), the moment you close the database connection, the **REF** cursor becomes unavailable. This is because the result set of a **REF** cursor actually resides in server memory, not at the client.

---

A question that might instantly pop in the back of your mind is, "Why return **REF** cursors instead of just returning the result set directly from the stored procedure?" There are a few reasons to favor a **REF** cursor:

- You need to modify the result of a query inside a stored procedure before returning it.

- You might be planning to pass the result set from one stored procedure directly into another stored procedure as input, with as little overhead as possible.

- The accessing code does not have direct access to the tables.

- As mentioned earlier, the REF cursor does not immediately return data until it is requested. This may be desirable (to reduce network traffic) under certain circumstances.

You will see that a **REF** cursor can be pretty versatile. It can be used as both an **IN** and **OUT** parameter. In the next few sections, we will explore how you can use the **OracleDataReader** and **OracleDataAdapter** classes to retrieve a result set generated from a PL/SQL stored procedure via a REF cursor. This result set will contain all the records in the **Products** table. Run the following two statements in SQL*Plus to create this stored procedure:

```
CREATE OR REPLACE PACKAGE ProductsPackage IS
        TYPE refCursor IS REF CURSOR;
        PROCEDURE proc_GetProductsInfo(ProdInfo OUT refCursor);
```

```
END ProductsPackage;
CREATE OR REPLACE PACKAGE BODY ProductsPackage IS
        PROCEDURE proc_GetProductsInfo(ProdInfo OUT refCursor)
        IS
        BEGIN
                OPEN ProdInfo FOR
                SELECT * FROM Products;
        END;
END ProductsPackage;
```

---

▪ **Tip** The OPEN . . . FOR statement is used to execute a query associated with a cursor. It positions the cursor variable before the first row in the result set.

---

## Reading a Result Set from a REF Cursor Using the OracleDataReader

To read a result set from a **REF** cursor, you only need to add a **REF** cursor output parameter to the **OracleCommand** object. When you run the **ExecuteDataReader()** method on this OracleCommand object, it will create and return an **OracleDataReader** object that internally maps to the result set referenced by the **REF** cursor.

Let's look at the code to do this. Create a new form, and place a button named **btnGetReader** on it. Write the code from Listing 5-14 in the click event of this button.

*Listing 5-14. Reading from a REF Cursor Using OracleDataReader*

```
private void btnGetReader_Click(object sender, EventArgs e)
{
        String _connstring = "Data Source=localhost/NEWDB;User
                Id=EDZEHOO;Password=PASS123;";
        try
        {
                OracleConnection _connObj = new OracleConnection(_connstring);
                _connObj.Open();
                OracleCommand _cmdObj = _connObj.CreateCommand();
                _cmdObj.CommandText = "ProductsPackage.proc_GetProductsInfo";
                _cmdObj.CommandType = CommandType.StoredProcedure;

                OracleParameter _RefParam = new OracleParameter();
                _RefParam.ParameterName = "ProdInfo";
                _RefParam.OracleDbType = OracleDbType.RefCursor;
                _RefParam.Direction = ParameterDirection.Output;
                _cmdObj.Parameters.Add(_RefParam);
                OracleDataReader _rdrObj = _cmdObj.ExecuteReader();

                //This should remind you of Chapter 4. We use an OracleDataReader object to
                //loop through the result set and display a summary of the retrieved
                //information in a popup message box
```

```
                    if (_rdrObj.HasRows)
                    {
                        while (_rdrObj.Read())
                        {
                            String _data="";
                            _data = "ID:" + _rdrObj.GetString(_rdrObj.GetOrdinal("ID")) + "\n" +
                                "Name:" + _rdrObj.GetString(_rdrObj.GetOrdinal("Name")) + "\n" +
                                "Price:" + _rdrObj.GetDecimal(_rdrObj.GetOrdinal("Price"));

                            MessageBox.Show(_data);
                        }
                    }
                    _connObj.Close();
                    _connObj.Dispose();
                    _connObj = null;
            }
            catch (Exception ex)
            {
                    MessageBox.Show(ex.ToString());
            }
    }
```

When you run the preceding code sample, you will be able to see the summary of the retrieved information show up in a series of pop-up message boxes (one of which is shown in Figure 5-5).

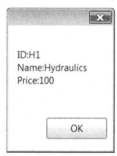

*Figure 5-5. Reading a result set from a REF cursor using OracleDataReader*

## Reading a Result Set from a REF Cursor Using the OracleDataAdapter

You can also similarly read from a REF cursor into a **Dataset** object using the **OracleDataAdapter** class. Let's try to also display the retrieved dataset in a **Datagridview** control. You can reuse the same **proc_GetProductsInfo** stored procedure you've created earlier. Create a new form, and place a **Datagridview** control named **Datagridview1** on the form. Place a button on the same form. In the click event of this button, write the code from Listing 5-14.

*Listing 5-15. Reading from a REF Cursor into a Dataset*

```
private void btnGetDataset_Click(object sender, EventArgs e)
{
        String _connstring = "Data Source=localhost/NEWDB;User
            Id=EDZEHOO;Password=PASS123;";
        try
        {

                OracleConnection _connObj = new OracleConnection(_connstring);
                _connObj.Open();
                OracleCommand _cmdObj = _connObj.CreateCommand();
                _cmdObj.CommandText = "ProductsPackage.proc_GetProductsInfo";
                _cmdObj.CommandType = CommandType.StoredProcedure;

                OracleParameter _RefParam = new OracleParameter();
                _RefParam.ParameterName = "ProdInfo";
                _RefParam.OracleDbType = OracleDbType.RefCursor;
                _RefParam.Direction = ParameterDirection.Output;
                _cmdObj.Parameters.Add(_RefParam);

                OracleDataAdapter _adapterObj = new OracleDataAdapter(_cmdObj);
                DataSet _datasetObj = new DataSet ();
                _adapterObj.Fill(_datasetObj);
                dataGridView1.DataSource = _datasetObj.Tables[0];
                _connObj.Close();
                _connObj.Dispose();
                _connObj = null;
        }
        catch (Exception ex)
        {
                MessageBox.Show(ex.ToString());
        }
}
```

When you run the code, the **DataSet** will be displayed in the **DataGridView** control. You should see results such as those in Figure 5-6.

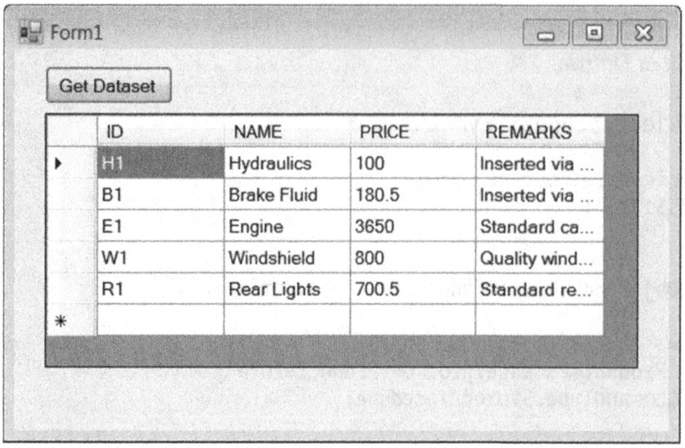

***Figure 5-6.*** *Reading a result set from a REF cursor into a Dataset*

## Retrieving Multiple Active Result Sets

The cool thing about **REF** cursors is that you can also retrieve multiple active result sets (MARs) from a single stored procedure run. You can do this by adding multiple **REF** cursor parameters to an **OracleCommand** object. First of all, let's change the previous section's stored procedure slightly. Instead of just retrieving the whole list of products, you will return two result sets—the first returning the list of products that are below $500 dollars, and the second returning the list of products above $500. The following highlighted code shows you what you need to change:

```
CREATE OR REPLACE PACKAGE ProductsPackage IS
        TYPE refCursor IS REF CURSOR;
        PROCEDURE proc_GetProductsInfo(cheapProducts OUT refCursor, expensiveProducts OUT
                refCursor);
END ProductsPackage;
CREATE OR REPLACE PACKAGE BODY ProductsPackage IS
        PROCEDURE proc_GetProductsInfo (cheapProducts OUT refCursor,
                expensiveProducts OUT refCursor)
        IS
        BEGIN
                OPEN cheapProducts FOR
                SELECT * FROM Products WHERE Price<500;
                OPEN expensiveProducts FOR
                SELECT * FROM Products WHERE Price>500;
        END;
END ProductsPackage;
```

If you return multiple **REF** cursors from your stored procedure and the **OracleDataAdapter.Fill()** method to obtain a **DataSet**, the various result sets are populated into separate **Datatable** objects in the same dataset.

Let's build the code sample to try this out now. You can use the same form you created earlier in the previous section. This time, you'd probably want to add another **DataGridView** control (named

Datagridview2) to your form to display the second result set. In the click event of the **btnGetDataset** button, write the code from Listing 5-16.

*Listing 5-16. Retrieving Multiple REF Cursors*

```csharp
private void btnGetDataset_Click(object sender, EventArgs e)
{
        String _connstring = "Data Source=localhost/NEWDB;User
                Id=EDZEHOO;Password=PASS123;";
        try
        {
                OracleConnection _connObj = new OracleConnection(_connstring);
                _connObj.Open();
                OracleCommand _cmdObj = _connObj.CreateCommand();
                _cmdObj.CommandText = "ProductsPackage.proc_GetProductsInfo";
                _cmdObj.CommandType = CommandType.StoredProcedure;

                //Create the REF cursor parameter for the products that are < $500
                OracleParameter _chpProdParam = new OracleParameter();
                _chpProdParam.ParameterName = "cheapProducts";
                _chpProdParam.OracleDbType = OracleDbType.RefCursor;
                _chpProdParam.Direction = ParameterDirection.Output;
                _cmdObj.Parameters.Add(_chpProdParam);

                //Create the REF cursor parameter for the products that are > $500
                OracleParameter _expProdParam = new OracleParameter();
                _expProdParam.ParameterName = "expensiveProducts";
                _expProdParam.OracleDbType = OracleDbType.RefCursor;
                _expProdParam.Direction = ParameterDirection.Output;
                _cmdObj.Parameters.Add(_expProdParam);

                OracleDataAdapter _adapterObj = new OracleDataAdapter(_cmdObj);
                DataSet _datasetObj = new DataSet();
                _adapterObj.Fill(_datasetObj);

                //The result sets are stored in separate Datatables in the same dataset
                dataGridView1.DataSource = _datasetObj.Tables[0];
                dataGridView2.DataSource = _datasetObj.Tables[1];

                _connObj.Close();
                _connObj.Dispose();
                _connObj = null;
        }
        catch (Exception ex)
        {
                MessageBox.Show(ex.ToString());
        }
}
```

When you run the code from Listing 5-16, you can see the data sets in the corresponding **DataGridView** controls. You should see results similar to those in Figure 5-7. In fact, there is nothing stopping you from running stored procedures that return more than two result sets. You can increase the performance of your application this way by reducing the number of round trips taken to the server for each request.

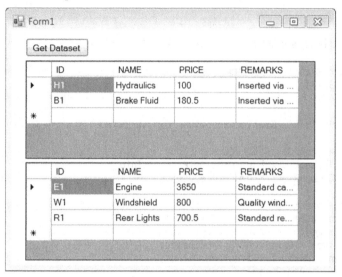

*Figure 5-7. Reading a result set from multiple REF cursors into multiple datatables*

## User Defined Types (UDT) / OBJECT Types

The Oracle database allows you to use UDTs in PL/SQL. UDTs are basically data types that allow you to model the structure of the data in your application. For example, you can represent real-world objects such as customers, as objects in an Oracle database using the following UDT definition:

```
CREATE OR REPLACE TYPE Customer AS OBJECT
(
        CustomerID VARCHAR2(10),
        CustomerName VARCHAR2(255),
        CustomerDOB DATE
);
```

UDTs are convenient because they extend object-oriented design into the database, making it easier for database administrators and developers to understand how individual fields relate to each other. It also makes for clearer and neater code; instead of passing parameters field by field to a stored procedure, you can pass them as a single UDT. Perhaps one of the most important benefits of using UDTs is that an Oracle UDT can map directly to a .NET class. This allows you to read from a UDT directly into a .NET class, with each UDT column mapping to a .NET property with the same name.

Let's take a look at how this mapping can be achieved. You will build a sample application to try to insert a new record into the **Products** table (by passing its details to a stored procedure as a UDT object). First, you must grant yourself the rights to create UDT objects. Log on under the **SYSTEM** account in SQL*Plus, and run the following statement:

```
GRANT CREATE ANY TYPE TO "EDZEHOO";
```

Next, you must define the UDT object itself. Log on under your own user account in SQL*Plus, and run the following statement:

```
CREATE OR REPLACE TYPE ProductType AS OBJECT
(
        ID VARCHAR2(10),
        Name VARCHAR2(255),
        Price NUMBER
);
```

The next thing you need to do is to create a stored procedure that will take in the UDT object and insert its details into the **Products** table. You can do this by running the following script in SQL*Plus. Notice that you can refer to the member variables of the UDT using the dot (.) separator.

```
CREATE OR REPLACE PROCEDURE proc_InsertProduct(udtProduct IN ProductType) IS
BEGIN
        INSERT INTO Products(ID, Name, Price) VALUES(udtProduct.ID, udtProduct.Name,
                udtProduct.Price);
END;
```

Now, you will need to create a class that maps to the UDT you've just created. Create a new class in your project called **ProductType**. This class must implement the **INullable** and **IOracleCustomType** interfaces. The code for this class follows in Listing 5-17.

*Listing 5-17. The ProductType Class*

```csharp
using System;
using Oracle.DataAccess.Client;
using Oracle.DataAccess.Types;

public class PRODUCTTYPE : INullable, IOracleCustomType {
        private bool m_IsNull;
        private string m_ID;
        private string m_NAME;
        private decimal m_PRICE;
        private bool m_PRICEIsNull;

        public PRODUCTTYPE() {
            this.m_PRICEIsNull = true;
        }

        public virtual bool IsNull {
            get {
                return this.m_IsNull;
            }
        }

        public static PRODUCTTYPE Null {
            get {
                PRODUCTTYPE obj = new PRODUCTTYPE();
```

```
            obj.m_IsNull = true;
            return obj;
        }
    }

    [OracleObjectMappingAttribute("ID")]
    public string ID {
        get {
            return this.m_ID;
        }
        set {
            this.m_ID = value;
        }
    }

    [OracleObjectMappingAttribute("NAME")]
    public string NAME {
        get {
            return this.m_NAME;
        }
        set {
            this.m_NAME = value;
        }
    }

    [OracleObjectMappingAttribute("PRICE")]
    public decimal PRICE {
        get {
            return this.m_PRICE;
        }
        set {
            this.m_PRICE = value;
        }
    }

    public bool PRICEIsNull {
        get {
            return this.m_PRICEIsNull;
        }
        set {
            this.m_PRICEIsNull = value;
        }
    }

    //The FromCustomObject method is required as part of the IOracleCustomType
    //interface. This function allows you to define the mapping to use when filling a
    //UDT object with data from your UDT class
    public virtual void FromCustomObject(Oracle.DataAccess.Client.OracleConnection con,
            System.IntPtr pUdt)
    {
            Oracle.DataAccess.Types.OracleUdt.SetValue(con, pUdt, "ID", this.ID);
            Oracle.DataAccess.Types.OracleUdt.SetValue(con, pUdt, "NAME", this.NAME);
```

```
            if ((PRICEIsNull == false))
            {
                    Oracle.DataAccess.Types.OracleUdt.SetValue(con, pUdt, "PRICE",
                            this.PRICE);
            }
    }

    //This method is the opposite. It allows you to define the mapping to use when
    //populating your UDT class with data from a retrieved UDT object.
    public virtual void ToCustomObject(Oracle.DataAccess.Client.OracleConnection con,
            System.IntPtr pUdt)
    {
            this.ID = ((string)(Oracle.DataAccess.Types.OracleUdt.GetValue(con, pUdt,
                    "ID")));
            this.NAME = ((string)(Oracle.DataAccess.Types.OracleUdt.GetValue(con, pUdt,
                    "NAME")));
            this.PRICEIsNull = Oracle.DataAccess.Types.OracleUdt.IsDBNull(con, pUdt,
                    "PRICE");
            if ((PRICEIsNull == false))
            {
                    this.PRICE =
                            ((decimal)(Oracle.DataAccess.Types.OracleUdt.GetValue(con,
                            pUdt, "PRICE")));
            }
    }
}
```

---

■ **Tip** Your class property names do not necessarily need to be the same as the column names in your UDT object. You can define your own mapping and behavior in the `FromCustomObject` and `ToCustomObject` methods in the class shown in Listing 5-17.

---

You will also need to create an accompanying factory class. To that end, execute the code in Listing 5-18.

*Listing 5-18. The ProductTypeFactory Class*

```
[OracleCustomTypeMappingAttribute("EDZEHOO.PRODUCTTYPE")]
public class PRODUCTTYPEFactory : IOracleCustomTypeFactory
{
        public virtual IOracleCustomType CreateObject()
        {
                PRODUCTTYPE obj = new PRODUCTTYPE();
                return obj;
        }
}
```

Now that you've done this, you can finally write the code to instantiate the UDT class and pass it to the stored procedure you've created. Create a new form, place a button on the form, and in the click event of this button, write the code from Listing 5-19.

*Listing 5-19. Inserting a New Record Using a UDT*

```
private void btnInsertProduct_Click(object sender, EventArgs e)
{
        String _connstring = "Data Source=localhost/NEWDB;User
            Id=EDZEHOO;Password=PASS123;";
        try
        {
            OracleConnection _connObj = new OracleConnection(_connstring);
            _connObj.Open();
            OracleCommand _cmdObj = _connObj.CreateCommand();
            _cmdObj.CommandText = " proc_InsertProduct";
            _cmdObj.CommandType = CommandType.StoredProcedure;

            //Instantiate your UDT class here and specify the data for your new record
            PRODUCTTYPE _product = new PRODUCTTYPE();
            _product.NAME = "SPARETYRE";
            _product.PRICE = 400;
            _product.ID = "Y1";

            //Declare a UDT-based parameter and pass the instantiated class into this
            //parameter
            OracleParameter param = new OracleParameter();
            param.OracleDbType = OracleDbType.Object;
            param.Direction = ParameterDirection.Input;
            param.UdtTypeName = "EDZEHOO.PRODUCTTYPE";
            param.Value = _product;
            _cmdObj.Parameters.Add(param);

            int result = _cmdObj.ExecuteNonQuery();
            if (result > 0)
            {
                MessageBox.Show("Product successfully added");
            }
            _connObj.Close();
            _connObj.Dispose();
            _connObj = null;
        }
        catch (Exception ex)
        {
            MessageBox.Show(ex.ToString());
        }
}
```

You can now run this code. You will find the **SpareTyre** product created in the **Products** table. Retrieving a UDT object is similar; you simply reverse the **ParameterDirection** in your code and in the stored procedure definition.

# Handling Custom-Defined PL/SQL Errors

The PL/SQL language allows you to raise exceptions in PL/SQL code. If you think about it, that ability to raise exceptions makes sense too. PL/SQL stored procedures take in all sorts of input parameters. A prudent PL/SQL developer would check the input parameters before they are used. For instance, if you wanted to update the product price in a stored procedure, you should at least check if the new **Price** passed in was a negative number (which would be invalid). If the validation failed, your PL/SQL stored procedure could then raise an error to the calling .NET code by executing a call to **RAISE_APPLICATION_ERROR**, as shown in the following code:

```
CREATE OR REPLACE PROCEDURE proc_UpdatePrice(ProdPrice IN DECIMAL, ProdName IN
        VARCHAR2)
IS
BEGIN
        IF ProdPrice<=0 THEN
                RAISE_APPLICATION_ERROR(-20000, 'Invalid price value');
        END IF;
        UPDATE Products SET Price=ProdPrice WHERE Name=ProdName;
END;
```

In your .NET code, you can detect an exception using the **OracleException** class you learned in the previous chapter. The highlighted code in Listing 5-20 shows how you can trap this exception and show a message to the user based on the retrieved error number.

*Listing 5-20. Handling Custom PL/SQL Errors*

```
private void btnUpdateNow_Click(object sender, EventArgs e)
{
        string _connstring = "Data Source=localhost/NEWDB;User
                Id=EDZEHOO;Password=PASS123;";
        try
        {
                OracleConnection _connObj = new OracleConnection(_connstring);
                _connObj.Open();
                OracleCommand _cmdObj = _connObj.CreateCommand();
                _cmdObj.CommandText = "proc_UpdatePrice";
                _cmdObj.CommandType = CommandType.StoredProcedure;

                OracleParameter _PriceParam = new OracleParameter();
                _PriceParam.ParameterName = "ProdPrice";
                _PriceParam.OracleDbType = OracleDbType.Int32;
                _PriceParam.Direction = ParameterDirection.Input;
                _PriceParam.Value = numPriceIncrement.Value;
                _cmdObj.Parameters.Add(_PriceParam);

                OracleParameter _NameParam = new OracleParameter();
                _NameParam.ParameterName = "ProdName";
                _NameParam.OracleDbType = OracleDbType.Varchar2;
                _NameParam.Direction = ParameterDirection.Input;
                _NameParam.Value = txtProductName.Text;
```

```
            _cmdObj.Parameters.Add(_NameParam);

            _recordsAffected = _cmdObj.ExecuteNonQuery();
            MessageBox.Show("Updating done!");

            _connObj.Close();
            _connObj.Dispose();
            _connObj = null;
        }
        catch (OracleException ex)
        {
            if (ex.Number == 20000)
                MessageBox.Show("Sorry, invalid price value!");
            else
                MessageBox.Show(ex.ToString());
        }
    }
}
```

If you run this code sample and pass in a negative number as the **Price**, an exception will be raised. Your application will trap and display the appropriate message, as shown in Figure 5-8.

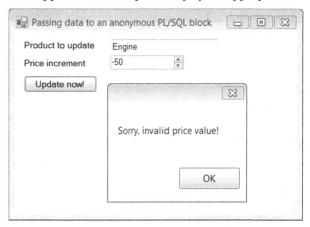

***Figure 5-8.*** *Handling custom-defined PL/SQL errors*

# Creating Your First .NET CLR Stored Procedure

.NET CLR stored procedures are stored procedures that can be written in a .NET language like C# or VB.NET, compiled into a .NET assembly (DLL file), registered with the Oracle database, and called like any other ordinary Oracle stored procedure. Unlike a PL/SQL stored procedure, a .NET CLR stored procedure executes outside of the Oracle database. When a call is made to execute this stored procedure, the assembly (DLL) hosting the stored procedure is loaded as an external process. Oracle then communicates with this external process (passing **IN/OUT** parameters for execution and so on).

.NET CLR stored procedures are a part of the Oracle Database Extensions for .NET package. You can create a .NET CLR stored procedure by creating a project based on the Oracle Project type in Visual Studio (shown in the screenshot in Figure 5-9).

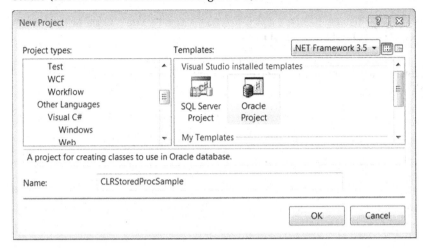

*Figure 5-9. Creating a new .NET CLR stored procedure*

In your new project, create a new class called **ProductClass**. Use the code from Listing 5-21.

The class in Listing 5-21 defines a **static** method named **UpdateProductPrice**, which will be your .NET CLR stored procedure. Let's use this method to update the price of a product by passing in the ID of the product you wish to update and the new price amount. Inside this method, you can use the **OracleConnection** and **OracleCommand** objects to execute SQL statements against the database. Listing 5-21 does exactly that.

*Listing 5-21. The .NET CLR Stored Procedure*

```
public class ProductClass
{
        public static void UpdateProductPrice(String ProdID, Decimal ProdPrice)
        {
                String _connString = "Data Source=localhost/NEWDB;User
                        Id=EDZEHOO;Password=PASS123;";
                OracleConnection _connObj = new OracleConnection(_connString);
                _connObj.Open();
                OracleCommand _cmdObj = _connObj.CreateCommand ();
                _cmdObj.CommandText ="UPDATE Products SET Price=" + ProdPrice + " WHERE
                        ID='" + ProdID + "'";
                _cmdObj.ExecuteNonQuery ();
                _connObj.Close();
                _connObj.Dispose ();
                _connObj = null;
        }
}
```

That's all there is to it! Listing 5-21 is, of course, a very basic example. You can create .NET stored procedures of any complexity and behavior in this fashion. In the next section, we'll take a look at how you can deploy what you've just written to the Oracle database.

## Deploying a .NET CLR Stored Procedure

To deploy a .NET CLR stored procedure, right click your project in the Solution window of the Visual Studio IDE. Choose the Deploy menu option to launch the deployment wizard for your CLR stored procedure. Figure 5-10 illustrates.

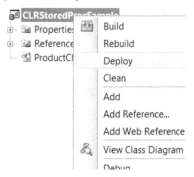

**Figure 5-10.** *Launching the .NET CLR stored procedure deployment wizard*

The first step of the deployment wizard allows you to configure an Oracle database connection to use for the deployment. Fill in your database connection settings. After that is done, proceed to the next step. The next window (shown in Figure 5-11) allows you to choose a deployment option. Since you will need to copy and load the DLL to the database, select the first option.

---

■ **Note** Take note that you are required to log on with SYSDBA privileges to use the .NET CLR stored procedure deployment wizard in Visual Studio.

---

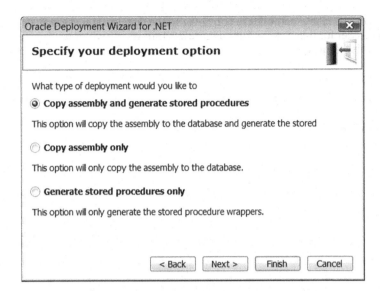

*Figure 5-11. Choosing the deployment option*

The next window (shown in Figure 5-12) allows you to specify the name of the assembly and library. You can use the defaults provided in this window.

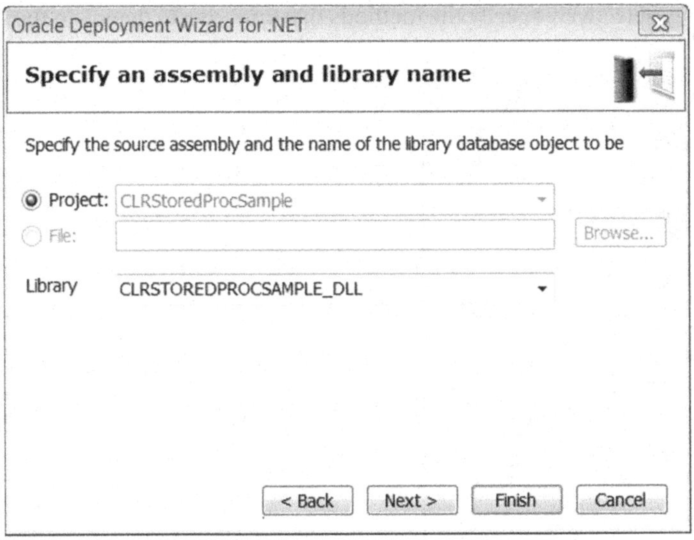

*Figure 5-12. Specifying an assembly and library name*

The subsequent step allows you to choose the assemblies to copy over to the Oracle database and also to specify an alternate destination folder for these assemblies. Figure 5-13 shows the window involved. Use the defaults provided in this window.

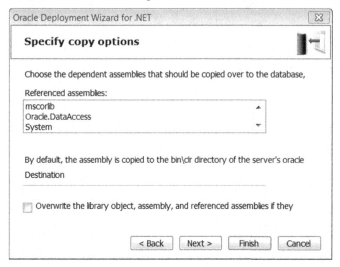

*Figure 5-13. Specifying copy options*

As a last step, the wizard allows you to selectively specify the methods that you wish to deploy to the database. See Figure 5-14 for an example.

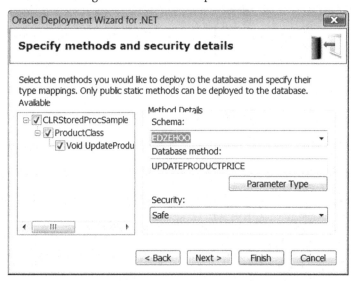

*Figure 5-14. Specifying method and security details*

Select your CLR stored procedure method, and change its schema to the desired schema. Click the Next or Finish button to proceed. Your stored procedure will be generated and deployed in the Oracle database, and you will see a message similar to that in Figure 5-15 in the output window of your Visual Studio IDE.

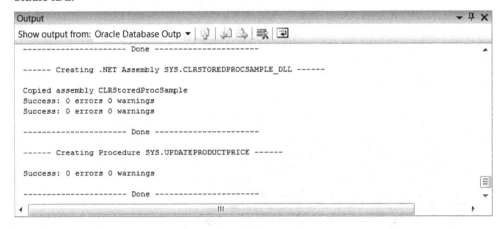

*Figure 5-15. .NET CLR stored procedure successfully created*

---

■ **Tip** You need to make sure that the ORACLECLRDIR environment variable has been configured appropriately before attempting to deploy your CLR stored procedure. This variable points to the output CLR directory that will house your CLR stored procedure assemblies. It typically takes on the value of $ORACLE_HOME\BIN\CLR. You can set this value manually in SQL*Plus by executing the following command under the SYSTEM account: CREATE OR REPLACE DIRECTORY ORACLECLRDIR AS '$ORACLE_HOME\BIN\CLR '. Replace the $ORACLE_HOME keyword with the full Oracle home path on your system.

---

## Executing the .NET CLR Stored Procedure

Executing a .NET CLR stored procedure from .NET code using ODP.NET is no different from executing any other ordinary PL/SQL stored procedure. You can pass **IN** and **OUT** parameters into the .NET CLR stored procedure the same way you did earlier. Create a new form with the layout shown in Figure 5-16.

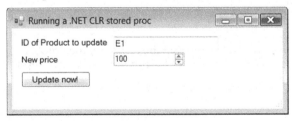

*Figure 5-16. Sample form to test your .NET CLR stored procedure*

In the click event of the "Update now!" button, you need to call the stored procedure you've just created. You can reapply what you learned earlier in this chapter to achieve this. The code to do so is shown in Listing 5-22.

*Listing 5-22. Testing the .NET CLR Stored Procedure*

```
private void btnUpdateNow_Click(object sender, EventArgs e)
{
        string _connstring = "Data Source=localhost/NEWDB;User
            Id=EDZEHOO;Password=PASS123;";
        try
        {
            OracleConnection _connObj = new OracleConnection(_connstring);
            _connObj.Open();
            OracleCommand _cmdObj = _connObj.CreateCommand();
            _cmdObj.CommandText = "EDZEHOO.UpdateProductPrice";
            OracleParameter _PriceParam = new OracleParameter();
            _PriceParam.ParameterName = "ProdPrice";
            _PriceParam.OracleDbType = OracleDbType.Decimal;
            _PriceParam.Direction = ParameterDirection.Input;
            _PriceParam.Value = numNewPrice.Value;
            _cmdObj.Parameters.Add(_PriceParam);

            OracleParameter _IDParam = new OracleParameter();
            _IDParam.ParameterName = "ProdID";
            _IDParam.OracleDbType = OracleDbType.Varchar2;
            _IDParam.Direction = ParameterDirection.Input;
            _IDParam.Value = txtProductName.Text;
            _cmdObj.Parameters.Add(_IDParam);

            _cmdObj.ExecuteNonQuery();
            MessageBox.Show("Updating done!");

            _connObj.Close();
            _connObj.Dispose();
            _connObj = null;
        }
        catch (Exception ex)
        {
            MessageBox.Show(ex.ToString());
        }
}
```

Now you can try to run your code sample. You may need to ensure that the record for the product you intend to update exists in the **Products** table. You will find the price of the product (ID) you've keyed in updated.

# Summary

In this chapter, you've taken a look at how to execute PL/SQL stored procedures, functions, and anonymous PL/SQL blocks from your code via ODP.NET. You've seen how they differ from each other and how input and output parameters can be used to pass in and retrieve data from these PL/SQL blocks.

As far as parameters go, you've also taken a look at how to handle the following PL/SQL complex data types:

- Associative arrays

- **VARRAY**s

- Nested tables

- UDTs

- **REF** cursors and multiple **REF** cursors

You've also closed this chapter by trying your hand at creating and deploying your first .NET CLR stored procedure using the integrated Oracle wizard in Visual Studio. In the next chapter, you'll learn how to make use of ODP.NET's globalization features to make your database and application work with an international audience.

# CHAPTER 6

■■■

# ODP.NET Globalization

I'll start this chapter by relating an incident that happened at a comic book retail company in Singapore a few years back. The headquarters in Singapore initially deployed an online marketing tool that allowed its sales team to launch and coordinate online marketing campaigns. The system ran on an Oracle database of course.

The problem came when the company officiated its Japanese online store. The Singaporeans wanted the Japanese to use the same set of tools and data, so they sent it all to a translator, who translated everything into Japanese. They were planning a hotly anticipated product launch at midnight. What they didn't notice, however, was that all the dates and times in the translated database were still in the Singaporean time zone! Tokyo leads Singapore by 1 hour.

You can guess what happened next. The Japanese online store launched an hour earlier without its Singaporean counterpart. The extra traffic to the Japanese site turned up frequent Denial of Service messages for its visitors. Worse, buyers who bought the comics an hour earlier posted storyline spoilers online, and that ruined the experience for many who were actually waiting for the Singaporean launch.

The bottom line is that data, especially dates and currencies, can sometimes be tightly coupled with locality. Often, conversion needs to be done to make that data available to an international audience. Oracle (and ODP.NET) provides classes that help do this conversion automatically for you.

In this chapter, we explore the following topics:

- Working with double byte data

- Using the `OracleGlobalization` class to handle currencies, dates, timestamps, and strings in different localities

- Using safe type mapping in the `OracleDataAdapter` class

## Storing and Retrieving Double-Byte Data

The first step in making your application work in different localities is to ensure that it supports the local language. You probably work with single-byte languages (such as English) most of the time, so let's give double-byte languages (like Japanese) a try for a change.

---

■ **Tip** To type East Asian characters, you can either enable the Chinese, Korean, or Japanese Input Method Editor (IME) provided by Microsoft, or simply copy and paste East Asian text from the Internet.

---

Technically, the only difference databasewise between using single- and double-byte characters is that you must use the **NCHAR**, **NVARCHAR2**, and **NCLOB** data types to store double-byte data instead of the usual **CHAR**, **VARCHAR2**, and **CLOB** data types that you use for single-byte data.

Let's try out an example. You probably recall from one of the earlier chapters that you've created an **NVARCHAR2** column named **RemarksInJapanese** in the **Products** table. Let's try to store some Japanese text in this field. Create a new form with the layout and controls shown in Figure 6-1. When the user clicks the Update button, the **RemarksInJapanese** field will be updated with the double-byte remarks for the specified product.

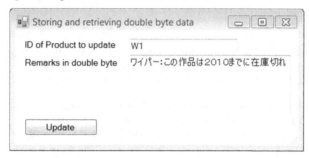

**Figure 6-1.** *Storing japanese text*

In the click event of the Update button, write the code from Listing 6-1. Take note that the **RemarksInJapanese** parameter is defined as an **OracleDbType.NVarchar2** data type.

*Listing 6-1. Writing Double-Byte Data to Oracle*

```
private void btnUpdateNow_Click(object sender, EventArgs e)
{
        string _connstring = "Data Source=localhost/NEWDB;User
                Id=EDZEHOO;Password=PASS123;";
        int _recordsAffected;
        try
        {
                OracleConnection _connObj = new OracleConnection(_connstring);
                _connObj.Open();
                OracleCommand _cmdObj = _connObj.CreateCommand();
                _cmdObj.CommandText = "UPDATE Products SET RemarksInJapanese=:DblByteRemarks
                        WHERE ID=:ProdID";
                _cmdObj.CommandType = CommandType.Text;

                OracleParameter _RemarksParam = new OracleParameter();
                _RemarksParam.ParameterName = "DblByteRemarks";
                _RemarksParam.OracleDbType = OracleDbType.NVarchar2;
                _RemarksParam.Direction = ParameterDirection.Input;
                _RemarksParam.Value = txtRemarks.Text;
                _cmdObj.Parameters.Add(_RemarksParam);
```

```
                    OracleParameter _NameParam = new OracleParameter();
                    _NameParam.ParameterName = "ProdID";
                    _NameParam.OracleDbType = OracleDbType.Varchar2;
                    _NameParam.Direction = ParameterDirection.Input;
                    _NameParam.Value = txtProductID.Text;
                    _cmdObj.Parameters.Add(_NameParam);

                    _recordsAffected = _cmdObj.ExecuteNonQuery();
                    MessageBox.Show("Updating done!");

                    _connObj.Close();
                    _connObj.Dispose();
                    _connObj = null;
            }
            catch (OracleException ex)
            {
                    MessageBox.Show(ex.ToString());
            }
    }
```

Now try running the code. Specify the ID of a product that exists in your **Products** table, and type some Japanese text.

---

■ **Tip**  To type East Asian characters, you need to install an IME. Microsoft provides Chinese, Japanese, and Korean IMEs. You can install them via the Regional Settings tool in the Windows Control Panel. To save time, you could also alternatively grab some East Asian text off the Internet.

---

Click the Update button to save the text to the database. Now that you've done that, you probably want to retrieve that same data to ensure you've typed them correctly. The code to retrieve double-byte data is the same as that to retrieve single-byte data and is shown in Listing 6-2.

*Listing 6-2. Reading Double-Byte Data from Oracle*

```
private void btnGetRemarks_Click(object sender, EventArgs e)
{
        string _connstring = "Data Source=localhost/NEWDB;User
                Id=EDZEHOO;Password=PASS123;";
        string _result;
        try
        {
                OracleConnection _connObj = new OracleConnection();
                _connObj.ConnectionString = _connstring;
                _connObj.Open();

                OracleCommand _cmdObj = _connObj.CreateCommand();
                _cmdObj.CommandText = "SELECT RemarksInJapanese FROM Products";
```

```
OracleDataReader _reader = _cmdObj.ExecuteReader();

_result = "Results:";
if (_reader.HasRows)
{
        while (_reader.Read())
        {
                if (_reader.IsDBNull(_reader.GetOrdinal
                        ("RemarksInJapanese")) == false)
                {
                        String _price = _reader.GetString(_reader.GetOrdinal
                                ("RemarksInJapanese"));
                        _result = _result + "\n" + _price.ToString();
                }
        }
}
MessageBox.Show(_result);
_reader.Dispose();
_cmdObj.Dispose();
_connObj.Dispose();
_reader.Close();
_connObj.Close();
_reader = null;
_connObj = null;
_cmdObj = null;
}
catch (Exception ex)
{
        MessageBox.Show(ex.ToString());
}
}
```

If you run this code sample, you will see the Japanese text retrieved correctly. You should see results similar to those in Figure 6-2.

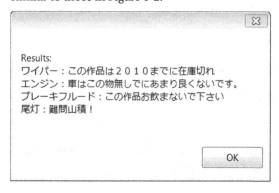

*Figure 6-2.* *Retrieving Japanese text*

# Using the OracleGlobalization class

The ODP.NET **OracleGlobalization** class allows you to develop multilingual applications that can be accessed from anywhere in the world simultaneously using each country's local language, currency, date, time, and string formatting conventions. It provides a set of properties that allow you to control the following locale-specific attributes:

- Language
- Date/timestamp format
- Calendar system
- Currency
- Time zone
- Text-sorting algorithm to use

Table 6-1 illustrates how **OracleGlobalization** attributes can be applied at different levels in your application.

*Table 6-1.* *OracleGlobalization Attributes at Different Scopes*

| Scope | Description |
|-------|-------------|
| Client level | Local computer-level (read only) |
| Session level | At the OracleConnection level (The specified OracleGlobalization attributes are used only within the scope of each connection, or session.) |
| Thread level | At the thread level (The specified OracleGlobalization attributes are used only within the scope of the currently executing thread.) |

Globalization attributes defined at the thread-level overrides those defined at the session level, and that, in turn, overrides those defined at the client level. The globalization attributes at all levels are initialized to the client-level settings by default.

## Setting Attributes at the Client Level

At the client level, **OracleGlobalization** attributes are read only. They depend on your operating system's regional settings. You can retrieve these attributes via the following code:

```
OracleGlobalization info = OracleGlobalization.GetClientInfo();
MessageBox.Show("Language:" + info.Language + "\n" +
             "Currency:" + info.Currency + "\n" +
             "Calendar:" + info.Calendar + "\n" +
             "Date format:" + info.DateFormat + "\n" +
```

```
                    "Territory:" + info.Territory + "\n" +
                    "Timezone:" + info.TimeZone);
```

If you run this code, you will see results similar to those in Figure 6-3.

Language:AMERICAN
Currency:$
Calendar:GREGORIAN
Date format:DD-MON-RR
Territory:AMERICA
Timezone:+08:00

OK

*Figure 6-3.* *Displaying client-level globalization settings*

## Setting Attributes at the Session Level

You can also specify a set of attributes that are used throughout a particular Oracle connection (that is, the session). Once the connection is closed, the attributes are no longer used. You can set globalization attributes on an Oracle connection via the **OracleConnection.SetSessionInfo()** method, as shown in the following code that sets the language attribute for the session to Japanese:

```
OracleConnection _connObj = new OracleConnection();
_connObj.ConnectionString = _connstring;
_connObj.Open();

//Retrieve the globalization attributes from the local computer, and change the language to
//Japanese
OracleGlobalization info = OracleGlobalization.GetClientInfo();
info.Language = "JAPANESE";

//Save the new globalization settings to the connection object
_connObj.SetSessionInfo(info);

//Do something
  .
  .
  .
_connObj.Close();
```

> ■ **Tip** Setting attributes at the session level is the most common method used to define globalization settings. In web-based applications, for instance, each connecting user would likely use a different database connection. You can thus set the appropriate globalization settings for each database connection depending on the connecting user's country of origin.

## Setting Attributes at the Thread Level

You can also set globalization attributes at the currently executing thread level. The globalization settings go out of scope when the thread goes out of scope. You can set the globalization settings for the currently executing thread using the **OracleGlobalization.SetThreadInfo()** method shown here:

```
OracleGlobalization info = OracleGlobalization.GetClientInfo();
info.Language = "JAPANESE";
OracleGlobalization.SetThreadInfo(info);
```

# Changing the Session Language

You can easily change the language used throughout an Oracle session by setting the desired language in the **OracleGlobalization.Language** property. This language change is automatically applied to month names, error messages, notifications, and so on.

Now, let's try to get the Invalid Identifier error message in Oracle printed in Italian. Set the **OracleGlobalization.Language** property to **ITALIAN** (see the highlighted code in Listing 6-3). To get the error message to show up, try to reference a nonexistent field in your SQL **SELECT** statement.

*Listing 6-3. Changing the Language for the Session*

```
private void btnGetPrice_Click(object sender, EventArgs e)
{
        String _connstring = "Data Source=localhost/NEWDB;User
             Id=EDZEHOO;Password=PASS123;";
        try
        {
                OracleConnection _connObj = new OracleConnection();
                _connObj.ConnectionString = _connstring;
                _connObj.Open();

                OracleGlobalization info = OracleGlobalization.GetClientInfo();
                info.Language = "ITALIAN";
                _connObj.SetSessionInfo(info);

                OracleCommand _cmdObj = _connObj.CreateCommand();
                _cmdObj.CommandText = "SELECT NonExistentField FROM Products";
                OracleDataReader _reader = _cmdObj.ExecuteReader();
                _reader.Dispose();
```

```
                    _cmdObj.Dispose();
                    _connObj.Dispose();
                    _reader.Close();
                    _connObj.Close();
                    _reader = null;
                    _connObj = null;
                    _cmdObj = null;
            }
            catch (Exception ex)
            {
                    MessageBox.Show(ex.Message.ToString());
            }
    }
```

If you try to run the code in the listing, you will see the expected error message pop up. The message will be displayed in Italian. It should appear as in Figure 6-4.

**Figure 6-4.** *The Invalid Identifier error in Italian*

# Formatting Calendar Dates

Using the **OracleGlobalization** class, you can define the custom format and language to use when displaying dates and times. This is an important step to globalizing your application because different countries have different ways of representing dates. For instance, consider the differences in date formatting shown in Table 6-2.

**Table 6-2.** *Date Formats in Different Countries*

| Country | Date Format |
| --- | --- |
| United States | MON-DD-YYYY |
| Southeast Asia | DD-MON-YYYY |
| Japan | YYYY-MON-DD |

There are two aspects to think about when working with dates. Most commonly, we encounter variations in formats and languages. Table 6-2 illustrates the variation in formats very well. A less commonly encountered aspect is that of calendar systems. We'll look at both aspects next. We begin with formats and languages.

## Displaying Various Date Formats and Languages

You can set the language to use when displaying month names using the
OracleGlobalization.DateLanguage property and the date format using the
OracleGlobalization.DateFormat property. In Listing 6-4, we will attempt to display the list of dates from the **Products** table in Finnish.

*Listing 6-4. Changing Date Format and Language*

```
private void btnGetDates_Click(object sender, EventArgs e)
{
        string _connstring = "Data Source=localhost/NEWDB;User
        Id=EDZEHOO;Password=PASS123;";
        string _result;
        try
        {
                OracleConnection _connObj = new OracleConnection();
                _connObj.ConnectionString = _connstring;
                _connObj.Open();

                OracleGlobalization info = OracleGlobalization.GetClientInfo();
                info.DateLanguage = "FINNISH";
                info.DateFormat = "DD-MON-YYYY";
                OracleGlobalization.SetThreadInfo(info);

                OracleCommand _cmdObj = _connObj.CreateCommand();
                _cmdObj.CommandText = "SELECT ExpiryDate FROM Products ORDER BY ExpiryDate
                        ASC";
                OracleDataReader _reader = _cmdObj.ExecuteReader();
                _result = "Results:";
                if (_reader.HasRows)
                {
                    while (_reader.Read())
                    {
                        OracleDate _odate =
                                _reader.GetOracleDate(_reader.GetOrdinal("ExpiryDate"));
                        _result = _result + "\n" + _odate.ToString();
                    }
                }
                MessageBox.Show(_result);
                _reader.Dispose();
                _cmdObj.Dispose();
                _connObj.Dispose();
                _reader.Close();
                _connObj.Close();
```

```
                    _reader = null;
                    _connObj = null;
                    _cmdObj = null;
            }
        catch (Exception ex)
        {
                MessageBox.Show(ex.ToString());
        }
    }
}
```

If you run the preceding code, you will see the months January to April displayed in the Finnish language.

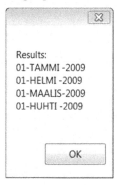

*Figure 6-5.* *"January" to "April" in Finnish*

Let's try a double-byte East Asian language next. Replace the language with **JAPANESE** and change the date formats (in Japan, the year comes first followed by the month and then the day). Here is the code to use:

```
OracleGlobalization info = OracleGlobalization.GetClientInfo();
info.DateLanguage = "JAPANESE";
info.DateFormat = "YYYY-MON-DD";
OracleGlobalization.SetThreadInfo(info);
```

Assuming you have support for East Asian languages on your operating system, you will see the pop-up message box shown in Figure 6-6.

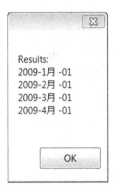

*Figure 6-6. "January" to "April" in Japanese*

# Designating Calendar Systems

The Gregorian calendar is the default calendar that we all know and use every day in our lives, but there are other calendars too. For example, the Persian calendar has 31 days for each of the first 6 months, 30 days for the next 5 months, and 29 or 30 days for the remaining month. Then there is the Buddhist calendar, used mostly in Southeast Asia (in Cambodia, Laos, Thailand, and Myanmar), which alternates between 29 and 30 days every month.

You can explicitly specify the calendar format to use when returning dates using the **OracleGlobalization.Calendar** property. The following code sample sets the calendar to Persian. To try this code sample, substitute the globalization section in the previous **btnGetDates_Click** function with the following code:

```
OracleGlobalization info = OracleGlobalization.GetClientInfo();
info.Calendar = "PERSIAN";
info.DateFormat = "DD/MON/YYYY";
OracleGlobalization.SetThreadInfo(info);
```

Figure 6-7 shows the dates that you'll see returned if you run the sample. Take note that the Gregorian year 2009 translates to the Persian years 1387 and 1388—the boundary between 1387 and 1388 falls sometime during 2009.

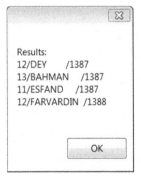

*Figure 6-7. 2009 according to the Persian calendar*

# Representing Currencies

Oracle provides three ways to represent the currency of any country. They are summarized in Table 6-3.

*Table 6-3.* *The Different Currency Formats and Identifiers*

| Country | Currency | ISO Currency | Secondary currency |
|---|---|---|---|
| (Oracle format element) | (L) | (C) | (U) |
| Sweden | Krona (Kr) | SEK | Euro |
| America | Dollar ($) | USD | -- |
| France | Euro (€) | EUR | Euro |

You can define custom symbols for each currency format and have Oracle use either one for display via the formatting elements specified in the **TO_CHAR** SQL function. For instance, Listing 6-5 establishes the yen character as the standard currency symbol for the session.

*Listing 6-5. Using a Custom Currency Symbol*

```
private void btnGetPrice_Click(object sender, EventArgs e)
{
        string _connstring = "Data Source=localhost/NEWDB;User
                Id=EDZEHOO;Password=PASS123;";
        string _result;
        try
        {
                OracleConnection _connObj = new OracleConnection();
                _connObj.ConnectionString = _connstring;
                _connObj.Open();

                OracleGlobalization info = OracleGlobalization.GetClientInfo();
                info.Currency = "¥";
                _connObj.SetSessionInfo(info);

                OracleCommand _cmdObj = _connObj.CreateCommand();
                _cmdObj.CommandText = "SELECT TO_CHAR(Price,'L99G999D99') Price FROM
                        Products WHERE Price IS NOT NULL";
                OracleDataReader _reader = _cmdObj.ExecuteReader();
                _result = "Results:";
                if (_reader.HasRows)
                {
                        while (_reader.Read())
```

```
            {
                    String _price = _reader.GetString
                            (_reader.GetOrdinal("Price"));
                    _result = _result + "\n" + _price;
            }
        }
        MessageBox.Show(_result);
        _reader.Dispose();
        _cmdObj.Dispose();
        _connObj.Dispose();
        _reader.Close();
        _connObj.Close();
        _reader = null;
        _connObj = null;
        _cmdObj = null;
    }
    catch (Exception ex)
    {
            MessageBox.Show(ex.ToString());
    }
}
```

If you run the code in Listing 6-5, you will see that all retrieved currencies will be formatted with the yen symbol (as shown in Figure 6-8).

*Figure 6-8. Defining a custom currency symbol*

Now, the use of a symbol such as the yen symbol that you see in Figure 6-8 might present a problem—some countries share currency symbols. For example, both Australia and Canada share the use of the dollar ($) symbol. Displaying currency amounts prefaced by just the $ symbol might be dangerous, because an end user would not be able to tell the difference between 50 Australian dollars and 50 Canadian dollars.

ISO currency abbreviations help alleviate the problem just described by assigning three-letter symbols that uniquely identify the currency of each nation. For example, US, Australian, and Singaporean currency would be USD, AUD, and SGD respectively. You can set a session to use a specific ISO currency abbreviation using the **OracleGlobalization.ISOCurrency** property. Let's try this out in Listing 6-6.

*Listing 6-6. Using ISO Currencies*

```
private void btnGetPrice_Click(object sender, EventArgs e)
{
        string _connstring = "Data Source=localhost/NEWDB;User
                Id=EDZEHOO;Password=PASS123;";
        string _result;
        try
        {
                OracleConnection _connObj = new OracleConnection();
                _connObj.ConnectionString = _connstring;
                _connObj.Open();

                OracleGlobalization info = OracleGlobalization.GetClientInfo();
                info.ISOCurrency = "AUSTRALIA";
                _connObj.SetSessionInfo(info);

                OracleCommand _cmdObj = _connObj.CreateCommand();
                _cmdObj.CommandText = "SELECT TO_CHAR(Price,'C99G999D99') Price FROM
                        Products";
                OracleDataReader _reader = _cmdObj.ExecuteReader();
                _result = "Results:";
                if (_reader.HasRows)
                {
                        while (_reader.Read())
                        {
                                String _price = _reader.GetString
                                        (_reader.GetOrdinal("Price"));
                                _result = _result + "\n" + _price.ToString();
                        }
                }
                MessageBox.Show(_result);
                _reader.Dispose();
                _cmdObj.Dispose();
                _connObj.Dispose();
                _reader.Close();
                _connObj.Close();
                _reader = null;
                _connObj = null;
                _cmdObj = null;
        }
        catch (Exception ex)
        {
                MessageBox.Show(ex.ToString());
        }
}
```

If you run the code sample in Listing 6-6, you should see a message box like the one shown in Figure 6-9. In it, you will see AUD instead of $. Thus, it's clear that the amounts are in Australian dollars; the use of "AUD" removes the ambiguity surrounding the dollar symbol.

*Figure 6-9. Using ISO currencies*

Displaying amounts using ISO currency abbreviations (for example, CAN) is better than using currency symbols (for example, $) for the following reasons:

- Your application does not need to know the currency symbol of a country in advance—just specify the country name, and Oracle will use the correct symbol. That's one less piece of information to track in your application.

- ISO currencies can uniquely represent each country's currency. There are no overlapping symbols such as the dollar symbol.

There is one more thing you need to know about currencies. Some European countries have dual currencies. For example, Sweden uses the krona and the euro. You can specify a secondary currency using the **OracleGlobalization.DualCurrency** field, as shown in the following code:

```
OracleGlobalization info = OracleGlobalization.GetClientInfo();
info.DualCurrency = "EUR";
_connObj.SetSessionInfo(info);
```

To display the secondary currency, you need to use the **U** formatting element like so:

```
_cmdObj.CommandText = "SELECT TO_CHAR(Price,'U99G999D99') Price FROM Products";
```
You can see a comparison between the standard currency (L) and secondary currency (U) for Sweden shown side by side in Figure 6-10.

*Figure 6-10. Swedish dual currency*

# Formatting Numbers

In the United States (and most parts of the world), the decimal point is a period (.), whereas in France, it is a comma (,). Therefore, $1,250 may mean entirely different things to these two countries. Needless to say, it is especially important to present the right information to the end user when dealing with financial data.

To specify your own custom numeric formatting, you can use the `OracleGlobalization.NumericCharacters` property in the following fashion:

```
OracleGlobalization info = OracleGlobalization.GetClientInfo();
info.NumericCharacters = ".,";
_connObj.SetSessionInfo(info);
```

The first character specifies the character used for the decimal point, and the second character specifies the character used for the thousand separator (digit grouping).

# Dealing with Time Zones

You've seen many times how the **DATE** data types in Oracle can be used to store both date and time data. Now, what if you needed a date that was heavily dependent on time zone?

Let's say your company decides to launch a particular product on a certain date at 3 p.m. Pacific Standard time in Los Angeles, Tokyo, and India simultaneously. If you stored the product launch date as a **DATE** field, the result would be disastrous. Unless you wrote extra code to apply the correct time zone conversion to the retrieved date or time, each country would see the product at 3 p.m. local time, which is incorrect, since they are all in different time zones.

The following statements create a new product launch date field that stores time zone data in the **Products** table. It will also set the launch date of all the products on Christmas day in 2010 at 3 p.m. (Eastern Standard time; GMT –05:00). Run these statements in SQL*Plus:

```
ALTER TABLE Products ADD LaunchDate TIMESTAMP WITH TIME ZONE;
UPDATE Products SET LaunchDate=TO_TIMESTAMP_TZ('2010-12-25 15:00:00 -5:00','YYYY/MM/DD
    HH24:MI:SS TZH:TZM');
```

---

■ **Tip** You can also specify the time zone using its representative name, like this: `UPDATE Products SET LaunchDate=TO_TIMESTAMP_TZ('2010-12-25 15:00:00 America/New_York','YYYY/MM/DD HH24:MI:SS TZR');`.

---

Let's take a look at what December 25, 2010, 3 p.m. translates to in Hong Kong. Once you've set the `OracleGlobalization.TimeZone` property to **Asia/Hong_Kong**, Oracle will assume Hong Kong time as the local time throughout the session. You can convert a timestamp into the local time using the **AT LOCAL** SQL predicate in Oracle. Let's write some code to try this out. Create a new form and place a button named **btnGetTimezoneCorrectDate** on the form. In the click event of the button, write the code from Listing 6-7.

*Listing 6-7. Retrieving Timezone-Correct Dates*

```
private void btnGetTimezoneCorrectDate_Click(object sender, EventArgs e)
{
        string _connstring = "Data Source=localhost/NEWDB;User
                Id=EDZEHOO;Password=PASS123;";
        try
        {
                OracleConnection _connObj = new OracleConnection();
                _connObj.ConnectionString = _connstring;
                _connObj.Open();

                OracleGlobalization info = OracleGlobalization.GetClientInfo();
                info.Territory = "Hong Kong";
                info.TimeZone = "Asia/Hong_Kong";
                OracleGlobalization.SetThreadInfo(info);
                _connObj.SetSessionInfo(info);

                OracleCommand _cmdObj = _connObj.CreateCommand();
                _cmdObj.CommandText = "SELECT LaunchDate AT LOCAL LaunchDateLocal FROM
                        Products";
                OracleDataReader _reader = _cmdObj.ExecuteReader();
                if (_reader.HasRows)
                {
                        if (_reader.Read())
                        {
                                OracleTimeStampTZ _launchDate = _reader.GetOracleTimeStampTZ
                                        (_reader.GetOrdinal("LaunchDateLocal"));
                                MessageBox.Show(_launchDate.ToString ());
                        }
                }
                _reader.Dispose();
                _cmdObj.Dispose();
                _connObj.Dispose();
                _reader.Close();
```

```
                        _connObj.Close();
                        _reader = null;
                        _connObj = null;
                        _cmdObj = null;
            }
            catch (Exception ex)
            {
                        MessageBox.Show(ex.ToString());
            }
}
```

If you run this code sample, you will see the pop-up window shown in Figure 6-11. From this result, it looks like the product launch date would fall on the morning of December 26, 2010, at 4 a.m. in Hong Kong (GMT +08:00).

26-DEC-10 04.00.00.000000 AM ASIA/HONG_KONG

OK

*Figure 6-11. Displaying Hong Kong time*

# Sorting and Comparing Strings

When you have data in different languages, you will obviously have strings that sort and compare differently. For example, consider the Spanish language: "CH" is actually considered a distinct character and it comes after "C" in the alphabet. This means that words like "chiquito," "chispa," and "chiflar" actually come after words like "cilantro" or "coriandro." Another example is the Norwegian language, where "Æ," "Ø," and "Å" are all part of its alphabet set, and all of them come after "Z." East Asian languages are yet another example; sorting order in these scripts would be based on the number of strokes in each character.

Let's take a look at the Spanish example. You will write a program to see the difference between a Spanish sort and an English sort when applied to two words—"cilantro" and "chiquito." First, you'll need to create these words in your **Products** table. Run the following statements in SQL*Plus:

```
INSERT INTO Products (ID, NAME) VALUES ('S1', 'Cilantro');
INSERT INTO Products (ID, NAME) VALUES ('S2', 'Chiquito');
```

Next, put the code from Listing 6-8 behind a button in your test application. The code retrieves the list of products in default (English) sorted order.

*Listing 6-8. Default English Sorting*

```
private void btnGetProductsEnglishOrdering_Click(object sender, EventArgs e)
{
        String _connstring = "Data Source=localhost/NEWDB;User
              Id=EDZEHOO;Password=PASS123;";
        string _result;
        try
        {
                OracleConnection _connObj = new OracleConnection();
                _connObj.ConnectionString = _connstring;
                _connObj.Open();

                OracleCommand _cmdObj = _connObj.CreateCommand();
                _cmdObj.CommandText = "SELECT Name FROM Products ORDER BY Name ASC";
                OracleDataReader _reader = _cmdObj.ExecuteReader();
                _result = "Results:";
                if (_reader.HasRows)
                {
                        while (_reader.Read())
                        {
                                String _Name = _reader.GetString
                                      (_reader.GetOrdinal("Name"));
                                _result = _result + "\n" + _Name.ToString();
                        }
                }
                MessageBox.Show(_result);
                _reader.Dispose();
                _cmdObj.Dispose();
                _connObj.Dispose();
                _reader.Close();
                _connObj.Close();
                _reader = null;
                _connObj = null;
                _cmdObj = null;
        }
        catch (Exception ex)
        {
                MessageBox.Show(ex.ToString());
        }
}
```

If you run the code from Listing 6-8, you will get the ordered list in Figure 6-12. Take note that Cilantro correctly comes after Chiquito in the results if you use an English sort.

*Figure 6-12. A list sorted via default English sorting*

Now, let's enable Spanish sorting. Execute the following code before you run `ExecuteReader()`:

```
OracleGlobalization info = OracleGlobalization.GetClientInfo();
info.Sort ="SPANISH_M";
_connObj.SetSessionInfo(info);
```

If you run the same code now, you'll notice that Chiquito comes after Cilantro, as is the case in the Spanish language and in the results shown in Figure 6-13.

*Figure 6-13. The same list resorted using Spanish language sorting*

In ODP.NET, there are essentially two different types of sorting:

- *Binary sorting* is based on the numeric representation of each character (as defined by the character's encoding scheme). This type of sorting is the fastest but produces results that are of little value when used on foreign languages (especially East Asian languages).

- *Linguistic sorting*, like the Spanish example in Figure 6-13, works by assigning a numeric value to each character to reflect its proper linguistic order. The algorithms used by Oracle differ between each language. In Chinese, for instance, this numeric value constitutes the number of strokes in each character, which defines its linguistic order.

You can apply binary sorting if you wish (although that would not be advisable if you are dealing with a foreign language) by setting the `OracleGlobalization.Sort` field to `BINARY`:

```
OracleGlobalization info = OracleGlobalization.GetClientInfo();
info.Sort ="BINARY";
_connObj.SetSessionInfo(info);
```

# Applying Country-Based Formatting

One convenient way to have Oracle automatically use the correct date, currency, time, and string settings for each country is to set `OracleGlobalization.Territory` and `OracleGlobalization.Language` to the desired country and language respectively.

Setting the `OracleGlobalization.Territory` property automatically defines the following settings internally:

- Date format

- Decimal character or group separator

- Local, ISO, and dual currency symbol

- First day of week

- Credit and debit symbols

- List separators

At minimum, you need to set both territory *and* language properties; setting the `OracleGlobalization.Territory` alone is not enough due to the existence of multilingual countries. For instance, although defining India as the territory allows Oracle to correctly default to the rupee as its currency, it has no clue of the language you intend to use—India has 11 different languages and dialects in total, including Malayalam, Marathi, Punjabi, Tamil, Telugu, and Hindi.

Setting the territory and language is, in fact, the best way for your application to handle locale-specific formatting. You can let Oracle determine the correct sorting algorithm, and currency, date, and time formats to use. Let's take a look at how these two settings can influence the formatting of various data types. Create a new form and place a button named **btnGetCulturedData** on the form. In the click event of the button, write the code shown in Listing 6-9.

*Listing 6-9. Specifying the Territory and Language*

```
private void btnGetCulturedData_Click(object sender, EventArgs e)
{
        string _connstring = "Data Source=localhost/NEWDB;User
            Id=EDZEHOO;Password=PASS123;";
        string _result;
```

```
try
{
        OracleConnection _connObj = new OracleConnection();
        _connObj.ConnectionString = _connstring;
        _connObj.Open();

        OracleGlobalization info = OracleGlobalization.GetClientInfo();
        info.Territory = "Sweden";
        info.Language = "Swedish";
        OracleGlobalization.SetThreadInfo(info);
        _connObj.SetSessionInfo(info);

        OracleCommand _cmdObj = _connObj.CreateCommand();
        _cmdObj.CommandText = "SELECT TO_CHAR(Price,'L99G999D99') PriceDefCurrency,
                TO_CHAR(Price,'U99G999D99') PriceDualCurrency, TO_CHAR(ExpiryDate,
                'DL') ExpiryDate FROM Products WHERE ID='B1'";
        OracleDataReader _reader = _cmdObj.ExecuteReader();
        if (_reader.HasRows)
        {
                if (_reader.Read())
                {
                        String _priceDefCurrency = _reader.GetString
                                (_reader.GetOrdinal("PriceDefCurrency"));
                        String _priceDualCurrency = _reader.GetString
                                (_reader.GetOrdinal("PriceDualCurrency"));
                        String _expiryDate = _reader.GetString
                                (_reader.GetOrdinal("ExpiryDate"));
                        _result = _priceDefCurrency + "\n" +
                                _priceDualCurrency + "\n" +
                                _expiryDate;
                        MessageBox.Show(_result);
                }
        }
        _reader.Dispose();
        _cmdObj.Dispose();
        _connObj.Dispose();
        _reader.Close();
        _connObj.Close();
        _reader = null;
        _connObj = null;
        _cmdObj = null;
}
catch (Exception ex)
{
        MessageBox.Show(ex.ToString());
}
}
```

If you run this code sample, you can see the message box shown Figure 6-14. That message box shows all the appropriately formatted data for Sweden.

*Figure 6-14. Territory-specific data*

# Safely Mapping to .NET Data Types

When populating data from Oracle into an ADO.NET **Dataset** object, the **OracleDataAdapter** class attempts to map Oracle native data types to .NET data types. This conversion can sometimes be lossy because not all the data types are supported natively in the **Dataset** class. Globalization actually makes this issue a bigger one than it otherwise might be. For example, time zone information gets lost when you try to load an Oracle timestamp containing a time zone into a **Dataset**. This can lead to the display of incorrect dates or time in your application!

In another example, the **NUMBER** data type in Oracle holds up to 38 digits of precision, while the .NET equivalent, the **Decimal** data type, can only hold up to 28 digits. The full list of fields that suffer from this or a similar predicament follows:

NUMBER

DATE

TIMESTAMP

TIMESTAMP WITH LOCAL TIME ZONE

TIMESTAMP WITH TIME ZONE

INTERVAL DAY TO SECOND

Because of the precision and related problems, Oracle decided that the best way to store these types of data in a **Dataset** object without losing any detail would be either as a byte array or a string. The only downside is that you have to manually define this mapping. Oracle provides the **OracleDataAdapter.SafeMapping** property that allows you to define whether to map one of the data types listed previously to a byte array or to a string in this fashion:

```
_myAdapter.SafeMapping.Add("LaunchDate", typeof(string));
_myAdapter.SafeMapping.Add("ExpiryDate", typeof(byte[]));
```

Let's write some code to see how safe type mapping works. You can use the **LaunchDate** field you created earlier (which is a **TIMESTAMP WITH TIME ZONE** data type). The idea is simple: If you don't define any safe type mapping, you will lose time zone detail in your **Dataset**. If safe mapping was defined, you would be able to retrieve time zone data. Create a new form; place a button named **btnSafeTypeMapping** on the form, and write the code from Listing 6-10 in the click event of the button.

*Listing 6-10. Retrieving Timestamp (with Time Zone Data) With and Without Safe Type Mapping*

```
private void btnSafeTypeMapping_Click(object sender, EventArgs e)
{
        string _connstring = "Data Source=localhost/NEWDB;User
            Id=EDZEHOO;Password=PASS123;";
        try
        {
                OracleConnection _connObj = new OracleConnection();
                _connObj.ConnectionString = _connstring;
                _connObj.Open();

                OracleCommand _cmdObj = _connObj.CreateCommand();
                DataSet _datasetObj = new DataSet();
                _cmdObj.CommandText = "SELECT LaunchDate FROM Products WHERE LaunchDate IS
                    NOT NULL";

                //Without safe mapping
                OracleDataAdapter _adapterObj = new OracleDataAdapter(_cmdObj);
                _adapterObj.Fill(_datasetObj);

                //Display the data type name and the data
                MessageBox.Show("Type:" + _datasetObj.Tables[0].Rows[0]
                    ["LaunchDate"].GetType().ToString () + "\nData:" + Convert.ToString
                    (_datasetObj.Tables[0].Rows[0]["LaunchDate"]));

                //With safe mapping
                _datasetObj = new DataSet();
                _adapterObj.SafeMapping.Add("LAUNCHDATE", typeof(string));
                _adapterObj.Fill(_datasetObj);

                //Display the data type name and the data again
                MessageBox.Show("Type:" + _datasetObj.Tables[0].Rows[0]
                    ["LaunchDate"].GetType().ToString () + "\nData:" + Convert.ToString
                    (_datasetObj.Tables[0].Rows[0]["LaunchDate"]));

                _adapterObj.Dispose();
                _cmdObj.Dispose();
                _connObj.Dispose();
                _connObj.Close();
                _adapterObj = null;
                _connObj = null;
                _cmdObj = null;
        }
        catch (Exception ex)
        {
                MessageBox.Show(ex.ToString());
        }
}
```

> ■ **Note** The name of the field passed in to `OracleDataAdapter.SafeMapping` is case sensitive. The mapping will not be applied if you use the wrong case format.

When you run the code in Listing 6-10, you will first see the message in Figure 6-15, indicating that `OracleDataAdapter` has decided to use the `System.Date` data type to store your timestamp. Take note that the time zone detail is missing.

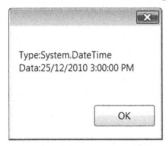

*Figure 6-15. Retrieving a timestamp (with timezone) value without safe type mapping*

You will then see the message box in Figure 6-16 (which is displayed after you have applied safe mapping). Take note that this time, the specified `System.String` data type was used to store your timestamp. As a result, it was able to capture the time zone information.

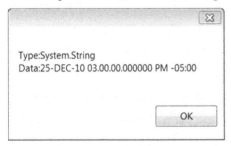

*Figure 6-16. Retrieving a timestamp (with timezone) value with safe type mapping*

# Summary

In this chapter, you've taken an overall look at how you can create applications that are locale sensitive. You have seen how you can use the features in ODP.NET's `OracleGlobalization` class to

- Store and retrieve double-byte data.
- Change the language for a particular session.
- Handle custom calendar dates, currencies, strings, and timestamps.

You've also taken a look at how you can use the **SafeMapping** property of **OracleDataAdapter** to define safe type mappings for Oracle data types that don't have a .NET equivalent.

In the next chapter, we'll move on to the topic of Oracle transactions and how you can run multiple database commands together as a single unit of transaction.

# CHAPTER 7

■ ■ ■

# Transactions with ODP.NET

When programming systems with data distributed in different locations, your application must take on the responsibility of managing data integrity. In complex systems, such as those of a financial institution, applications have to frequently update data that resides in different databases. If something goes wrong somewhere in the chain, chaos can ensue if nothing is done to ensure that data integrity is maintained.

For example, if you were updating the address of a customer in three different databases, the operation can only be considered complete if all three databases were updated. If any one of these three updates failed, the updates that were successfully done on the other two databases must also be undone. If this were not done, a scenario would arise where you have the correct address in two databases but an incorrect one in the remaining database. In financial systems, and when you are dealing with monetary amounts instead of addresses, this requirement is not only important but a necessity to the correct functioning of the system.

When you pool multiple commands into single unit of execution, this unit is called a transaction. Oracle provides transactional support through the `OracleTransaction` class, which we will cover in detail via the following topics:

- An introduction to transactions and the `OracleTransaction` class

- Using save points in a transaction and how to use a partial rollback

- Running distributed transactions

- An introduction to promotable transactions and how this setting can be configured via the ODP.NET connection string

## Understanding Transactions and the OracleTransaction Class

A transaction is simply a block of code that needs to be executed as one single unit; if any part of it fails, the entire block of code will be considered to have failed. It follows the "all or nothing" principle—either all operations in the transaction succeed or all of them fail. In such cases, transaction managers usually provide rollback functionality to undo parts of the transaction that were successful up to the point where it failed.

Applying this concept to the database, let's consider the example of a master-detail table relationship. If you've worked in any business, you will be familiar with invoices. An invoice is a legally binding document issued by a seller to a buyer indicating the products or items delivered to a buyer and the amount that the buyer must now pay the seller. The screenshot in Figure 7-1 shows a sample invoice.

| The Ariel Sportsware Company | Invoice INV001 Created 15 July 2005 Page 1 of 1 |
|---|---|

Address : 31 Kaki Bukit Road 3, Techlink #06-20, Singapore

## INVOICE

Attn : ABC Retail Co.

Date : 15 July 2005

Remarks : Sample Invoice

| Item Description | Unit Price (RM) | Qty | Total (RM) |
|---|---|---|---|
| Size A White shoes | 52.00 | 100 | 5200.00 |
| Size B White shoes | 30.00 | 10 | 300.00 |
| XXL Size T-Shirt | 15.00 | 10 | 150.00 |
| **TOTAL** | | | **5650.00** |

**Figure 7-1.** *A sample invoice*

When you attempt to create an invoice record in the database, it is obvious that if any part of the invoice (such as one of the invoice detail rows) was not created successfully in the database, the half-complete invoice should be discarded from the database, and a new attempt should be made.

Your code can create an invoice via a transaction. The inserting of data records into the invoice master table and the invoice details child table can be done under the same transaction. This means that if any one of the **INSERT** statements fail, whatever changes that were made to the database up to that point will be rolled back.

The **OracleTransaction** class is ODP.NET's transaction class. It will allow you to achieve our example scenario rather easily. For your information, this class is also synonymous with the **System.Transactions.Transaction** class provided by Microsoft for the SQL Server database. Through **OracleTransaction**, you can commit, roll back, or create a save point in a transaction. The standard usage of this class is shown in Listing 7-1.

*Listing 7-1. Standard Usage of the OracleTransaction Class*

```
OracleTransaction.BeginTransaction();
try
{
        //Do something
        .
        .
        .
        //Successful so far, so we can signal a commit
        OracleTransaction.Commit();
```

```
}
else
{
        //An error has occurred, initiate a rollback
        OracleTransaction.Rollback();
}
```

Before you write any code to start trying out transactions, set up the following tables in your database via SQL*Plus. The **Invoice** table will be the master table that holds the master invoice record, while the **InvoiceDetails** table is the child table that will hold the details of the invoice (such as the items ordered and their quantities).

```
CREATE TABLE "EDZEHOO"."INVOICE" (
"INVID" VARCHAR2(10) NOT NULL,
"INVDATE" DATE,
"REMARKS" VARCHAR2(4000),
CONSTRAINT "INVOICEPRIMKEY" PRIMARY KEY ("INVID") VALIDATE);

CREATE TABLE "EDZEHOO"."INVOICEDETAILS" (
"INVID" VARCHAR2(10) NOT NULL,
"DESCRIPTION" VARCHAR2(255),
"QUANTITY" NUMBER(10,2),
"UNITPRICE" NUMBER(10,2));
```

# Executing Your First Transaction

You will now write an application that demonstrates a transaction. As shown earlier, you can signal the start of a transaction using the **OracleConnection.BeginTransaction** method. You will attempt to write a record to each of the **Invoice** and **InvoiceDetails** tables. If any of these two SQL statements fail, it will initiate a rollback. Execute the code shown in Listing 7-2.

*Listing 7-2. Executing Your First Transaction*

```
private void btnInsert_Click(object sender, EventArgs e)
{
        string _connstring = "Data Source=localhost/NEWDB;User
            Id=EDZEHOO;Password=PASS123;";
        try
        {
            OracleConnection _connObj = new OracleConnection(_connstring);
            OracleTransaction _tranObj;
            _connObj.Open();
            _tranObj=_connObj.BeginTransaction();
            OracleCommand _cmdObj = _connObj.CreateCommand();
            try
            {
                    //Insert a record into the Invoice table
                    _cmdObj.CommandText = "INSERT INTO Invoice(InvID, InvDate, Remarks)
                        VALUES(:InvID, SYSDATE, :Remarks)";
```

```
            _cmdObj.Parameters.Add(new OracleParameter("InvID", "A01"));
            _cmdObj.Parameters.Add(new OracleParameter("Remarks", "Sample
                invoice"));
            _cmdObj.ExecuteNonQuery();

            //Insert a record into the InvoiceDetails table
            _cmdObj.CommandText = "INSERT INTO InvoiceDetails(InvID,
                Description, Quantity, UnitPrice) VALUES(:InvID,
                :Description, :Quantity, :UnitPrice)";
            _cmdObj.Parameters.Clear();
            _cmdObj.Parameters.Add(new OracleParameter("InvID", "A01"));
            _cmdObj.Parameters.Add(new OracleParameter("Description", "Exhaust
                pipe"));
            _cmdObj.Parameters.Add(new OracleParameter("Quantity", "5"));
            _cmdObj.Parameters.Add(new OracleParameter("UnitPrice", "99.50"));
            _cmdObj.ExecuteNonQuery();
            _tranObj.Commit();
            MessageBox.Show("Records inserted successfully");
        }
        catch (Exception)
        {
            MessageBox.Show("Uh oh, rollback initiated...");
            _tranObj.Rollback();
        }
        finally
        {
            _connObj.Close();
            _connObj.Dispose();
            _connObj = null;
        }
    }
    catch (Exception ex)
    {
        MessageBox.Show(ex.ToString());
    }
}
```

If you run the form, you will notice that it generates a single record in each of the **Invoice** and **InvoiceDetails** tables. Now, let's see what happens if we intentionally cause the second SQL statement (on the **InvoiceDetails** table) to fail. Change the second SQL statement in the code to the following:

```
_cmdObj.CommandText = "INSERT INTO NonExistentTable(InvID,
                    Description, Quantity, UnitPrice) VALUES(:InvID,
                    :Description, :Quantity, :UnitPrice)";
```

Now, clear both the **Invoice** and **InvoiceDetails** tables of any data. Run the code sample again (this time with the changes). You will find at the end that no records were inserted in either table even though only the second statement failed. This is because both statements are part of a transaction. If the second SQL statement fails, it will roll back the changes made by the first.

# Executing Stored Procedures in a Transaction

Transactions can also involve other types of commands, such as stored procedures. You can roll back the changes made via a stored procedure. To test this, create the following stored procedure in your database via SQL*Plus. This stored procedure will insert two records in the **InvoiceDetails** table.

```
CREATE OR REPLACE PROCEDURE proc_InsertSamplePODetails IS
BEGIN
        INSERT INTO InvoiceDetails(InvID, Description, Quantity, UnitPrice)
               VALUES('A02','Seatbelts',100,50.00);
        INSERT INTO InvoiceDetails(InvID, Description, Quantity, UnitPrice)
               VALUES('A02','Gearstick',50,30.00);
END;
```

Now, write the code shown in Listing 7-3. This function will first call the preceding stored procedure and subsequently insert a record into the **Invoice** table.

*Listing 7-3. Including a Stored Procedure in a Transaction*

```
private void btnInsertData_Click(object sender, EventArgs e)
{
        string _connstring = "Data Source=localhost/NEWDB;User
               Id=EDZEHOO;Password=PASS123;";
        try
        {
               OracleConnection _connObj = new OracleConnection(_connstring);
               OracleTransaction _tranObj;
               _connObj.Open();
               _tranObj = _connObj.BeginTransaction();
               OracleCommand _cmdObj = _connObj.CreateCommand();
               try
               {
                       _cmdObj.CommandText = "proc_InsertSamplePODetails";
                       _cmdObj.CommandType = CommandType.StoredProcedure;
                       _cmdObj.Parameters.Clear();
                       _cmdObj.ExecuteNonQuery();

                       _cmdObj.CommandText = "INSERT INTO Invoice(InvID, InvDate,
                               Remarks) VALUES(:InvID, SYSDATE, :Remarks)";
                       _cmdObj.CommandType = CommandType.Text;
                       _cmdObj.Parameters.Clear();
                       _cmdObj.Parameters.Add(new OracleParameter("InvID", "A02"));
                       _cmdObj.Parameters.Add(new OracleParameter("Remarks", "Sample
                               invoice 2"));
                       _cmdObj.ExecuteNonQuery();

                       _tranObj.Commit();
                       MessageBox.Show("Records inserted successfully");
               }
               catch (Exception ex)
```

```
            {
                    MessageBox.Show(ex.ToString());
                    MessageBox.Show("Uh oh, rollback initiated...");
                    _tranObj.Rollback();
            }
            finally
            {
                    _connObj.Close();
                    _connObj.Dispose();
                    _connObj = null;
            }
        }
        catch (Exception ex)
        {
                MessageBox.Show(ex.ToString());
        }
    }
```

Clear both the **Invoice** and **InvoiceDetails** tables, and run the code in Listing 7-3. You will notice that one record is written in the **Invoice** table and two records in the **InvoiceDetails** table. Now, change the second SQL statement to the following:

```
_cmdObj.CommandText = "INSERT INTO NonExistentTable(InvID, InvDate, Remarks) VAL↵
UES(:InvID, SYSDATE, :Remarks)";
```

Clear both the **Invoice** and **InvoiceDetails** tables, and run this code sample again. You will notice that this time, none of the records are written into either table. The error encountered with the second SQL statement initiated a rollback, which rolled back the changes made by the stored procedure.

# Performing Partial Rollbacks

There might also be times when you need a partial rollback instead of a full one. For example, consider the following transaction:

1.  Create invoice master record.
2.  Create invoice detail records.
3.  Create receipt record.

Step 1 might take the longest in terms of processing time. To improve performance, instead of rolling back all three steps completely when something goes wrong, you could have the transaction roll back to the state it was right after step 1. You can create these save points anywhere in a transaction using the **Save** function and designate each one with a name. To roll back to a particular save-point, you simply need to pass the name of the save point to the **Rollback** function. You can try this by writing the code in Listing 7-4.

*Listing 7-4. Performing a Partial Rollback*

```
private void btnSavepoints_Click(object sender, EventArgs e)
{
        string _connstring = "Data Source=localhost/NEWDB;User
               Id=EDZEHOO;Password=PASS123;";
        try
        {
                OracleConnection _connObj = new OracleConnection(_connstring);
                OracleTransaction _tranObj;
                _connObj.Open();
                _tranObj = _connObj.BeginTransaction();
                OracleCommand _cmdObj = _connObj.CreateCommand();
                try
                {
                        _cmdObj.CommandText = "INSERT INTO Invoice(InvID, InvDate, Remarks)
                               VALUES(:InvID, SYSDATE, :Remarks)";
                        _cmdObj.Parameters.Add(new OracleParameter("InvID", "A01"));
                        _cmdObj.Parameters.Add(new OracleParameter("Remarks", "Sample
                               invoice"));
                        _cmdObj.ExecuteNonQuery();
                        _tranObj.Save("MySavepoint1");

                        _cmdObj.CommandText = "INSERT INTO InvoiceDetails(InvID,
                               Description, Quantity, UnitPrice) VALUES(:InvID,
                               :Description, :Quantity, :UnitPrice)";
                        _cmdObj.Parameters.Clear();
                        _cmdObj.Parameters.Add(new OracleParameter("InvID", "A01"));
                        _cmdObj.Parameters.Add(new OracleParameter("Description", "Exhaust
                               pipe"));
                        _cmdObj.Parameters.Add(new OracleParameter("Quantity", "5"));
                        _cmdObj.Parameters.Add(new OracleParameter("UnitPrice", "99.50"));
                        _cmdObj.ExecuteNonQuery();
                        _tranObj.Save("MySavepoint2");

                        _cmdObj.CommandText = "INSERT INTO NonExistentTable(InvID,
                               Description, Quantity, UnitPrice) VALUES(:InvID,
                               :Description, :Quantity, :UnitPrice)";
                        _cmdObj.Parameters.Clear();
                        _cmdObj.Parameters.Add(new OracleParameter("InvID", "B01"));
                        _cmdObj.Parameters.Add(new OracleParameter("Description",
                               "Windshield wipers"));
                        _cmdObj.Parameters.Add(new OracleParameter("Quantity", "20"));
                        _cmdObj.Parameters.Add(new OracleParameter("UnitPrice", "25.50"));
                        _cmdObj.ExecuteNonQuery();
                        _tranObj.Save("MySavepoint3");
                        _tranObj.Commit();
                        MessageBox.Show("Records inserted successfully");
                }
                catch (Exception)
```

```
                {
                        MessageBox.Show("Uh oh, rollback initiated...");
                        _tranObj.Rollback("MySavepoint1");
                        _tranObj.Commit();
                }
                finally
                {
                        _connObj.Close();
                        _connObj.Dispose();
                        _connObj = null;
                }
        }
        catch (Exception ex)
        {
                MessageBox.Show(ex.ToString());
        }
}
```

Before running this code sample, clear both the **Invoice** and **InvoiceDetails** tables. Take note that we intentionally cause the third SQL statement to fail by using a table name that does not exist. The exception will be caught, and a rollback will occur. We pass the name **MySavepoint1** to the **RollBack** method, so it will roll back to the state it was right after the first SQL statement.

Based on the rollback logic in Listing 7-4, you will find that only the invoice record is written to the **Invoice** table. None of the invoice details will be written to the database because the rollback skips these sections, as demonstrated in Figure 7-2.

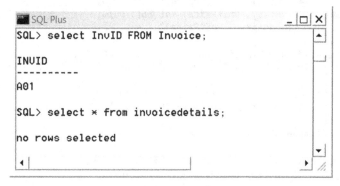

*Figure 7-2.* A partial rollback

# Working with Distributed Transactions

There are times when you might need to update two or more database instances as part of a single transaction. For example, a large organization might keep outgoing invoices in one database instance and the corresponding receipts in another database instance. Thus, whenever the application creates an invoice record in the first database, it must always create a corresponding receipt record in the second database. If creation of the receipt fails, we must roll back the creation of the invoice as well. This process is depicted in Figure 7-3.

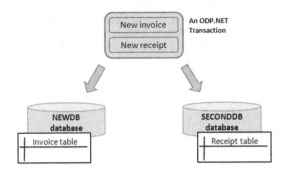

*Figure 7-3. A distributed transaction*

Through the use of transactions, you can preserve data integrity in a system across multiple databases. Given Figure 7-3's scenario, you will always be sure that there is a receipt record for every corresponding invoice record. Now, let's take a look at what you need to do to run and test distributed transactions on Oracle.

# Creating a Second Database Instance

First, you need to create a second database instance to use for the examples to follow. You can create a new database instance by navigating to $ORACLE_HOME → Configuration and Migration Tools → Database Configuration Assistant from the Windows Start menu. A window like the one shown in Figure 7-4 will appear.

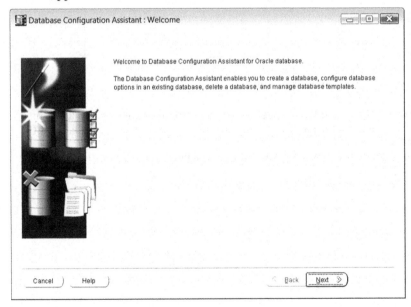

*Figure 7-4. Creating a new database instance*

In the next screen, choose to "Create a new database". You will need to click the Next button through 14 additional pages before Oracle creates the database instance for you. You can use most of the default settings given in this wizard. One of the important screens is at step 3, shown in Figure 7-5, where the wizard allows you to define a name for the second database. For the examples in this book, I choose the name **SECONDDB**.

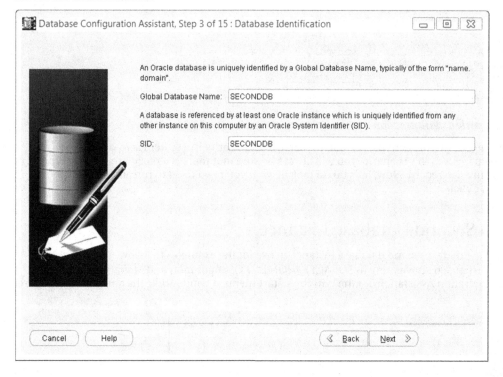

**Figure 7-5.** *Specifying the name of the new database instance*

At step 5, take note that you will be prompted to specify the password for various system accounts. For the sake of brevity, choose to use the same password for all accounts. In my code example, I went with the password **admin** (See Figure 7-6).

After all these steps are completed, the new database instance will be created. You can immediately connect to it via ODP.NET or SQL*Plus.

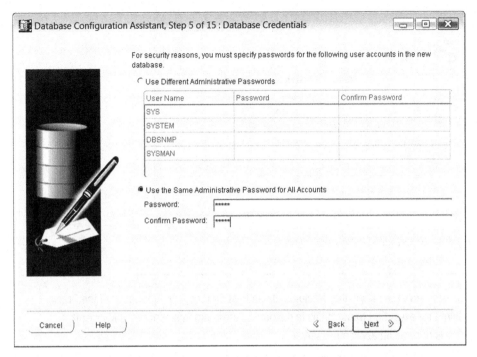

*Figure 7-6. Specifying the system password for the new database instance*

You will now need to create the **Receipt** table in the **SECONDDB** database. Log in to SQL*Plus, and issue the following command:

```
CONNECT SYSTEM@SECONDDB AS SYSDBA
```

Because the **NEWDB** instance was first created when you installed Oracle, it has become the local database for the machine. To connect to the second database, you must explicitly specify the second database with the **CONNECT** SQL*Plus command. After running the preceding command, Oracle will prompt you for a password. Enter the password you've specified earlier in the wizard for the system account.

After you've done that, you need to create the **Receipt** table by running the following code:

```
CREATE TABLE "SYSTEM"."RECEIPT" (
"RECEIPTID" VARCHAR2(10) NOT NULL,
"RECEIPTDATE" DATE,
"TOTALAMOUNT" NUMBER(10,2),
"REMARKS" VARCHAR2(4000),
CONSTRAINT "RECEIPTPRIMKEY" PRIMARY KEY ("RECEIPTID") VALIDATE);
```

Before running the examples in the sections that follow, you should also clear the **Invoice** and **InvoiceDetail** tables of data. As a last step, you will need to ensure that **OracleMTSRecoveryService** has started. You can see the list of services on your machine from the Start → Control Panel → Administrative Tools → Services menu in Windows. You'll see a list similar to the one shown in Figure 7-7.

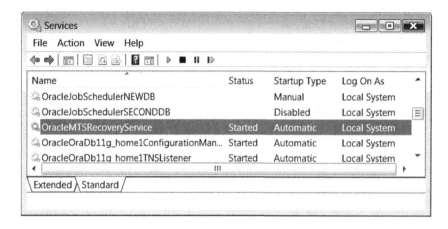

*Figure 7-7. Ensuring that the OracleMTSRecoveryService has started*

---

■ **Note** `OracleMTSRecoveryService` allows the Oracle database to store recovery information in the Oracle database. It is also required for executing transactions in distributed environments, where the Microsoft Transaction Server (MTS) is used as an application server.

---

## Executing Implicit Distributed Transactions

An implicit transaction is one where you don't have to interact with the transaction object itself. The **System.Transactions.TransactionScope** class provided by the .NET Framework allows you to mark a block of code as being part of a transaction. The rest of the work, including the rollback, is all handled automatically by this class—hence the term "implicit."

To use the **TransactionScope** class, you must first add a reference to the **System.Transactions** library. Figure 7-8 shows how to do that.

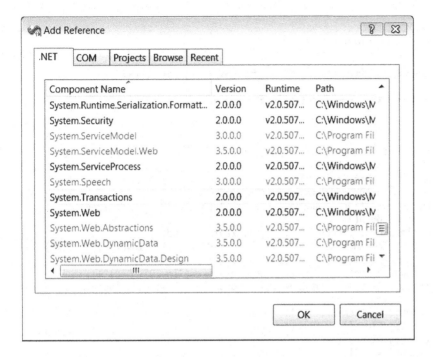

**Figure 7-8.** *Importing the System.Transactions library*

To designate a block of code as part of a transaction, you can place it inside a **using** tag, as shown here:

```
using (TransactionScope _ts = new TransactionScope())
{
        //Your code goes here...
        _ts.Complete();
}
```

That is all there is to it. You need to call the **TransactionScope.Complete()** method to signal a commit. Unlike the previous examples, however, you do not need to specify a rollback. If the **TransactionScope.Complete()** method is called, the transaction is committed, but if it isn't called, the transaction will automatically roll back after the **TransactionScope** object is disposed.

Let's try this out. Using the same invoice and receipt scenario outlined earlier, we will attempt to write a record into the **Invoice** and **Receipt** tables (on different database instances) as part of a transaction. Create a new form, and place a button on the form. In the click event of the button, write the code from Listing 7-5.

*Listing 7-5. Performing an Implicit Distributed Transaction*

```
private void btnCreateInvoiceAndReceipt_Click(object sender, EventArgs e)
{
        using (TransactionScope _ts = new TransactionScope())
        {
                try
                {
                        //Connect to the first database instance and create a new record in
                        //the Invoice table
                        string _connstring = "Data Source=localhost/NEWDB;User
                                Id=EDZEHOO;Password=PASS123;";
                        OracleConnection _connObj = new OracleConnection(_connstring);
                        _connObj.Open();
                        OracleCommand _cmdObj = _connObj.CreateCommand();
                        _cmdObj.CommandText = "INSERT INTO Invoice(InvID, InvDate, Remarks)
                                VALUES(:InvID, SYSDATE, :Remarks)";
                        _cmdObj.Parameters.Add(new OracleParameter("InvID", "B01"));
                        _cmdObj.Parameters.Add(new OracleParameter("Remarks", "Sample
                                invoice"));
                        _cmdObj.ExecuteNonQuery();
                        _connObj.Close();
                        _connObj.Dispose();
                        _connObj = null;

                        //Connect to the second database instance and create a new record in
                        //the Receipt table
                        _connstring = "Data Source=localhost/SECONDDB;User
                                Id=SYSTEM;Password=admin;";
                        _connObj = new OracleConnection(_connstring);
                        _connObj.Open();
                        _cmdObj = _connObj.CreateCommand();
                        _cmdObj.CommandText = "INSERT INTO Receipt(ReceiptID, ReceiptDate,
                                Remarks) VALUES(:ReceiptID, SYSDATE, :Remarks)";
                        _cmdObj.Parameters.Add(new OracleParameter("ReceiptID", "R01"));
                        _cmdObj.Parameters.Add(new OracleParameter("Remarks", "Sample
                                receipt"));
                        _cmdObj.ExecuteNonQuery();
                        _connObj.Close();
                        _connObj.Dispose();
                        _connObj = null;
                        _ts.Complete();
                        MessageBox.Show("Records inserted successfully");
                }
                catch(Exception ex)
                {
                    MessageBox.Show(ex.ToString());
                }
        }
}
```

If you run the code sample in Listing 7-5, you will notice that a record is created in each of the **Invoice** and **Receipt** tables. Now, let's see what happens if we intentionally cause the second SQL statement to fail. Change the **INSERT** statement for the **Receipt** table to the following:

```
INSERT INTO NonExistentTable (ReceiptID, ReceiptDate, Remarks) VALUES↵
(:ReceiptID, SYSDATE, :Remarks)
```

Clear both the **Invoice** and **Receipt** tables, and run the same code sample again. This time, you will find that no data was written to both the **Invoice** and **Receipt** tables (although only the **Receipt** table SQL was incorrect). This demonstrates that these two operations (across multiple database instances) executed as a single transaction.

## Executing Explicit Distributed Transactions

The second type of distributed transaction is explicit. This means that you have to explicitly designate each connection as part of a transaction. The concept is simple: You first create a **System.Transactions.CommittableTransaction** object. You can then designate any **OracleConnection** object as part of this transaction using the **OracleConnection.EnlistTransaction** method. Any commands that execute under this connection will be part of the transaction. Listing 7-6 gives an example of an explicit distributed transaction.

*Listing 7-6. Performing an Explicit Distributed Transaction*

```
private void btn_CreateInvoiceAndReceipt_Click(object sender, EventArgs e)
{
        CommittableTransaction _cmtTran = new CommittableTransaction();
        try
        {
                //Connect to the first database instance and create a new record in
                //the Invoice table
                string _connstring = "Data Source=localhost/NEWDB;User
                        Id=EDZEHOO;Password=PASS123;";
                OracleConnection _connObj = new OracleConnection(_connstring);
                _connObj.Open();
                _connObj.EnlistTransaction(_cmtTran);
                OracleCommand _cmdObj = _connObj.CreateCommand();
                _cmdObj.CommandText = "INSERT INTO Invoice(InvID, InvDate, Remarks)
                        VALUES(:InvID, SYSDATE, :Remarks)";
                _cmdObj.Parameters.Add(new OracleParameter("InvID", "B01"));
                _cmdObj.Parameters.Add(new OracleParameter("Remarks", "Sample invoice"));
                _cmdObj.ExecuteNonQuery();
                _connObj.Close();
                _connObj.Dispose();
                _connObj = null;

                //Connect to the second database instance and create a new record in
                //the Receipt table
                _connstring = "Data Source=localhost/SECONDDB;User
                        Id=SYSTEM;Password=admin;";
```

```
                    _connObj = new OracleConnection(_connstring);
                    _connObj.Open();
                    _connObj.EnlistTransaction(_cmtTran);
                    _cmdObj = _connObj.CreateCommand();
                    _cmdObj.CommandText = "INSERT INTO Receipt(ReceiptID, ReceiptDate, Remarks)
                            VALUES(:ReceiptID, SYSDATE, :Remarks)";
                    _cmdObj.Parameters.Add(new OracleParameter("ReceiptID", "R01"));
                    _cmdObj.Parameters.Add(new OracleParameter("Remarks", "Sample receipt"));
                    _cmdObj.ExecuteNonQuery();
                    _connObj.Close();
                    _connObj.Dispose();
                    _connObj = null;
                    _cmtTran.Commit();
                    MessageBox.Show("Records inserted successfully");
            }
            catch (Exception ex)
            {
                    _cmtTran.Rollback();
                    MessageBox.Show(ex.ToString());
            }
    }
}
```

You will notice that you need to explicitly specify when to **Commit** and **Rollback**. You can test out this code the same way as before. First, clear the **Invoice** and **Receipt** tables. After running the code sample, you will find both tables populated with one record each. Clear these two tables again. If you now intentionally change the second SQL statement (for the **Receipt** table) so that it fails and run the same code sample again, you will find that neither record is created.

---

■ **Tip** Choosing when to use implicit or explicit transactions depends entirely on your code structure. For example, if you wish to use the same transaction across multiple function calls or threads, you will need to use explicit transactions.

---

## Executing Promotable Transactions

Sometimes, it is difficult to know beforehand whether a transaction is going to be local or distributed. In such cases, developers usually assume that a transaction is distributed by default. This assumption consumes more resources than necessary.

Oracle supports the concept of a promotable transaction. When you have support for promotable transactions enabled, all transactions are assumed to be local but are automatically promoted to distributed if more than one database instance is found to be involved in a transaction.

By default, a connection is opened in promotable mode. You can override that default by setting a connection to be only local or distributed in the following fashion:

```
string _connstring = "Data Source=localhost/NEWDB;User Id=EDZEHOO;Password=PASS↵
123; Promotable Transaction=LOCAL";
```

Transactions are promotable by default so that Oracle can operate in minimal resource usage mode when it is a local transaction, yet still cater for distributed transactions when the need arises. However, if you know for certain that your transactions will always be local, you can further optimize performance by specifying the transaction as **LOCAL**, as shown in the preceding code snippet.

---

■ **Note** Oracle does not support transactions, local or distributed, in .NET stored procedures, so you cannot start, commit, or roll back any transaction in a .NET stored procedure. However, the execution of a .NET stored procedure can still be part of a transaction; it will inherit the current transaction of an Oracle connection.

---

## Summary

In this chapter, you've taken an overall look at the following:

- Using the **OracleTransaction** class
- Performing a partial rollback using save points
- Running distributed transactions

In the next chapter, we'll move on to the topic of database change notifications, and you'll see how your code can be automatically notified when your data changes.

# CHAPTER 8

■ ■ ■

# Oracle Database Change Notifications with ODP.NET

Imagine that you're eagerly anticipating a parcel to be delivered to your home. You keep looking out your window to see if the mail man has arrived. Besides being extremely inefficient, you can't concentrate on your work, and you get a sore neck from all that craning. Wouldn't it be nice if the mail man could call you on your phone when the parcel was delivered? Many scenarios in the workplace are similar. You have to keep checking every day to see if your colleague has already created that sales quotation. Your e-mail program has to keep checking the mail server to see if you have any new e-mail.

Similarly, in the database, your application has no idea of knowing if data has changed. Take an electronic terminal displaying a list of flight schedules for example. The only way for you to keep this display updated is to continuously poll the database for changes and to periodically refresh the display. This approach (often referred to as the pull approach) raises some disadvantages, such as a constant performance hit on the server, even when there is no change in data.

The Oracle database offers a push alternative via database change notifications. This exciting technology allows Oracle to alert your application through ODP.NET when any changes are detected on a query set or database object.

In this chapter, you will learn how you can

- Register your application to receive change notifications on a table or on a query result set

- Register multiple change notifications in one go

- Retrieve detailed change notification information

- Apply change notification technology to real-world usage scenarios

- Adopt best practices when using change notification technology

## Understanding Database Change Notification

ODP.NET change notification uses the Continuous Query Notification feature in the Oracle database. The following lists some of the core features of Oracle change notification technology:

- Notifications are supported only on Oracle database versions 10.2 and above.

- Database change notifications happen instantaneously. The moment data is altered, the database raises the notification.

- Notifications provide information about the type of change in the data—whether they are **INSERT**, **UPDATE**, **DELETE**, or **ALTER** statements.

- Notifications are initiated from within the Oracle database. ODP.NET is merely used to register these notifications.

- There are generally two types of change notifications that can be registered:

- Query-based notifications

- Object-based notifications

Query-based change notification is actually a new feature introduced with version 11.1 of the Oracle database. With query-based notifications, you can configure Oracle in such a way that if a particular result set changes in any way, a notification will be raised. With this type of notification, you can choose, for example, to watch a particular record and only be notified when it is updated or deleted.

Object-based notifications work on a wider scale; they are based on changes in a table as a whole. When any change (**INSERT**, **DELETE**, or **UPDATE**) occurs on a table, a notification is raised. In the following sections, we will explore how to register both types of change notifications.

---

■ **Note** Although you can use database change notifications in your .NET code, take note that you cannot use them from within a .NET stored procedure. They can be used in PL/SQL stored procedures, but their setup and invocation is not configured through ODP.NET, and thus falls outside the scope of this book.

---

# Registering for Query-Based Change Notifications

Before you can register for any change notifications, you must grant the **CHANGE NOTIFICATION** privilege to the accessing user account. Remember to log in under the **SYSTEM** account so that you are able to grant this privilege. Here is the **GRANT** statement:

**GRANT CHANGE NOTIFICATION TO EDZEHOO;**

ODP.NET provides the **OracleDependency** class, which lets you register for change notifications with an **OracleCommand** object. The registration process for change notifications consists roughly of the following steps:

1. Create an OracleDependency instance.

2. Bind it to an OracleCommand object.

3. Add an event handler to handle notifications.

4. Register for change notifications, and start the notification listener.

In the first two steps, you need to create an **OracleDependency** instance and bind it to an **OracleCommand** object in the following manner; you can specify an active command object to bind to in the constructor of the **OracleDependency** instance:

```
OracleDependency.Port = 1200;
OracleDependency _dep = new OracleDependency(_cmdObj);
```

The port number specifies a port number for the notification listener to listen to. By default, this port number is set to –1. If you do not define any port number, ODP.NET will randomly pick a port number when you attempt to register a change notification.

---

■ **Tip** You should ensure that the port number used for the `OracleDependency` object is not obstructed by any firewall installed on your system.

---

In the second line of code, an `OracleNotificationRequest` object is internally created and assigned to the `OracleCommand.Notification` property. You can change the details of this notification request by accessing this property directly.

The next thing you need to do is to register an event handler for the change notification. Whenever a notification is raised, your event handler will be called. You can do this with the following code:

```
_dep.OnChange += new OnChangeEventHandler(OnNotificationReceived);

//Change notification handler
public static void OnNotificationReceived(object src, OracleNotificationEventArgs arg)
{
        MessageBox.Show("Notification Received");
}
```

In this notification handler, you can access the details of the change notification via the `OracleNotificationEventArgs` object. We will explore more on this later. The next thing you need to do is to register a query. The query will allow you to define a result set that you wish to register notifications for. For example, the following SQL query will raise a notification only when a change occurs on the ACME record:

```
SELECT * FROM Customers WHERE CustomerID= 'ACME'
```

You can also register notifications on result sets containing multiple records. For example, the following SQL query will raise a notification when changes occur to any customer record that has a name beginning with the letter "A." A separate notification will be received for each record (in this result set) that is altered.

```
SELECT * FROM Customers WHERE CustomerName LIKE 'A%'
```

There are some requirements to register query-based change notifications successfully:

- First, you can register most query types except for the following:

    - *Queries on fixed tables or views*. For example, many of the Oracle internal configuration data are stored using fixed tables.

    - *Queries over materialized views*. These are also known as snapshots in previous Oracle releases. Materialized views are commonly used in replication environments to make local copies of remotely located data.

- You need to have at least version 11.1 of the Oracle database installed.

- Also, the SELECT list must not contain data types other than VARCHAR2 and NUMBER. For this same reason, only use SELECT * FROM XXXX when you know that all the columns returned are either of these two data types.

- The COMPATIBLE initialization parameter of the database is set to at least 11.0.0 (this is set by default).

- Finally, Automatic Undo Management (AUM) must be enabled (this is enabled by default).

If the second and third criteria are not met, the change notification will default to an object-based change notification, which means that it will track all changes on the table instead of just the query set. If the fourth and fifth criteria are not met, you will not even be able to register the change notification.

To register the query, you can run the following code:

```
_cmdObj.CommandText = "SELECT * FROM Customers WHERE CustomerID= 'ACME'";
_cmdObj.ExecuteNonQuery();
```

When you call the ExecuteNonQuery() method, ODP.NET will internally register the change notification on the result set and also set up a notification listener on the specified port number. The notification listener is only set up once (on the first successful registration). Once this is done, you can no longer change the port number.

That's all you need to do. After this, anytime you make any changes to the customer record 'ACME' (whether from a different application or directly in the database), your event handler will be automatically called.

---

▒ **Note** If you drop a registered table from the database and re-create another table with the same name, you will still need to reregister the table to receive database change notifications.

---

Now, let's take a look at the full code you need to write to test this. Create a form, and place two buttons on the form. Make them like those in Figure 8-1.

*Figure 8-1. Your first change notification application*

You will now need to write the code to register the change notification event handler. You can see how to do this in Listing 8-1.

*Listing 8-1. Raising a Query-Based Change Notification*

```
//Declare a global variable to indicate whether the notification has been raised
private static bool _NotificationRaised=false;
private void btnRegisterChangeNotifications(object sender, EventArgs e)
{
        string _connstring = "Data Source=localhost/NEWDB;User
                Id=EDZEHOO;Password=PASS123;";
        try
        {
                //Register the change notification
                OracleConnection _connObj = new OracleConnection(_connstring);
                _connObj.Open();
                OracleCommand _cmdObj = _connObj.CreateCommand();
                _cmdObj.CommandText = "SELECT Price FROM Products WHERE ID='LD1'";
                OracleDependency.Port = 1200;
                OracleDependency _dep = new OracleDependency(_cmdObj);
                _dep.OnChange += new OnChangeEventHandler(OnNotificationReceived);
                _cmdObj.ExecuteNonQuery();

                //Wait in a loop for the notification
                while (_NotificationRaised==false)
                {
                    Application.DoEvents();
                }

                _connObj.Close();
                _connObj.Dispose();
                _connObj = null;
        }
        catch (Exception ex)
        {
                MessageBox.Show(ex.ToString());
        }
}

//The event handler for the change notification
public static void OnNotificationReceived(object src, OracleNotificationEventArgs arg)
{
        DataTable changeDetails = arg.Details;
    _NotificationRaised = true;
    MessageBox.Show("Table has changed: " + changeDetails.Rows[0]["ResourceName"]);
}

private void btnUpdateTable_Click(object sender, EventArgs e)
{
        string _connstring = "Data Source=localhost/NEWDB;User
                Id=EDZEHOO;Password=PASS123;";
        try
        {
                OracleConnection _connObj2 = new OracleConnection(_connstring);
```

```
            _connObj2.Open();
            OracleTransaction _txn = _connObj2.BeginTransaction();

            //Update the particular record that we've registered the change notification
            //for
            string _sql = "UPDATE Products SET Price=550 WHERE ID='LD1'";
            OracleCommand _cmdObj2 = new OracleCommand(_sql, _connObj2);
            _cmdObj2.ExecuteNonQuery();
            _txn.Commit();
            _connObj2.Close();
        }
        catch (Exception ex)
        {
            MessageBox.Show(ex.ToString());
        }
}
```

To try running this code sample, click the first button to register the change notification. You will see a message showing that the change notification was registered. That message should look like the one shown in Figure 8-2.

*Figure 8-2. Change notification successfully registered*

Once that is done, click the second button. Your change notification event handler will be instantly called; you will see a message appear displaying the name of the table that was modified, as in Figure 8-3.

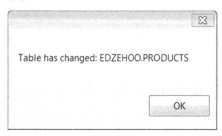

*Figure 8-3. Displaying the name of the changed table*

# Registering for Object-Based Change Notifications

If you tried to change the **UPDATE** SQL query in the previous section's source code into an **INSERT** query, you will have found that the notification is not raised. The reason is simple—a query-based notification only keeps track of changes to the data in the query result set. How do you go about tracking changes in the table as a whole?

Object-based change notification is the default type of change notification request in the Oracle database. With object-based change notifications, you can track any changes made to the data (using **INSERT**, **UPDATE**, or **DELETE**) and schema (using **ALTER**) of a table.

To register object-based change notifications, you need to set the **QueryBasedNotification** property of the **OracleDependency** object to **false**, as shown below:

```
_dep.QueryBasedNotification = false;
```

---

■ **Note** If you are using an Oracle database earlier than version 11.1, you will be automatically defaulted to object-based change notifications. Take note that if your SQL select list contains columns other than columns of type **VARCHAR2** and **NUMBER**, you will also be automatically defaulted to object-based change notifications.

---

The changes you need to make to your code are highlighted in bold in Listing 8-2. This time, try doing an **INSERT** instead of an **UPDATE** in the second button on the form.

*Listing 8-2. Raising an Object-Based Change Notification*

```
private void btnRegisterChangeNotifications(object sender, EventArgs e)
{
        string _connstring = "Data Source=localhost/NEWDB;User
               Id=EDZEHOO;Password=PASS123;";
        try
        {
                //Register the change notification
                OracleConnection _connObj = new OracleConnection(_connstring);
                _connObj.Open();
                OracleCommand _cmdObj = _connObj.CreateCommand();
                _cmdObj.CommandText = "SELECT * FROM Products";
                OracleDependency.Port = 1200;
                OracleDependency _dep = new OracleDependency(_cmdObj);
                _dep.QueryBasedNotification = false;
                _dep.OnChange += new OnChangeEventHandler(OnNotificationReceived);
                _cmdObj.ExecuteNonQuery();

                //Wait in a loop for the notification
                while (_NotificationRaised==false)
                {
                    Application.DoEvents();
                }
```

```
                        _connObj.Close();
                        _connObj.Dispose();
                        _connObj = null;
            }
            catch (Exception ex)
            {
                        MessageBox.Show(ex.ToString());
            }
}

private void btnUpdateTable_Click(object sender, EventArgs e)
{
            string _connstring = "Data Source=localhost/NEWDB;User
                        Id=EDZEHOO;Password=PASS123;";
            try
            {
                        OracleConnection _connObj2 = new OracleConnection(_connstring);
                        _connObj2.Open();
                        OracleTransaction _txn = _connObj2.BeginTransaction();

                        //Insert a new record into the table
                        string _sql = "INSERT INTO Products (ID, Price, Name) VALUES('ZL1', 300,
                                    'TestProduct')";
                        OracleCommand _cmdObj2 = new OracleCommand(_sql, _connObj2);
                        _cmdObj2.ExecuteNonQuery();
                        _txn.Commit();
                        _connObj2.Close();
            }
            catch (Exception ex)
            {
                        MessageBox.Show(ex.ToString());
            }
}
```

You will find that a notification is raised after you click the second button, indicating that the INSERT operation has successfully triggered a notification.

# Grouping Multiple Notification Requests

You can add more than one notification request in a single registration using the AddCommandDependency() method of the OracleDependency object. You might decide to do group requests when you need to listen on a few OracleCommand objects at the same time. Listing 8-3 shows how.

*Listing 8-3. Adding Multiple Notification Requests in a Single Registration*

```
OracleConnection _connObj = new OracleConnection(_connstring);
_connObj.Open();

//Here we create three different query sets
```

```
OracleCommand _cmdObj = _connObj.CreateCommand();
_cmdObj.CommandText = "SELECT Price FROM Products WHERE ID='LD1'";
OracleCommand _cmdObj2 = _connObj.CreateCommand();
_cmdObj2.CommandText = "SELECT CustName FROM Customer WHERE CustName LIKE 'A%'";
OracleCommand _cmdObj3 = _connObj.CreateCommand();
_cmdObj3.CommandText = "SELECT TotalAmount FROM Sales WHERE SaleMonth ='FEB'";
OracleDependency.Port = 1200;

//We register all three OracleCommand objects with the OracleDependency object
OracleDependency _dep = new OracleDependency(_cmdObj);
_dep.AddCommandDependency(_cmdObj2);
_dep.AddCommandDependency(_cmdObj3);
```

You will notice that after registering the change notifications once via the code in Listing 8-3, you will receive a notification when you try to update any of the three tables. The OracleNotificationEventArgs property will provide information on the row or table that has changed.

# Removing a Registration

Removing a registration is a simple and straightforward process. There are three ways to remove a registration:

- Explicitly removing a registration by code

- Specifying a timeout for the registration

- Specifying that notifications should only be raised once

You can explicitly remove a registration via code by simply calling the RemoveRegistration() method of the OracleDependency object. You need to specify the connection object that you've registered the notification on earlier as the first argument of this method, for example:

```
_dep.RemoveRegistration(_cmdObj);
```
Besides explicitly removing the registration by code, you can also set a timeout value on each registration. After you've bound the OracleCommand object to the OracleDependency object, you can access the OracleCommand.Notification.Timeout property to set this timeout value (in seconds). The code to do this follows:

```
OracleDependency _dep = new OracleDependency(_cmdObj);
//Listen for changes for only 10 seconds
_cmdObj.Notification.Timeout = 10;
```

You can also specify that the notification is raised only once. The notification registration will be automatically removed after this happens. The code to do this follows.

```
OracleDependency _dep = new OracleDependency(_cmdObj);
_cmdObj.Notification.IsNotifiedOnce = true;
```

# Retrieving Change Notification Information

The **OracleNotificationEventArgs** object passed to the event handler of your change notification contains information about the specific change. It represents the invalidation message generated for the notification—called so because when a query set is externally changed, it is said to be invalidated.

The **OracleNotificationEventArgs.Details** property returns a **DataTable** object containing detailed information about the particular change, such as the row and the names of the tables that were changed. To see what it contains, let's plug this **DataTable** into a **DataGridView** control. Add a **DataGridView** control to your form. You will also need to make some changes to the **OnNotificationReceived** event handler. These changes are highlighted in bold in Listing 8-4.

*Listing 8-4. Retrieving Detailed Change Notification Information*

```
public void OnNotificationReceived(object src, OracleNotificationEventArgs arg)
{
        DataTable changeDetails = arg.Details;
        _NotificationRaised = true;
        DisplayDataInGrid(changeDetails);
}

//You need to write some extra code below because .NET will not allow you to update a
//DataGridView control directly from a callback function

private delegate void DisplayDataInGridDelegate(DataTable sourceData);
private void DisplayDataInGrid(DataTable sourceData)
{
        if (this.InvokeRequired)
        {
                DisplayDataInGridDelegate _displayDataFunc = new
                        DisplayDataInGridDelegate(DisplayDataInGrid);
                this.BeginInvoke(_displayDataFunc,sourceData);
                return;
        }
        //This is the code that displays the OracleNotificationEventArgs object in the
        //DataGridView control
        dataGridView1.DataSource = sourceData;
        dataGridView1.Refresh();
}
```

If you run your code again, instead of a pop-up message box, you will see the details of the change notification show in the **DataGridView** control. Your output should look like Figure 8-4.

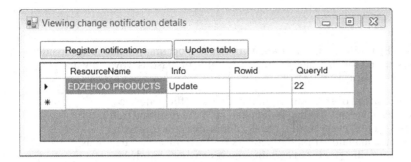

*Figure 8-4. Retrieving change notification details*

There are a few useful pieces of information you can retrieve from this **DataTable**. They are outlined in Table 8-1.

*Table 8-1. Information Stored in OracleNotificationEventArgs*

| Field name | Description |
|---|---|
| **ResourceName** | This is the name of the invalidated table that raised the notification. |
| **Info** | This field indicates the type of change that has occurred, and can take any one of the following values:<br>**Insert:** A new record was inserted.<br>**Delete:** A record was deleted.<br>**Update:** A record was updated.<br>**Startup:** A database was started.<br>**Shutdown:** A database was shut down.<br>**Shutdown_Any:** A database instance in an RAC was shut down.<br>**Alter:** A database object was altered.<br>**Drop:** An object or database was dropped.<br>**End:** A registration was removed.<br>**Error:** A notification error has occurred. |
| **RowID** | The **RowID** for the invalidated table row. You can use this field to find out which records have changed in a query set containing more than one record. |
| **QueryID** | This field contains the query ID, an internal Oracle value that is maintained by ODP.NET and retrieved when running the **SELECT** query. |

# Choosing to Poll

If you don't wish to be automatically notified when a change notification occurs, you can also consider using the **OracleDependency** class to poll for changes. There are a couple of reasons why you would choose to poll for changes instead of using a callback:

- You need fine-grained control over the amount of network traffic generated. Callbacks are raised whenever any change is detected, and the resulting traffic can be unpredictable. Using a poll every fixed number of minutes cuts down this uncertainty and lets you calculate estimated network traffic more accurately. This can be a crucial cost-controlling factor in certain scenarios where bandwidth is chargeable by the amount of network traffic generated.

- The database table is expected to change very frequently over time. In such a case, using a callback is bad, since it will be called very frequently, putting unnecessary load on the database. By polling every few minutes, for example, you can significantly reduce the load on the database.

You can poll the database for changes by checking the **OracleDependency.HasChanges** property. For example, the code in Listing 8-5 shows how you can use a timer to keep polling for changes every second using the **HasChanges** property. To test this code, create a form, and drop two buttons (**btnRegisterNotificationWithTimer** and **btnInsertData**) and a timer control onto the form.

*Listing 8-5. Using the OracleDependency.HasChanges Property*

```
//Declare a global OracleDependency object
private static OracleDependency _globalDep;
private void btnRegisterNotificationWithTimer_Click(object sender, EventArgs e)
{
        string _connstring = "Data Source=localhost/NEWDB;User
                Id=EDZEHOO;Password=PASS123;";
        try
        {
                OracleConnection _connObj = new OracleConnection(_connstring);
                _connObj.Open();
                OracleCommand _cmdObj = _connObj.CreateCommand();
                _cmdObj.CommandText = "SELECT * FROM Products";
                OracleDependency.Port = 1200;
                _globalDep = new OracleDependency(_cmdObj);
                _cmdObj.ExecuteNonQuery();
                MessageBox.Show("Change Notification Registered!");
                _connObj.Close();
                _connObj.Dispose();
                _connObj = null;
        }
        catch (Exception ex)
        {
                MessageBox.Show(ex.ToString());
        }
```

```
        //Start a timer to keep polling for changes in the table every 1 second
        timer1.Tick += new EventHandler(TimerTick);
        timer1.Start();
}

//The timer tick event handler. Show a message if a change is detected
private static void TimerTick(object sender,EventArgs e)
{
        if (_globalDep.HasChanges)
        {
                MessageBox.Show("Change detected!");
        }
}

private void btnInsertData(object sender, EventArgs e)
{
        string _connstring = "Data Source=localhost/NEWDB;User
                Id=EDZEHOO;Password=PASS123;";
        try
        {
                OracleConnection _connObj2 = new OracleConnection(_connstring);
                _connObj2.Open();
                OracleTransaction _txn = _connObj2.BeginTransaction();
                string _sql = "INSERT INTO Products(ID, Name, Price) VALUES('AZ1','Test
                        Product',300)";
                OracleCommand _cmdObj2 = new OracleCommand(_sql, _connObj2);
                _cmdObj2.ExecuteNonQuery();
                _txn.Commit();
                _connObj2.Close();
        }
        catch (Exception ex)
        {
                MessageBox.Show(ex.ToString());
        }
}
```

Run the sample in Listing 8-5, and click the **btnRegisterNotificationWithTimer** button. You should see a message prompt showing that the registration was successful. This would also kick off the timer to poll the database for changes every second. Now, click the **btnInsertData** button. You should be able to see the "Change detected!" message box displayed.

# Considering Typical Usage Scenarios

You can realize the full benefits of change notifications when it is used under the correct conditions. Table 8-2 describes a few scenarios where change notifications can help create smarter and more responsive applications.

*Table 8-2. Sample Usage Scenarios for Change Notifications*

| Usage Scenario | Description |
| --- | --- |
| A data grid that automatically updates itself | This is the most common use for change notifications and is suitable for terminals that need to always display the latest data. Examples include stock price displays, flight schedule terminals, and job boxes. |
| A system that alerts the administrator when the database schema has changed | Change notifications can also be used to ensure database integrity. When a table crucial to an application is deleted, for example, the administrator can be automatically notified, or a database repair operation can be automatically initiated. |
| A system that drives information flow or a business process | Another creative use of change notifications is to drive information flow. For example, a clerk receives a purchase order from a customer and creates a purchase order record in the database. Through change notification, this may automatically generate a corresponding sales order record in the sales order database, and so on, creating a chain of automatically triggered **INSERT** commands. |
| A data cache that automatically invalidates and refreshes itself | When used in caching, change notification can effectively ensure that your cache is always up to date, increasing the hit/miss ratio. |

One of the more useful applications arising from the use of database change notifications is the self-updating data grid. The concept is simple: You bind a **DataGridView** control to a table and register a change notification on this table. When any data inside this table changes, your application is notified. It can then repopulate the grid with the latest data. The code to do this is detailed in Listing 8-6.

*Listing 8-6. Building a Self-Updating Data Grid Control*

```
private bool _BoundToDB = false;
private int _globalID = 1;

//The event handler for the change notification. Here we initiate a refresh of the grid data
public void OnNotificationReceived(object src, OracleNotificationEventArgs arg)
{
        RefreshGrid();
}
```

```csharp
//Extra code to update the DataGridView control from a callback thread
private delegate void RefreshGridDelegate();
private void RefreshGrid()
{
        if (this.InvokeRequired)
        {
                RefreshGridDelegate _displayDataFunc = new RefreshGridDelegate(RefreshGrid);
                this.BeginInvoke(_displayDataFunc);
                return;
        }

        //Write the code to populate the DataGridView control with latest data from the
        //Products table
        string _connstring = "Data Source=localhost/NEWDB;User
                Id=EDZEHOO;Password=PASS123;";
        try
        {
                OracleConnection _connObj = new OracleConnection(_connstring);
                _connObj.Open();
                OracleCommand _cmdObj = _connObj.CreateCommand();
                _cmdObj.CommandText = "SELECT * FROM Products";
                OracleDataAdapter _adapObj = new OracleDataAdapter (_cmdObj);
                DataSet _products = new DataSet();
                _adapObj.Fill(_products);
                dataGridView1.DataSource = _products.Tables[0];
                dataGridView1.Refresh();
                _cmdObj.Dispose();
                _connObj.Close();
                _connObj.Dispose();
                _connObj = null;
                _cmdObj = null;
        }
        catch (Exception ex)
        {
                MessageBox.Show(ex.ToString());
        }
}

//Clicking on the Bind button registers change notification for the Products table
private void btnBind_Click(object sender, EventArgs e)
{
        string _connstring = "Data Source=localhost/NEWDB;User
                Id=EDZEHOO;Password=PASS123;";
        try
        {
                OracleConnection _connObj = new OracleConnection(_connstring);
                _connObj.Open();
                OracleCommand _cmdObj = _connObj.CreateCommand();
                _cmdObj.CommandText = "SELECT * FROM Products";
                OracleDependency.Port = 1200;
                OracleDependency _dep = new OracleDependency(_cmdObj);
```

```csharp
                //Set notification settings
                _dep.QueryBasedNotification = false;
                _cmdObj.Notification.IsNotifiedOnce = false;

                _dep.OnChange += new OnChangeEventHandler(OnNotificationReceived);
                _cmdObj.ExecuteNonQuery();
                MessageBox.Show("Change Notification Registered!");
                _BoundToDB = true;

                //Populate the DataGridView with data from the Products table
                RefreshGrid();
                while (_BoundToDB == true)
                {
                    Application.DoEvents();
                }
                _connObj.Close();
                _connObj.Dispose();
                _connObj = null;
        }
        catch (Exception ex)
        {
                MessageBox.Show(ex.ToString());
        }
}

//Quit the listening loop initiated in btnBind_Click
private void btnUnBind_Click(object sender, EventArgs e)
{
        _BoundToDB = false;
}

//Insert a new record directly into the Products table - calling this function should cause
//the notification to be raised and the DataGridView control to refresh itself automatically
private void btnInsert_Click(object sender, EventArgs e)
{
        string _connstring = "Data Source=localhost/NEWDB;User
                Id=EDZEHOO;Password=PASS123;";
        _globalID += 1;
        try
        {
                OracleConnection _connObj2 = new OracleConnection(_connstring);
                _connObj2.Open();
                OracleTransaction _txn = _connObj2.BeginTransaction();
                string _sql = "INSERT INTO Products(ID, Name, Price) VALUES('TP" +
                        _globalID.ToString() + "','Test Product',100)";
                OracleCommand _cmdObj2 = new OracleCommand(_sql, _connObj2);
                _cmdObj2.ExecuteNonQuery();
                _txn.Commit();
                _connObj2.Close();
        }
        catch (Exception ex)
        {
```

```
                    MessageBox.Show(ex.ToString());
            }
    }
}
```

You can try running the code in Listing 8-6 by clicking the "Bind to Database" button. Once you've done that, the **DataGridView** control will be populated with data from the **Products** table. After that, click the "Insert a new product" button to insert a new product into the **Products** table. Because change notification is already set up, the **DataGridView** control will instantaneously refresh its list of data. To quit the application, click the "Unbind from Database" button, and close the window. You can see a screenshot of this application in action in Figure 8-5.

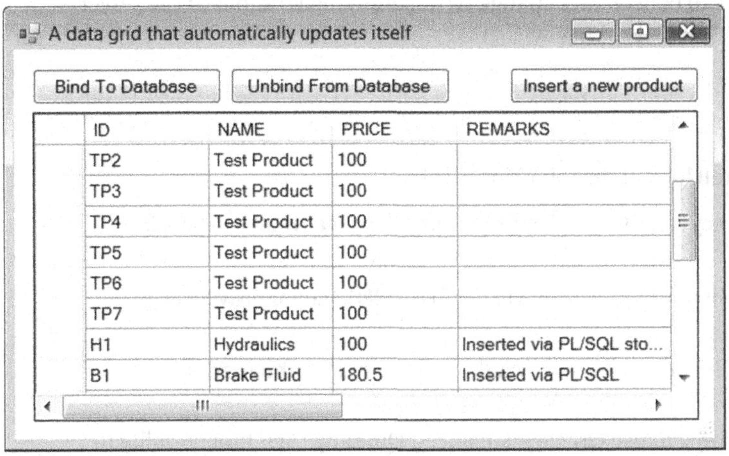

*Figure 8-5. A self-updating data grid control*

# Thinking About Performance

There are certain performance caveats when using change notifications. You can probably foresee that for a database that is frequently updated, you will get a large number of notifications, and your event handler will be invoked many times. Needless to say, it is not a good idea to stuff heavy processing or blocking calls in your event handler. For example, it's a bad idea to try to generate a report file in your notification event handler, especially if you know in advance that the table will be updated frequently.

Outside your code, you should also take note that notifications do take up space and processing power in the Oracle database internally. Oracle recommends the following best practices when using change notifications:

- Use change notifications with mostly read-only tables.

- When updating a change-registered table, try to update as little rows as possible.

- Limit the number of change notification registrations for the same query.

All three approaches attempt to reduce the number of notifications raised. Large numbers of notifications require a lot of space in the invalidation queue. For example, consider a database table containing the list of products of a company. This is a good candidate to register for change notifications, since product listings don't usually change by the minute.

The rationale behind the second best practice listed is that too many rows being updated in a single transaction may cause the size of an invalidation message to become very large. Therefore, it is a good idea to keep the number of rows updated to a minimum in a single transaction when working with change-registered tables.

You should also try to limit the number of change notification registrations for the same query whenever possible. For example, it is convenient to register change notifications for every client that connects to the database so that they can be notified when the data changes. In scenarios with thousands of clients connecting to the database, this can quickly lead to a significant performance drain on the database. A better approach is to consolidate change notification registrations at the server instead to minimize the number of notifications raised.

# Summary

In this chapter, you've taken an overall look at the following areas:

- Using the **OracleDependency** class to register both query-based and object-based change notifications

- Retrieving information about a notification via the **OracleNotificationEventArgs** object

- Configuring change notification properties via the **OracleNotificationRequest** object

In the next chapter, you'll learn how to use Oracle's Advanced Queuing (AQ) functionality to implement wait queues.

# CHAPTER 9

■ ■ ■

# Using Oracle Database Streams Advanced Queuing with ODP.NET

The landscape of enterprise software today is populated with thousands of different systems that need to talk to each other reliably. I'm not specifically referring to the communication standards or protocols that allow heterogeneous applications to share data, but rather to the underlying technologies that these applications use to send and receive data. Even homogeneous applications residing in the same server would command the same necessity. For example, sending data between two processes, a Windows Service and a web application. Most developers have learned that this task might not turn out to be as simple as they'd thought it to be.

In the past, developers would open TCP/IP sockets between two applications so that they could send data to one another. Pipes were another alternative provided by Microsoft. These various methods suffered from various problems—the biggest complaint being that they were extremely messy and difficult to program.

When Microsoft introduced message queuing via the Microsoft Messaging Queue (MSMQ) server component, it provided developers another interesting concept for data sharing: an application would send a message to a remote queue server (via the MSMQ API), and the intended recipient could then retrieve it from this queue. This simple idea allowed applications to receive data even when they were offline because the messages could be temporarily stored in a queue and read any time the intended application went online.

Oracle provides a similar feature, known as Advanced Queuing (AQ) that extends this same concept to the database: it uses the Oracle database as a temporary storage area for queue messages. Since these messages are stored in a table like any other ordinary table in Oracle, all the features of the Oracle database (for instance, indexing) could be applied on this message store.

In this chapter, you will learn the basics of using AQ to send and receive messages between different applications, specifically:

- How to create queues via SQL*Plus

- How to pass data from one application to another using ODP.NET's enqueue and dequeue functionality

- How to use RAW, XML, and UDT data types for messaging queuing

- How to dequeue a message synchronously and asynchronously

# Understanding the Basics of AQ

In the world of AQ, there are two basic terms you will need to be familiar with: enqueue and dequeue. Enqueuing refers to the act of adding (or sending) a message to a queue. Dequeuing refers to the act of removing or retrieving the message from a queue.

Figure 9-1 briefly summarizes how AQ works.

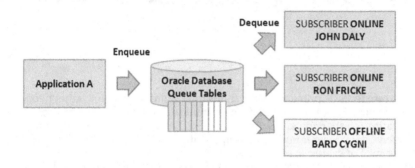

***Figure 9-1.*** *An overview of AQ*

An application can enqueue any number of messages to a queue (stored in an Oracle table). The intended recipients (subscribers) of the queue will be able to retrieve these messages when they connect to the queue. As an analogy, the queue can be said to be somewhat the equivalent of a mail server, and the dequeuing process the equivalent of a mail client connecting to the mail server to retrieve e-mail.

The important point underlying this concept is that you do not have to be connected to your mail server 24 hours a day to receive mail. This is the same for AQ.

# Creating a Single-Consumer Queue

You can use a single-consumer queue if you know in advance that there will only be one single sender and one single receiver (also known as a point-to-point scenario). A single-consumer queue is one of the simplest queues to set up and is typically used in single-user environments. For example, a job order system that might need to trigger a message to a backend processing system for each incoming job order could make use of a single-consumer queue.

## Setting Up a Single-Consumer Queue

Before you can set up a queue or run any of the examples in this chapter, you must first grant permissions to the database user to use the **DBMS_AQADM** package. This PL/SQL package contains the routines that allow you to create and manage queues in Oracle. You can grant this permission by logging on as the **SYSTEM** account and executing the following in SQL*Plus:

```
GRANT EXECUTE on DBMS_AQADM to EDZEHOO;
```

You are now ready to create your first queue. You must always fulfill these three steps before you attempt to use a queue:

1. Create the table to hold the queue messages.

2. Create the queue.

3. Start the queue.

You can accomplish these steps by logging on to SQL*Plus again under your user account and running the following PL/SQL block:

```
BEGIN
        DBMS_AQADM.CREATE_QUEUE_TABLE(
                queue_table=>'EDZEHOO.MY_JOBS_QUEUE_TABLE',
                queue_payload_type=>'RAW',
                multiple_consumers=>FALSE);

        DBMS_AQADM.CREATE_QUEUE(
                queue_name=>'EDZEHOO.MY_JOBS_QUEUE',
                queue_table=>'EDZEHOO.MY_JOBS_QUEUE_TABLE');
        DBMS_AQADM.START_QUEUE(queue_name=>'EDZEHOO.MY_JOBS_QUEUE');
END;
/
```

Take note that there are a few parameters that must be defined in the PL/SQL block. These are listed in Table 9-1.

*Table 9-1. Queue Creation Parameters*

| Parameter Name | What It Represents |
|---|---|
| queue_table | Defines the name of the table used to store queue messages |
| queue_payload_type | The data type of the payload (the data carried in the message), which can be **RAW** (byte array), **UDT** (user defined type), or **XML** (XML data) |
| multiple_consumers | Specifies whether this queue supports multiple consumers |
| queue_name | The name of the queue |

■ **Tip** You can also create and manage queues via a GUI within the Visual Studio environment by way of the Oracle Developer Tools (ODT.NET) suite. You can read more about this in Chapters 14 and 15 of this book.

# Enqueuing and Dequeuing a Single Message

Once you've created a queue, you can start to enqueue a message. The process of enqueuing a message usually follows these steps:

1. Connect to the database.

2. Create an **OracleAQQueue** object that points to a desired queue.

3. Create an **OracleAQMessage** object, and load the payload data into the message.

4. Call the **OracleAQQueue**.Enqueue method.

5. Disconnect from the database.

To be able to send messages to a queue from your .NET code, you must first create an **OracleAQQueue** object. You can do this with the following code. The first argument is the name of the queue that you created earlier via SQL*Plus. The second argument is an open database connection. You must also inform ODP.NET that you wish to send byte data (**RAW**) to this queue.

```
OracleAQQueue _queueObj = new OracleAQQueue("EDZEHOO.MY_JOBS_QUEUE", _connObj);
_queueObj.MessageType = OracleAQMessageType.Raw;
```

The next step is to create an **OracleAQMessage** object and load the data you wish to send into the **Payload** property of this object:

```
OracleAQMessage _msg = new OracleAQMessage();
String Data = "HELLO, HOW ARE YOU!";
_msg.Payload = ConvertToByteArray(Data);
```

As the last step, you will need to call the **Enqueue** method to send this message to the queue:

```
_queueObj.Enqueue(_msg);
```

That wasn't difficult at all, was it? Let's begin to write your first AQ application. Create a new form, and place a single button on it (**btnEnqueue**). Write the code from Listing 9-1.

*Listing 9-1. Enqueuing a Single Message*

```
using System.Text;

private void btnEnqueue_Click(object sender, EventArgs e)
{
        string _connstring = "Data Source=localhost/NEWDB;User
              Id=EDZEHOO;Password=PASS123;";
        try
        {
                OracleConnection _connObj = new OracleConnection(_connstring);

                // Create a new queue object
                OracleAQQueue _queueObj = new OracleAQQueue("EDZEHOO.MY_JOBS_QUEUE",
```

```csharp
                _connObj);
            _connObj.Open();
            OracleTransaction _txn = _connObj.BeginTransaction();

            // Set payload type to RAW (byte array)
            _queueObj.MessageType = OracleAQMessageType.Raw;

            // Create a new message object
            OracleAQMessage _msg = new OracleAQMessage();

            String Data = "HELLO, HOW ARE YOU!";
            _msg.Payload = ConvertToByteArray(Data);

            //You can also attach additional custom data to a message via the
            //Correlation property
            _msg.Correlation = "MY ADDITIONAL MISC DATA";

            //The Visibility property OnCommit makes the enqueue part of a transaction
            _queueObj.EnqueueOptions.Visibility = OracleAQVisibilityMode.OnCommit;

            // Enqueue the message
            _queueObj.Enqueue(_msg);

            // Display the payload data that was enqueued
            MessageBox.Show("Payload Data : " + Data + "\n" +
                    "Payload Hex value : " + ConvertToHexString((byte[])_msg.Payload) +
                    "\n" + "Message ID : " + ConvertToHexString(_msg.MessageId) + "\n" +
                    "Correlation : " + _msg.Correlation);
            _txn.Commit();

            _queueObj.Dispose();
            _connObj.Close();
            _connObj.Dispose();
            _connObj = null;
        }
        catch (Exception ex)
        {
            MessageBox.Show(ex.ToString());
        }
    }


// Converts a byte array to a Hexadecimal string
static private string ConvertToHexString(byte[] Data)
{
        StringBuilder _stringObj = new StringBuilder();
        for (int i = 0; i < Data.Length; i++)
        {
                _stringObj.Append((int.Parse(Data[i].ToString())).ToString("X"));
        }
        return _stringObj.ToString();
}
```

```
// Converts a String to a byte array
static private byte[] ConvertToByteArray(String Data)
{
        char[] _charArray = Data.ToCharArray();
        byte[] _byteArray = new byte[Data.Length];
        for (int i = 0; i < _charArray.Length; i++)
        {
                _byteArray[i] = (byte)_charArray[i];
        }
        return _byteArray;
}
```

Now that you have the enqueue function ready, you need to do the opposite equivalent—the dequeue. Since you probably want to test the sending of messages across different processes, you can create a new project and new form for the dequeue. In this form, create a button with the name **btnDequeue**. Write the code shown in Listing 9-2 for this button.

*Listing 9-2. Dequeuing a Single Message*

```
private void btnDequeue_Click(object sender, EventArgs e)
{
        string _connstring = "Data Source=localhost/NEWDB;User
                Id=EDZEHOO;Password=PASS123;";
        try
        {
                OracleConnection _connObj = new OracleConnection(_connstring);

                // Create a new queue object
                OracleAQQueue _queueObj = new OracleAQQueue("EDZEHOO.MY_JOBS_QUEUE",
                        _connObj);
                _connObj.Open();
                OracleTransaction _txn = _connObj.BeginTransaction();

                //The Visibility property OnCommit makes the dequeue part of the transaction
                //The Wait property specifies the number of seconds to wait for the Dequeue.
                //The default value of this property is set to wait forever
                _queueObj.DequeueOptions.Visibility = OracleAQVisibilityMode.OnCommit;
                _queueObj.DequeueOptions.Wait = 10;

                // Dequeue the message.
                OracleAQMessage _deqMsg = _queueObj.Dequeue();

                MessageBox.Show("Dequeued Payload Data: " +
                        ConvertFromByteArray((byte[])_deqMsg.Payload) + "\n"
                        + "Dequeued Payload Hex: " +
                        ConvertToHexString((byte[])_deqMsg.Payload) + "\n"
                        + "Message ID of Dequeued Payload : " +
                        ConvertToHexString(_deqMsg.MessageId) + "\n" +
                         "Correlation : " + _deqMsg.Correlation);
```

```
                _txn.Commit();
                _queueObj.Dispose();
                _connObj.Close();
                _connObj.Dispose();
                _connObj = null;
        }
        catch (Exception ex)
        {
                MessageBox.Show(ex.ToString());
        }
}

// Converts a byte array to a String
static private String ConvertFromByteArray(byte[] Data)
{
        StringBuilder _stringObj = new StringBuilder();
        for (int i = 0; i < Data.Length; i++)
        {
                _stringObj.Append((char)Data[i]);
        }
        return _stringObj.ToString();
}
```

■ **Note** The `Correlation` property behaves much like a `Tag` property; it allows you to attach additional custom data to a message. As sample usage scenario, you could mark each outgoing message with an ID number specific to your application (a job ID for example).

Now, let's try this application! Launch the Enqueue application, and click the Enqueue button. Your application will display the details of the message that was enqueued. You can now close this application. If you now launch the Dequeue application and click the Dequeue button, you will instantly be presented with a pop-up message like the one shown in Figure 9-2 containing the details of the enqueued message.

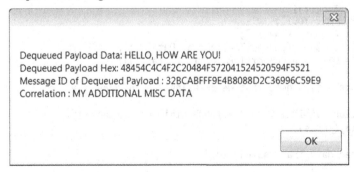

*Figure 9-2. Dequeued message*

229

Through AQ, this simple test demonstrates that you can send a message from one application to another, even when the second application is not running at the same time.

## Enqueuing and Dequeuing Multiple Messages

As you create applications that handle substantial business traffic, you will find that you might need to send more than one message at one time. It is possible to enqueue more than one message at one go. The **EnqueueArray** method allows you to pass in multiple messages (as a single array) for enqueuing. Listing 9-3 demonstrates this.

*Listing 9-3. Enqueuing Multiple Messages*

```
private void btnEnqueueMultiple_Click(object sender, EventArgs e)
{
        string _connstring = "Data Source=localhost/NEWDB;User
            Id=EDZEHOO;Password=PASS123;";
        try
        {
            OracleConnection _connObj = new OracleConnection(_connstring);

            // Create a new queue object
            OracleAQQueue _queueObj = new OracleAQQueue("EDZEHOO.MY_JOBS_QUEUE",
                _connObj);
            _connObj.Open();
            OracleTransaction _txn = _connObj.BeginTransaction();

            // Set payload type
            _queueObj.MessageType = OracleAQMessageType.Raw;

            // Create an array of OracleAQMessage objects
            OracleAQMessage[] _msgs = new OracleAQMessage[2];

            // Fill the array with strings
            String[] Data = new String[2];
            Data[0] =  "HELLO, HOW ARE YOU!";
            Data[1] =  "... AND WHAT'S YOUR NAME?";
            _msgs[0] = new OracleAQMessage(ConvertToByteArray(Data[0]));
            _msgs[1] = new OracleAQMessage(ConvertToByteArray(Data[1]));

            // Enqueue the message - take note that we're using the EnqueueArray
            // function now
            _queueObj.EnqueueOptions.Visibility = OracleAQVisibilityMode.OnCommit;
            _queueObj.EnqueueArray(_msgs);

            // Display the payload data that was enqueued
            for (int i = 0; i < 2; i++)
            {
                MessageBox.Show("Payload Data : " + Data[i] + "\n" +
                    "Payload Hex value : " +
                    ConvertToHexString((byte[])_msgs[i].Payload) + "\n" +
```

```
                            "Message ID : " + ConvertToHexString(_msgs[i].MessageId));
                }
                _txn.Commit();
                _queueObj.Dispose();
                _connObj.Close();
                _connObj.Dispose();
                _connObj = null;
        }
        catch (Exception ex)
        {
                MessageBox.Show(ex.ToString());
        }
}
```

You can also dequeue multiple messages at once if you know in advance how many messages are waiting in a queue. You can do this via the **DequeueArray** method. This method returns an array of **OracleAQMessage** objects that you can use to inspect each retrieved message, and the code to use it is in Listing 9-4.

*Listing 9-4. Dequeuing Multiple Messages*

```
private void btnDequeueMultiple_Click(object sender, EventArgs e)
{
        string _connstring = "Data Source=localhost/NEWDB;User
                Id=EDZEHOO;Password=PASS123;";
        try
        {

                OracleConnection _connObj = new OracleConnection(_connstring);

                // Create a new queue object
                OracleAQQueue _queueObj = new OracleAQQueue("EDZEHOO.MY_JOBS_QUEUE",
                        _connObj);
                _connObj.Open();
                OracleTransaction _txn = _connObj.BeginTransaction();
                _queueObj.DequeueOptions.Visibility = OracleAQVisibilityMode.OnCommit;
                _queueObj.DequeueOptions.Wait = 10;
                _queueObj.DequeueOptions.ProviderSpecificType = true;

                // Dequeue the messages - take note that you can specify the number of
                // messages you wish to retrieve from the queue
                OracleAQMessage[] _deqMsgs = _queueObj.DequeueArray(2);

                for (int i = 0; i < _deqMsgs.Length ; i++)
                {
                        // If you enqueued a byte array, the dequeued object is an
                        // OracleBinary object. You can retrieve the byte array using the
                        // OracleBinary.Value property

                        OracleBinary _payload = (OracleBinary)_deqMsgs[i].Payload;
                        MessageBox.Show("Dequeued Payload Data: " +
                                ConvertFromByteArray(_payload.Value) + "\n"
```

```
                                        + "Dequeued Payload Hex: " +
                                        ConvertToHexString(_payload.Value) + "\n");
                    }

                    _txn.Commit();
                    _queueObj.Dispose();
                    _connObj.Close();
                    _connObj.Dispose();
                    _connObj = null;
            }
            catch (Exception ex)
            {
                    MessageBox.Show(ex.ToString());
            }
    }
}
```

You can test the code from Listing 9-4 in the same fashion. Take note that, this time, you will receive two pop-up notifications when you press each of the Enqueue and Dequeue buttons. The second pop-up notification is shown in Figure 9-3.

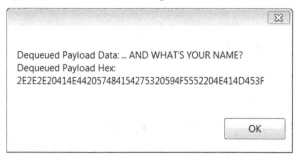

*Figure 9-3. The second pop-up notification message*

---

▪ **Tip** You don't have to execute a multiple message enqueue to perform a multiple message dequeue. For instance, you could execute a single message enqueue routine five consecutive times and, after that, perform a multiple message dequeue with the number of messages set to 5: `OracleAQQueue.DequeueArray(5)`.

---

# Creating a Multiple-Consumer Queue

Now that you've seen how single-consumer queues work, let's take a look at one that is meant for a multiuser environment. For instance, you might want to setup a jobs queue, where multiple technicians might need to retrieve jobs from this queue.

Multiple-consumer queues in Oracle work like this: you must explicitly define the recipients for the queue. Only the defined recipients would be able to dequeue messages from the queue. There are two ways to define recipients:

- *At the queue level*: During the creation of a multiple-consumer queue, you can use the DBMS_AQADM package to add a subscriber to the queue.

- *At the message level*: You can also define a list of recipients for each message that you enqueue.

The same name defined for the subscriber or recipient must be specified in the `OracleAQQueue.DequeueOptions.ConsumerName` property during dequeuing. This allows Oracle to know who's attempting to dequeue.

## Defining Recipients at the Queue Level

Before you proceed with the examples in this section, you must first create a multiple-consumer queue. Again, you can use SQL*Plus for this. Take note that you will also be adding a subscriber with the name **JOHNDALY** to the queue and then mapping this subscriber to a database user. When you do this, you are defining the recipients at the queue-level. Execute the code in Listing 9-5.

*Listing 9-5. Defining Recipients at the Queue Level*

```
DECLARE
      SUBSCRIBER SYS.AQ$_AGENT;
BEGIN
      DBMS_AQADM.CREATE_QUEUE_TABLE
      (
              queue_table => 'EDZEHOO.JobsQueue_Table',
              queue_payload_type => 'RAW',
              sort_list => 'ENQ_TIME',
              message_grouping => DBMS_AQADM.NONE,
              compatible => '10.0',
              comment => '',
              multiple_consumers => TRUE,
              secure => TRUE
      );

      DBMS_AQADM.CREATE_QUEUE
      (
              queue_name => 'EDZEHOO.JobsQueue',
              queue_table => 'EDZEHOO.JobsQueue_Table',
              queue_type => DBMS_AQADM.NORMAL_QUEUE,
              max_retries => 0,
              retry_delay => 0,
              retention_time => 0,
              comment => ''
      );

      SUBSCRIBER := SYS.AQ$_AGENT('JOHNDALY', NULL, NULL);
      DBMS_AQADM.ADD_SUBSCRIBER
      (
              queue_name => 'EDZEHOO.JobsQueue',
              subscriber => SUBSCRIBER,
```

```
            queue_to_queue => FALSE,
            delivery_mode => DBMS_AQADM.PERSISTENT
    );

    DBMS_AQADM.ENABLE_DB_ACCESS
    (
            agent_name => 'JOHNDALY',
            db_username => 'EDZEHOO'
    );

    DBMS_AQADM.start_queue(queue_name=>'EDZEHOO.JobsQueue');
END;
/
```

Some of the properties used in the preceding listing are described in Table 9-2.

*Table 9-2.* *Properties Used in ADD_SUBSCRIBER and ENABLE_DB_ACCESS*

| Property Name | What It Represents |
|---|---|
| queue_name | This property is the name of the queue to add a subscriber to. |
| subscriber | This property is the name of the agent subscribing to the queue. |
| queue_to_queue | This one specifies whether to enable queue to queue propagation for the subscriber (propagating a messaging from a queue to another). |
| delivery_mode | This specifies whether to use **BUFFERED** or **PERSISTENT** delivery of messages for the subscriber. Buffered messaging is faster than persistent messaging, because the messages reside in shared memory and are written to disk only when the shared memory limit is approached. The downside of buffered messaging is reduced reliability; if the Oracle instance crashed, for instance, messages that were not written to disk are lost. |
| agent_name | This property tells the name of the subscribing agent. |
| db_username | This one is the name of the database user to map to. |

You can now write the full code for the enqueue function as shown in Listing 9-6. For multiple-consumer queues, you are required to define the sender ID. You can set it to any name you wish.

*Listing 9-6. Recipient-Specific Enqueuing*

```
private void btnEnqueueMCQ_Click(object sender, EventArgs e)
{
        string _connstring = "Data Source=localhost/NEWDB;User
            Id=EDZEHOO;Password=PASS123;";
        try
        {
                OracleConnection _connObj = new OracleConnection(_connstring);

                // Create a new queue object
                OracleAQQueue _queueObj = new OracleAQQueue("EDZEHOO.JobsQueue", _connObj);
                _connObj.Open();
                OracleTransaction _txn = _connObj.BeginTransaction();

                // Set payload type
                _queueObj.MessageType = OracleAQMessageType.Raw;

                // Create a new message object
                OracleAQMessage _msg = new OracleAQMessage();

                String Data = "HELLO, HOW ARE YOU!";
                _msg.Payload = ConvertToByteArray(Data);

                // Define the sender ID and enqueue the message
                _queueObj.EnqueueOptions.Visibility = OracleAQVisibilityMode.OnCommit;
                _msg.SenderId = new OracleAQAgent("EDZEHOO");
                _queueObj.Enqueue(_msg);

                // Display the payload data that was enqueued
                MessageBox.Show("Payload Data : " + Data + "\n" +
                  "Payload Hex value : " + ConvertToHexString((byte[])_msg.Payload) + "\n" +
                  "Message ID : " + ConvertToHexString(_msg.MessageId));
                _txn.Commit();

                _queueObj.Dispose();
                _connObj.Close();
                _connObj.Dispose();
                _connObj = null;
        }
        catch (Exception ex)
        {
                MessageBox.Show(ex.ToString());
        }
}
```

The code for the corresponding dequeue function is shown in Listing 9-7. Take note that you will be declaring who you are to ODP.NET (by defining the **ConsumerName**).

235

*Listing 9-7. Recipient-Specific Dequeuing*

```
private void btnDequeueMCQ_Click(object sender, EventArgs e)
{
        string _connstring = "Data Source=localhost/NEWDB;User
                Id=EDZEHOO;Password=PASS123;";
        try
        {
                OracleConnection _connObj = new OracleConnection(_connstring);

                // Create a new queue object
                OracleAQQueue _queueObj = new OracleAQQueue("EDZEHOO.JobsQueue", _connObj);
                _connObj.Open();
                OracleTransaction _txn = _connObj.BeginTransaction();

                // Dequeue the message.
                _queueObj.DequeueOptions.Visibility = OracleAQVisibilityMode.OnCommit;
                _queueObj.DequeueOptions.Wait = 10;

                // Here set the consumer name to the registered queue subscriber
                // This queue subscriber was registered when you setup the queue
                // in SQL*Plus
                _queueObj.DequeueOptions.ConsumerName = "JOHNDALY";
                OracleAQMessage _deqMsg = _queueObj.Dequeue();

                MessageBox.Show("Dequeued Payload Data: " +
                    ConvertFromByteArray((byte[])_deqMsg.Payload) + "\n"
                    + "Dequeued Payload Hex: " +
                    ConvertToHexString((byte[])_deqMsg.Payload) + "\n"
                    + "Message ID of Dequeued Payload : " +
                    ConvertToHexString(_deqMsg.MessageId));

                _txn.Commit();
                _queueObj.Dispose();
                _connObj.Close();
                _connObj.Dispose();
                _connObj = null;
        }
        catch (Exception ex)
        {
                MessageBox.Show(ex.ToString());
        }
}
```

Now, what's interesting is that if you change the consumer name in the dequeue code to another person, as illustrated here, you will find that there are no messages found in the queue:

```
_queueObj.DequeueOptions.ConsumerName = "RONFRICKE";
```

The reason is simple—only subscribers to a queue will be able to access messages enqueued in that queue, which could be useful, for example, in the following scenario: You could set up multiple announcement boards (with each board represented by a queue) and a list of subscribers for each announcement board. The subscribers will only receive announcements for the boards they are subscribed to.

## Defining Recipients at the Message Level

In some cases, your application cannot know in advance who the subscribers to a queue are. Or you might need the list of recipients to be different for each message in the same queue. You can set different recipients for each message in the same queue by defining recipients at the message level using the `OracleAQMessage.Recipients` property. The code for this enqueue function is in Listing 9-8.

*Listing 9-8. Defining Recipients at the Message Level*

```
private void btnEnqueueRecipients_Click(object sender, EventArgs e)
{
        string _connstring = "Data Source=localhost/NEWDB;User
            Id=EDZEHOO;Password=PASS123;";
        try
        {
                OracleConnection _connObj = new OracleConnection(_connstring);

                // Create a new queue object
                OracleAQQueue _queueObj = new OracleAQQueue("EDZEHOO.JobsQueue", _connObj);
                _connObj.Open();
                OracleTransaction _txn = _connObj.BeginTransaction();

                // Set payload type
                _queueObj.MessageType = OracleAQMessageType.Raw;

                // Create a new message object
                OracleAQMessage _msg = new OracleAQMessage();

                String Data = "HELLO, HOW ARE YOU!";
                _msg.Payload = ConvertToByteArray(Data);

                // Enqueue the message
                _queueObj.EnqueueOptions.Visibility = OracleAQVisibilityMode.OnCommit;

                // Register the subscriber at the message-level using the
                // OracleAQMessage.Recipients property
                OracleAQAgent[] agent = new OracleAQAgent[1];
                agent[0] = new OracleAQAgent("RONFRICKE");
                _msg.Recipients = agent;
                _msg.SenderId = new OracleAQAgent("EDZEHOO");

                _queueObj.Enqueue(_msg);

                // Display the payload data that was enqueued
                MessageBox.Show("Payload Data : " + Data + "\n" +
                   "Payload Hex value : " + ConvertToHexString((byte[])_msg.Payload) + "\n" +
```

```
                    "Message ID : " + ConvertToHexString(_msg.MessageId));
                _txn.Commit();

                _queueObj.Dispose();
                _connObj.Close();
                _connObj.Dispose();
                _connObj = null;
        }
        catch (Exception ex)
        {
                MessageBox.Show(ex.ToString());
        }
}
```

You can use the same code (in **btnDequeueMCQ_Click**) for the dequeue function. Ensure that the **ConsumerName** property has been set to **RONFRICKE**. If you run this code sample, you will find that even though **RONFRICKE** isn't a subscriber to the queue, he will be able to receive the particular message (because he is on the recipient list of that message).

---

■ **Note** Recipients defined at the message level override the subscribers defined at the queue level.

---

# Enqueuing and Dequeuing Various Data Types in AQ

AQ allows for three different types of data to be enqueued or dequeued:

- **RAW**: Data consisting of a stream of binary data

- **UDT**: Values of a user-defined type

- **XML**: Data formatted as an XML document

In the previous sections, you've been working with **RAW** data types, which are pretty much byte arrays. In this section, let's explore how you can use **UDT** or **XML** data types.

## Using UDT Data Types

You've seen and worked with UDTs earlier on in Chapter 5 of this book. UDTs are a great way to pass entire business objects from one application to another (without the need to do any serialization), since Oracle can represent UDTs natively in the database.

Let's first define the UDT object via SQL*Plus:

```
CREATE TYPE EDZEHOO.Jobs_Type AS object(
        JobID                   VARCHAR2(10),
        JobName                 VARCHAR2(255),
        JobPrice                NUMBER,
        JobDescription          VARCHAR2(255));
/
```

You will also need to create a new queue, with the payload type set to the name of the UDT you've just created. Run the following PL/SQL block in SQL*Plus:

```
BEGIN
        DBMS_AQADM.CREATE_QUEUE_TABLE(
                queue_table=>'EDZEHOO.SmallJobs_table',
                queue_payload_type=>'EDZEHOO.Jobs_Type',
                multiple_consumers=>FALSE);

        DBMS_AQADM.CREATE_QUEUE(
                queue_name=>'EDZEHOO.SmallJobs',
                queue_table=>'EDZEHOO.SmallJobs_table');
        DBMS_AQADM.START_QUEUE(queue_name=>'EDZEHOO.SmallJobs');
END;
/
```

You must now create the .NET class that represents this UDT object you've created. Listing 9-9 does that for you. This class must inherit from the **INullable** and **IOracleCustomType** interfaces. Each field in the UDT object must be exposed as a property in this class. You must use the **[OracleObjectMappingAttribute("FieldName")]** directive to tell ODP.NET how to map each property to its represented UDT field. The **ToCustomObject** and **FromCustomObject** interface methods allow you to define how the UDT object in the database is read into your UDT class, and vice versa.

*Listing 9-9. Defining the UDT Class*

```
using System;
using System.Text;
using Oracle.DataAccess.Client;
using Oracle.DataAccess.Types;

public class JobClass : INullable, IOracleCustomType
{
        private bool _isNull;
        private int _jobPrice;
        private string _jobDescription;
        private string _jobID;
        private string _jobName;

        public virtual bool IsNull
        {
                get
                {
                        return _isNull;
                }
        }

        [OracleObjectMappingAttribute("JOBPRICE")]
        public int JobPrice
        {
                get
                {
```

```csharp
                    return _jobPrice;
        }
        set
        {
                    _jobPrice = value;
        }
}

[OracleObjectMappingAttribute("JOBNAME")]
public string JobName
{
        get
        {
                    return _jobName;
        }
        set
        {
                    _jobName = value;
        }
}

[OracleObjectMappingAttribute("JOBID")]
public string JobID
{
        get
        {
                    return _jobID;
        }
        set
        {
                    _jobID = value;
        }
}

[OracleObjectMappingAttribute("JOBDESCRIPTION")]
public string JobDescription
{
        get
        {
                    return _jobDescription;
        }
        set
        {
                    _jobDescription = value;
        }
}

// IOracleCustomType.FromCustomObject() implementation
// Writes a JobClass object into the JOBS_TYPE Oracle UDT
public virtual void FromCustomObject(OracleConnection con, IntPtr pUdt)
{
        if (_jobID != null)
```

```
        {
                OracleUdt.SetValue(con, pUdt, "JOBID", _jobID);
        }
        if (_jobName != null)
        {
                OracleUdt.SetValue(con, pUdt, "JOBNAME", _jobName);
        }
        if (_jobPrice != null)
        {
                OracleUdt.SetValue(con, pUdt, "JOBPRICE", _jobPrice);
        }
        if (_jobDescription != null)
        {
                OracleUdt.SetValue(con, pUdt, "JOBDESCRIPTION", _jobDescription);
        }
    }

    // IOracleCustomType.ToCustomObject() implementation
    // Writes a JOBS_TYPE Oracle UDT into a JobClass object
    public virtual void ToCustomObject(OracleConnection con, IntPtr pUdt)
    {
            _jobID = (string) OracleUdt.GetValue(con, pUdt, "JOBID");
            _jobName = (string)OracleUdt.GetValue(con, pUdt, "JOBNAME");
            _jobDescription = (string)OracleUdt.GetValue(con, pUdt, "JOBDESCRIPTION");
            _jobPrice = (int)OracleUdt.GetValue(con, pUdt, "JOBPRICE");
    }

    // Prints out a summary of the job record this object represents
    public override string ToString()
    {
            return "Job ID : " + _jobID + "\n"
                    + "Job Name : " + _jobName + "\n"
                    + "Job Description : " + _jobDescription + "\n"
                    + "Job Price : " + _jobPrice;
    }
}
```

The next step is to create the factory class that generates instances of your **JobClass** class. Here's the code to write:

```
//JobClass factory class
[OracleCustomTypeMappingAttribute("EDZEHOO.JOBS_TYPE")]
public class OrderFactory : IOracleCustomTypeFactory
{
        // Implementation of IOracleCustomTypeFactory.CreateObject()
        public IOracleCustomType CreateObject()
        {
                return new JobClass();
        }
}
```

Finally, with that out of the way, you can now write the code shown in Listing 9-10 for your enqueue function. The payload this time is an instance of your UDT class.

*Listing 9-10. Enqueuing a UDT Object*

```
private void btnEnqueueUDT_Click(object sender, EventArgs e)
{
        string _connstring = "Data Source=localhost/NEWDB;User
            Id=EDZEHOO;Password=PASS123;";
        try
        {

                OracleConnection _connObj = new OracleConnection(_connstring);

                // Create a new queue object
                OracleAQQueue _queueObj = new OracleAQQueue("EDZEHOO.SmallJobs", _connObj);
                _connObj.Open();
                OracleTransaction _txn = _connObj.BeginTransaction();

                // Set the payload type to your UDT
                _queueObj.MessageType = OracleAQMessageType.Udt;
                _queueObj.UdtTypeName = "EDZEHOO.JOBS_TYPE";

                // Create a new message object
                OracleAQMessage _msg = new OracleAQMessage();

                // Create an instance of JobClass and pass it in as the payload for the
                // message
                JobClass _job = new JobClass();
                _job.JobID = "J1234";
                _job.JobName = "Feed Snuppy";
                _job.JobPrice = 15;
                _job.JobDescription = "Feed Rice Crispies twice a day";
                _msg.Payload = _job;

                // Enqueue the message
                _queueObj.EnqueueOptions.Visibility = OracleAQVisibilityMode.OnCommit;
                _queueObj.Enqueue(_msg);

                // Display the payload data that was enqueued
                MessageBox.Show("Payload Data : " + _job.ToString());
                _txn.Commit();

                _queueObj.Dispose();
                _connObj.Close();
                _connObj.Dispose();
                _connObj = null;
        }
        catch (Exception ex)
        {
                MessageBox.Show(ex.ToString());
        }
}
```

The code for the dequeue function follows in Listing 9-11. You can dequeue directly into an instance of your UDT class.

*Listing 9-11. Dequeuing a UDT Object*

```
private void btnDequeueUDT_Click(object sender, EventArgs e)
{
        string _connstring = "Data Source=localhost/NEWDB;User
                Id=EDZEHOO;Password=PASS123;";
        try
        {
                OracleConnection _connObj = new OracleConnection(_connstring);

                // Create a new queue object
                OracleAQQueue _queueObj = new OracleAQQueue("EDZEHOO.SmallJobs", _connObj);

                // Set the payload type to your UDT
                _queueObj.MessageType = OracleAQMessageType.Udt;
                _queueObj.UdtTypeName = "EDZEHOO.JOBS_TYPE";

                _connObj.Open();
                OracleTransaction _txn = _connObj.BeginTransaction();

                // Dequeue the message.
                _queueObj.DequeueOptions.Visibility = OracleAQVisibilityMode.OnCommit;
                _queueObj.DequeueOptions.Wait = 10;
                OracleAQMessage _deqMsg = _queueObj.Dequeue();
                JobClass _Data = (JobClass)_deqMsg.Payload;
                MessageBox.Show(_Data.ToString ());

                _txn.Commit();
                _queueObj.Dispose();
                _connObj.Close();
                _connObj.Dispose();
                _connObj = null;
        }
        catch (Exception ex)
        {
                MessageBox.Show(ex.ToString());
        }
}
```

If you run the code samples from the previous two listings, you will see the pop-up shown in Figure 9-4 displayed when you perform the dequeue.

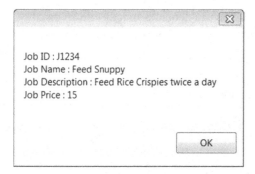

**Figure 9-4.** *Dequeued UDT object*

## Using XML Data Types

Now, let's turn to **XML** data types. You will need to define a new queue (via SQL*Plus) with the payload type set to **SYS.XMLType**, for example:

```
BEGIN
        DBMS_AQADM.CREATE_QUEUE_TABLE(
                queue_table=>'EDZEHOO.JobsXML_table',
                queue_payload_type=>'SYS.XMLType',
                multiple_consumers=>FALSE);

        DBMS_AQADM.CREATE_QUEUE(
                queue_name=>'EDZEHOO.JobsXML',
                queue_table=>'EDZEHOO.JobsXML_table');

        DBMS_AQADM.START_QUEUE(queue_name=>'EDZEHOO.JobsXML');
END;
/
```

The enqueue function for XML data follows in Listing 9-12. ODP.NET provides the **OracleXmlType** class, which you must use to encapsulate the raw XML data you wish to send.

*Listing 9-12. Enqueuing XML Data*

```
private void btnEnqueueXML_Click(object sender, EventArgs e)
{
        string _connstring = "Data Source=localhost/NEWDB;User
                Id=EDZEHOO;Password=PASS123;";
        try
        {
                OracleConnection _connObj = new OracleConnection(_connstring);

                // Create a new queue object
                OracleAQQueue _queueObj = new OracleAQQueue("EDZEHOO.JobsXML", _connObj);
```

```
        _connObj.Open();
        OracleTransaction _txn = _connObj.BeginTransaction();

        // Set payload type to XML
        _queueObj.MessageType = OracleAQMessageType.Xml;

        // Create a new message object
        OracleAQMessage _msg = new OracleAQMessage();
        OracleXmlType _jobXML = new OracleXmlType(_connObj ,
                "<JOB><JOBID>J1234</JOBID><JOBNAME>Feed Snuppy</JOBNAME></JOB>");
        _msg.Payload = _jobXML;

        // Enqueue the message
        _queueObj.EnqueueOptions.Visibility = OracleAQVisibilityMode.OnCommit;
        _queueObj.Enqueue(_msg);

        // Display the payload data that was enqueued
        MessageBox.Show("Payload Data : \n" + _jobXML.Value);
        _txn.Commit();

        _queueObj.Dispose();
        _connObj.Close();
        _connObj.Dispose();
        _connObj = null;
    }
    catch (Exception ex)
    {
        MessageBox.Show(ex.ToString());
    }
}
```

To dequeue the message, write the code in Listing 9-13. You can access the XML data (as a **String**) via the **OracleXmlType.Value** property.

*Listing 9-13. Dequeuing XML Data*

```
private void btnDequeueXML_Click(object sender, EventArgs e)
{
        string _connstring = "Data Source=localhost/NEWDB;User
            Id=EDZEHOO;Password=PASS123;";
        try
        {
                OracleConnection _connObj = new OracleConnection(_connstring);

                // Create a new queue object
                OracleAQQueue _queueObj = new OracleAQQueue("EDZEHOO.JobsXML", _connObj);

                // Set the payload type to XML
                _queueObj.MessageType = OracleAQMessageType.Xml;

                _connObj.Open();
```

```
OracleTransaction _txn = _connObj.BeginTransaction();

// Dequeue the message.
_queueObj.DequeueOptions.Visibility = OracleAQVisibilityMode.OnCommit;
_queueObj.DequeueOptions.Wait = 10;
_queueObj.DequeueOptions.ProviderSpecificType = true;

OracleAQMessage _deqMsg = _queueObj.Dequeue();
OracleXmlType _jobXML = (OracleXmlType)_deqMsg.Payload;
MessageBox.Show("Dequeued Payload Data: \n" + _jobXML.Value);

_txn.Commit();
_queueObj.Dispose();
_connObj.Close();
_connObj.Dispose();
_connObj = null;
}
catch (Exception ex)
{
MessageBox.Show(ex.ToString());
}
}
```

If you run the code sample from Listing 9-13, you will see the pop-up shown in Figure 9-5.

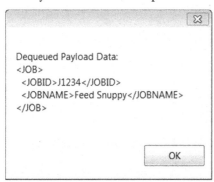

**Figure 9-5.** *Dequeued XML data*

# Waiting for Incoming Messages

So far, you have been manually retrieving messages from queues. You retrieve a message by clicking the Dequeue button, because you know there's a message in the queue. But when your application goes live, how does it know if there's something in the queue? There are two approaches to take:

- Do a synchronous (blocking) call that waits for an incoming message.

- Get notified via an asynchronous callback function when there is an incoming message.

# Dequeuing Messages Synchronously (Blocking)

You can get your code to wait indefinitely for an incoming message by calling the `OracleAQQueue.Listen` method. This function does not return until a message is detected in the queue. The code to do this follows in Listing 9-14.

*Listing 9-14. Listening for Incoming Messages*

```
private void btnStartListener_Click(object sender, EventArgs e)
{
        string _connstring = "Data Source=localhost/NEWDB;User
                Id=EDZEHOO;Password=PASS123;";
        try
        {
                OracleConnection _connObj = new OracleConnection(_connstring);

                // Create a new queue object
                OracleAQQueue _queueObj = new OracleAQQueue("EDZEHOO.MY_JOBS_QUEUE",
                        _connObj);
                _connObj.Open();

                // The Listen function is a blocking call - it will wait
                // indefinitely until a message is received.
                _queueObj.Listen(null);

                // Once we're here this means a message has been detected in the queue.
                // We can now proceed to dequeue that message
                OracleTransaction _txn = _connObj.BeginTransaction();

                // Dequeue the message.
                _queueObj.DequeueOptions.Visibility = OracleAQVisibilityMode.OnCommit;
                _queueObj.DequeueOptions.Wait = 10;
                OracleAQMessage _deqMsg = _queueObj.Dequeue();

                MessageBox.Show("Dequeued Payload Data: " +
                            ConvertFromByteArray((byte[])_deqMsg.Payload) + "\n"
                        + "Dequeued Payload Hex: " +
                            ConvertToHexString((byte[])_deqMsg.Payload) + "\n"
                        + "Message ID of Dequeued Payload : " +
                            ConvertToHexString(_deqMsg.MessageId) + "\n" +
                             "Correlation : " + _deqMsg.Correlation);

                _txn.Commit();
                _queueObj.Dispose();
                _connObj.Close();
                _connObj.Dispose();
                _connObj = null;
        }
        catch (Exception ex)
        {
```

```
                            MessageBox.Show(ex.ToString());
          }
}
```

The **OracleAQQueue.Listen** method may choke up your UI, since it is a blocking call. To test this, run two instances of your application, so that you could set one instance to listen indefinitely for messages and then run an enqueue on the second instance. You will find that the moment you've enqueued a message via the second instance, the listening instance would return immediately from the blocking call. The dequeued message is then subsequently displayed.

Although the use of (nonblocking) asynchronous notifications would seem to be useful for most applications, synchronous notifications might make development easier sometimes. Take, for example, an application that needs to wait for a particular sequence of messages to arrive before it can do something. This would be easier to set up by just calling the **Listen** method a specified consecutive number of times, rather than setting up callback functions (where you must then worry about sorting the messages that come through the callback).

---

■ **Tip** You can prevent the UI from choking every time you call the blocking **OracleAQQueue.Listen** method by placing it inside a thread.

---

## Dequeuing Messages Asynchronously (Nonblocking)

As I highlighted in the previous chapter, notifications are useful by nature because they adopt a push approach rather than a pull approach. You can also be automatically notified by callback when a message arrives at a particular queue. Listing 9-15 shows some code that implements this nonblocking approach to dequeuing. For the enqueue functionality, you can reuse the code from the **btnEnqueue_Click** button in Listing 9-1.

*Listing 9-15. Registering an Asynchronous Callback*

```
private static bool _notified = false;
private void btnDequeueNotification_Click(object sender, EventArgs e)
{
        string _connstring = "Data Source=localhost/NEWDB;User
                Id=EDZEHOO;Password=PASS123;";
        try
        {
                OracleConnection _connObj = new OracleConnection(_connstring);

                // Create a new queue object
                OracleAQQueue _queueObj = new OracleAQQueue("EDZEHOO.MY_JOBS_QUEUE",
                        _connObj);
                _connObj.Open();
                OracleTransaction _txn = _connObj.BeginTransaction();

                _queueObj.DequeueOptions.Visibility = OracleAQVisibilityMode.OnCommit;
                _queueObj.DequeueOptions.Wait = 10;
```

```
//Register the callback function
_queueObj.MessageAvailable += new
        OracleAQMessageAvailableEventHandler(IncomingMessageCallback);

_txn.Commit();

MessageBox.Show("Notification registered. Entering loop...");

// Loop while waiting for notification
while (_notified == false)
{
    System.Threading.Thread.Sleep(2000);
}

_queueObj.Dispose();
_connObj.Close();
_connObj.Dispose();
_connObj = null;
}
catch (Exception ex)
{
    MessageBox.Show(ex.ToString());
}
}
```

Listing 9-16 shows the code for the callback function. You can retrieve a myriad of information about the incoming message via the **OracleAQMessageAvailableEventArgs** object.

*Listing 9-16. The Callback Function*

```
static void IncomingMessageCallback(object src, OracleAQMessageAvailableEventAr↵
gs arg)
{
    try
    {
        MessageBox.Show("Notification Received...\n" +
                "QueueName : " + arg.QueueName + "\n" +
                "Notification Type : " + arg.NotificationType);
        _notified = true;
    }
    catch (Exception e)
    {
        MessageBox.Show("Error : " + e.ToString());
    }
}
```

To test asynchronous dequeuing, launch two instances of the same application (just like you did earlier for the synchronous example). Click the Dequeue Notification button in the first instance to register the callback. After that, click the Enqueue button in the second instance. You will find that the message in the callback function is immediately displayed, as shown in Figure 9-6.

**Figure 9-6.** *Callback function message box*

# Understanding the Useful OracleAQMessage Properties

Several properties of the **OracleAQMessage** class are worth a look. They give you control over how messages are stored and delivered. Table 9-3 summarizes some of the useful properties of this class.

**Table 9-3.** *Miscellaneous Properties of the OracleAQMessage Class*

| Property Name | What It Represents |
| --- | --- |
| Delay | This specifies the delay (in seconds) between an enqueue and a subsequent dequeue attempt, which allows the developer to delay immediate consumption of an enqueued message. |
| DeliveryMode | This specifies the delivery mode of the message and can take one of two different values: buffered or persistent. Buffered delivery, a new feature in Oracle Streams AQ 10.2, allows messages to be stored in a shared memory are, making it faster than persistent delivery (which stores messages in the database). The downside to using buffered delivery is that messages stored in this memory area would be lost if the server shutdown unexpectedly. Persistent delivery is more reliable but performs slower. |
| DequeueAttempts | This property returns the number of attempts at dequeuing a particular message. |

| EnqueueTime | This property specifies the time the message was enqueued. |
|---|---|
| ExceptionQueue | This specifies the name of a queue that a message will be automatically moved to if either one of the following conditions are met: the message has expired, or the number of unsuccessful dequeue attempts exceeds the **max_retries** counter configured for the queue. |
| Expiration | This property specifies the duration (in seconds) that a message will remain enqueued in a queue. |
| Priority | This specifies the priority of a message (with smaller numbers representing higher priority). It is used when dequeuing messages based on priority. |

# Summary

In this chapter, you've taken a look at the following:

- Using DDL statements to create a queue

- Using the **OracleAQQueue** and **OracleAQMessage** classes to enqueue and dequeue messages to and from a queue

- Enqueuing messages with **RAW**, **XML**, and **UDT** data types

- Using the **OracleAQQueue.Listen** method to wait for messages synchronously

- Implementing an asynchronous callback function with **OracleAQQueue**'s automatic notification capability

In the next chapter, you'll learn how Oracle natively handles XML data types and the various functions provided by ODP.NET to manipulate XML data.

251

■ ■ ■

# CHAPTER 10

# Oracle XML Support

XML, short for Extensible Markup Language has become one of the most widely used formats in the business world to represent data since it was first published by the World Wide Web Consortium (W3C) in 1996. XML provides a representation for semistructured data that is human readable and platform independent yet flexible enough to overcome the rigidity of two-dimensional data representation models (such as the standard relational databases we all know today).

To get an idea of how XML can be effectively used, consider the following example, which captures the details of a purchase order in a structured fashion and is highly portable to other systems:

```
<PurchaseOrder PoNumber="PO0001">
    <InitiatedBy>Preston Cole</InitiatedBy>
    <DateIssued>25 Dec 2009</DateIssued>
    <Supplier>
        <Name>ACME Ammunition Co.</Name>
        <Address>
                <Street>20 Depot Road</Street>
                <City>Singapore</City>
                <State>NA</State>
                <Postcode>806110</Postcode>
        </Address>
    </Supplier>
    <PODetails>
        <Item>
                <Name>M5 Minigun</Name>
                <UnitPrice>50.00</UnitPrice>
                <Qty>20</Qty>
        </Item>
        <Item>
                <Name>Frag Grenade</Name>
                <UnitPrice>8.00</UnitPrice>
                <Qty>10</Qty>
        </Item>
    </PODetails>
</PurchaseOrder>
```

If you tried to represent the same thing using a relational database, you would need three separate tables, one each to store the purchase order, purchase order details, and supplier details respectively. On top of that, you would have to define the join relationships between these tables and maintain a set of indices and a set of data constraints to ensure data integrity.

Life can be made simpler when dealing with XML data, and your application can be made to perform faster by storing data as XML natively in the database. The Oracle database provides support for native XML data storage. In addition, it even allows you to generate XML from relational record sets. ODP.NET allows you to access these features from within your .NET applications. In this chapter, you will learn how to:

- Retrieve and manipulate native XML data (stored in **XMLTYPE** columns) in the Oracle database

- Pass XML data to and from PL/SQL stored procedures

- Use XSLT to transform raw XML data from one schema to another

- Retrieve and manipulate relational data using XML

- Use XQuery to perform XML-aware search in the database

# Accessing Native XML Data (XMLTYPE)

The **XMLTYPE** data type is an Oracle data type that stores XML data natively in the database. **XMLTYPE** is essentially made out of a **CLOB**, so it has a large size limit, allowing you to store a large amount of XML data in it.

Storing data objects natively as XML is a good idea if you don't expect the individual constituents of that data object to be reused in any way. For instance, in the purchase order example introduced earlier, the purchase order details will always be retrieved together with their master Purchase Order record – there is hardly any use of retrieving just the purchase order details on their own. However, consider another scenario where you have a customer, and each customer has **1:many** invoices. You might be tempted to store this relationship (one record for each customer) in the database as follows:

```
<Customer Name='ABC Co.'>
        <Invoice ID='Inv001'>
        .
        .
        </Invoice>
        <Invoice ID='Inv002'>
        .
        .
        </Invoice>
</Customer>
```

In such a case, using XML may not be advisable, since at some point in your application, you will likely need to pull out the list of available invoices across all customers.

When done in the right context, storing an entire business object whole in XML can yield better performance than if you were to represent it using separate relational tables. In the sections to follow, you will explore how to manipulate **XMLTYPE** data using three different objects: Microsoft's **System.Xml.XmlReader** class, ODP.NET's **OracleXmlType** class, and last but not least, ODP.NET's **OracleString** class.

## Creating an XMLTYPE Column

Before you proceed to those sections, let's create a new table that contains an **XMLTYPE** column and insert some test data. This table, **Product_ExtraInfo**, will contain additional information about a product such as the category it belongs to, the person in charge, and pricing information for different regions. You can do this by running the following statements in SQL*Plus:

```
CREATE TABLE "EDZEHOO"."PRODUCT_EXTRAINFO" (
"ID" VARCHAR2(10) NOT NULL,
"INFO" XMLTYPE,
CONSTRAINT "EXTRAINFO_PRIMKEY" PRIMARY KEY ("ID") VALIDATE);

INSERT INTO PRODUCT_EXTRAINFO (ID, INFO)
VALUES('E1','<PRODUCT><CATEGORY>Engines</CATEGORY>
<PERSON_IN_CHARGE>Johnson Adams</PERSON_IN_CHARGE>
<REGIONAL_PRICING><EASTASIA>45.00</EASTASIA><AMERICAS>20.00</AMERICAS>
</REGIONAL_PRICING></PRODUCT>');

INSERT INTO PRODUCT_EXTRAINFO (ID, INFO)
VALUES('R1','<PRODUCT><CATEGORY>Lamps</CATEGORY>
<PERSON_IN_CHARGE>Kathy Wick</PERSON_IN_CHARGE>
<REGIONAL_PRICING><EASTASIA>50.00</EASTASIA><AMERICAS>15.00</AMERICAS>
</REGIONAL_PRICING></PRODUCT>');
```

## Receiving XMLTYPE Data with XMLReader

The **XMLReader** class belongs to **System.Xml** namespace in the .NET Framework. You can use the **GetXmlReader** method of the **OracleDataReader** object to read a column in a table using the **XMLReader** class, as shown in the following code:

```
string _sql = "SELECT INFO FROM PRODUCT_EXTRAINFO";
OracleCommand _cmdObj = new OracleCommand(_sql, _connObj);
OracleDataReader _rdrObj = _cmdObj.ExecuteReader ();
XmlReader _xmlRdr = _rdrObj.GetXmlReader(_rdrObj.GetOrdinal("INFO"));
```

To iterate through the elements of the XML and individually retrieve its values, you will need to use an **XMLDocument** object (which also belongs to the **System.Xml** namespace). You can do this using the following code:

```
XmlDocument _xmlDoc = new XmlDocument();
_xmlDoc.Load(_xmlRdr);
```

Let's take a look at the full example in code. You will attempt to read an **XMLTYPE** column into an **XmlReader** object, pass that into an **XMLDocument** object to retrieve each individual element, and finally, display them in a pop-up message box. Create a new form, and place a button on it. In the click event of that button, write the code shown in Listing 10-1.

*Listing 10-1. Using the XmlReader Class*

```
private void btnXMLReader_Click(object sender, EventArgs e)
{
        string _connstring = "Data Source=localhost/NEWDB;User
            Id=EDZEHOO;Password=PASS123;";
```

```
try
{
        OracleConnection _connObj = new OracleConnection(_connstring);
        _connObj.Open();
        string _sql = "SELECT INFO FROM PRODUCT_EXTRAINFO";
        OracleCommand _cmdObj = new OracleCommand(_sql, _connObj);
        OracleDataReader _rdrObj = _cmdObj.ExecuteReader ();
        if (_rdrObj.HasRows) {
        while (_rdrObj.Read())
        {
                String _message ="";
                String _regionalprices="";
                XmlReader _xmlRdr = _rdrObj.GetXmlReader
                        (_rdrObj.GetOrdinal("INFO"));

                //Now that we have an XMLReader object, we create an XMLDocument
                //object so that we can manipulate its elements
                XmlDocument _xmlDoc = new XmlDocument();
                _xmlDoc.Load(_xmlRdr);
                XmlNode _xmlRoot = _xmlDoc.FirstChild;
                XmlNode _xmlCategory = _xmlRoot.SelectSingleNode("CATEGORY");
                XmlNode _xmlPerson = _xmlRoot.SelectSingleNode
                        ("PERSON_IN_CHARGE");
                XmlNode _xmlRegionalPricing = _xmlRoot.SelectSingleNode
                        ("REGIONAL_PRICING");
                for (int i = 0; i < _xmlRegionalPricing.ChildNodes.Count; i++)
                {
                        XmlNode _xmlRegion = _xmlRegionalPricing.ChildNodes.Item(i);
                        if (_regionalprices.Length > 0) _regionalprices += ",";
                        _regionalprices += _xmlRegion.Name + " : " +
                                _xmlRegion.InnerText;
                }
                _message = "Category name:\t" + _xmlCategory.InnerText + "\n" +
                        "Person in charge:\t" + _xmlPerson.InnerText + "\n" +
                        "Regional Pricing:\t" + _regionalprices + "\n" +
                        "Raw XML:\n" + _xmlDoc.OuterXml;
                MessageBox.Show(_message);
        }
        }
        _rdrObj.Close();
        _connObj.Close();
        _connObj.Dispose();
        _connObj = null;
}
catch (Exception ex)
{
        MessageBox.Show(ex.ToString());
}
}
```

If you run this code sample, you will see the message box shown in Figure 10-1 displaying the retrieved values of the individual XML elements.

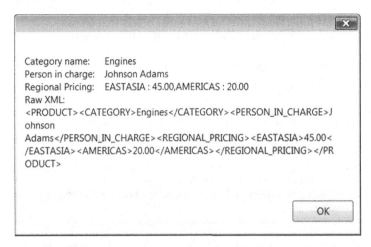

*Figure 10-1. Individual XML elements of an XML*

## Receiving XMLTYPE Data with OracleXMLType

You can also use ODP.NET's **OracleXmlType** class to receive data from an **XMLTYPE** column. In much the same way, you start off with an **OracleDataReader** object and then use its **GetOracleXmlType** method to return an **OracleXmlType** object.

```
string _sql = "SELECT INFO FROM PRODUCT_EXTRAINFO";
OracleCommand _cmdObj = new OracleCommand(_sql, _connObj);
OracleDataReader _rdrObj = _cmdObj.ExecuteReader ();
OracleXmlType _oracleXmlType = _rdrObj.GetOracleXmlType(_rdrObj.GetOrdinal("INFO"));
```

The **OracleXmlType** class contains a set of useful methods, such as the ability to extract individual elements from the XML without the need to create an **XMLDocument** object, or to check if an element is present in the XML. Let's take a look at some of these functions in Table 10-1.

*Table 10-1. Useful Methods and Properties in the OracleXmlType Class*

| Method/Property Definition | Description |
| --- | --- |
| IsExists(xpathExpr, nsMap) | This function takes in an XPath expression (and namespace) and checks if the requested element exists. For example, you could run **IsExists("/PRODUCT/CATEGORY", null)** to check if the **CATEGORY** element was present in the XML. |
| IsEmpty | This property returns **true** or **false** and indicates |

|  |  |
|---|---|
|  | whether the current **OracleXmlType** object holds any data. |
| GetXmlReader() | This function returns an **XMLReader** object that allows you to read a stream of XML from the **XMLTYPE** column. |
| GetXMLDocument() | This function returns an **XMLDocument** object directly that allows you to access and manipulate individual elements in the XML |
| Extract(xpathExpr, nsMap) | This function extracts the element specified by the XPath expression. The extracted element is returned in a new **OracleXmlType** object. |
| Update(xpathExpr, nsMap, Value) | This function updates the element specified by the XPath expression with a new **OracleXmlType** or **String** value. |

Let's take a look at some of these functions in action. In Listing 10-2, you will attempt to read the **XMLTYPE** data into an **OracleXmlType** object, extract the **CATEGORY** element of each product and display it alongside the full raw XML.

*Listing 10-2. Using the OracleXmlType Class*

```
private void btnOracleXMLType_Click(object sender, EventArgs e)
{
        string _connstring = "Data Source=localhost/NEWDB;User
                Id=EDZEHOO;Password=PASS123;";
        try
        {
                OracleConnection _connObj = new OracleConnection(_connstring);
                _connObj.Open();
                string _sql = "SELECT INFO FROM PRODUCT_EXTRAINFO";
                string _message="";
                OracleCommand _cmdObj = new OracleCommand(_sql, _connObj);
                OracleDataReader _rdrObj = _cmdObj.ExecuteReader();
                if (_rdrObj.HasRows)
                {
                        while (_rdrObj.Read())
                        {
                                OracleXmlType _oracleXmlType = _rdrObj.GetOracleXmlType
                                        (_rdrObj.GetOrdinal("INFO"));
                                if (!_oracleXmlType.IsNull)
                                {
                                        string _xPath = "/PRODUCT/CATEGORY";
                                        string _nsMap = null;
                                        if (_oracleXmlType.IsExists(_xPath, _nsMap))
                                        {
                                                OracleXmlType _oracleXmlTypeNode =
```

```
                                        _oracleXmlType.Extract(_xPath,
                                           _nsMap);
                                if (!_oracleXmlTypeNode.IsEmpty)
                                {
                                        _message = "Category tag:\t" +
                                                _oracleXmlTypeNode.Value;
                                }
                        }
                        _message += "Raw XML:\n" + _oracleXmlType.Value;
                        MessageBox.Show(_message);
                    }
                }
            }
            _rdrObj.Close();
            _connObj.Close();
            _connObj.Dispose();
            _connObj = null;
        }
        catch (Exception ex)
        {
            MessageBox.Show(ex.ToString());
        }
    }
}
```

Running the code in Listing 10-2 would yield the message box display shown in Figure 10-2.

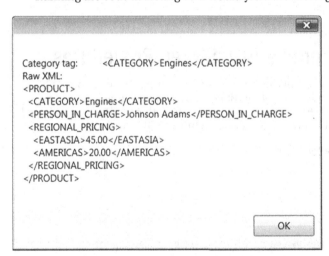

*Figure 10-2.* A tag extracted using the OracleXmlType Extract method

## Receiving XMLTYPE Data as a String

If all you need is to read data from the **XMLTYPE** column and output it somewhere without parsing or checking its individual elements, you can also choose to retrieve it as a flat string object. The code to do this is relatively simple: just use the **GetOracleString** function instead of the **GetXmlReader** or **GetOracleXmlType** functions. This will return you an **OracleString** object, as illustrated below in Listing 10-3.

*Listing 10-3. Retrieving XMLTYPE Data as an OracleString*

```
string _sql = "SELECT INFO FROM PRODUCT_EXTRAINFO";
OracleCommand _cmdObj = new OracleCommand(_sql, _connObj);
OracleDataReader _rdrObj = _cmdObj.ExecuteReader();
if (_rdrObj.HasRows)
{
        while (_rdrObj.Read())
        {
                OracleString _oracleStrRdr =
                        _rdrObj.GetOracleString(_rdrObj.GetOrdinal("INFO"));
                if (!_oracleStrRdr.IsNull)
                {
                        MessageBox.Show(_oracleStrRdr.Value);
                }
        }
}
```

# Passing XML Data to and from PL/SQL Stored Procedures

If you use **XMLTYPE** columns in your database, you will (sooner or later) encounter the need to pass XML data to and from PL/SQL stored procedures. You can declare **XMLTYPE** data types as input, output, or return parameters just like any other data type. Before you try out the code in this section, you will need to create the relevant stored procedures first by running these statements in SQL*Plus:

```
CREATE OR REPLACE PROCEDURE proc_GetProdInfo
(
        ProductID IN VARCHAR2,
        xmlProductInfo OUT XMLTYPE
)
IS
BEGIN
        SELECT INFO INTO xmlProductInfo FROM Product_ExtraInfo WHERE ID=ProductID;
END;
/

CREATE OR REPLACE PROCEDURE proc_InsertProdInfo
(
        ProductID IN VARCHAR2,
        xmlProductInfo IN XMLTYPE
)
```

```
IS
BEGIN
        INSERT INTO Product_ExtraInfo(ID, INFO) VALUES(ProductID,xmlProductInfo);
END;
/
```

You can pass XML data around by encapsulating it in the **OracleXmlType** class. For example, you can retrieve XML from a stored procedure by declaring an output parameter and setting its type to **OracleDbType.XmlType**. This is illustrated in Listing 10-4.

*Listing 10-4. Retrieving XML from a Stored Procedure*

```
private void btnGetProductInfo_Click(object sender, EventArgs e)
{
        string _connstring = "Data Source=localhost/NEWDB;User
            Id=EDZEHOO;Password=PASS123;";
        try
        {
                OracleConnection _connObj = new OracleConnection(_connstring);
                _connObj.Open();
                OracleCommand _cmdObj = new OracleCommand("proc_GetProdInfo", _connObj);
                _cmdObj.CommandType = CommandType.StoredProcedure;

                //Define the first parameter - we want to retrieve the XML info for the
                //product with the ID "E1"
                OracleParameter _ProductIDParam = new OracleParameter("ProductID",
                        OracleDbType.Varchar2);
                _ProductIDParam.Value = "E1";
                _cmdObj.Parameters.Add(_ProductIDParam);

                //Define the output parameter that receives the XMLType data
                OracleParameter _ProductInfoParam = new OracleParameter("ProductInfo",
                        OracleDbType.XmlType);
                _ProductInfoParam.Direction = ParameterDirection.Output;
                _cmdObj.Parameters.Add(_ProductInfoParam);
                _cmdObj.ExecuteNonQuery();
                OracleXmlType _returnValue = (OracleXmlType)_ProductInfoParam.Value;
                MessageBox.Show(_returnValue.Value);

                _connObj.Close();
                _connObj.Dispose();
                _connObj = null;
        }
        catch (Exception ex)
        {
                MessageBox.Show(ex.ToString());
        }
}
```

You can also send XML in the opposite direction the same way. This is illustrated in Listing 10-5.

*Listing 10-5. Passing XML into a Stored Procedure*

```
private void btnInsertProdInfo_Click(object sender, EventArgs e)
{
        string _connstring = "Data Source=localhost/NEWDB;User
                Id=EDZEHOO;Password=PASS123;";
        try
        {
                OracleConnection _connObj = new OracleConnection(_connstring);
                _connObj.Open();
                OracleCommand _cmdObj = new OracleCommand("proc_InsertProdInfo", _connObj);
                _cmdObj.CommandType = CommandType.StoredProcedure;

                //Define first input parameter
                OracleParameter _ProductIDParam = new OracleParameter("ProductID",
                        OracleDbType.Varchar2);
                _ProductIDParam.Value = "W1";
                _cmdObj.Parameters.Add(_ProductIDParam);

                //Define the second input parameter
                OracleParameter _ProductInfoParam = new OracleParameter("ProductInfo",
                        OracleDbType.XmlType);
                OracleXmlType _ProductInfoXML = new OracleXmlType(_connObj,
                        "<PRODUCT><CATEGORY>Accessories</CATEGORY><PERSON_IN_CHARGE>Mary
                        Sabbath</PERSON_IN_CHARGE><REGIONAL_PRICING><EASTASIA>3.00
                        </EASTASIA><AMERICAS>8.00</AMERICAS></REGIONAL_PRICING></PRODUCT>");
                _ProductInfoParam.Value = _ProductInfoXML;
                _cmdObj.Parameters.Add(_ProductInfoParam);

                _cmdObj.ExecuteNonQuery();
                _connObj.Close();
                _connObj.Dispose();
                _connObj = null;
                MessageBox.Show("Product inserted");
        }
        catch (Exception ex)
        {
                MessageBox.Show(ex.ToString());
        }
}
```

# Validating Against XML Schema

XML represents not just data but also schema (the structure of the data). However, the Oracle database does not automatically check the validity of incoming XML that you store in a column. The responsibility of ensuring that a given XML document conforms to its schema falls to you. For instance, consider the following XML:

```
<FRUITS>
        <APPLE>
                <RETAIL_PRICE>5.50</RETAIL_PRICE >
                <WHOLESALER_PRICE>3.00</WHOLESALER_PRICE>
        </APPLE>
        <DURIAN>
                <RETAIL_PRICE>8.00</RETAIL_PRICE >
                <WHOLESALER_PRICE>4.50</WHOLESALER_PRICE>
        </DURIAN>
</FRUITS>
```

This XML doesn't just tell you the price of different fruits but also that each fruit is expected to have two different prices—retail and wholesale. If one of these fruits was missing a wholesale price, for example, the XML would be incorrect.

Oracle allows you to validate XML against a schema using the **OracleXmlType.Validate** function. This function validates XML data against a schema defined in the XML Schema Definition (XSD) format. A rough overview of how you can use this function follows:

1.  Create an XSD schema.

2.  Register the schema.

3.  Call the **OracleXmlType.Validate** function to validate all incoming XML.

Before you can register a schema with Oracle, you will need to grant some rights to your user account. Login as the SYSTEM account and run the following statements in SQL*Plus:

```
GRANT RESOURCE TO EDZEHOO;
GRANT ALTER SESSION TO EDZEHOO;
GRANT CREATE VIEW TO EDZEHOO;
```

After that, log in again under your own user account. You will now need to declare the XSD schema.

---

■ **Note** XSD is a schema language published by the World Wide Web Consortium (W3C) and is used to define a set of rules that an XML must conform to so that it can be considered valid. We will not cover the specifics and syntax of the XSD language in this book. For more information on XSD syntax, please visit http://www.w3.org/TR/xmlschema-0/.

---

Listing 10-6 defines a schema named **PRODUCT.xsd** that enforces a structure such that a **<PRODUCT>** tag must contain the **<CATEGORY>**, **<PERSON_IN_CHARGE>**, and **<REGIONAL_PRICING>** tags, and that **<EASTASIA>** and **<AMERICAS>** tag is a subtag of the **<REGIONAL_PRICING>** tag. After defining this schema, you will need to register it. You can do that using the **RegisterSchema** method in the **DBMS_XMLSCHEMA** PL/SQL package. We, therefore, place the entire operation in a single PL/SQL block that you can easily run off SQL*Plus:

*Listing 10-6. Defining and Registering an XSD Schema*

```
DECLARE
        SCHEMASTRING VARCHAR2(4000);
BEGIN
        SCHEMASTRING:= '<schema xmlns="http://www.w3.org/2001/XMLSchema" ' ||
                        'targetNamespace="PRODUCT.xsd" ' ||
                        'xmlns:PRODUCT="PRODUCT.xsd" ' ||
                        'xmlns:xdb="http://xmlns.oracle.com/xdb" ' ||
                        'elementFormDefault="qualified" version="1.0"> ' ||
                        '<complexType name = "PRODUCTTYPE"> ' ||
                        '<sequence> ' ||
                        '   <element name = "CATEGORY" type="string"/> ' ||
                        '   <element name = "PERSON_IN_CHARGE" type="string"/> ' ||
                        '   <element name = "REGIONAL_PRICING"> ' ||
                        '       <complexType>' ||
                        '           <sequence>' ||
                        '               <element name = "EASTASIA" type="float"/> ' ||
                        '               <element name = "AMERICAS" type="float"/> ' ||
                        '           </sequence>' ||
                        '       </complexType>' ||
                        '   </element>' ||
                        '</sequence> ' ||
                        '</complexType> ' ||
                        '<element name = "PRODUCT" type="PRODUCT:PRODUCTTYPE"/> ' ||
                        '</schema>';

        DBMS_XMLSCHEMA.RegisterSchema('PRODUCT.xsd', SCHEMASTRING, true, true, false);
END;
/
```

After running the PL/SQL block from Listing 10-6, you will see a "PL/SQL procedure successfully completed" message. For your additional reference, you can also unregister a schema using the following PL/SQL block (if you need to):

```
BEGIN
    dbms_xmlschema.DeleteSchema('PRODUCT.xsd', DBMS_XMLSCHEMA.DELETE_CASCADE);
END;
/
```

After you've registered the schema, you can refer to it from your .NET application at any time using the **OracleXmlType.Validate** function. You simply need to pass in the name of your schema (**PRODUCT.xsd**) as the sole argument to the **Validate** function. It will check the data held in the **OracleXmlType** object against this schema and return either a **true** (if it conforms to the schema) or **false**.

---

■ **Note** You have to make sure that the XML data being validated declares the XSD as its namespace (using the `xmlns` tag). If this is not done the `Validate` method will return false.

---

In Listing 10-7, we pass in a block of XML data to validate against the schema you have registered.

*Listing 10-7. Validating Against an XSD Schema*

```
private void btnValidateXML_Click(object sender, EventArgs e)
{
        string _connstring = "Data Source=localhost/NEWDB;User
            Id=EDZEHOO;Password=PASS123;";
        try
        {

            OracleConnection _connObj = new OracleConnection(_connstring);
            _connObj.Open();

            string _data = "";
            _data = "<PRODUCT xmlns=\"PRODUCT.xsd\">" +
                    "   <CATEGORY>Slipspace drives</CATEGORY>" +
                    "   <PERSON_IN_CHARGE>Fujikawa</PERSON_IN_CHARGE>" +
                    "   <REGIONAL_PRICING>" +
                    "       <EASTASIA>5000</EASTASIA>" +
                    "       <AMERICAS>8000</AMERICAS>" +
                    "   </REGIONAL_PRICING> " +
                    "</PRODUCT>";

            OracleXmlType _oracleXmlType = new OracleXmlType(_connObj, _data);
            MessageBox.Show("Validation result is : " +
                    _oracleXmlType.Validate("PRODUCT.xsd"));

            _connObj.Close();
            _connObj.Dispose();
            _connObj = null;
        }
        catch (Exception ex)
        {
            MessageBox.Show(ex.ToString());
        }
}
```

If you run the preceding code, you will notice that it first returns **true**, indicating that the XML data conforms to the schema. Now, try changing the XML data slightly; intentionally misspell or remove one of the tags (as highlighted in bold):

```
_data = "<PRODUCT xmlns=\"PRODUCT.xsd\">" +
        "   <CATEGORY_NAME>Slipspace drives</CATEGORY_NAME>" +
        "   <PERSON_IN_CHARGE>Fujikawa</PERSON_IN_CHARGE>" +
```

```
"    <REGIONAL_PRICING>" +
"        <EASTASIA>5000</EASTASIA>" +
"        <AMERICAS>8000</AMERICAS>" +
"    </REGIONAL_PRICING> " +
"</PRODUCT>";
```

Try running the same validation routine again. Although the XML is well formed and correct, its structure does not conform to the specified schema, and the **Validation** function ultimately returns **false**.

# Using XSLT to Transform XML Data

Extensible Stylesheet Language Transformations (XSLT) is yet another tool that you will need to be familiar with if you are going to manipulate XML data. XSLT is commonly used to transform the existing schema of an XML into a different one. For instance, let's consider your **PRODUCT** XML again:

```
<PRODUCT>
        <CATEGORY>Engines</CATEGORY>
        <PERSON_IN_CHARGE>John Malcolm</PERSON_IN_CHARGE>
        <REGIONAL_PRICING>
                <EASTASIA>45.00</EASTASIA>
                <AMERICAS>20.00</AMERICAS>
        </REGIONAL_PRICING>
</PRODUCT>
```

This is all fine and dandy, but what if you wanted your schema to look like the following instead (so that it could be exported to some other system, for example).

```
<ProductExtraInfo>
        <CategoryName>Engines</CategoryName>
        <EastAsianPrice>45.00</EastAsianPrice>
        <AmericaPrice>20.00</AmericaPrice>
</ProductExtraInfo >
```

You could either write code to iterate through the original XML using the **XMLDocument** class and then rebuild a new one element by element, or you could just use XSLT. XSLT allows you to define a set of mappings to convert the schema of an XML to a different one.

---

■ **Note** XSLT is published by the World Wide Web Consortium. We will not cover the specifics and syntax of XSLT in this book. For more information on XSLT, you can visit **http://www.w3.org/TR/xslt**.

---

The code in Listing 10-8 shows how you can define an XSL block to map the original tag names to a set of new ones and to also break the **<EASTASIA>** and **<AMERICAS>** tags out of the **<REGIONAL_PRICING>** tag. Notice that the **<PERSON_IN_CHARGE>** tag is intentionally left out; the transformed XML will not include this information. After you've defined your XSL block, you can use the **OracleXmlType.Transform** method to initiate the transform. You will, of course, need to pass in the XSL to use for the transformation. The full code to do this follows in Listing 10-8.

*Listing 10-8. Using XSLT to Transform the Schema of an XML Block*

```
private void btnTranslateXML_Click(object sender, EventArgs e)
{
        string _connstring = "Data Source=localhost/NEWDB;User
            Id=EDZEHOO;Password=PASS123;";
        try
        {
            OracleConnection _connObj = new OracleConnection(_connstring);
            _connObj.Open();
            string _sql = "SELECT INFO FROM PRODUCT_EXTRAINFO";
            OracleCommand _cmdObj = new OracleCommand(_sql, _connObj);
            OracleDataReader _rdrObj = _cmdObj.ExecuteReader();

            if (_rdrObj.HasRows)
            {
            while (_rdrObj.Read())
            {
                OracleXmlType _oracleXmlType =
                    _rdrObj.GetOracleXmlType(_rdrObj.GetOrdinal("INFO"));
                string _xsl;
                _xsl = "<?xml version=\"1.0\"?>" +
                    "<xsl:stylesheet version=\"1.0\" " +
                    "   xmlns:xsl=\"http://www.w3.org/1999/XSL/Transform\">" +
                    "   <xsl:template match=\"/\">" +
                    "       <ProductExtraInfo>" +
                    "           <xsl:apply-templates select=\"PRODUCT\"/>" +
                    "       </ProductExtraInfo>" +
                    "   </xsl:template>" +
                    "   <xsl:template match=\"PRODUCT\">" +
                    "       <xsl:apply-templates select=\"CATEGORY\"/>" +
                    "       <xsl:apply-templates select=\"REGIONAL_PRICING\"/>"+
                    "   </xsl:template>" +
                    "   <xsl:template match=\"CATEGORY\">" +
                    "       <CategoryName>" +
                    "           <xsl:value-of select=\".\"/>" +
                    "       </CategoryName>" +
                    "   </xsl:template>" +
                    "   <xsl:template match=\"REGIONAL_PRICING\">" +
                    "       <xsl:apply-templates select=\"EASTASIA\"/>" +
                    "       <xsl:apply-templates select=\"AMERICAS\"/>" +
                    "   </xsl:template>" +
                    "   <xsl:template match=\"EASTASIA\">" +
                    "       <EastAsianPrice>" +
                    "           <xsl:value-of select=\".\"/>" +
                    "       </EastAsianPrice>" +
                    "   </xsl:template>" +
                    "   <xsl:template match=\"AMERICAS\">" +
```

```
                         "            <AmericanPrice>" +
                         "                 <xsl:value-of select=\".\"/>" +
                         "            </AmericanPrice>" +
                         "       </xsl:template>" +
                        "</xsl:stylesheet>";
                    OracleXmlType _transformedXML = _oracleXmlType.Transform(_xsl, "");
                    MessageBox.Show(_transformedXML.Value);
                }
            }
            _rdrObj.Close();
            _connObj.Close();
            _connObj.Dispose();
            _connObj = null;
        }
        catch (Exception ex)
        {
                MessageBox.Show(ex.ToString());
        }
}
```

If you run this code sample, you will see the transformed XML display in a pop-up message box (as shown in Figure 10-3).

*Figure 10-3. Transformed XML*

---

■ **Tip** You can even use XSLT to transform XML directly into a HTML document. XSLT syntax allows you to transform tag names into tag attributes and vice versa, insert completely new tags (such as the <TR> and <TD> tags used in a HTML table) and so on. XSLT is a powerful language that allows you to segregate transformation rules from code and should be used whenever possible.

---

# Retrieving Relational Data as XML

In the examples so far in this chapter, you've been manipulating native XML data within the confines of the **XMLTYPE** data type. The Oracle database supports yet another cool feature—the ability to read and manipulate relational data as XML!

---

■ **Note** Relational data, as opposed to hierarchical data, refers to the standard two dimensional table-column data format that you are familiar with. The ADO.NET **DataSet** object, for example holds relational data. The **XMLTYPE** column holds hierarchical data.

---

This means that you can run an SQL query on any table in Oracle and have it return XML instead of a record set, for instance. You can also do this in the opposite direction—inserting records into a table by passing the data in as XML. There are three different ways that you can retrieve relational data as XML, of which you will learn in the following individual sections:

- Using the **XMLCommandType** property

- Using the **Dataset.GetXML** method

- Using the **DBMS_XMLGEN.GETXML** stored procedure

## Using the XMLCommandType property

Retrieving relational data as XML consists of two steps:

1.  Define the Root and Row tags to use for the generated raw XML.

2.  Define an XSLT to transform the raw XML to the desired schema and format.

To tell ODP.NET to retrieve relational data as XML, you must first set the **XmlCommandType** property of the OracleCommand object:

```
_cmdObj.XmlCommandType = OracleXmlCommandType.Query;
```

The **OracleCommand** object also contains an **XmlQueryProperties** object, which allows you to define a set of rules that govern the query. There are four main properties to set in this object. These properties are explained in Table 10-2.

*Table 10-2. Properties in the XMLQueryProperties Object*

| Property Definition | Description |
| --- | --- |
| MaxRows | This is the maximum number of rows to retrieve in the query. To retrieve all rows, leave this value as the default (–1). |

269

RootTag and RowTag · These two properties define the name of the root tag and row tag to use when the raw XML is generated.

Xslt · This property allows you to set the XSLT to use to transform the raw XML into the desired schema and format.

As mentioned earlier, the **RootTag** and **RowTag** properties allow you to define the name of the root and row XML tags to use when generating raw XML. For instance, if you set them to **MYRECORDSET** and **MYROW** respectively, the raw generated XML from the **PRODUCTS** table might look something like this:

```
<MYRECORDSET>
        <MYROW>
                <ID>E1</ID>
                <NAME>Engine</NAME>
                <PRICE>50.00</PRICE>
        </MYROW>
        <MYROW>
                <ID>R1</ID>
                <NAME>Rear mirror</NAME>
                <PRICE>5.00</PRICE>
        </MYROW>
</MYRECORDSET>
```

Listing 10-9 shows how you can retrieve a maximum of two records from the **PRODUCTS** table and have it formatted nicely with their appropriate tags in XML.

*Listing 10-9. Retrieving Relational Data As XML*

```
private void btnXMLQuery_Click(object sender, EventArgs e)
{
        string _connstring = "Data Source=localhost/NEWDB;User
                Id=EDZEHOO;Password=PASS123;";
        string _xsltString = "";
        try
        {
                OracleConnection _connObj = new OracleConnection(_connstring);
                OracleCommand _cmdObj = new OracleCommand("SELECT * FROM Products",
                        _connObj);
                _connObj.Open();
                _cmdObj.BindByName = true;
                _cmdObj.XmlCommandType = OracleXmlCommandType.Query;
                _cmdObj.XmlQueryProperties.MaxRows = 2;
                _cmdObj.XmlQueryProperties.RootTag = "MYRECORDSET";
                _cmdObj.XmlQueryProperties.RowTag = "MYRECORD";

                //Define the XSL to transform the relational dataset to XML
                _xsltString =   "<?xml version=\"1.0\"?>" +
                                "<xsl:stylesheet version=\"1.0\" " +
```

```
    "    xmlns:xsl=\"http://www.w3.org/1999/XSL/Transform\">" +
    "    <xsl:output encoding=\"utf-8\"/>\n" +
    "    <xsl:template match=\"/\">" +
    "        <Products>" +
    "            <xsl:apply-templates select=\"MYRECORDSET\"/>" +
    "        </Products>" +
    "    </xsl:template>" +
    "    <xsl:template match=\"MYRECORDSET\">" +
    "        <xsl:apply-templates select=\"MYRECORD\"/>" +
    "    </xsl:template>" +
    "    <xsl:template match=\"MYRECORD\">" +
    "        <Product>" +
    "        <ID>" +
    "            <xsl:value-of select=\"ID\"/>" +
    "        </ID>" +
    "        <Name>" +
    "            <xsl:value-of select=\"NAME\"/>" +
    "        </Name>" +
    "        <Price>" +
    "            <xsl:value-of select=\"PRICE\"/>" +
    "        </Price>" +
    "        <Remarks>" +
    "            <xsl:value-of select=\"REMARKS\"/>" +
    "        </Remarks>" +
    "        </Product>" +
    "    </xsl:template>" +
    "</xsl:stylesheet>";

        _cmdObj.XmlQueryProperties.Xslt = _xsltString;
        XmlReader xmlReader = _cmdObj.ExecuteXmlReader();
        XmlDocument xmlDocument = new XmlDocument();
        xmlDocument.PreserveWhitespace = true;
        xmlDocument.Load(xmlReader);
        MessageBox.Show(xmlDocument.OuterXml);

        _connObj.Close();
        _connObj.Dispose();
        _connObj = null;
    }
    catch (Exception ex)
    {
        MessageBox.Show(ex.ToString());
    }
}
```

If you run the preceding code, you will see the message box shown in Figure 10-4 displaying the result set as formatted XML.

```
<Products>
<Product>
<ID>E1</ID>
<Name>Engine</Name>
<Price>3000</Price>
<Remarks>Standard car engine</Remarks>
</Product>
<Product>
<ID>W1</ID>
<Name>Windshield</Name>
<Price>500</Price>
<Remarks>Quality windshields</Remarks>
</Product>
</Products>
```

OK

*Figure 10-4. The data from the Products table retrieved as XML*

## Using the Dataset.GetXML Method

While reading the previous section, you might have realized that you could also do the same thing using the ADO.NET record set object. You can do so using the **GetXml** method of the ADO.NET **DataSet** object, as shown in Listing 10-10. There are two disadvantages to using this method:

- You have to write additional code to transform the XML.

- Since the **GetXml** method is available only in the **DataSet** object, you need to use **OracleDataAdapter**, which is slower in comparison to **XmlReader.**

*Listing 10-10. Using GetXml() to Format a Relational dataset as XML*

```
private void btnADOGetXML_Click(object sender, EventArgs e)
{
        string _connstring = "Data Source=localhost/NEWDB;User
                Id=EDZEHOO;Password=PASS123;";
        string _sql;
        try
        {
                OracleConnection _connObj = new OracleConnection(_connstring);
                _ds = new DataSet();
                _connObj.Open();
                _sql = "SELECT * FROM Products";
                OracleDataAdapter _adapterObj = new OracleDataAdapter(_sql, _connObj);
```

```
                _adapterObj.Fill(_ds);
                MessageBox.Show(_ds.GetXml());
                _connObj.Close();
                _connObj.Dispose();
                _connObj = null;
        }
        catch (Exception ex)
        {
                MessageBox.Show(ex.ToString());
        }
}
```

## Using the DBMS_XMLGEN.GETXML Stored Procedure

Another method that you can use to do the same thing is through the **DBMS_XMLGEN** PL/SQL package. This package easily converts the results of an SQL statement into XML:

```
SELECT DBMS_XMLGEN.GETXML('<YOUR_SQL_STATEMENT_GOES_HERE>') FROM DUAL;
```

---

■ **Note** You need to have Oracle XML DB installed to have access to the DBMS_XMLGEN package.

---

You can try this by running the following PL/SQL block in SQL*Plus:

```
//Set some display settings in the SQL*Plus console window so that you can see the
//full generated XML
SET PAGES 0
SET LONG 9999999
SET HEAD OFF

//Run the query
SELECT DBMS_XMLGEN.GETXML('SELECT * FROM PRODUCTS') FROM DUAL;
```

You will be able to see the output shown in Figure 10-5.

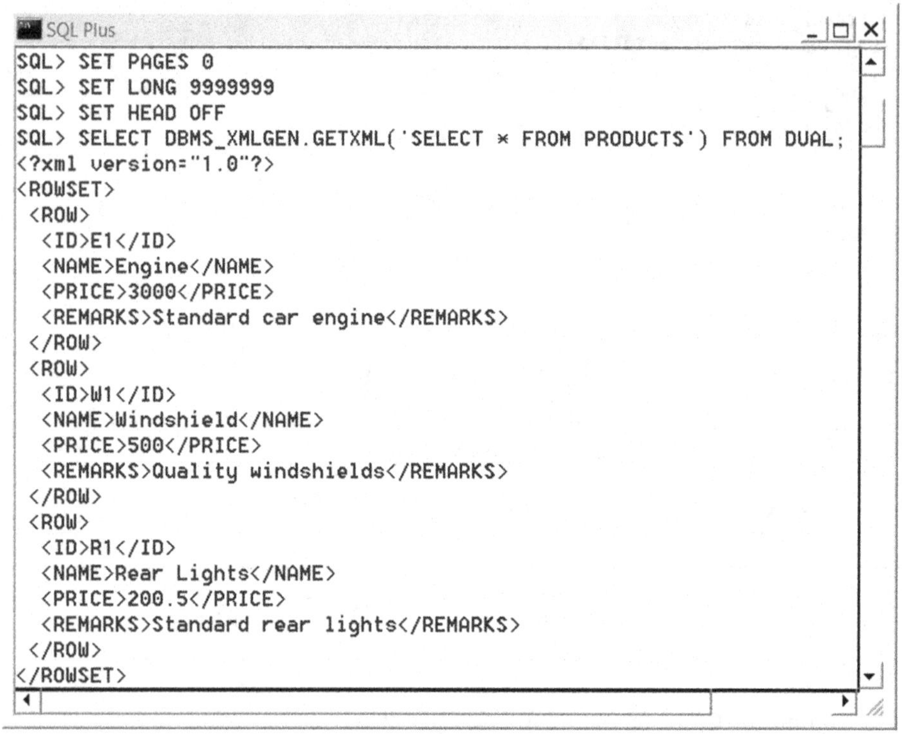

```
SQL Plus                                                              _ □ ×
SQL> SET PAGES 0
SQL> SET LONG 9999999
SQL> SET HEAD OFF
SQL> SELECT DBMS_XMLGEN.GETXML('SELECT * FROM PRODUCTS') FROM DUAL;
<?xml version="1.0"?>
<ROWSET>
 <ROW>
  <ID>E1</ID>
  <NAME>Engine</NAME>
  <PRICE>3000</PRICE>
  <REMARKS>Standard car engine</REMARKS>
 </ROW>
 <ROW>
  <ID>W1</ID>
  <NAME>Windshield</NAME>
  <PRICE>500</PRICE>
  <REMARKS>Quality windshields</REMARKS>
 </ROW>
 <ROW>
  <ID>R1</ID>
  <NAME>Rear Lights</NAME>
  <PRICE>200.5</PRICE>
  <REMARKS>Standard rear lights</REMARKS>
 </ROW>
</ROWSET>
```

*Figure 10-5. Output of the DBMS_XMLGEN.GETXML method*

# Manipulating Relational Data as XML

In this next section, you will explore the transformation between relational and XML data in the opposite direction—inserting, updating, and deleting data via XML.

## Inserting Relational Data Using XML

You will now learn how to insert records to the **PRODUCTS** table using XML. Inserting relational data via XML consists of four steps:

1. Define the update columns list, the set of columns that will be updated in the table during the insert operation.

2. Define an XSL block to transform the incoming XML into the raw XML format that Oracle recognizes so that the insert operation can be performed.

3. Set the various properties in the **OracleCommand.XmlSaveProperties** object for the insert operation.

4. Assign the XML data (that you wish to insert) to the **CommandText** property of the **OracleCommand** object, and call the **ExecuteNonQuery** method.

Take note that you also need to change the **XmlCommandType** property to denote an insert:

```
_cmdObj.XmlCommandType = OracleXmlCommandType.Insert;
```

Next, you have to define the set of columns that you will be updating during the insert operation. This can be easily done by setting up an array in the following fashion:

```
string[] _updColList = new string[4];
_updColList[0] = "ID";
_updColList[1] = "NAME";
_updColList[2] = "PRICE";
_updColList[3] = "REMARKS";
_cmdObj.XmlSaveProperties.UpdateColumnsList = _updColList;
```

After that, you need to define the properties outlined in Table 10-3.

*Table 10-3. Properties in the XMLSaveProperties Object*

| Property Definition | Description |
| --- | --- |
| UpdateColumnsList | This is a list of names of the columns that you will be updating in the table |
| KeyColumnsList | This is only used for **UPDATE** and **DELETE** operations, where the columns used as the identifier for each record must be specified. |
| RowTag | This property denotes the name of the tag identifying each row in the XML. When you transform the incoming XML, each row will need to begin with this tag name. Take note that the **RootTag** property is no longer required. |
| Table | This is the name of the underlying Oracle table that you will be updating. |
| Xslt | This property allows you to set the XSL to use to transform the incoming XML into the raw XML recognized by Oracle. |

The next step is to define the XSLT so that you can map the incoming XML into the raw XML format that Oracle needs to update the table. The tag names in the raw XML format usually correlates with the actual Oracle table and column names.

Listing 10-11 shows how you can declare two new records (in XML) and insert them at one go to the **Products** table.

*Listing 10-11. Inserting Multiple Records to the Products Table via XML*

```
private void btnXMLManipulate_Click(object sender, EventArgs e)
{
        string _connstring = "Data Source=localhost/NEWDB;User
                Id=EDZEHOO;Password=PASS123;";
        string _xsltString = "";
        try
        {
                OracleConnection _connObj = new OracleConnection(_connstring);
                OracleCommand _cmdObj = new OracleCommand("", _connObj);
                _connObj.Open();

                string[] _updColList = new string[4];
                _updColList[0] = "ID";
                _updColList[1] = "NAME";
                _updColList[2] = "PRICE";
                _updColList[3] = "REMARKS";

                //The XSL used to transform the incoming XML data into the raw XML format
                //that Oracle recognizes to perform the Insert.
                _xsltString =   "<?xml version=\"1.0\"?>" +
                                "<xsl:stylesheet version=\"1.0\" " +
                                "   xmlns:xsl=\"http://www.w3.org/1999/XSL/Transform\">" +
                                "  <xsl:output encoding=\"utf-8\"/>\n" +
                                "  <xsl:template match=\"/\">" +
                                "      <RECORDSET>" +
                                "          <xsl:apply-templates select=\"MYPRODUCTS\"/>" +
                                "      </RECORDSET>" +
                                "  </xsl:template>" +
                                "  <xsl:template match=\"MYPRODUCTS\">" +
                                "      <xsl:apply-templates select=\"MYPRODUCT\"/>" +
                                "  </xsl:template>" +
                                "  <xsl:template match=\"MYPRODUCT\">" +
                                "      <RECORD>" +
                                "      <ID>" +
                                "          <xsl:value-of select=\"PROD_ID\"/>" +
                                "      </ID>" +
                                "      <NAME>" +
                                "          <xsl:value-of select=\"PROD_NAME\"/>" +
                                "      </NAME>" +
                                "      <PRICE>" +
                                "          <xsl:value-of select=\"PROD_PRICE\"/>" +
                                "      </PRICE>" +
                                "      <REMARKS>" +
                                "          <xsl:value-of select=\"PROD_REMARKS\"/>" +
                                "      </REMARKS>" +
                                "      </RECORD>" +
                                "  </xsl:template>" +
                                "</xsl:stylesheet>";
```

```
            _cmdObj.BindByName = true;
            _cmdObj.XmlCommandType = OracleXmlCommandType.Insert;
            _cmdObj.XmlSaveProperties.RowTag = "RECORD";
            _cmdObj.XmlSaveProperties.Table = "PRODUCTS";
            _cmdObj.XmlSaveProperties.KeyColumnsList = null;
            _cmdObj.XmlSaveProperties.UpdateColumnsList = _updColList;
            _cmdObj.XmlSaveProperties.Xslt = _xsltString;

            //Declare two records in XML to insert
            _cmdObj.CommandText =   "<?xml version=\"1.0\"?>\n" +
                                    "<MYPRODUCTS>\n" +
                                    "   <MYPRODUCT>\n" +
                                    "      <PROD_ID>G1</PROD_ID>\n" +
                                    "      <PROD_NAME>Grille</PROD_NAME>\n" +
                                    "      <PROD_PRICE>30.20</PROD_PRICE>\n" +
                                    "      <PROD_REMARKS>The front grille of the
                                           car</PROD_REMARKS>\n" +
                                    "   </MYPRODUCT>\n" +
                                    "   <MYPRODUCT>\n" +
                                    "      <PROD_ID>M1</PROD_ID>\n" +
                                    "      <PROD_NAME>Mirrors</PROD_NAME>\n" +
                                    "      <PROD_PRICE>50.50</PROD_PRICE>\n" +
                                    "      <PROD_REMARKS>Front mirrors of the
                                           car</PROD_REMARKS>\n" +
                                    "   </MYPRODUCT>\n" +
                                    "</MYPRODUCTS>";

        int _result = _cmdObj.ExecuteNonQuery();
        MessageBox.Show("Rows Inserted:" + _result);

        _connObj.Close();
        _connObj.Dispose();
        _connObj = null;
    }
    catch (Exception ex)
    {
        MessageBox.Show(ex.ToString());
    }
}
```

After you run the code in Listing 10-11, you will see the message box shown in Figure 10-6, denoting that two records were inserted successfully. You can cross-check this by running a query on the **PRODUCTS** table in SQL*Plus.

*Figure 10-6. Records inserted successfully*

# Updating Relational Data Using XML

Performing an update operation on relational data using XML is rather similar to performing an insert. It consists of the following steps:

1. Define the update columns list, the set of columns that will be updated in the table during the update operation.

2. Define the key columns list, the set of columns to use as the identifier for each record. This is typically set to the primary key of the table.

3. Define an XSL block to transform the incoming XML into the raw XML format that Oracle recognizes so that the update operation can be performed.

4. Set the various properties in the **OracleCommand.XmlSaveProperties** object for the update operation.

5. Assign the XML data (that you wish to update) to the **CommandText** property of the **OracleCommand** object, and call the ExecuteNonQuery method.

The differences here are that you need to set the **XmlCommandType** property to denote an update:

```
_cmdObj.XmlCommandType = OracleXmlCommandType.Update;
```

Next, you need to define the key list:

```
string[] _keyColList = new string[1];
_keyColList[0] = "ID";
_cmdObj.XmlSaveProperties.KeyColumnsList = _keyColList;
```

You can reuse the same XSL to transform the incoming data. The full code to execute the update is shown in Listing 10-12.

*Listing 10-12. Updating Multiple Records in the Products Table via XML*

```
private void btnUpdate_Click(object sender, EventArgs e)
{
        string _connstring = "Data Source=localhost/NEWDB;User
                Id=EDZEHOO;Password=PASS123;";
```

```
string _xsltString = "";
try
{
        OracleConnection _connObj = new OracleConnection(_connstring);
        OracleCommand _cmdObj = new OracleCommand("", _connObj);
        _connObj.Open();

        // Set the Update Column List
        string[] _updColList = new string[2];
        _updColList[0] = "NAME";
        _updColList[1] = "PRICE";

        // Set the Key List
        string[] _keyColList = new string[1];
        _keyColList[0] = "ID";

        _xsltString =       "<?xml version=\"1.0\"?>" +
                            "<xsl:stylesheet version=\"1.0\" " +
                            "  xmlns:xsl=\"http://www.w3.org/1999/XSL/Transform\">" +
                            "  <xsl:output encoding=\"utf-8\"/>\n" +
                            "  <xsl:template match=\"/\">" +
                            "      <RECORDSET>" +
                            "          <xsl:apply-templates select=\"MYPRODUCTS\"/>" +
                            "      </RECORDSET>" +
                            "  </xsl:template>" +
                            "  <xsl:template match=\"MYPRODUCTS\">" +
                            "      <xsl:apply-templates select=\"MYPRODUCT\"/>" +
                            "  </xsl:template>" +
                            "  <xsl:template match=\"MYPRODUCT\">" +
                            "      <RECORD>" +
                            "      <ID>" +
                            "          <xsl:value-of select=\"PROD_ID\"/>" +
                            "      </ID>" +
                            "      <NAME>" +
                            "          <xsl:value-of select=\"PROD_NAME\"/>" +
                            "      </NAME>" +
                            "      <PRICE>" +
                            "          <xsl:value-of select=\"PROD_PRICE\"/>" +
                            "      </PRICE>" +
                            "      <REMARKS>" +
                            "          <xsl:value-of select=\"PROD_REMARKS\"/>" +
                            "      </REMARKS>" +
                            "      </RECORD>" +
                            "  </xsl:template>" +
                            "</xsl:stylesheet>";

        _cmdObj.BindByName = true;
        _cmdObj.XmlCommandType = OracleXmlCommandType.Update ;
        _cmdObj.XmlSaveProperties.RowTag = "RECORD";
        _cmdObj.XmlSaveProperties.Table = "PRODUCTS";
        _cmdObj.XmlSaveProperties.KeyColumnsList = _keyColList;
        _cmdObj.XmlSaveProperties.UpdateColumnsList = _updColList;
```

279

```
            _cmdObj.XmlSaveProperties.Xslt = _xsltString;

            //Notice that you don't have to include all the fields - only the fields you
            //wish to update (together with the record identifiers)
            _cmdObj.CommandText =   "<?xml version=\"1.0\"?>\n" +
                                    "<MYPRODUCTS>\n" +
                                    "  <MYPRODUCT>\n" +
                                    "    <PROD_ID>G1</PROD_ID>\n" +
                                    "    <PROD_NAME>Grille Revision 2</PROD_NAME>\n" +
                                    "    <PROD_PRICE>50.00</PROD_PRICE>\n" +
                                    "  </MYPRODUCT>\n" +
                                    "  <MYPRODUCT>\n" +
                                    "    <PROD_ID>M1</PROD_ID>\n" +
                                    "    <PROD_NAME>Titanium Enforced
                                        Mirror</PROD_NAME>\n" +
                                    "    <PROD_PRICE>60.50</PROD_PRICE>\n" +
                                    "  </MYPRODUCT>\n" +
                                    "</MYPRODUCTS>";

        int _result = _cmdObj.ExecuteNonQuery();
        MessageBox.Show("Rows Updated:" + _result);
        _connObj.Close();
        _connObj.Dispose();
        _connObj = null;
    }
    catch (Exception ex)
    {
        MessageBox.Show(ex.ToString());
    }
}
```

## Deleting Relational Data Using XML

A delete operation is also somewhat similar. It consists of the following steps:

1. Define the key columns list, the set of columns to use as the identifier for each record. This is typically set to the primary key of the table.

2. Define an XSL block to transform the incoming XML into the raw XML format that Oracle recognizes so that the delete operation can be performed.

3. Set the various properties in the **OracleCommand.XmlSaveProperties** object for the delete operation.

4. Assign the XML data (that you wish to delete) to the **CommandText** property of the **OracleCommand** object, and call the **ExecuteNonQuery** method.

You need to set the **XmlCommandType** property to denote a delete:

```
_cmdObj.XmlCommandType = OracleXmlCommandType.Delete;
```

Since a delete does not update any columns in a table, you will not need to define an update columns list. You need to define only a key columns list. The full code to perform the delete operation is shown in Listing 10-13.

*Listing 10-13. Deleting Multiple Records in the Products Table via XML*

```
private void btnDelete_Click(object sender, EventArgs e)
{
        string _connstring = "Data Source=localhost/NEWDB;User
            Id=EDZEHOO;Password=PASS123;";
        string _xsltString = "";
        try
        {
                OracleConnection _connObj = new OracleConnection(_connstring);
                OracleCommand _cmdObj = new OracleCommand("", _connObj);
                _connObj.Open();

                // Define the Key Columns List
                string[] _keyColList = new string[1];
                _keyColList[0] = "ID";

                _xsltString =   "<?xml version=\"1.0\"?>" +
                                "<xsl:stylesheet version=\"1.0\" " +
                                "   xmlns:xsl=\"http://www.w3.org/1999/XSL/Transform\">" +
                                "   <xsl:output encoding=\"utf-8\"/>\n" +
                                "   <xsl:template match=\"/\">" +
                                "       <RECORDSET>" +
                                "           <xsl:apply-templates select=\"MYPRODUCTS\"/>" +
                                "       </RECORDSET>" +
                                "   </xsl:template>" +
                                "   <xsl:template match=\"MYPRODUCTS\">" +
                                "       <xsl:apply-templates select=\"MYPRODUCT\"/>" +
                                "   </xsl:template>" +
                                "   <xsl:template match=\"MYPRODUCT\">" +
                                "       <RECORD>" +
                                "       <ID>" +
                                "           <xsl:value-of select=\"PROD_ID\"/>" +
                                "       </ID>" +
                                "       <NAME>" +
                                "           <xsl:value-of select=\"PROD_NAME\"/>" +
                                "       </NAME>" +
                                "       <PRICE>" +
                                "           <xsl:value-of select=\"PROD_PRICE\"/>" +
                                "       </PRICE>" +
                                "       <REMARKS>" +
                                "           <xsl:value-of select=\"PROD_REMARKS\"/>" +
                                "       </REMARKS>" +
                                "       </RECORD>" +
                                "   </xsl:template>" +
                                "</xsl:stylesheet>";
```

```
_cmdObj.BindByName = true;
_cmdObj.XmlCommandType = OracleXmlCommandType.Delete;
_cmdObj.XmlSaveProperties.RowTag = "RECORD";
_cmdObj.XmlSaveProperties.Table = "PRODUCTS";
_cmdObj.XmlSaveProperties.KeyColumnsList = _keyColList;
_cmdObj.XmlSaveProperties.UpdateColumnsList = null;
_cmdObj.XmlSaveProperties.Xslt = _xsltString;

//Define the records to delete. Only the record identifier field is needed
_cmdObj.CommandText = "<?xml version=\"1.0\"?>\n" +
        "<MYPRODUCTS>\n" +
        "  <MYPRODUCT>\n" +
        "    <PROD_ID>G1</PROD_ID>\n" +
        "  </MYPRODUCT>\n" +
        "  <MYPRODUCT>\n" +
        "    <PROD_ID>M1</PROD_ID>\n" +
        "  </MYPRODUCT>\n" +
        "</MYPRODUCTS>";

int _result = _cmdObj.ExecuteNonQuery();
MessageBox.Show("Rows Deleted:" + _result);
_connObj.Close();
_connObj.Dispose();
_connObj = null;
}
catch (Exception ex)
{
        MessageBox.Show(ex.ToString());
}
}
```

## Using XQuery to Query Data

XQuery is yet another powerful language introduced by the W3C. Whereas an SQL **LIKE** statement can only match phrases in a string, XQuery gives you the ability to do an XML-aware search. For instance, consider the **PRODUCT_EXTRAINFO** table you've been using throughout this chapter. The **INFO** column contains XML data describing the product category, person in charge, and so on. How would you, for example, issue a query to retrieve all products belonging to the **ENGINES** category? You could, of course, argue that it could be done with the following SQL:

```
SELECT * FROM PRODUCT_EXTRAINFO WHERE INFO LIKE '%ENGINES%'
```

However, this solution is crude and inelegant. What if the XML stored in the **INFO** column contained the word **ENGINES** in the **<PERSON_IN_CHARGE>** tag instead of the **<CATEGORY>** tag? For instance, the person in charge could have a name like **GONZALEZ MENGINES**. Your query would then retrieve the (logically) wrong results. It is obvious you need a way to perform an XML-element aware search.

---

■ **Note**  XQuery is a standard defined by the W3C. We will not cover the specifics and syntax of XQuery in this book. To read more on XQuery, please visit http://www.w3.org/TR/xquery/.

---

XQuery fits this job like a glove. Its syntax might seem a little cryptic to newcomers, but underlying it, there is enough flexibility to allow for a large number of powerful queries. Consider the following XQuery for example:

```
for $i in ora:view("PRODUCT_EXTRAINFO")
where $i/ROW/INFO/PRODUCT/CATEGORY = $MyCategory
return $i'
PASSING :MyCategory AS \"MyCategory\"
RETURNING CONTENT
```

The **for** loop iterates through each row in the **PRODUCT_EXTRAINFO** table and is able to extend its reach right into the **<PRODUCT><CATEGORY>** tag inside the **INFO XMLTYPE** column. It is then able to do a direct comparison on the value held in the **<CATEGORY>** tag. The **PASSING** keyword allows you to pass in an external parameter that can be used in the XQuery statement. The matching results are then returned as XML.

To run the XQuery statement, you need to encapsulate it within an SQL statement:

```
SELECT XMLQuery(<YOUR_XQUERY_STMT_GOES_HERE>) FROM DUAL;
```

To see how all this fits in to your .NET application, take a look at the code in Listing 10-14.

*Listing 10-14. Using XQuery to Retrieve All Products Belonging to the ENGINES Category*

```
private void btnXQuery_Click(object sender, EventArgs e)
{
        string _connstring = "Data Source=localhost/NEWDB;User
            Id=EDZEHOO;Password=PASS123;";
        try
        {
                OracleConnection _connObj = new OracleConnection(_connstring);
                OracleCommand _cmdObj = new OracleCommand("", _connObj);
                _connObj.Open();
                _cmdObj.CommandType = CommandType.Text;
                string _sql;
                _sql =  "SELECT XMLQuery('" +
                        "for $i in ora:view(\"PRODUCT_EXTRAINFO\") " +
                        "where $i/ROW/INFO/PRODUCT/CATEGORY = $MyID " +
                        "return $i' " +
                        "PASSING :MyID AS \"MyID\" RETURNING CONTENT) " +
                        "FROM DUAL";
                _cmdObj.CommandText = _sql;

                //Pass in "Engines" as the category to search for
                _cmdObj.Parameters.Add("MyID", OracleDbType.Varchar2, "Engines",
                        ParameterDirection.Input);
```

```
                    OracleDataReader _rdrObj = _cmdObj.ExecuteReader();
                    _rdrObj.Read();
                    OracleXmlType xml = _rdrObj.GetOracleXmlType(0);
                    MessageBox.Show(xml.Value);
                    _connObj.Close();
                    _connObj.Dispose();
                    _connObj = null;
            }
            catch (Exception ex)
            {
                    MessageBox.Show(ex.ToString());
            }
    }
```

If you run the code in Listing 10-14, you will see the message box shown in Figure 10-7.

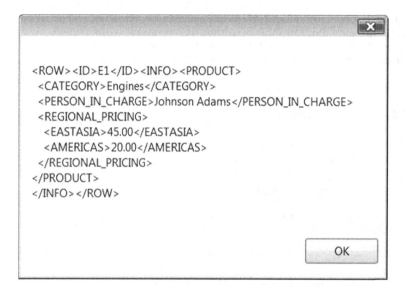

*Figure 10-7. Records retrieved through XQuery*

# Summary

You've seen in this chapter that the hierarchical organization of XML may be better suited for certain scenarios compared to relational models and that ODP.NET provides a set of powerful XML functions and packages to manipulate XML data in the database. In this chapter, you've taken a specific look at the following:

- Manipulating **XMLTYPE** data using the **XmlReader**, **OracleXmlType**, and **OracleString** classes

- Passing XML data to and from PL/SQL stored procedures via the **OracleXmlType** object

- Validating **OracleXmlType** objects against an XSD schema

- Using **OracleXmlType** and XSLT to transform the schema of an XML to a different one

- Retrieving and manipulating relational data as XML

In the next chapter, you'll learn how to protect your .NET applications via ODP.NET's security model.

# CHAPTER 11

# ODP.NET Security Features

"Security" is a big word conjuring up images of hackers working away late at night in their seedy offices trying to crack through your application to get at that precious financial data. As exciting as it sounds, most developers seem to pay the least attention to security, preferring to work first on getting the flashy features of an application running.

In fact, many seasoned development teams don't even start out with any proper security plan in place; the scene of a team of developers deploying their application on a security hardened server only to find that half their application does not work because it ran afoul of the local security policies isn't uncommon. Just like you can't play poker without knowing your hand, it is important to know every bit of your deployment environment upfront even before you start developing your application! This allows you to formulate a security strategy that lets you choose the security model most suitable for your application early, thus avoiding last-minute surprises and clunky workarounds.

This chapter intends to highlight the areas of a typical ODP.NET application where security would matter. In this chapter, you will learn the following:

- The security stack of a typical ODP.NET application

- The different authentication modes available to you in Oracle

- The .NET code access security mechanism and how you can use it to secure your ODP.NET applications

- How to secure your ASP.NET applications using trust levels

- Best practices you can adopt in your code to avoid exposing common vulnerabilities

## Securing Your .NET Applications

When you design any database-driven application, you should think about which security technology to employ for each of the following aspects of database programming:

- Authentication

- Code security

- Data access

- Data storage

- Data transmission

Authentication is the most basic concern. Any application that needs to use a database needs to authenticate its users against the database. There are a few different modes of authentication to choose from (we'll look at these in detail in the next section).

Code access security is a security model introduced with the .NET Framework. Because all .NET code runs in a managed environment, system administrators can prevent parts of the code from accessing a particular resource (in this case, the Oracle database) by externally configuring the allowed permissions for a machine or user at the .NET Framework level. ODP.NET provides you classes that allow you to build applications that conform to this security model. Using code access security, you can ensure that only trusted code assemblies can gain access to the Oracle database.

Security for data access, data storage, and data transmission can be configured at the database level. For example, to properly access data in the database, you need to ensure that the appropriate rights for each database object have been granted to the appropriate roles or users.

When you store data in the Oracle database, you should also consider activating Transparent Data Encryption (TDE), a feature that allows you to apply encryption on your data at the database level without having to write a single line of code.

Finally, when the database passes any data to your application over the network, you should also consider encrypting the data before it is transmitted over the network, by means of Secure Sockets Layer (SSL) or some other encryption method.

The security stack for a typical ODP.NET application may look like Figure 11-1.

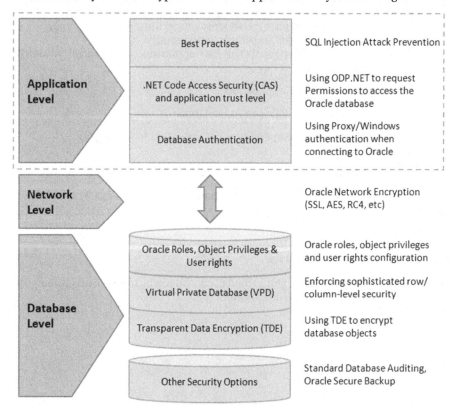

*Figure 11-1. Security stack of a typical ODP.NET application*

In the following sections, we will take a look at the various security options that you can implement at the application level: authentication, code access security, and best practices to overcome common database vulnerabilities in your code.

# Authenticating Data

When embarking on building your application, it is always a good idea to decide on the mode of authentication for your application. The Oracle database supports three different modes of authentication:

- Standard username/password authentication
- Proxy authentication
- Windows authentication

It is important to know the drawbacks of each mode so that you can choose the one most suitable for your project. For example, if your concerns are stronger audit trails in the database, you should consider Windows authentication or proxy authentication over standard username/password authentication. On the other hand, if all you need is to get your database application up and running quickly with as little code as possible, standard username/password authentication is a better choice. In the following sections, you will learn the reasons behind this logic.

## Implementing Username/Password Authentication

You've been using standard username/password authentication in most of the examples in this book. The following shows how you could pass a user ID and password in the connection string:

```
Data Source=localhost/NEWDB;User Id=EDZEHOO;Password=PASS123;
```

The obvious benefit of this mode of authentication is its simplicity. You need only manage a single database account in Oracle (the **EDZEHOO** account). All the users of your application will be made to access the database through this single database account. You can also almost immediately spot the problem with this arrangement—since everyone goes through the same database account, the database has no idea who the actual users are. Audit trails will always reflect **EDZEHOO**, regardless of whether the accessing user is really Jane, John, or Thomas.

## Implementing Proxy Authentication

Proxy authentication addresses the anonymity problem with standard username/password authentication. The solution is simple—since Oracle has no idea of knowing who the actual users are, why not just declare the actual users in the connection string as well!

In proxy authentication, two user accounts are passed in via the connection string for authentication: the actual user's credentials and the pooled (proxy) user's credentials. It adds two new keywords to the connection string: **Proxy User ID** and **Proxy Password**. For example, if Thomas accesses the database, he will use the following connection string:

```
Data Source=localhost/NEWDB;User Id=Thomas;Password=THOM123; Proxy User
ID=EDZEHOO;Proxy Password=PASS123;
```

---

■ **Note** Take careful note that the pooled database account is now declared as the proxy user, and the `User ID` and `Password` fields are set to the actual user's credentials.

---

The `User ID` and `Password`, for example, can be retrieved from an application's login page and the connection string dynamically constructed using these credentials. Before you can log in using proxy authentication for a particular user, you must grant that user rights to do this. You can grant these rights by running the following command in SQL*Plus:

```
ALTER USER Thomas GRANT CONNECT THROUGH EDZEHOO;
```

The benefit of using proxy authentication is that it can maintain the same connection pool (through the proxy account) yet produce accurate audit trails (since it knows who the actual users are).

---

■ **Tip** You can also choose not to specify a password for the actual user in the connection string. If this is done, no authentication is performed on the `User ID` field. `User ID` simply becomes an identifier field to distinguish different users (when audit trails are generated). In such a case, you can assign any string you wish to the `User ID` field.

---

## Implementing ClientId-Based Username/Password Authentication

Another way to specify the actual users when you are using standard username/password authentication is by programmatically setting the **ClientId** property for each **OracleConnection** object to any string (preferably a unique identifier for each user), as shown in the highlighted code in Listing 11-1.

*Listing 11-1. Programmatically Setting the ClientId*

```
string _connstring = "Data Source=localhost/NEWDB;User
      Id=EDZEHOO;Password=PASS123;";
try
{
      OracleConnection _connObj = new OracleConnection(_connstring);
      _connObj.Open();
      _connObj.ClientId = "THIS_IS_THOMAS";
      //Do something
      _connObj.Close();
      _connObj.Dispose ();
}
```

```
catch (Exception ex)
{
        MessageBox.Show(ex.ToString());
}
```

When you do this, all updates made to the database under this connection will be made under the name specified in the `ClientId` property, which will be reflected in the audit trail records.

You can use any unique identifier for the `ClientId` property: social security numbers, employee IDs, network IP addresses, or even Window credentials (such as `MYCOMPANY\THOMAS`).

You might also come across the need to retrieve the current `ClientId` for a particular session. You can do so using the following SQL statement:

```
SELECT SYS_CONTEXT('USERENV','CLIENT_IDENTIFIER') FROM DUAL;
```

You can retrieve the audit trail records for a specific table and specific `ClientId` by running the SQL in Listing 11-2 through SQL*Plus.

*Listing 11-2. Retrieving Audit Trails Using the Client Identifier*

```
SELECT * FROM dba_audit_object
WHERE username = 'EDZEHOO'
AND client_id = 'THIS_IS_THOMAS'
AND OBJ_NAME = 'Products'
```

## Implementing Windows Authentication

As you saw in Chapter 3, you can also authenticate users against the Oracle database using integrated Windows authentication. You can log on via Windows authentication using the following connection string:

```
Data Source=localhost/NEWDB;User Id=/;
```

The benefit of using Windows authentication is the ability to achieve single sign-on functionality with the database, but the downside is that you also have to ensure that each Windows user account has been explicitly given access to the desired objects in the database.

---

■ **Tip** The `ClientId` property behaves the same way for both username/password authenticated and Windows-authenticated sessions.

---

# Understanding Code Access Security

Back in the old days, when unmanaged code ran, the system resources it could access was restricted only by the user account it ran under—all that was needed to get access to these resources was to be given the appropriate permissions in their access control lists (ACLs). This simple form of security worked but had its limitations. Any user with high enough privileges could execute malicious code (with or without intention) on the system and end up damaging the file system, registry, or database.

The objective of CAS is to provide another security layer; it allows (or disallows) managed code to execute based not only on the user account the code ran under but also other attributes such as the originating publisher of the code, the zone it executed in, the strong name of the code, and so on. In the following sections, we will cover some of the basic concepts and terminology of CAS.

## Using Code Groups

Through the .NET Framework Configuration tool, the system administrator can create a code group. A code group can declare a set of membership conditions; any assembly that matches these conditions will belong to that specific code group. Figure 11-2 shows multiple code groups in the Configuration tool.

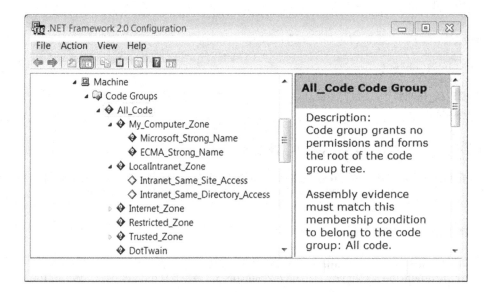

*Figure 11-2. Code groups in the configuration tool*

Table 11-1 lists some of the membership conditions that can be set on a code group.

*Table 11-1. Various Code Group Membership Conditions*

| Membership Condition | Description |
|---|---|
| Hash | Any assembly that matches the specified hash |
| Publisher | Any assembly that matches the specified publisher's name, issuer name, and hash |
| Site | Any assembly that originates from the specified site name |
| Strong name | Any assembly that matches the specified strong name (and public key) |
| URL | Any assembly that originates from the specified URL |
| Zone | Any assembly that originates from the specified zone (e.g., **Internet**, **Intranet**, **My Computer**, **Trusted Sites**, or **Untrusted Sites**) |

The administrator can grant each code group a set of permissions (also called a **PermissionSet**). A typical **PermissionSet**, for example, specifies if the code group has access to the file system, registry, or Windows events log.

# Using Permission Sets

As I mentioned earlier, a permission set defines a list of permissions for each specific type of resource present on the system. For instance, a permission set for a highly secure code group may only contain user interface (UI) permissions, while a permission set for a less secure one might contain file I/O permissions, UI permissions, registry permissions, Oracle database access permissions, sockets access permissions, and so on. Figure 11-3 shows the list of permissions in a particular permission set.

*Figure 11-3. List of permissions in a code group permission set*

Any assembly in a code group will automatically inherit the permission set assigned to the code group.

## Resolving Permissions in .NET

You might have noticed in Figure 11-2 that you could configure code groups at three different policy levels: Enterprise, Machine, and User. How would CAS behave if you gave a user permission to access the Oracle database at the machine level but denied access at the enterprise level? Or what happens when your application, by way of membership conditions, falls into two different code groups (at the same policy level) with contradicting permissions? You will explore how CAS permission arithmetic works in detail in this section.

---

■ **Note** There is also a fourth policy level (`AppDomain`) that is controlled by code rather than by the .NET Framework Configuration tool.

---

Within the same policy level, your application could fall into more than one code group if it matches the membership conditions of multiple code groups. When this happens, the permission sets of these code groups are collectively added together. This becomes the total permission set available to your application at that policy level. Figure 11-4 illustrates this concept.

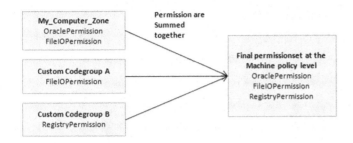

*Figure 11-4. Summation of permission sets from multiple code groups at a policy level*

This same process occurs at all three policy levels. After that, CAS would need to finally combine the permission sets from each of these three policy levels. This time, the combining is done differently from before. Instead of taking the sum of the permission sets from the three policy levels, CAS takes the intersection of these three policy level permission sets, which means that if your application needs access to Oracle (for instance), Oracle permissions must be granted at all three policy levels. Denying this permission at any one of these policy levels would prevent your application from accessing Oracle. This is visually represented as a Venn diagram shown in Figure 11-5. The intersection is highlighted in gray.

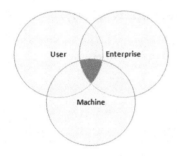

*Figure 11-5. How the permission sets from the three policy levels are combined*

It is important to note that the default CAS policy configuration gives the **All_Code** code group **FullTrust** permissions at the user and enterprise policy levels. What this means is that the machine policy level effectively becomes the control policy; the permission set at this policy level ultimately defines which resources your application has access to. You could, of course, change this behavior by changing the permission sets at the user and enterprise policy levels, but you should always proceed with caution since using the wrong settings might break applications that otherwise work fine.

## Seeing CAS in Action

The diagram in Figure 11-6 shows how a set of CAS security policies can be configured by the administrator and used when your application's assembly loads up. The .NET Common Language

Runtime (CLR) will determine which code group your assembly belongs to and grant the corresponding permissions (defined in the permission set) to the assembly.

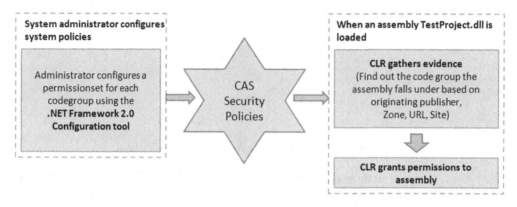

*Figure 11-6. Configuring and using CAS security policies*

Let's say you wanted your assembly to access an Oracle database. You can force your assembly to check against CAS to ensure that your assembly has the **OraclePermission** permission. You can do this using ODP.NET's **OraclePermission** class, as shown here:

```
OraclePermission _perm = new OraclePermission(PermissionState.Unrestricted);
_perm.Demand();
```

If the permission was found in the permission set, your code is allowed to run. Otherwise, an exception is raised, as Figure 11-7 depicts in detail.

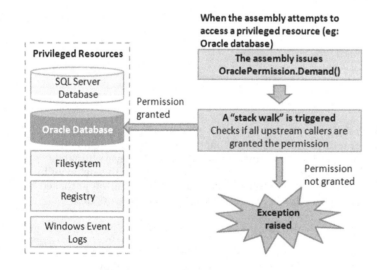

*Figure 11-7. Requesting permissions*

You will notice that a stack walk is triggered when you call the **Demand** method. It is important to note that each assembly might be called by several higher assemblies. For example, take a look at Figure 11-8. When the **DataLayerFunctions.dll** assembly attempts to access the Oracle database, a **Demand** method call placed there would trigger a stack walk upward to check the permissions of each calling assembly. This makes sense, because if **CustomDataGrid.dll**, for example, was not given permissions to access the Oracle database, the request in the **DataLayerFunctions.dll** assembly should ultimately fail.

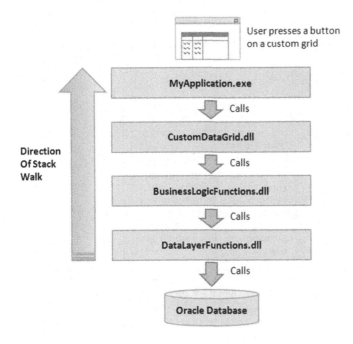

*Figure 11-8. The stack walk*

# Configuring CAS Policies

The usage of CAS consists of two polarities. One side is the configuring of CAS policies (typically done by system administrators), and the other side is the requesting of permissions from within your application. CAS policies can be configured via a couple different ways: an administrator could do it manually using the .NET Framework configuration tool or programmatically using the **OraclePermission** class.

## Configuring CAS Policies via the GUI

You can configure CAS policies manually using the .NET Framework Configuration tool. You can launch the .NET Framework Configuration tool by selecting Start ➤ Control Panel ➤ Administrative Tools ➤ .NET Framework 2.0 Configuration Tool.

> **Note** You may have noticed that the .NET Framework Configuration tool shows as Microsoft .NET Framework 2.0 Configuration on your machine. Do not be alarmed by the version number; this tool can also be used to manage CAS policies for the .NET Framework 3.0 and 3.5. If you cannot see this specific version of the tool on your machine, you can install it by installing the .NET Framework 2.0 SDK.

The .NET Configuration tool window is depicted in Figure 11-9. You can define a security policy at the Enterprise, Machine, or User level.

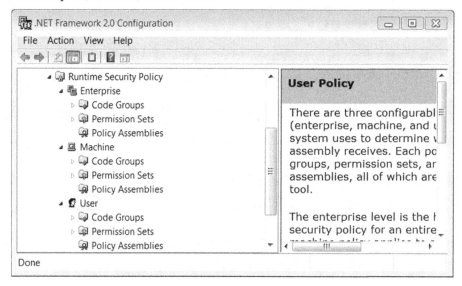

**Figure 11-9.** *The .NET Configuration Tool main window*

If you expand the User node, you can see the main code group (**All_Code**); its permission set has been set to Full Trust. This means that it has unrestricted access to all system resources. Change the permission set to Everything instead. The Everything permission set has a list of permissions defined for most of the basic resources on the system. You can see this list of permissions by navigating to the Everything permission set under the Permission Sets node. Click the Change Permissions link in the right panel. You will see a list of permissions similar to the one shown in Figure 11-10.

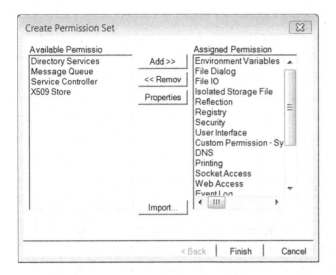

*Figure 11-10. Permissions in the Everything permission set*

But wait—you don't see **OraclePermission** anywhere in the list! This is so because **OraclePermission** is a custom permission and will not show by default. You can use the Import button to import a custom permission into that list. Before you can do that, you must first define an XML file for **OraclePermission**. Create a text file (using Notepad or a similar editing program) and write the following declaration in the file:

```
<IPermission class="Oracle.DataAccess.Client.OraclePermission, Oracle.DataAccess,
Version=2.111.7.20, Culture=neutral, PublicKeyToken=89b483f429c47342"
version="1"
Unrestricted="true"/>
```

Save this file as an XML file (using any filename you wish). On the Everything permission set window, click the Import button, and browse for this XML file. When you've clicked Open, you will be able to see the new entry for **OraclePermission** added to the list on the right (as shown in Figure 11-11).

---

■ **Caution** Be careful when making any changes to the CAS security policies via the .NET Framework Configuration tool. If you remove too many privileges, you may find that you cannot launch any application on your system (including the .NET Framework Configuration tool itself!). Always set the security policies back to their original values after testing, or use sandboxing to create a test environment for your applications.

---

*Figure 11-11.* *The newly added OraclePermission*

---

■ **Note** The `Unrestricted` keyword in the XML declaration means that you are granting the assembly full access to the Oracle database, as opposed to being partially restricted (in which you can define certain restrictions, such as "Connection string must not contain blank passwords" or "Connection string cannot have any keywords other than User ID, Password, and Datasource").

---

Instead of granting full, unrestricted access to the Oracle database, you can also choose to grant access with some restrictions. For example, you might restrict the connection string used to connect to the database to the **User ID**, **Password**, and **Datasource** keywords and not allow blank passwords. In such an example, any code that attempts to connect to the database using a connection string like this would fail (since the **Pooling** keyword violates the restriction):

```
Data Source=localhost/NEWDB;User Id=EDZEHOO;Password=PASS123;Pooling=true;
```

You can declare such a restriction by rewriting the XML used in the preceding line as follows:

```
<IPermission class="Oracle.DataAccess.Client.OraclePermission, Oracle.DataAccess,
Version=2.111.7.20, Culture=neutral, PublicKeyToken=89b483f429c47342"
version="1" AllowBlankPassword="False">
        <add ConnectionString="Data Source=localhost/NEWDB;"
                KeyRestrictions="Data Source=;User ID=;Password=;"
                KeyRestrictionBehavior="AllowOnly" />
</IPermission>
```

---

■ **Tip** `KeyRestrictionBehavior` can be either `AllowOnly` or `PreventUsage`. Both behaviors apply to the keywords defined in the `KeyRestrictions` attribute. The `ConnectionString` attribute lets you define the data sources that an assembly is allowed to connect to. You can, of course, define multiple `<add>` entries in the permission.

---

## Configuring CAS Policies Programmatically

You can also write code to programmatically configure CAS policies using the **OraclePermission** class. To enforce the same restrictions on the connection strings, you can use the **OraclePermission.Add** method, as shown here:

```
OraclePermission _perm = new OraclePermission(PermissionState.Unrestricted);
_perm.AllowBlankPassword = false;
_perm.Add("Data Source=localhost/NEWDB;", "Data Source=;User Id=;Password=;",
        KeyRestrictionBehavior.AllowOnly);
```

The first, second, and third arguments to the **OraclePermission.Add** method correspond to the **ConnectionString**, **KeyRestrictions**, and **KeyRestrictionBehavior** attributes covered earlier.

# Requesting Permissions

Now, let's explore the other end of CAS. You can request permissions in one of two ways from your managed code: declaratively and imperatively. Let's take a look at how you can perform each one.

## Requesting Permissions Declaratively

You can request permission to access Oracle via the **OraclePermission** class at the assembly level. When your application is first loaded by the CLR, it will check to ensure you are granted this permission. If the permission is not granted, an exception is thrown, and your application will fail to even load. You can enforce permission checking at the assembly level by declaring the highlighted tag shown in Listing 11-3 at the top of the main class in your application.

*Listing 11-3. Requesting Permissions Declaratively at the Assembly Level*

```
using System;
using System.Collections.Generic;
using System.Windows.Forms;
using Oracle.DataAccess.Client;
using System.Security;
using System.Security.Permissions;
using System.IO;

[assembly: OraclePermission(SecurityAction.RequestMinimum, Unrestricted = true)]
namespace MyNamespace
{
        static class Program
        {
                [STAThread]
                static void Main()
                {
                    ConnectToDatabase();
                }
```

301

```
private static void ConnectToDatabase()
{
        string _connstring = "Data Source=localhost/NEWDB;User
                Id=EDZEHOO;Password=PASS123;";
        try
        {
                OracleConnection _connObj = new
                        OracleConnection(_connstring);
                _connObj.Open();
                _connObj.Close();
                _connObj.Dispose ();
                MessageBox.Show("The database was just opened and closed
                        successfully!");
        }
        catch (Exception ex)
        {
                MessageBox.Show(ex.ToString());
        }
}
}
}
```

You can try this code by explicitly removing **OraclePermission** from the **PermissionSet** of the Everyone code group in the **User** node (via the .NET Framework Configuration tool). When you try running your application, it will show an error message similar to the one in Figure 11-12 (assuming you tried to run your application from within Visual Studio).

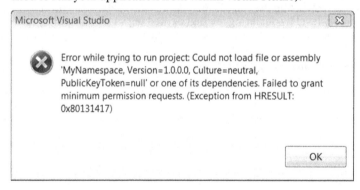

*Figure 11-12. Security exception thrown at the assembly level*

Instead of checking at the assembly level, you can also opt to do this checking at each individual method, as shown in Listing 11-4. Take note that you must use the **SecurityAction.Demand** action at the method level.

*Listing 11-4. Requesting Permissions Declaratively at the Method Level*

```
using System;
using System.Collections.Generic;
using System.Windows.Forms;
using Oracle.DataAccess.Client;
using System.Security;
using System.Security.Permissions;
using System.IO;

namespace MyNamespace
{
        static class Program
        {
                [STAThread]
                static void Main()
                {
                    ConnectToDatabase();
                }

                [method: OraclePermissionAttribute(SecurityAction.Demand , Unrestricted =
                        true)]
                private static void ConnectToDatabase()
                {
                        string _connstring = "Data Source=localhost/NEWDB;User
                                Id=EDZEHOO;Password=PASS123;";
                        try
                        {
                                OracleConnection _connObj = new
                                        OracleConnection(_connstring);
                                _connObj.Open();
                                _connObj.Close();
                                _connObj.Dispose ();
                                MessageBox.Show("The database was just opened and closed
                                        successfully!");
                        }
                        catch (Exception ex)
                        {
                                MessageBox.Show(ex.ToString());
                        }
                }
        }
}
```

When you run the preceding code in Visual Studio, (assuming you have removed **OraclePermission**), you will see an error message similar to the one shown in Figure 11-13.

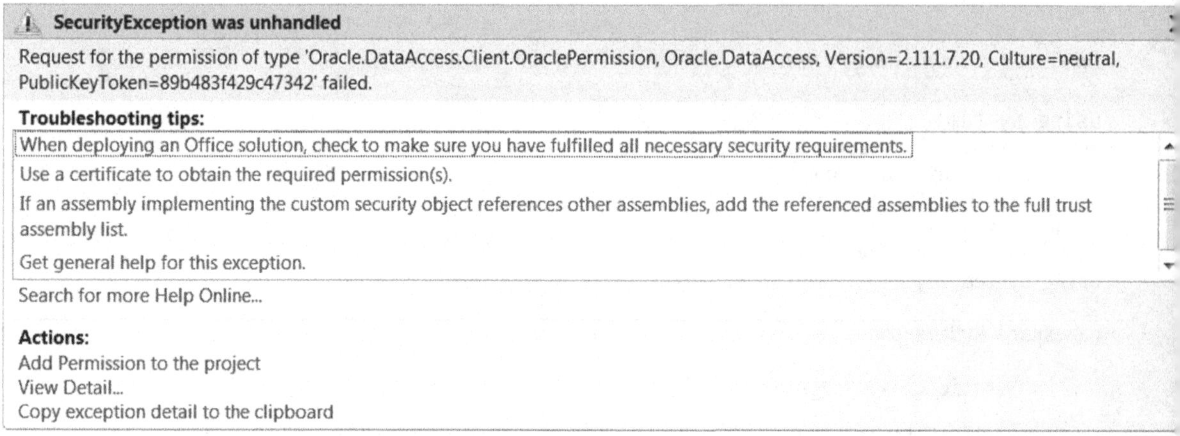

**⚠ SecurityException was unhandled**

Request for the permission of type 'Oracle.DataAccess.Client.OraclePermission, Oracle.DataAccess, Version=2.111.7.20, Culture=neutral, PublicKeyToken=89b483f429c47342' failed.

**Troubleshooting tips:**

When deploying an Office solution, check to make sure you have fulfilled all necessary security requirements.

Use a certificate to obtain the required permission(s).

If an assembly implementing the custom security object references other assemblies, add the referenced assemblies to the full trust assembly list.

Get general help for this exception.

Search for more Help Online...

**Actions:**

Add Permission to the project
View Detail...
Copy exception detail to the clipboard

*Figure 11-13. Security exception thrown at the method level*

## Requesting Permissions Imperatively

You can also request permissions imperatively (programmatically), as you've seen earlier, using the following code:

```
OraclePermission _perm = new OraclePermission(PermissionState.Unrestricted);
_perm.Demand();
```

Let's see how this looks like in the big picture (Listing 11-5).

*Listing 11-5. Requesting Permissions Programmatically at the Method Level*

```
using System;
using System.Collections.Generic;
using System.Windows.Forms;
using Oracle.DataAccess.Client;
using System.Security;
using System.Security.Permissions;
using System.IO;

namespace MyNamespace
{
        static class Program
        {
                [STAThread]
                static void Main()
                {
                    ConnectToDatabase();
                }
```

```
private static void ConnectToDatabase()
{
        string _connstring = "Data Source=localhost/NEWDB;User
                Id=EDZEHOO;Password=PASS123;";
        try
        {
                //If the request fails, an exception is raised, and the
                //error message will be displayed
                OraclePermission _perm = new
                        OraclePermission(PermissionState.Unrestricted);
                _perm.Demand();

                OracleConnection _connObj = new
                        OracleConnection(_connstring);
                _connObj.Open();
                _connObj.Close();
                _connObj.Dispose ();
                MessageBox.Show("The database was just opened and closed
                        successfully!");
        }
        catch (Exception ex)
        {
                MessageBox.Show(ex.Message());
        }
}
}
```

If you run the code in Listing 11-5, you will see an error message similar to the one shown in Figure 11-14.

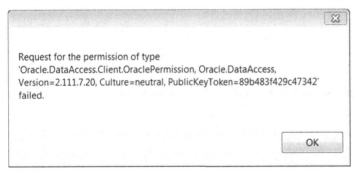

*Figure 11-14. Security exception caught at the method level*

# Ensuring That an Assembly Can Never Access Oracle

Let's say you've created a DLL component that will never need to access the Oracle database. When you deploy such a component in a highly sensitive environment (where any slight change to the database would bring dire consequences), how do you ensure that your DLL will never be able to access the Oracle database? After all, it is quite possible for a malicious application to misuse your DLL.

The safest way is to prevent your application code (at the .NET Framework level) from ever being given these Oracle permissions. You can insert a declaration in your assembly to do so.

Preventing access to Oracle can be useful, for instance, when you've written a multivendor database manager tool, but you don't want your users to ever use this tool to attempt a connection to the Oracle databases on the network (maybe because the tool is used for mission-critical purposes).

There are three ways to achieve this in your application:

- Refusing permissions at the assembly level

- Denying permissions at the method level

- Denying permissions programmatically at runtime

## Refusing Permissions Declaratively at the Assembly Level

Using the **RequestRefuse** security action, you can prevent an assembly from ever being given the **FileIOPermission** permission using the following declaration:

```
[assembly: FileIOPermission(SecurityAction.RequestRefuse , Unrestricted = true)]
```

You can refuse permissions by writing the highlighted declaration shown in Listing 11-6 at the top of the assembly.

*Listing 11-6. Refusing Permissions Declaratively at the Assembly Level*

```
using System;
using System.Collections.Generic;
using System.Windows.Forms;
using Oracle.DataAccess.Client;
using System.Security;
using System.Security.Permissions;
using System.IO;

[assembly: OraclePermission(SecurityAction.RequestRefuse, Unrestricted = true)]
namespace MyNamespace
{
        static class Program
        {
                [STAThread]
                static void Main()
                {
                    ConnectToDatabase();
                }

                private static void ConnectToDatabase()
                {
                        string _connstring = "Data Source=localhost/NEWDB;User
                            Id=EDZEHOO;Password=PASS123;";
```

```
        try
        {
                OracleConnection _connObj = new
                        OracleConnection(_connstring);
                _connObj.Open();
                _connObj.Close();
                _connObj.Dispose ();
                MessageBox.Show("The database was just opened and closed
                        successfully!");
        }
        catch (Exception ex)
        {
                MessageBox.Show(ex.ToString());
        }
    }
  }
}
```

# Denying Permissions Declaratively at the Method Level

In some cases, preventing an entire assembly from accessing the Oracle database might be a little too wide in scope. You might prefer to narrow down the restriction to a particular method (for instance, a method that is exposed to calling applications). You can do this by declaring the restriction at the beginning of the method instead using the **Deny** security action, as shown in Listing 11-7.

*Listing 11-7. Denying Permissions Declaratively at the Method Level*

```
[method: OraclePermissionAttribute(SecurityAction.Deny, Unrestricted = true)]
private static void ConnectToDatabase()
{
        string _connstring = "Data Source=localhost/NEWDB;User
                Id=EDZEHOO;Password=PASS123;";
        try
        {
                OracleConnection _connObj = new OracleConnection(_connstring);
                _connObj.Open();
                _connObj.Close();
                _connObj.Dispose ();
                MessageBox.Show("The database was just opened and closed successfully!");
        }
        catch (Exception ex)
        {
                MessageBox.Show(ex.ToString());
        }
}
```

## Denying Permissions Imperatively at the Method Level

You can also deny Oracle permissions at runtime using the **OraclePermission.Deny** method call. You can do this by writing the highlighted code shown in Listing 11-8.

*Listing 11-8. Denying Permissions Programmatically at the Method Level*

```
private static void ConnectToDatabase()
{
        string _connstring = "Data Source=localhost/NEWDB;User
                Id=EDZEHOO;Password=PASS123;";
        try
        {
                //Deny Oracle Permissions
                OraclePermission _perm = new OraclePermission(PermissionState.Unrestricted);
                _perm.Deny();

                OracleConnection _connObj = new OracleConnection(_connstring);
                _connObj.Open();
                _connObj.Close();
                _connObj.Dispose ();
                MessageBox.Show("The database was just opened and closed successfully!");
        }
        catch (Exception ex)
        {
                MessageBox.Show(ex.ToString());
        }
}
```

# Using CAS with ASP.NET Applications

By default, when you create ASP.NET applications, they run with full trust—your web-based applications, as far as security is concerned, only need to ensure that they have the appropriate ACL permissions to the various objects they are accessing. There is no security layer between your ASP.NET application and the Oracle database other than the basic database authentication feature.

---

▪ **Note** ASP.NET applications, unlike Windows Form applications, fall under the application domain security policy. The application domain security policy cannot be configured using the .NET Framework Configuration tool.

---

You can introduce an additional layer of security by having your web applications operate in medium trust. There are five default trust levels in total (in order of most privileges to least):

- Full
- High

- Medium

- Low

- Minimal

You can set the desired trust level in the **web.config** file of each individual ASP.NET application or in the machine-level **web.config** file (so that it can apply generally to all web sites deployed on the machine). When you run a web site in medium trust, your web site is immediately subject to the security restrictions shown in Table 11-2.

*Table 11-2. Medium Trust Security Restrictions*

| Security Privilege | Granted? | Description |
|---|---|---|
| OleDbPermission | Not granted | Your application cannot make use of the Active Data Objects (ADO.NET) and Object Linking and Embedding, Database (OLEDB) data provider to access any database. |
| EventLogPermission | Not granted | Your application cannot access the Windows event logs. |
| ReflectionPermission | Not granted | Your application cannot use the .NET reflection features. |
| RegistryPermission | Not granted | Your application cannot access the registry. |
| OraclePermission | Not granted | Your application cannot access the Oracle database using ODP.NET. |
| FileIOPermission | Limited grant | Your application can only access files in the same virtual folder (and subfolders) of your ASP.NET application. |
| WebPermission | Limited grant | Your application can only communicate with addresses defined in the **<trust>** element. |

You can view the individual filenames for each different security policy in the machine level **web.config** file located in the following folder:

**\<Windows Folder>\Microsoft.NET\Framework\<Framework Version>\CONFIG**

You will notice a section that looks like the following:

```
<location allowOverride="true">
     <system.web>
          <securityPolicy>
                <trustLevel name="Full" policyFile="internal"/>
                <trustLevel name="High" policyFile="web_hightrust.config"/>
                <trustLevel name="Medium" policyFile="web_mediumtrust.config"/>
                <trustLevel name="Low" policyFile="web_lowtrust.config"/>
                <trustLevel name="Minimal" policyFile="web_minimaltrust.config"/>
          </securityPolicy>
```

```
        <trust level="Full" originUrl=""/>
    </system.web>
</location>
```

You can see that the trust level for all applications is currently set to Full. You should now change the trust level to Medium in the following manner:

```
<trust level="Medium" originUrl=""/>
```

---

■ **Tip** Besides the five default trust levels, you can also create your own custom trust levels. You can declare your own custom trust level by adding another <trustLevel> tag (that points to a custom policy file) to the list. You can use any name you wish for the trust level (and policy file name) as long as the <trust> tag points to that same name.

---

The allowOverride keyword in the <location> tag allows you to specify whether an application-level web.config file can override the trust level and policies specified in this machine-level web.config file. For instance, you might want to prevent your individual ASP.NET developers from granting themselves full trust to their web applications. You can do this by setting allowOverride=false in the machine-level web.config file in the following manner:

```
<location allowOverride="false">
```

To see all the permissions available to the medium trust policy, you can view the web_mediumtrust.config file. If you scroll down this file a little bit, you should be able to see a section similar to the one shown in Listing 11-9. This section declares the allowed permissions for medium trust. Notice that OraclePermission is nowhere in this list! You will encounter problems if you try to connect to Oracle from your ASP.NET application at this time.

*Listing 11-9. The ASP.Net Permission Set Declaration in the web_mediumtrust.config File*

```
<PermissionSet class="NamedPermissionSet" version="1" Name="ASP.Net">
    <IPermission class="AspNetHostingPermission" version="1" Level="Medium"/>
    <IPermission class="DnsPermission" version="1" Unrestricted="true"/>
    <IPermission class="EnvironmentPermission" version="1"
            Read="TEMP;TMP;USERNAME;OS;COMPUTERNAME"/>
    <IPermission class="FileIOPermission" version="1" Read="$AppDir$" Write="$AppDir$"
            Append="$AppDir$" PathDiscovery="$AppDir$"/>
    <IPermission class="IsolatedStorageFilePermission" version="1"
            Allowed="AssemblyIsolationByUser" UserQuota="9223372036854775807"/>
    <IPermission class="PrintingPermission" version="1" Level="DefaultPrinting"/>
    <IPermission class="SecurityPermission" version="1" Flags="Assertion, Execution,
            ControlThread, ControlPrincipal, RemotingConfiguration"/>
    <IPermission class="SmtpPermission" version="1" Access="Connect"/>
    <IPermission class="SqlClientPermission" version="1" Unrestricted="true"/>
    <IPermission class="WebPermission" version="1">
```

```
            <ConnectAccess>
                    <URI uri="$OriginHost$"/>
            </ConnectAccess>
        </IPermission>
        <IPermission class="ReflectionPermission" version="1"
                Flags="RestrictedMemberAccess"/>
</PermissionSet>
```

You now need to add the relevant **OraclePermission** entries to this file. Add an entry to declare the **OraclePermission** security class under the **<SecurityClasses>** tag:

```
<SecurityClass Name="OraclePermission"
Description="Oracle.DataAccess.Client.OraclePermission, Oracle.DataAccess.Clien↵
t, Version=2.111.7.20, Culture=neutral, PublicKeyToken=89b483f429c47342"/>
```

Under the **ASP.Net** permission set, add the following **<IPermission>** declaration:

```
<IPermission class="OraclePermission" version="1" Unrestricted="true"/>
```

The contents of your **web_mediumtrust.config** file should now look something like the one shown in Listing 11-10 (changes are highlighted in bold).

*Listing 11-10. The web_mediumtrust.config file After Adding OraclePermission*

```
<configuration>
        <mscorlib>
        <security>
        <policy>
        <PolicyLevel version="1">
        <SecurityClasses>
                <SecurityClass Name="AllMembershipCondition"
                        Description="System.Security.Policy.AllMembershipCondition,
                        mscorlib, Version=2.0.0.0, Culture=neutral,
                        PublicKeyToken=b77a5c561934e089"/>
                <SecurityClass Name="AspNetHostingPermission"
                        Description="System.Web.AspNetHostingPermission, System,
                        Version=2.0.0.0, Culture=neutral, PublicKeyToken=b77a5c561934e089"/>
                <SecurityClass Name="DnsPermission" Description="System.Net.DnsPermission,
                        System, Version=2.0.0.0, Culture=neutral,
                        PublicKeyToken=b77a5c561934e089"/>
                <SecurityClass Name="OraclePermission"
                        Description="Oracle.DataAccess.Client.OraclePermission,
                        Oracle.DataAccess.Client, Version=2.111.7.20, Culture=neutral,
                        PublicKeyToken=89b483f429c47342"/>
        </SecurityClasses>
        <NamedPermissionSets>
                <PermissionSet class="NamedPermissionSet" version="1"
                        Unrestricted="true" Name="FullTrust" Description="Allows
                        full access to all resources"/>
                <PermissionSet class="NamedPermissionSet" version="1" Name="Nothing"
```

```
                              Description="Denies all resources, including the right to
                              execute"/>
                    <PermissionSet class="NamedPermissionSet" version="1"
                              Name="ASP.Net">
                        <IPermission class="AspNetHostingPermission" version="1"
                                Level="Medium"/>
                        <IPermission class="DnsPermission" version="1"
                                Unrestricted="true"/>
                        <IPermission class="OraclePermission" version="1"
                                Unrestricted="true"/>
                        <IPermission class="EnvironmentPermission" version="1"
                                Read="TEMP;TMP;USERNAME;OS;COMPUTERNAME"/>
                        <IPermission class="FileIOPermission" version="1"
                                Read="$AppDir$" Write="$AppDir$" Append="$AppDir$"
                                PathDiscovery="$AppDir$"/>
                        <IPermission class="IsolatedStorageFilePermission"
                                version="1" Allowed="AssemblyIsolationByUser"
                                UserQuota="9223372036854775807"/>
                        <IPermission class="PrintingPermission" version="1"
                                Level="DefaultPrinting"/>
                        <IPermission class="SecurityPermission" version="1"
                                Flags="Assertion, Execution, ControlThread,
                                ControlPrincipal, RemotingConfiguration"/>
                        <IPermission class="SmtpPermission" version="1"
                                Access="Connect"/>
                        <IPermission class="SqlClientPermission" version="1"
                                Unrestricted="true"/>
                        <IPermission class="WebPermission" version="1">
                            <ConnectAccess>
                                    <URI uri="$OriginHost$"/>
                            </ConnectAccess>
                        </IPermission>
                        <IPermission class="ReflectionPermission" version="1"
                                Flags="RestrictedMemberAccess"/>
                    </PermissionSet>
                </NamedPermissionSets>
                <CodeGroup class="FirstMatchCodeGroup" version="1" PermissionSetName="Nothing">
                        .
                        .
                        .
                </CodeGroup>
            </PolicyLevel>
            </policy>
            </security>
            </mscorlib>
        </configuration>
```

If you now try to access the Oracle database from your web application, you should be able to do so without any further problem. Now that the security policies for Oracle have been configured, your ASP.NET applications can also demand or refuse permissions (as you did in the earlier sections) using the **OraclePermission** object.

# Implementing Best Practices

It is important to note that the biggest security flaws in your application can most often be avoided by simply keeping to best practices when writing code to access the database. For example, SQL injection attacks are one of the most common forms of attack involving the database, and they can be easily avoided just by using parameterized queries instead of dynamically generated SQL statements. In the following sections, you'll see how SQL injection attacks work and how you can write better code to reduce the chances of it happening.

## Preventing SQL Injection Attacks

An SQL injection attack is an ingenious method of injecting malicious SQL code directly into your application by way of input-collecting text boxes. When you create a login page that looks like the screenshot shown in Figure 11-15, for example, your code expects the user to type in a username and a password.

*Figure 11-15. A typical login window*

If you dynamically construct your SQL statement by directly incorporating input from the user, a malicious user could manipulate this SQL statement by typing in carefully formatted data through the text boxes. For example, let's say that your application builds up the SQL statement using the following code:

```
_cmdObj.CommandText = "SELECT * FROM Useraccounts WHERE UserID='" +
        txtUsername.Text + "' AND Password='" + txtPassword.Text + "'";
OracleDataReader _rdrObj = _cmdObj.ExecuteReader();
if (_rdrObj.HasRows)
{
        MessageBox.Show("Access Granted!");
}
```

Now, think about what happens if your user types in exactly the following in the Username text box:

```
' OR UserID<>'
```
and the following in the Password text box:

```
' OR Password<>'
```

When these pieces of data are used to construct the final SQL, your final SQL becomes:

```
SELECT * FROM Useraccounts WHERE UserID='' OR UserID<>'' AND Password='' OR Pass↵
word<>''
```

This SQL statement will now return every single user account in the system, and the malicious user will always have access to your application.

As shown in this example, this problem stems mostly from not formatting the input data appropriately. It could be avoided, for example, by having your application look for a single apostrophe in the input data and stripping out or replacing any that it finds. A safer way, however, is to pass input to an SQL statement as parameters instead of directly appending them as strings.

For example, you could stamp out SQL injection attacks by simply rewriting the code snippet as follows:

```
_cmdObj.CommandText = "SELECT * FROM Useraccounts WHERE UserID=:UserID AND
        Password=:Password";
_cmdObj.Parameters.Add(new OracleParameter("UserID", txtUsername.Text));
_cmdObj.Parameters.Add(new OracleParameter("Password", txtPassword.Text));
```

It is always better to use parameterized queries or PL/SQL stored procedures to pass user input safely to an SQL. In scenarios where dynamically generated SQL is unavoidable, parse and check all input for special characters and escape them appropriately before appending them to any SQL statement.

## Preventing Nonpersistent Cross-Site Scripting Attacks

Nonpersistent cross-site scripting (XSS) is a type of attack that targets web-based applications that send data from one webpage to another via form **POST** or through the query string segment of the URL of a requested web page.

For instance, consider a web page that generates a list of products for display, each product represented by a harmless-looking link:

```
http://localhost/myapp/viewproduct.aspx?ProductID=333888
```

Let's assume that the **viewproduct.aspx.vb** page contained the following code:

```
_cmdObj.CommandText = "SELECT * FROM Products WHERE ProductID='"
        + Request.QueryString["ProductID"] + "'";
```

A malicious user could replace the **ProductID** in the URL with the following:

```
http://localhost/myapp/viewproduct.aspx?ProductID=' UNION SELECT * FROM Prohibi↵
tedProducts WHERE ProhibitedProductID=100 AND ProhibitedProductID<>'
```

When this **ProductID** value is eventually plugged into the SQL statement, your SQL will read as follows:

```
SELECT * FROM Products WHERE ProductID='' UNION SELECT * FROM ProhibitedProducts
WHERE ProhibitedProductID=100 AND ProhibitedProductID<>''
```

The malicious user is now able to access data in a prohibited table that would otherwise be normally inaccessible.

---

■ **Note** As you can see from this example, users can still introduce malicious code even when you don't expect them to pass in any input data. If your application passes any data internally, it is important to ensure that the receiving web pages validate and check any incoming data appropriately before usage.

---

The following are precautions that you can take to prevent nonpersistent XSS attacks:

- Always scramble or encrypt the query string portion of a URL.

- Always double-check input data. For example, if the product ID is a number, you should check if the incoming product ID is a numerical value.

- Whenever possible, place checks on a web page to ensure that the currently logged-on user has rights to view the desired page and its data.

- Input data that is eventually fed into an SQL statement should always be passed in as parameters.

# Summary

You've seen in this chapter how you could create secure ODP.NET applications through three different methods:

- Authentication

- Code access security

- Adopting best practices when accessing the database

- You've learned the following in detail:

- The three different authentication modes available in Oracle and when to use each one

- How to use the **OraclePermission** and **OraclePermissionAttribute** classes to request and refuse permissions to the Oracle database in your code (declaratively and imperatively)

- How to secure your ASP.NET applications by changing the trust level associated with your web application

- How to prevent your ODP.NET code from being exploited in SQL Injection and non-persistent cross-site scripting attacks

In the next chapter, you'll learn how to optimize your ODP.NET code for performance.

# CHAPTER 12

■ ■ ■

# ODP.NET Performance

My gym instructor (who's a self-professed authority on the ninja arts) once remarked that the sharpest blade in the world is useless if one cannot wield it fast enough. Extending these wise words into the realm of ODP.NET, I find that the same can be said of development teams that frequently make the mistake of classifying performance optimization as something optional to do after development rather than as a habit that is practiced from the very first line of code.

A lack of knowledge about the inner workings of the Oracle database and best performance practices can lead development teams to write tons of code affixed to a particular style that make it difficult to alter later on in the project without rewriting the entire data layer. You need to master this knowledge before you even embark on your first ODP.NET project.

In the world of Oracle, your sword is ODP.NET, your training the skill set you possess, and your enemy time. In this chapter, you will conquer the following techniques to write lightning fast ODP.NET applications:

- Enable the ODP.NET performance counters and programmatically measure performance in your code.

- Establish faster connections.

- Perform faster floating point arithmetic.

- Execute SQL statements more efficiently.

- Pass parameters more efficiently.

- Manage large objects (**LOB**s) more efficiently.

- Retrieve data more efficiently.

- Load bulk data into Oracle more efficiently.

- Obtain detailed performance statistics for each of the techniques outlined.

## Measuring Performance

Carrying on the wisdom of my gym instructor, you cannot beat down an opponent that you don't know enough about. In your case, you need to know how your code fares against time. There are generally two ways to check on the performance of your application. One way is to inspect the set of performance counters published by ODP.NET, and the other is to programmatically time your code using a high-resolution timer.

# Enabling the Performance Counters

The ODP.NET performance counters are a set of counters that tell you the number of connections active, closed, and so on at any point in time. This tool allows you, for example, to detect connection leaks where your code unintentionally leaves database connections unclosed.

For example, you might run a particular function in your application, check the total number of new connections, and then cross-check that with the number of connections closed. If the numbers do not match over repeated experimentation, you can conclude you have a connection leak. You can also hook these performance counters up to the Windows Reliability and Performance Monitor, which allows you to visualize different aspects of database performance as a set of time graphs. You could, for instance use, them to analyze correlations between CPU and database utilization peaks by overlaying different charts together.

---

■ **Note** The Oracle performance counters are not installed by default. You can install them anytime by choosing the Custom installation option and selecting the Oracle for Windows Performance option in the Oracle installer.

---

You will need to perform one more step before you can use the performance counters. The Oracle performance counters are setup to monitor only one database instance. You need to register your database instance with it. Oracle provides the command-line **Operfcfg.exe** tool (in the **ORACLE_HOME\BIN** folder) that allows you to do this via the following syntax:

```
operfcfg U <system> P <password> D <instancename>
```

For instance, you can register the **NEWDB** database instance by running the following at the command line:

```
operfcfg U SYSTEM P admin D localhost\NEWDB
```

Once you have done that, you should also ensure that all the performance counters are enabled. Using the Windows Registry Editor (**regedit.exe**) tool, navigate to the following key:

```
HKEY_LOCAL_MACHINE\Software\ORACLE\ODP.NET\2.111.7.20\PerformanceCounters
```

This key will be set to **0** (disabled). To enable all the counters, change this value to **4095**. You will next need to restart the Oracle database instance. As mentioned earlier, you can also view the performance counters visually in the Reliability and Performance Monitor tool provided by Windows in the Start ➤ Control Panel ➤ Administrative Tools area.

Launch the monitoring tool, highlight the Performance Monitor node, and click the Add Counters menu item. This will pop open a window showing a list of counters. Locate the Oracle Data Provider for .NET counter, and move all the counters into the Added Counters list, as shown in Figure 12-1.

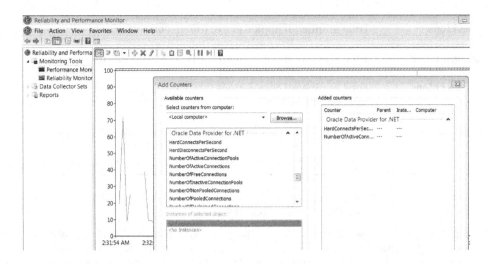

*Figure 12-1. ODP.NET performance counters in the Reliability and Performance Monitor tool*

Click the OK button to confirm. You will see the ODP.NET counters show up in the time graph area. Table 12-1 shows the list of performance counters available in Oracle and what each counter represents.

*Table 12-1. List of Performance Counters in Oracle*

| Performance Counter | Description |
|---|---|
| HardConnectsPerSecond | Total number of new database sessions established each second |
| HardDisconnectsPerSecond | Total number of database sessions closed each second |
| SoftConnectsPerSecond | Total number of cached connections retrieved from the connection pool |
| SoftDisconnectsPerSecond | Total number of cached connections released into the connection pool |
| NumberOfActiveConnectionPools | Total number of active connection pools |
| NumberOfInactiveConnectionPools | Total number of inactive connection pools |
| NumberOfActiveConnections | Total number of connections in use |
| NumberOfFreeConnections | Total number of connections available across all connection pools |

319

| NumberOfPooledConnections | Total number of pooled active (open) connections |
| NumberOfNonPooledConnections | Total number of non-pooled active (open) connections |
| NumberOfReclaimedConnections | Total number of connections internally disposed of by the garbage collector |
| NumberOfStasisConnections | Total number of connections that have been closed by the user but are in stasis—awaiting release back into the connection pool |

## Measuring Performance Programmatically

Measuring code performance has changed little over the years—you record the time before and after an event and calculate its delta. To achieve this, you need a high-resolution timer, one that can measure the time accurately to the millisecond. The .NET Framework, starting with version 2.0, provides a (in my opinion, well-named) **StopWatch** class that fits this job perfectly.

The **StopWatch** class attempts to use a hardware-based high-resolution timer (if one is found) or falls back on the system timer otherwise. The **StopWatch** class actually makes use of **kernel32.dll**'s **QueryPerformanceCounter** Windows API call to retrieve the time, so these two are functionally interchangeable. It is, of course, a better practice to use the **StopWatch** class since it is managed code.

You can use the **StopWatch** class in the following manner:

```
Stopwatch _stopwatch = new Stopwatch();
_stopwatch.Start();

// Do the task...

_stopwatch.Stop();
MessageBox.Show(_stopwatch.Elapsed.TotalSeconds.ToString () + " seconds");
```

This code **StopWatch.Elapsed.TotalSeconds** property can be used to retrieve the elapsed time. This will be displayed in the following format:

```
0.0917097 seconds
```

Take note that if you attempt to use the same **StopWatch** instance again after you have timed an event, you will need to call the **StopWatch.Reset** method to reset the total elapsed time internally stored in the object, as illustrated here:

```
Stopwatch _stopwatch = new Stopwatch();
_stopwatch.Start();
// Do first task ...
_stopwatch.Stop();
_stopwatch.Reset();
_stopwatch.Start();
//Do second task ...
_stopwatch.Stop();
```

---

■ **Tip** When measuring performance, it is usually not a good idea to take the measurement on the first run of the test code. When you run your code for the first time, you may have a lot of background-level loading, caching, and initialization going on, and all this can contribute to a larger time delta. A single, off-target measurement can drastically affect the measured average and produce inaccurate results.

---

# Speeding Up Connections with Connection Pooling

In the lifetime of an application, especially a web-based one, a large number of database connection instances will be opened and closed. To illustrate a case scenario, a web page may open two database connections on average. Assuming this web page receives 100 hits a minute (a realistic figure in the case of high-volume applications in some large organizations), that comes up to about 200 connections opened on the database every minute, a fairly large number for any database.

Connection pooling is Oracle's way of handling large number of connection requests. Opening a new connection to the database is usually a very slow and resource-intensive task. Connection pooling works by not destroying a connection object after it has been closed. It is merely kept in an "inactive" state until a new connection request arrives, whereby it is then reused. This allows the database to avoid the expensive operation of opening a totally new connection.

You can specify whether to enable or disable connection pooling in the connection string itself (although it is enabled by default). In fact, if you recall earlier from Chapter 3, there were a few other parameters that you could tweak in the connection string to adjust the performance of the connection pool. In this section, you will directly measure the performance difference between a code sample that uses connection pooling and one that doesn't. You can do this by measuring the time taken to open and close ten connections, in one case with connection pooling enabled and in the other case disabled. Create a new form, place a button on the form, and write the code shown in Listing 12-1.

*Listing 12-1. Opening and Closing Ten Connections With and Without Connection Pooling*

```
private void btnConnectionPooling_Click(object sender, EventArgs e)
{
        Stopwatch _stopwatch = new Stopwatch();
        String _Results;
        String _connstring = "Data Source=localhost/NEWDB;User
                Id=EDZEHOO;Password=PASS123;Pooling=false";
        try
        {
                //Open and close connections 10 times without connection pooling enabled
                OracleConnection _connObj = new OracleConnection(_connstring);
                _stopwatch.Start();
                for (int i = 1; i <= 10; i++)
                {
                    _connObj.Open();
                    _connObj.Close();
                }
                _stopwatch.Stop();
                _Results = "Without connection pooling:\t" +
```

```
                            _stopwatch.Elapsed.TotalSeconds.ToString() + " seconds\n";

                    //Open and close connections 10 times with connection pooling enabled
                    _connstring = "Data Source=localhost/NEWDB;User
                            Id=EDZEHOO;Password=PASS123;Pooling=true";
                    _connObj = new OracleConnection(_connstring);
                    _stopwatch.Reset();
                    _stopwatch.Start();
                    for (int i = 1; i <= 10; i++)
                    {
                        _connObj.Open();
                        _connObj.Close();
                    }
                    _stopwatch.Stop();
                    _Results = _Results + "With connection pooling:\t" +
                            _stopwatch.Elapsed.TotalSeconds.ToString() + " seconds\n";
                    MessageBox.Show(_Results);
                    _connObj.Close();
            }
            catch (Exception ex)
            {
                    MessageBox.Show(ex.ToString());
            }
    }
```

If you run this form and click the button, you will see a pop-up message showing you the elapsed time with connection pooling turned on and turned off. Note down these numbers, and run the same code again, but change the number of iterations from 10 to 50. If you repeat these steps with 100, 500, and 1,000 iterations, you will be able to tabulate results similar to the following:

| Iterations | Without connection pooling | With connection pooling | Performance boost |
|---|---|---|---|
| 10 | 0.4485831 | 0.2239234 | x 2.00 |
| 50 | 1.5553226 | 0.0757786 | x 20.52 |
| 100 | 3.0455792 | 0.0816510 | x 37.30 |
| 500 | 13.8253361 | 0.1356212 | x 101.94 |
| 1,000 | 25.8209253 | 0.2001342 | x 129.02 |

You can calculate the performance boost simply by dividing the elapsed time without connection pooling by the elapsed time with connection pooling. The preceding results indicate that by turning on connection pooling, the performance is twice as fast for ten iterations with connection pooling turned on than without.

Analyzing the results in more detail, you also find that the performance boost is, in fact, not linear, and the more connections that are opened and closed, the better the performance gain. This proves that connection pooling does indeed help and that it should always be used, even when you are not opening many connections to the database.

Use connection pooling in the following scenarios:

- When you need to open and close connections frequently, as in the case of web-based applications. Connection pooling can greatly reduce the amount of time required to establish subsequent connections to the database.

- It is always a good idea to keep connection pooling enabled, unless you have an always-connected application and you need full control over your database connections.

# Performing Faster Floating Point Arithmetic

One of the improvements of Oracle 10g was the introduction of the **BINARY_FLOAT** and **BINARY_DOUBLE** data types. These data types use machine arithmetic, which means that the computation works is passed to the operating system, and this makes them extremely efficient in handling floating point numbers.

You can gauge the performance of **BINARY_FLOAT** and **BINARY_DOUBLE** against the performance of the **NUMBER** data type. Create another button on the same form earlier, and write the code shown in Listing 12-2.

*Listing 12-2. One Million Additions Using BINARY_FLOAT, BINARY_DOUBLE, and NUMBER*

```
private void btnMeasureNumbers(object sender, EventArgs e)
{
        Stopwatch _stopwatch = new Stopwatch();
        String _Results;
        String _connstring = "Data Source=localhost/NEWDB;User
                Id=EDZEHOO;Password=PASS123;";
        try
        {
                OracleConnection _connObj = new OracleConnection(_connstring);
                _connObj.Open();
                OracleCommand _cmdObj = _connObj.CreateCommand();

                //Adding NUMBERs
                _cmdObj.CommandText = "DECLARE" +
                                "    Number1 NUMBER:=1;" +
                                "    Number2 NUMBER:=1;" +
                                "BEGIN" +
                                "    FOR i IN 1 .. 1000000 LOOP" +
                                "        Number1:=Number1 + Number2;" +
                                "    END LOOP;" +
                                "END;";
                _stopwatch.Start();
                _cmdObj.ExecuteNonQuery();
                _stopwatch.Stop();
```

```
        _Results = "Adding NUMBERs:\t" + _stopwatch.Elapsed.TotalSeconds.ToString()
                + " seconds\n";

        //Adding BINARY_FLOAT numbers
        _cmdObj.CommandText = "DECLARE" +
                        "    BinaryFloat1 BINARY_FLOAT:=1;" +
                        "    BinaryFloat2 BINARY_FLOAT:=1;" +
                        "BEGIN" +
                        "    FOR i IN 1 .. 1000000 LOOP" +
                        "        BinaryFloat1:=BinaryFloat1 + BinaryFloat2;" +
                        "    END LOOP;" +
                        "END;";
        _stopwatch.Reset();
        _stopwatch.Start();
        _cmdObj.ExecuteNonQuery();
        _stopwatch.Stop();
        _Results = _Results + "Adding BINARY_FLOATs:\t" +
                _stopwatch.Elapsed.TotalSeconds.ToString() + " seconds\n";

        //Adding BINARY_DOUBLE numbers
        _cmdObj.CommandText = "DECLARE" +
                        "    BinaryDouble1 BINARY_DOUBLE:=1;" +
                        "    BinaryDouble2 BINARY_DOUBLE:=1;" +
                        "BEGIN" +
                        "    FOR i IN 1 .. 1000000 LOOP" +
                        "        BinaryDouble1:=BinaryDouble1 + " +
                        "                    BinaryDouble2;" +
                        "    END LOOP;" +
                        "END;";
        _stopwatch.Reset();
        _stopwatch.Start();
        _cmdObj.ExecuteNonQuery();
        _stopwatch.Stop();
        _Results = _Results + "Adding BINARY_DOUBLEs:\t" +
                _stopwatch.Elapsed.TotalSeconds.ToString() + " seconds\n";

        MessageBox.Show(_Results);
        _connObj.Close();
    }
    catch (Exception ex)
    {
        MessageBox.Show(ex.ToString());
    }
}
```

If you record the elapsed times obtained for the following iterations in the same manner as before, you will roughly end up with the following results:

| Iterations | NUMBER | BINARY_FLOAT | Performance boost over NUMBER type | BINARY_DOUBLE | Performance boost over NUMBER type |
|---|---|---|---|---|---|
| 100 | 0.0004525 | 0.0001705 | x 2.65 | 0.0001590 | x 2.85 |
| 5,000 | 0.0008028 | 0.0003621 | x 2.22 | 0.0003468 | x 2.31 |
| 100,000 | 0.0084713 | 0.0043564 | x 1.94 | 0.0050087 | x 1.69 |
| 1,000,000 | 0.0779376 | 0.0397637 | x 1.96 | 0.0522518 | x 1.49 |
| 10,000,000 | 0.9389645 | 0.4426459 | x 2.12 | 0.5081020 | x 1.85 |

The test I've done on my PC shows that **BINARY_FLOAT** and **BINARY_DOUBLE** data types are consistently twice as fast (on average) as using **NUMBER** data types, even for a small number of iterations. It is therefore a good practice to always opt for **BINARY_FLOAT** and **BINARY_DOUBLE** data types when dealing with floating point numbers.

Use **BINARY_FLOAT** and **BINARY_DOUBLE** when you need performance over accuracy. Although they are fast, **BINARY_FLOAT** and **BINARY_DOUBLE** may not always represent fractional values accurately. If accuracy is important in your application, the **NUMBER** data type is a better choice.

# Executing Statements Faster

There are usually two performance bottlenecks when it comes to executing an SQL command. First, the SQL statement must be sent over the network to the Oracle server for processing before the results are returned. This sequence of events is commonly referred to as a database round-trip and is, by far, the most undesirable bottleneck, since it is subject to unknown variables such as network latency. Second, the SQL statement needs to be parsed by Oracle before it can actually be executed.

In the following sections, you will explore how to write code that improves the performance of these two tasks.

## Batching Your SQL Statements Together For Execution

One of the golden rules of improving data access performance is to reduce as much as possible the number of round-trips required to the database. This is because the amount of time required to send your SQL statements across the network is usually orders of magnitude higher than the amount of time needed to run the query at the server. There are two ways to reduce the number of database round trips:

- *Placing multiple SQL statements in a single stored procedure on the server:* This way, only a single round-trip is needed (to invoke the stored procedure) instead of making a round trip for each separate SQL statement.

- *Encasing multiple SQL statements within an anonymous PL/SQL block:* This is similar to the first method, except that you have the freedom of generating an anonymous PL/SQL block on the fly.

The following code sample shows how you can place multiple SQL statements within an anonymous PL/SQL block:

```
BEGIN
        UPDATE Products SET Price=100 WHERE ID='E1';
        UPDATE Products SET Price=200 WHERE ID='K1';
        DELETE FROM Products WHERE ID='A1';
END;
```

The entire preceding code snippet can simply be passed in as the **CommandText** property of an **OracleCommand** object. Let's take a look at the full code in detail. You will compare the performance of making one single database round trip (via a batched query) against the performance of making a separate database round trip for each SQL statement. Write the code shown in Listing 12-3.

*Listing 12-3. Updating 10,000 Records As Separate and Batched Commands*

```
private void btnBatchSQL(object sender, EventArgs e)
{
        Stopwatch _stopwatch = new Stopwatch();
        String _Results;
        String _connstring = "Data Source=localhost/NEWDB;User
                Id=EDZEHOO;Password=PASS123;";
        try
        {
                OracleConnection _connObj = new OracleConnection(_connstring);
                _connObj.Open();
                OracleCommand _cmdObj = _connObj.CreateCommand();

                //Update 10,000 products in separate statements
                _stopwatch.Start();
                for (int i = 1; i <= 10000; i++)
                {
                    _cmdObj.CommandText = "UPDATE Products SET Name='Test" +
                        Convert.ToString(i) + "' WHERE ID='E1'";
                    _cmdObj.ExecuteNonQuery();
                }
                _stopwatch.Stop();
                _Results = "Without Batch SQL:\t" +
                        _stopwatch.Elapsed.TotalSeconds.ToString() + " seconds\n";

                //Update 10,000 products in batch
                _cmdObj.CommandText = "BEGIN" +
                                "    FOR i IN 1 .. 10000 LOOP" +
                                "        UPDATE Products SET Name='Test' || i WHERE"+
                                "            ID='E1';" +
                                "    END LOOP;" +
                                "END;";
                _stopwatch.Reset();
                _stopwatch.Start();
                _cmdObj.ExecuteNonQuery();
                _stopwatch.Stop();
```

```
            _Results = _Results + "With Batch SQL:\t" +
                    _stopwatch.Elapsed.TotalSeconds.ToString() + " seconds\n";

            MessageBox.Show(_Results);
            _connObj.Close();
        }
        catch (Exception ex)
        {
            MessageBox.Show(ex.ToString());
        }
    }
}
```

If you run the preceding code sample for the different iterations shown here, you will roughly obtain the following results:

| No. of SQL commands | As separate statements | Batched in a single execution | Performance boost |
|---|---|---|---|
| 10 | 0.0013589 | 0.0007924 | x 1.71 |
| 100 | 0.0242765 | 0.0040843 | x 5.94 |
| 1,000 | 0.2767377 | 0.0347016 | x 7.97 |
| 5,000 | 4.4956063 | 0.2117111 | x 21.23 |
| 10,000 | 10.6515809 | 0.3819980 | x 27.88 |

By looking at these results, you can see that, even with a small number of SQL statements, you can already realize significant performance gains by batching your SQL commands together. The performance gains are more prominent if you batch more SQL commands together. The number of SQL commands you can batch together is limited by an internal size limit (which you can control in Oracle). If your application logic allows, always try to batch as many SQL commands as you can in a single database round-trip.

■ **Note** The actual performance gains are, in fact, higher than the results shown in the results table, because you are most likely running your code samples in the same machine as your Oracle database. You will see much higher performance gains if your code accesses a database server across the network. For this reason, it is a good idea to try to replicate your production environment as much as possible when you do performance testing. This will allow you to obtain performance measurements that are more reflective of your deployment environment.

Batch your SQL statements together in the following situations:

- *When you have different SQL statements that you need to execute together in a group:* If you have just a single SQL statement that you need to run repeatedly on a batch of data, you should consider using bind arrays instead (which will be covered later in this chapter).

- *When you don't have the option of placing the SQL statements in a stored procedure:* In terms of performance, stored procedures are always better since your SQL exists in compiled form. However, if your SQL statements need to be dynamically generated, you might want to consider using SQL statement batching.

## Using Statement Caching

Every time Oracle receives your SQL statement at the server, it will attempt to parse the statement and create the necessary cursors. It has to repeat this task for every SQL statement that it receives even if two statements are exactly the same. Now imagine having a long and complex SQL statement like this:

```
SELECT * FROM Products INNER JOIN ProductFiles ON
Products.ID=ProductFiles.ProductID
        INNER JOIN ProductComponents ON Products.ID=ProductComponents.ProductID
        INNER JOIN ProductImages ON Products.ID=ProductImages.ProductID
        WHERE Products.ID IN (SELECT ID FROM PurchasedProducts WHERE Amount>:Amount)
```

If this statement was executed many times (on every web page hit, for example), there would be a lot of wasted cycles parsing and processing the same thing over and over again. Statement caching allows the Oracle database to cache a statement, so that the next time it sees the same exact SQL, it will use the copy cached in memory instead of having to rebuild one from scratch. The result is better performance.

The statement cache can store a limited number of statements and push out the least recently used (LRU) statement when it is full. Take note that statement caching also works well with parameterized queries. For example, the following query is regarded as the same SQL statement regardless of the different parameters that are passed in, and will only take up one slot in the statement cache:

```
SELECT * FROM Products WHERE ID=:1 AND Name=:2
```

You can enable statement caching via a few methods. For example, you can enable it at the registry-level or at the connection instance level (in the connection string). Statement caching is enabled by default in ODP.NET, and the statement cache size (the maximum number of statements that the cache can hold), is set to 10 by default.

For example, to set the statement cache size of a particular connection to 20, you can declare it in the connection string as follows:

```
Data Source=localhost/NEWDB;User Id=EDZEHOO;Password=PASS123;Statement Cache Si↵
ze=20;Self Tuning=false;
```

---

■ **Tip** Self-tuning is a feature of the Oracle database (enabled by default) that can dynamically adjust the statement cache size on its own to improve application performance. When it is enabled, the automatically determined statement cache size will overwrite any other statement cache size setting. For this reason, you must set it to `false` if you want to define a fixed statement cache size of your own.

---

You can also control the statement cache programmatically through ODP.NET. For example, you might have enabled statement caching on a connection instance but do not wish to cache a particular statement (maybe because it is rarely called, and you prefer not to have it take up any cache slots). You can tell ODP.NET whether to add a statement to the cache or not by setting the `OracleCommand.AddToStatementCache` property to either **true** or **false**, in the fashion shown here:

```
OracleCommand _cmdObj = _connObj.CreateCommand();
_cmdObj.AddToStatementCache = false;
_cmdObj.CommandText = "SELECT * FROM Products";
_cmdObj.ExecuteNonQuery();
```

The code in Listing 12-4 shows the performance gains when you turn on statement caching. It attempts to run the same query 10,000 times on the **Products** table in two scenarios, one with statement caching disabled and the other with it enabled.

*Listing 12-4. Executing 10,000 Queries with Statement Caching Disabled and Enabled*

```
private void btnStatementCaching(object sender, EventArgs e)
{
        Stopwatch _stopwatch = new Stopwatch();
        String _Results;

        try
        {
                //Retrieve 10,000 products with statement caching disabled
                //Setting a cache size of 0 automatically disables the statement cache
                String _connstring = "Data Source=localhost/NEWDB;User
                        Id=EDZEHOO;Password=PASS123;Statement Cache Size=0;Self
                        Tuning=false;";
                OracleConnection _connObj = new OracleConnection(_connstring);
                _connObj.Open();
                OracleCommand _cmdObj = _connObj.CreateCommand();
                _stopwatch.Start();
                _cmdObj.CommandText = "SELECT * FROM Products WHERE ID=:IDValue";
                OracleParameter _paramObj =
                        _cmdObj.Parameters.Add("IDValue",OracleDbType.Varchar2);
                for (int i = 1; i <= 10000; i++)
                {
                        _paramObj.Value = "E" + Convert.ToString(i);
                        OracleDataReader _rdrObj = _cmdObj.ExecuteReader();
                        _rdrObj.Dispose();
                }
                _stopwatch.Stop();
```

```
        _Results = "Without Statement Caching:\t" +
                _stopwatch.Elapsed.TotalSeconds.ToString() + " seconds\n";
        _cmdObj.Dispose();
        _connObj.Close();

        //Retrieve 10,000 products with statement caching enabled
        _connstring = "Data Source=localhost/NEWDB;User
                Id=EDZEHOO;Password=PASS123;Statement Cache Size=5;Self
                Tuning=false;";
        _connObj.ConnectionString = _connstring;
        _connObj.Open();
        _cmdObj = _connObj.CreateCommand();
        _stopwatch.Reset();
        _stopwatch.Start();
        _cmdObj.CommandText = "SELECT * FROM Products WHERE ID=:IDValue";
        _paramObj = _cmdObj.Parameters.Add("IDValue", OracleDbType.Varchar2);
        for (int i = 1; i <= 10000; i++)
        {
                _paramObj.Value = "E" + Convert.ToString(i);
                OracleDataReader _rdrObj = _cmdObj.ExecuteReader();
                _rdrObj.Dispose();
        }
        _stopwatch.Stop();
        _Results = _Results + "With Statement Caching:\t" +
                _stopwatch.Elapsed.TotalSeconds.ToString() + " seconds\n";
        _cmdObj.Dispose();
        _connObj.Close();
        MessageBox.Show(_Results);
    }
    catch (Exception ex)
    {
            MessageBox.Show(ex.ToString());
    }
}
```

Running this form will produce the following results:

| Iterations | Without statement caching | With statement caching | Performance boost |
|---|---|---|---|
| 10 | 0.0058024 | 0.0021162 | x 2.74 |
| 100 | 0.0694805 | 0.0208891 | x 3.33 |
| 5,000 | 2.1803009 | 0.7888571 | x 2.76 |
| 10,000 | 5.0760874 | 1.6864191 | x 3.01 |
| 50,000 | 22.7099379 | 8.3316285 | x 2.73 |

You can observe that statement caching will consistently yield a performance gain if the executing statement is found in the cache.

Use statement caching when you have a small bunch of SQL statements that will be called very frequently in your application. Even if you have widely differing set of SQL statements, you can still enable statement caching (together with the self-tuning option) since Oracle will dynamically adjust the size of the statement cache for you.

## REF Cursors and Multiple Active Resultsets (MARs)

You took your first look at **REF** cursors and multiple active results (MARs) in Chapter 5. Essentially, these two features allow you to reduce the number of round-trips to the server by executing multiple statements and returning multiple datasets in a single round-trip to Oracle. They may not seem to contribute to any performance difference if your code and database resides on the same machine, but when accessing the database over the network, the performance gain becomes visibly higher.

# Passing Parameters More Efficiently

As mentioned earlier, one of the most common ways of improving performance is to reduce the number of round-trips required to the database server. One idea that has arisen from this objective thought is to pass a large number of parameters in bulk to the server in a single round-trip and have the SQL at the server side work on each row of data in the parameter set.

For instance, you might want to insert five records into a table. Instead of running five separate queries (five round-trips), you could put all five records into an array, send it to the server in a single round-trip, and have the SQL **INSERT** command work on each of the records at the server.

There are two ways to pass such arrays to the server: via bind arrays and PL/SQL associative arrays.

## Using Bind Arrays to Pass Parameters in Bulk

The bind array feature allows you to bind a standard .NET array to an **OracleParameter** object instead of the usual **VARCHAR2** or **DECIMAL** data types. To bind an array, simply pass in any .NET array to the **OracleParameter.Value**, and set the **OracleCommand.ArrayBindCount** property to the number of elements in the array. The code in Listing 12-5 shows how you can update the prices for three different products by specifying the data via a bind array.

*Listing 12-5. Updating the Prices for Three Different Products via a Bind Array*

```
//Declare the arrays and the SQL command
int[] _priceArray = new int[3] { 100, 300, 500 };
String[] _IDArray = new String[3] {"E1","E2","E3"};
OracleCommand _cmdObj = _connObj.CreateCommand();
_cmdObj.CommandText = "UPDATE Products SET Price=:Price WHERE ID=:ID";

//Declare the parameters
OracleParameter _priceParam = new OracleParameter("Price", OracleDbType.Decimal);
_priceParam.Value = _priceArray;
_cmdObj.Parameters.Add(_priceParam);
OracleParameter _IDParam = new OracleParameter("ID", OracleDbType.Varchar2);
```

```
_IDParam.Value = _IDArray;
_cmdObj.Parameters.Add(_IDParam);

//Define the number of elements in the arrays
_cmdObj.ArrayBindCount = 3;
_cmdObj.ExecuteNonQuery();
```

Now, let's take a look at the performance gains when you use bind arrays. You will insert three records into the **Products** table using a bind array and iterate this task 10,000 times. The results will be compared against a scenario in which three separate **ExecuteNonQuery** calls are executed to insert each of the three records. The code in Listing 12-6 shows the full code for this sample.

*Listing 12-6. Updating the Prices for Three Different Products via a Bind Array*

```
private void btnBindArray_Click(object sender, EventArgs e)
{
        Stopwatch _stopwatch = new Stopwatch();
        String _Results;
        String _connstring = "Data Source=localhost/NEWDB;User
              Id=EDZEHOO;Password=PASS123;";
        try
        {
                OracleConnection _connObj = new OracleConnection(_connstring);
                _connObj.Open();

                //Clear the table
                OracleCommand _cmdDelObj = _connObj.CreateCommand();
                _cmdDelObj.CommandText = "DELETE FROM Products";
                _cmdDelObj.ExecuteNonQuery();

                //Perform 10,000 iterations, inserting 3 records in every iteration without
                //using bind arrays
                OracleCommand _cmdObj = _connObj.CreateCommand();
                _cmdObj.CommandText = "INSERT INTO Products(ID, Name, Price) VALUES(:ID,
                      :Name, :Price)";
                OracleParameter _IDParam = new OracleParameter("ID", OracleDbType.Varchar2);
                _cmdObj.Parameters.Add(_IDParam);
                OracleParameter _nameParam = new OracleParameter("Name",
                      OracleDbType.Varchar2);
                _cmdObj.Parameters.Add(_nameParam);
                OracleParameter _priceParam = new OracleParameter("Price",
                      OracleDbType.Decimal);
                _cmdObj.Parameters.Add(_priceParam);

                _stopwatch.Start();
                for (int i = 1; i <= 10000; i++)
                {
                        _IDParam.Value = "EN" + Convert.ToString(i);
                        _nameParam.Value = "Engine" + Convert.ToString(i);
                        _priceParam.Value = 100;
                        _cmdObj.ExecuteNonQuery();
```

```
                    _IDParam.Value = "WS" + Convert.ToString(i);
                    _nameParam.Value = "Windshield" + Convert.ToString(i);
                    _priceParam.Value = 300;
                    _cmdObj.ExecuteNonQuery();

                    _IDParam.Value = "RL" + Convert.ToString(i);
                    _nameParam.Value = "Rear Lights" + Convert.ToString(i);
                    _priceParam.Value = 500;
                    _cmdObj.ExecuteNonQuery();
            }
            _stopwatch.Stop();
            _Results = "Without bind arrays:\t" +
                    _stopwatch.Elapsed.TotalSeconds.ToString() + " seconds\n";

            //Clear the table again
            _cmdDelObj.ExecuteNonQuery();
            _cmdDelObj.Dispose();

            //Perform 10,000 iterations, inserting 3 records in every iteration using
            //bind arrays
            _cmdObj.ArrayBindCount = 3;
            _stopwatch.Reset ();
            _stopwatch.Start();
            for (int i = 1; i <= 10000; i++)
            {
                    int[] _priceArray = new int[3] { 100, 300, 500 };
                    String[] _nameArray = new String[3] { "Engine" +
                            Convert.ToString(i), "Windshield" + Convert.ToString(i),
                            "Rear Lights" + Convert.ToString(i) };
                    String[] _IDArray = new String[3] { "EN" + Convert.ToString(i), "WS"
                            + Convert.ToString(i), "RL" + Convert.ToString(i) };
                    _IDParam.Value = _IDArray;
                    _nameParam.Value = _nameArray;
                    _priceParam.Value = _priceArray;
                    _cmdObj.ExecuteNonQuery();
            }
            _stopwatch.Stop();
            _cmdObj.Dispose();
            _Results = _Results + "With Bind Arrays:\t" +
                    _stopwatch.Elapsed.TotalSeconds.ToString() + " seconds\n";

            MessageBox.Show(_Results);
            _connObj.Close();
            _connObj.Dispose();
            _connObj = null;
    }
    catch (Exception ex)
    {
            MessageBox.Show(ex.ToString());
    }
}
```

By repeating the test with different iterations, you will roughly obtain the following results:

| Iterations | Using 3 separate statements | 1 single query via bind arrays | Performance boost |
|---|---|---|---|
| 10 | 0.0282477 | 0.0083203 | x 3.40 |
| 500 | 1.0320563 | 0.4317347 | x 2.39 |
| 1,000 | 2.1718022 | 0.8851226 | x 2.45 |
| 5,000 | 11.7337222 | 4.7723287 | x 2.46 |
| 10,000 | 25.3184049 | 11.7804309 | x 2.15 |

As you can see, there is a consistent performance gain greater than a factor of two even for a small number of iterations. This performance gain observed should be greater in a production environment where the database server sits on a different machine from your executing code.

Use bind arrays in the following scenarios:

- When you have a single SQL statement that you need to run repeatedly many times on a large set of data, a bind array would be suitable.

- Bind arrays, as opposed to PL/SQL associative arrays (which you will read about in the next section) support a larger number of data types (including **LOB** and **XMLType**). Use bind arrays when you need to pass in arrays that are based on these data types.

- Bind arrays are also faster than PL/SQL associative arrays. A bind array is copied as a chunk directly to the SQL engine, whereas a PL/SQL associative array first makes it into the PL/SQL engine as a chunk but is then sent to the SQL engine one row at a time.

## Using PL/SQL Associative Arrays

You first encountered PL/SQL associative arrays in Chapter 5. You've seen how you could pass a standard .NET array to a PL/SQL stored procedure as an associative array. This section aims to show the performance gains that arise from using associative arrays. The code shown in Listing 12-7 will first update three records in the **Products** table using three individual statements (repeated 10,000 times), and then perform the same function using associative arrays. For this sample, you will be making use of the **ProductsPackage.proc_UpdateMultiplePrices** package that you've created earlier in Chapter 5.

*Listing 12-7. Updating Three Records 10,000 times With and Without Associative Arrays*

```
private void btnAssociativeArrays(object sender, EventArgs e)
{
        Stopwatch _stopwatch = new Stopwatch();
```

```
String _Results;
String _connstring = "Data Source=localhost/NEWDB;User
        Id=EDZEHOO;Password=PASS123;";
try
{
        //Perform 10,000 iterations, updating 3 records in each iteration without
        //using associative arrays
        OracleConnection _connObj = new OracleConnection(_connstring);
        _connObj.Open();
        OracleCommand _cmdObj = _connObj.CreateCommand();
        _cmdObj.CommandText = "UPDATE Products SET Price = Price + :ProdPrice WHERE
                Name = :ProdName";
        OracleParameter _priceParam = new
                OracleParameter("ProdPrice",OracleDbType.Decimal);
        _cmdObj.Parameters.Add(_priceParam);
        OracleParameter _nameParam = new OracleParameter("ProdName",
                OracleDbType.Varchar2 );
        _cmdObj.Parameters.Add(_nameParam);

        _stopwatch.Start();
        for (int i = 1; i <= 10000; i++)
        {
            _priceParam.Value  = 100;
            _nameParam.Value = "Engine";
            _cmdObj.ExecuteNonQuery();

            _priceParam.Value = 300;
            _nameParam.Value = "Windshield";
            _cmdObj.ExecuteNonQuery();

            _priceParam.Value = 500;
            _nameParam.Value = "Rear Lights";
            _cmdObj.ExecuteNonQuery();
        }
        _stopwatch.Stop();
        _cmdObj.Dispose();
        _Results = "Without arrays:\t" + _stopwatch.Elapsed.TotalSeconds.ToString()
                + " seconds\n";

        //Perform 10,000 iterations, updating 3 records in each iteration using
        //associative arrays
        _cmdObj = _connObj.CreateCommand();
        _cmdObj.CommandText = "ProductsPackage.proc_UpdateMultiplePrices";
        _cmdObj.CommandType = CommandType.StoredProcedure;

        //Declare first parameter
        _priceParam = new OracleParameter();
        _priceParam.ParameterName = "ProdPrices";
        _priceParam.OracleDbType = OracleDbType.Decimal;
        _priceParam.Direction = ParameterDirection.Input;
        _priceParam.CollectionType = OracleCollectionType.PLSQLAssociativeArray;
        _cmdObj.Parameters.Add(_priceParam);
```

```
                //Declare second parameter
                _nameParam = new OracleParameter();
                _nameParam.ParameterName = "ProdNames";
                _nameParam.OracleDbType = OracleDbType.Varchar2;
                _nameParam.Direction = ParameterDirection.Input;
                _nameParam.CollectionType = OracleCollectionType.PLSQLAssociativeArray;
                _cmdObj.Parameters.Add(_nameParam);

                _stopwatch.Reset();
                _stopwatch.Start();
                for (int i = 1; i <= 10000; i++)
                {
                        Decimal[] decArray = new Decimal[3];
                        decArray[0] = 100;
                        decArray[1] = 300;
                        decArray[2] = 500;
                        _priceParam.Value = decArray;

                        String[] stringArray = new String[3];
                        stringArray[0] = "Engine";
                        stringArray[1] = "Windshield";
                        stringArray[2] = "Rear Lights";
                        _nameParam.Value = stringArray;

                        _cmdObj.ExecuteNonQuery();
                }
                _stopwatch.Stop();
                _cmdObj.Dispose();
                _Results = _Results + "With Associative Arrays:\t" +
                        _stopwatch.Elapsed.TotalSeconds.ToString() + " seconds\n";

                MessageBox.Show(_Results);
                _connObj.Close();
                _connObj.Dispose();
                _connObj = null;
        }
        catch (Exception ex)
        {
                MessageBox.Show(ex.ToString());
        }
}
```

As you can see from the following results (after running the same test for different each number of iterations), there is a consistent performance gain. This performance gain will be greater if data access is made over the network.

| Iterations | Using 3 separate | 1 single query via statements | Performance boost associative arrays |
|---|---|---|---|
| 10 | 0.0284687 | 0.0105727 | x 2.69 |
| 100 | 0.2164235 | 0.1016446 | x 2.13 |
| 1,000 | 2.3103020 | 1.0773094 | x 2.14 |
| 5,000 | 16.7329752 | 7.7061877 | x 2.17 |
| 10,000 | 26.1693986 | 12.1299475 | x 2.16 |

Use PL/SQL associative arrays when you need a high level of control in a stored procedure. PL/SQL associative arrays are powerful collection objects that let you do much more in PL/SQL. For instance, you could refer to the elements of an associative array using an index of any desired data type. It could, therefore, double as a lookup table. If you need this type of control in your stored procedure, passing your data to a stored procedure via a PL/SQL associative array would be better than a bind array.

# Managing LOBs More Efficiently

The official documentation from Oracle suggests using the large object data types (**BLOB**, **CLOB**, and **NCLOB**) instead of the **LONG** or **LONG RAW** data types when storing large objects (greater than 2GB) in the database, because the Oracle **LOB** data types yield better performance.

When using **LOB** data types, however, it is still possible to further boost performance in the following two ways:

- Enabling the **LOB** cache
- Setting the `InitialLOBFetchSize` property

## Enabling the LOB Cache

When you enable **LOB** caching on a **LOB** column, the data in that column is cached in a database buffer cache. You can immediately see the pros and cons of such an approach. If you cache a **LOB** column containing large amounts of stored data, this would frequently force other data blocks out of the cache. For this reason, **LOB** caching is disabled by default.

**LOB** caching is useful when you have small **LOB** objects that are retrieved very frequently. For example, you might have a bunch of 5-KB employee photos stored in a **LOB** column that you need very fast access to. However, if you were planning on storing 2-MB photos in the **LOB** column, disabling the **LOB** cache would be a better idea.

You can enable **LOB** caching on a **LOB** column by running the following query in SQL*Plus:

```
ALTER TABLE ProductFiles MODIFY LOB(FileAttachment) (CACHE);
```

To disable caching, run the same query but substitute **CACHE** with **NOCACHE**. The code in Listing 12-8 shows the performance gain when you enable **LOB** caching. You will first disable caching on the **FileAttachment BLOB** column in the **ProductFiles** table. After doing so, you will read the full length of the **BLOB** data from a record and repeat this task 100 times. The second part of the code does the same thing with **LOB** caching enabled.

*Listing 12-8. Retrieving LOB Data with LOB Caching Disabled and Enabled*

```
private void btnLOBS_Click(object sender, EventArgs e)
{
        //We first read the full contents of the file into a byte array
        Stopwatch _stopwatch = new Stopwatch();
        String _Results;
        String _connstring = "Data Source=localhost/NEWDB;User
                Id=EDZEHOO;Password=PASS123;";
        try
        {
                OracleConnection _connObj = new OracleConnection(_connstring);
                OracleDataReader _rdrObj;
                _connObj.Open();
                OracleCommand _cmdObj = _connObj.CreateCommand();

                //Disable the Cache
                _cmdObj.CommandText = "ALTER TABLE ProductFiles MODIFY LOB(FileAttachment)
                        (NOCACHE)";
                _cmdObj.ExecuteNonQuery();
                _cmdObj.CommandText = "SELECT FileAttachment FROM ProductFiles WHERE
                        ProductID=:ProductID";
                _cmdObj.Parameters.Add(new OracleParameter("ProductID", "Z1"));
                _stopwatch.Start();
                for (int i = 1; i <= 100; i++)
                {
                        _rdrObj = _cmdObj.ExecuteReader();
                        if (_rdrObj.HasRows)
                        {
                                if (_rdrObj.Read())
                                {
                                OracleBlob _blobObj =
                                        _rdrObj.GetOracleBlob(_rdrObj.GetOrdinal
                                        ("FileAttachment"));
                                byte[] dest = new byte[_blobObj.Length];
                                _blobObj.Read(dest, 0, (int)_blobObj.Length);
                                }
                        }
                        else
                        {
                                MessageBox.Show("The BLOB was not found!");
                        }
                }
                _stopwatch.Stop();
                _cmdObj.Dispose();
```

```
            _Results = "Without LOB caching:\t" +
                    _stopwatch.Elapsed.TotalSeconds.ToString() + " seconds\n";

            //Enable the Cache
            _cmdObj = _connObj.CreateCommand();
            _cmdObj.CommandText = "ALTER TABLE ProductFiles MODIFY LOB(FileAttachment)
                    (CACHE)";
            _cmdObj.ExecuteNonQuery();
            _cmdObj.CommandText = "SELECT FileAttachment FROM ProductFiles WHERE
                    ProductID=:ProductID";
            _cmdObj.Parameters.Add(new OracleParameter("ProductID", "Z1"));
            _stopwatch.Reset();
            _stopwatch.Start();
            for (int i = 1; i <= 100; i++)
            {
                    _rdrObj = _cmdObj.ExecuteReader();
                    if (_rdrObj.HasRows)
                    {
                            if (_rdrObj.Read())
                            {
                            OracleBlob _blobObj =
                                    _rdrObj.GetOracleBlob(_rdrObj.GetOrdinal
                                    ("FileAttachment"));
                            byte[] dest = new byte[_blobObj.Length];
                            _blobObj.Read(dest, 0, (int)_blobObj.Length);
                            }
                    }
                    else
                    {
                            MessageBox.Show("The BLOB was not found!");
                    }
            }
            _stopwatch.Stop();
            _Results = _Results + "With LOB Caching:\t" +
                    _stopwatch.Elapsed.TotalSeconds.ToString() + " seconds\n";
            MessageBox.Show(_Results);
            _connObj.Close();
            _connObj.Dispose();
            _connObj = null;
        }
        catch (Exception ex)
        {
                MessageBox.Show(ex.ToString());
        }
}
```

Before you run the preceding form, you will need to ensure that you have loaded a record (together with the **BLOB** data) into the **ProductFiles** table. Running the test yields the following result, showing that there is a consistent performance gain when **LOB** caching is enabled:

| Iterations | Without LOB caching | With LOB caching | Performance boost |
|------------|---------------------|------------------|-------------------|
| 1 | 0.2171803 | 0.0838123 | x 2.59 |
| 10 | 0.5357599 | 0.3057165 | x 1.75 |
| 50 | 2.2895203 | 1.3499337 | x 1.70 |
| 100 | 4.8449798 | 2.7377508 | x 1.77 |

Enable the **LOB** cache when you have small **LOB** objects that are retrieved very frequently from the database.

## Setting the InitialLOBFetchSize Property

The second way to boost **LOB** performance is to change the **InitialLOBFetchSize** property. This property defines the amount of **LOB** column data (in bytes) to fetch (and cache) from the database during an **OracleDataReader.Read** invocation. By default, this property is set to **0**. If you know the size (or size limit) of your **LOB** data in advance, you can set this property to that size or a higher value to give your code a performance boost.

You can set the **InitialLOBFetchSize** in the manner illustrated in Listing 12-9.

*Listing 12-9. Setting the InitialLOBFetchSize Property*

```
OracleConnection _connObj = new OracleConnection(_connstring);
OracleDataReader _rdrObj;
_connObj.Open();
OracleCommand _cmdObj = _connObj.CreateCommand();
//Set the LOB Fetch Size to 100,000 bytes
_cmdObj.InitialLOBFetchSize = 100000
_cmdObj.CommandText = "SELECT FileAttachment FROM ProductFiles WHERE
        ProductID=:ProductID";
_rdrObj = _cmdObj.ExecuteReader();
if (_rdrObj.HasRows)
{
        if (_rdrObj.Read())
        {
                OracleBlob _blobObj = _rdrObj.GetOracleBlob(_rdrObj.GetOrdinal
                        ("FileAttachment"));
        }
}
_connObj.Close();
_connObj.Dispose();
```

---

■ **Note** The official Oracle documentation recommends that you set the `InitialLOBFetchSize` property to the LOB size that is encountered 80 percent of the time. For example, in a table of 1,000 rows where 800 rows have LOB data sizes of 15KB and the other 200 rows 100KB, you should set the `InitialLOBFetchSize` property to 15KB.

---

Change the `InitialLOBCacheSize` property if you know in advance the size of the LOB objects you are frequently fetching from the database.

# Retrieving Data More Efficiently

After you've established a cursor to your data source, data retrieval can also be a performance-intensive affair. The objective of performance optimization in this area would be to cut down on as much round-trips to the server as possible to retrieve the data you need. This can be done via two methods:

- Changing the `FetchSize` property
- Enabling the client result cache

## Changing the FetchSize Property

The `FetchSize` property, as its name indicates, represents the size of the data to fetch during each round-trip made to the server. It directly affects the performance of the **OracleDataReader** object. The `FetchSize` property is set to 64KB by default. You can change this value if you would like to retrieve more data than this amount during each round-trip to the server.

The **OracleCommand** property also provides a **RowSize** property, which can come in pretty handy when you need to set the `FetchSize`. Rather than simply guessing a number to use for `FetchSize`, you can specify the amount to fetch in terms of number of rows instead. This can be done using this rather simple formula:

```
OracleDataReader.FetchSize = OracleCommand.RowSize * rowsNeeded;
```

In Listing 12-10, you can see performance gains when you attempt to retrieve 10,000 rows from the **Products** table when you change your `FetchSize` to fetch for instance, all 10,000 rows in one round-trip.

*Listing 12-10. Fetching 10,000 Rows from the Database with Different FetchSizes*

```
private void btnFetchData_Click(object sender, EventArgs e)
{
        Stopwatch _stopwatch = new Stopwatch();
        String _Results;
        string _connstring = "Data Source=localhost/NEWDB;User
                Id=EDZEHOO;Password=PASS123;";
        try
        {
```

```
OracleConnection _connObj = new OracleConnection(_connstring);
_connObj.Open();
OracleCommand _cmdObj = _connObj.CreateCommand();

//Insert 10,000 dummy records into the Products table
_cmdObj.CommandText = "DELETE FROM Products";
_cmdObj.ExecuteNonQuery();
for (int i = 1; i <= 10000; i++)
{
        _cmdObj.CommandText = "INSERT INTO Products(ID, Name, Remarks)
                VALUES('E' + Convert.ToString(i) + "','TestData','')";
        _cmdObj.ExecuteNonQuery();
}
MessageBox.Show("10,000 products inserted");

//Read all 10,000 products from the same table using the default FetchSize
//of 64K
_cmdObj.CommandText = "SELECT * FROM Products";
_stopwatch.Start();
OracleDataReader _rdrObj = _cmdObj.ExecuteReader();
while (_rdrObj.Read()) { }
_stopwatch.Stop();
_Results = "Default Fetchsize (64Kb):\t" +
        _stopwatch.Elapsed.TotalSeconds.ToString() + " seconds\n";

//Set the FetchSize to accommodate for 10,000 rows and execute the same
//query again
_stopwatch.Reset();
_stopwatch.Start();
_rdrObj = _cmdObj.ExecuteReader();
long _newFetchSize = _rdrObj.RowSize * 10000;
_rdrObj.FetchSize = _newFetchSize;
while (_rdrObj.Read()) { }
_stopwatch.Stop();
_Results = _Results + "Fetchsize (" + Convert.ToString (_newFetchSize) +
        "):\t" + _stopwatch.Elapsed.TotalSeconds.ToString() + " seconds\n";

MessageBox.Show(_Results);
_connObj.Close();
}
catch (Exception ex)
{
        MessageBox.Show(ex.ToString());
}
}
```

After you run this test, you will notice that performance gains become gradually higher as you attempt to retrieve more rows, because the first portion of the test is limited by its default fetch size of 64KB. Just like the earlier examples, you will also notice higher performance gains if your test runs with the database accessed across the network; this is due to the reduced numbered of round-trips to the server.

| Rows to retrieve | Default Fetchsize (64K) | Setting Fetchsize to full size of recordset | Performance boost |
|---|---|---|---|
| 100 | 0.0042696 | 0.0033354 | x 1.28 |
| 500 | 0.0091752 | 0.0062257 | x 1.47 |
| 1,000 | 0.0158941 | 0.0083665 | x 1.90 |
| 5,000 | 0.0653888 | 0.0296861 | x 2.20 |
| 10,000 | 0.1405070 | 0.0553485 | x 2.54 |

Change the FetchSize property if you know in advance how many rows you need from the database. For instance, if you know that you need the entire set of records from the Products table, and you know that you have about 800 products, you can attempt to fetch 1,000 rows from this table by changing the FetchSize property accordingly.

## Using the Client Result Cache

Unlike the earlier forms of caching, a client result cache is performed at the client side to cache query results, which means that data could be readily retrieved from the client cache instead of having to make a round-trip to the server. The client result cache is also automatically invalidated and refreshed by the server. Whenever data at the server changes, the client automatically receives a notification that updates the client-side cache. This is all done under the hood without requiring a single line of change to your code.

The client result cache is disabled by default and can only be enabled via the init.ora file. This file is the initialization file for your Oracle instance and can either be edited manually or via SQL*Plus. In both cases, a restart of your Oracle database instance is required. To enable the client result cache, you need to specify a size for the cache. You can enable it by typing the following in SQL*Plus under the SYSTEM account:

```
ALTER SYSTEM SET client_result_cache_size=64000 scope=spfile;
```

The scope=spfile keyword is mandatory; it tells SQL*Plus to make the changes directly to the SPFile (init.ora). After doing this, restart your Oracle database instance under Administrative Tools ➤ Services. When your database instance is back up, you can check to see if the client result cache size reflects the new size by typing the following commands in SQL*Plus:

```
SHOW PARAMETER client_result_cache_size;
SHOW PARAMETER result_cache_mode;
```

You should see the screenshot shown in Figure 12-2.

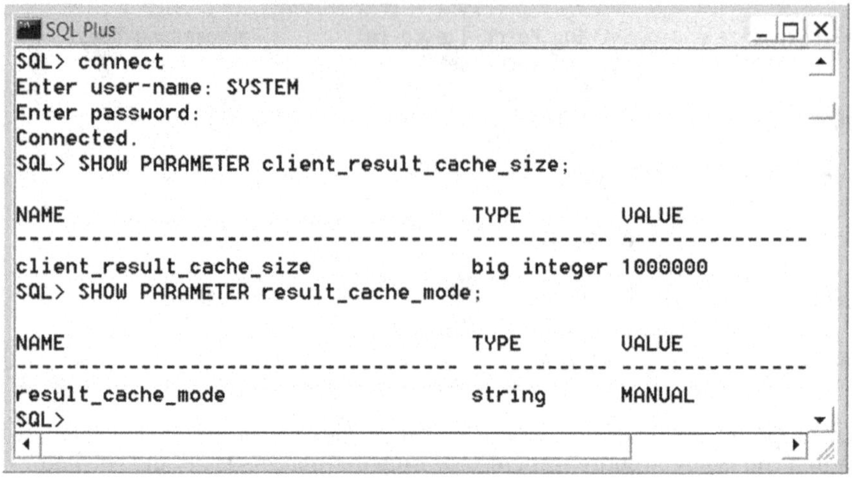

*Figure 12-2. Retrieving the result_cache_mode and client_result_cache_size parameters*

The result cache mode specifies whether statements should use the client result cache always or only when manually specified in the SQL statement itself. If this value is set to **MANUAL**, you can get an SQL statement to use the client result cache by specifying the **/*+ result_cache */** hint in the following manner:

```
SELECT /*+ result_cache */ ID,Name FROM Products
```

Let's measure the performance gains of using the client result cache. The code in Listing 12-11 measures the performance when 1,000 rows are retrieved from the **Products** table with the client result cache first disabled and then enabled.

*Listing 12-11. Fetching 1,000 Rows with Client Result Cache Disabled and Enabled*

```
private void btnClientResultCache_Click(object sender, EventArgs e)
{
        Stopwatch _stopwatch = new Stopwatch();
        String _Results;
        String _connstring = "Data Source=localhost/NEWDB;User
                Id=EDZEHOO;Password=PASS123;";
        try
        {
                OracleConnection _connObj = new OracleConnection(_connstring);
                _connObj.Open();
                OracleCommand _cmdObj = _connObj.CreateCommand();

                //Insert 1,000 dummy records into the Products table
                _cmdObj.CommandText = "DELETE FROM Products";
                _cmdObj.ExecuteNonQuery();
                for (int i = 1; i <= 1000; i++)
```

```
{
        _cmdObj.CommandText = "INSERT INTO Products(ID, Name, Remarks)
                VALUES('E" + Convert.ToString(i) + "','TestData','')";
        _cmdObj.ExecuteNonQuery();
}
MessageBox.Show("1,000 products inserted");

//Retrieve 1,000 rows without using the client result cache
_cmdObj.CommandText = "SELECT * FROM Products";
_stopwatch.Start();
for (int i = 1; i <=1000; i++)
{
        OracleDataReader _rdrObj = _cmdObj.ExecuteReader();
        while (_rdrObj.Read()) { }
        _rdrObj.Close();
}
_stopwatch.Stop();
_Results = "No client result cache:\t" +
        _stopwatch.Elapsed.TotalSeconds.ToString() + " seconds\n";

//Retrieve 1,000 rows using the client result cache
_cmdObj.CommandText = "SELECT /*+ result_cache */ * FROM Products";
_stopwatch.Reset();
_stopwatch.Start();
for (int i = 1; i <= 1000; i++)
{
        OracleDataReader _rdrObj = _cmdObj.ExecuteReader();
        while (_rdrObj.Read()) {  }
        _rdrObj.Close();
}
 _stopwatch.Stop();
_Results = _Results + "With client result cache:\t" +
        _stopwatch.Elapsed.TotalSeconds.ToString() + " seconds\n";

MessageBox.Show(_Results);
_connObj.Close();
}
catch (Exception ex)
{
        MessageBox.Show(ex.ToString());
}
}
```

The results show that a consistent performance gain when the client result cache is enabled:

| Iterations | Without client result caching | With client result caching | Performance boost |
|---|---|---|---|
| 10 | 0.0364982 | 0.0166926 | x 2.19 |
| 50 | 0.1925042 | 0.1326922 | x 1.45 |

| 100 | 0.3760727 | 0.1593220 | x 2.36 |
| 500 | 1.8196209 | 0.7860007 | x 2.32 |
| 1000 | 3.7780752 | 2.2051182 | x 1.71 |

Use the client result cache in the following situations:

- When you have queries that are repeatedly executed and that you know are expected to produce the same results set

- When you are reading from tables containing mostly read-only data

# Importing Data More Efficiently

The Oracle bulk loader was designed to let the user quickly upload a large amount of data to the database. It was responsible for many over-the-table quotes like "Mine did 50,000 rows in 2 seconds flat" during my casual lunch meetings with Oracle database administrators.

The Oracle bulk loader could load data so fast because it bypassed the entire SQL layer and directly wrote data into proprietary Oracle data blocks (via the Oracle Call Interface (OCI) layer). ODP.NET fortunately provides us with this same power, exposed through the **OracleBulkLoader** class.

You can load data through this class from a variety of sources—from a **DataReader** or from a **DataTable**, for instance. The following code snippet shows how this can be easily done:

```
OracleBulkCopy _bulkCopy = new OracleBulkCopy(_connObj);
_bulkCopy.DestinationTableName = "Products";
_bulkCopy.WriteToServer(SourceDataTable);
```

Even if the column names don't match between the source **DataTable** and the target table, you can specify column mappings using the **OracleBulkLoader** class to put the data in the right destination. The code in Listing 12-12 measures the performance when 50,000 records are loaded into the **Products** table first via standard SQL and then **OracleBulkLoader**.

Listing 12-12. Inserting 50,000 Records into the Table via Standard SQL and OracleBulkLoader

```
private void btnOracleBulkCopy_Click(object sender, EventArgs e)
{
        Stopwatch _stopwatch = new Stopwatch();
        String _Results;
        String _connstring = "Data Source=localhost/NEWDB;User
                Id=EDZEHOO;Password=PASS123;";
        try
        {
                OracleConnection _connObj = new OracleConnection(_connstring);
                _connObj.Open();
                OracleCommand _cmdObj = _connObj.CreateCommand();

                //Clear all records from the Products table
                _cmdObj.CommandText = "DELETE FROM Products";
```

```
_cmdObj.ExecuteNonQuery();

//Insert 50,000 records into the Products table using 50,000 individual SQL
//statements
_cmdObj.CommandText = "INSERT INTO Products(ID, Name, Price) VALUES(:ID,
        :Name, :Price)";
OracleParameter _IDParam = new OracleParameter("ID", OracleDbType.Varchar2);
_cmdObj.Parameters.Add(_IDParam);
OracleParameter _nameParam = new OracleParameter("Name",
        OracleDbType.Varchar2);
_cmdObj.Parameters.Add(_nameParam);
OracleParameter _priceParam = new OracleParameter("Price",
        OracleDbType.Decimal);
_cmdObj.Parameters.Add(_priceParam);
_stopwatch.Start();
for (int i = 1; i <= 50000; i++)
{
        _IDParam.Value = "E" + Convert.ToString(i);
        _nameParam.Value = "Test Product" + Convert.ToString(i);
        _priceParam.Value = 100;
        _cmdObj.ExecuteNonQuery();
}
_stopwatch.Stop();
_cmdObj.Dispose();
_Results = "Without Oracle Bulk Copy:\t" +
        _stopwatch.Elapsed.TotalSeconds.ToString() + " seconds\n";

//Clear the Products table again
_cmdObj = _connObj.CreateCommand();
_cmdObj.CommandText = "DELETE FROM Products";
_cmdObj.ExecuteNonQuery();
_cmdObj.Dispose();

//Inserting 50,000 records into the Products table using OracleBulkCopy
//First, create a DataTable to hold the source data
DataTable _dataTbl = new DataTable("SourceTable");
_dataTbl.Columns.Add(new DataColumn("ID",
        System.Type.GetType("System.String")));
_dataTbl.Columns.Add(new DataColumn("Name",
        System.Type.GetType("System.String")));
_dataTbl.Columns.Add(new DataColumn("Price",
        System.Type.GetType("System.String")));
_stopwatch.Reset();
_stopwatch.Start();
for (int i = 1; i <= 50000; i++)
{
    DataRow _newrow = _dataTbl.NewRow();
    _newrow["ID"] = "E" + Convert.ToString (i);
    _newrow["Name"] = "Test Product" + Convert.ToString(i);
    _newrow["Price"] = 100;
    _dataTbl.Rows.Add(_newrow);
}
```

```
            _stopwatch.Stop();
            OracleBulkCopy _bulkCopy = new OracleBulkCopy(_connObj);
            _bulkCopy.DestinationTableName = "Products";
            _stopwatch.Start();
            _bulkCopy.WriteToServer(_dataTbl);
            _stopwatch.Stop();
            _Results += "With Oracle Bulk Copy:\t" +
                    _stopwatch.Elapsed.TotalSeconds.ToString() + " seconds\n";
            _bulkCopy.Close();
            _bulkCopy.Dispose();
            _bulkCopy = null;

            MessageBox.Show(_Results);
            _connObj.Close();
        }
        catch (Exception ex)
        {
            MessageBox.Show(ex.ToString());
        }
    }
```

The following measurements show that, for large amounts of data, **OracleBulkCopy** is extremely effective, offering performance gains up to 30 times that of using individual SQL **INSERT** commands:

| Records to load | Using individual statements | Using OracleBulkCopy boost | Performance |
| --- | --- | --- | --- |
| 100 | 0.0917097 | 0.1652669 | x 0.55 (performance drain) |
| 1000 | 0.6572200 | 0.0689074 | x 9.54 |
| 5,000 | 3.4043001 | 0.1925245 | x 17.68 |
| 10,000 | 8.3390993 | 0.3059878 | x 27.25 |
| 50,000 | 50.8451298 | 1.5958709 | x 31.86 |

Use the Oracle bulk loader when you have a very large number of external records to insert into an Oracle table. As you can see from the performance results, small numbers of records may even cause a performance drain when using the bulk loader.

# Applying Optimization Best Practices

As I've hinted in the introduction to this chapter, performance optimization is a habit that begins with the first line of code you write. There are a few best practices and mindsets that, if consistently adopted, could ensure optimal performance to your ODP.NET code. Some of these best practices (in addition to the techniques outlined earlier in this chapter) are described in brief here.

## Using Stored Procedures Whenever Possible

Stored procedures (although not the ultimate solution for performance) are generally faster than dynamic queries simply because they exist in precompiled form. This means that your data manipulation commands are processed more efficiently since Oracle skips the parsing work required for dynamic queries. It also reduces network traffic and the number of round-trips required for a particular task.

There are also many other nonperformance benefits to using stored procedures, such as additional security and separation of database code from business logic.

## Using the Right Data Access Object

For most databases, the **DataReader** object will always outperform the **DataAdapter** object, because a **DataAdapter** object needs to spend additional time creating the dataset object and populating it. This holds true for the Oracle database as well. Whenever you need read-only access to data, such as populating a display-only grid or reading data into a drop-down list, you should always consider using the **OracleDataReader** object over the **OracleDataAdapter** object.

# Summary

In this chapter, you've taken a look at the various performance techniques and tips to adopt when building your application. You've written code to see the performance gains that you can squeeze from your application with each of the following techniques:

- Using connection pooling for more efficient database connections
- Using the **BINARY_FLOAT** and **BINARY_DOUBLE** floating point data types
- Batching SQL together for faster execution
- Using statement caching to cache frequently used SQL statements
- Passing data in bulk via bind arrays
- Passing data in bulk via PL/SQL associative arrays
- Managing large objects
- Changing the **FetchSize** and **RowSize** properties for efficient data retrieval
- Enabling the client result cache for efficient data retrieval
- Importing data in bulk into the Oracle database

In the next chapter, we will move on to the topic of design patterns. We will learn how the Gang of Four (GoF) design patterns can be applied to your ODP.NET projects.

# CHAPTER 13

■ ■ ■

# Design Patterns and Considerations in Using ODP.NET

In October 1994, Erich Gamma, Richard Helm, Ralph Johnson, and John Vlissides published a book they wrote on the topic of software engineering, identifying common problems in software design and classifying their solutions in groups of design patterns. After 500,000 copies sold in 13 different languages around the world, the original authors would come to be famously known as the Gang of Four (GoF), and their design patterns have since made it into countless articles, journals, books and software development kits (SDKs).

The idea is that most complex software consists of small recurring pieces of code that have a similar structure, or pattern. For example, the GoF noticed that a linked list, collection, and array would each work very differently under the hood, and programmers would typically create separate implementations of the same algorithm (for instance a search) for each type of data structure. The GoF realized that rather than having to iterate through each data structure differently like this:

```
//Searching a linked list
MyLinkedList.MoveFirst();
while (MyLinkedList.EOF()==false)
{
        if (MyLinkedList.GetItemByIndex(i)=='x') return true;
        MyLinkedList.Next();
}
//Searching a collection
for (i=0;<MyCollection.Count;i++) {if (MyCollection.item(i)=='x') return true;}
//Searching an array
for (i=0; i<UBound(MyArray);i++) { if (MyArray[i]=='x') return true;}
```

these data structures could implement an **Iterator**, which could shield the underlying implementation of the search for each data structure from the programmer. The previous could thus be rewritten like so:

```
public bool Search(Iterator objIterator)
{
        objIterator.First();
        for (Item item = objIterator.First(); objIterator.IsDone; item = objIterator.Next())
                {if (item =='x') return true;}
}

Search(MyLinkedList.GetIterator());
Search(MyCollection.GetIterator());
Search(MyArray.GetIterator());
```

This approach leads to improved clarity and flexibility of code. If you ever needed to search a new type of data structure, you would never need to change your **Search** implementation. You need only implement an **Iterator** for the new data structure.

The GoF identify 23 such design patterns in their book. In this chapter, you will only take a look at the design patterns that specifically apply to the data layer and how you can make use of them in your ODP.NET projects. Specifically, we will cover the following:

- Various design patterns and concepts relevant to the data tier

- Best practices to adopt to maintain clear separation of business logic from the data tier

- Using the data access application block in the Microsoft Enterprise Library to establish a robust data layer that you can readily use for your ODP.NET applications

# Programming to an Interface Instead of an Implementation

One of the main tenets of the GoF design principles is that two parts of an application never need to be aware of each other's underlying implementation. When these parts of the application need to communicate with each other, it is done through an interface.

By decoupling an underlying implementation from the calling code, changes pertaining to the underlying implementation can be localized to that layer alone. You wouldn't need to change any part of the calling code.

For instance, imagine that you've been using the ODP.NET classes (for example, **OracleConnection**, **OracleCommand**, **OracleDataAdapter**, and **OracleDataReader**) directly in your application code. In fact, you have been doing this since the early chapters of this book. Let's assume that you've peppered these classes throughout your entire application. Everything works fine, until your chief technical officer steps in to tell you that you now need to have your application support an Oracle Open Database Connectivity (ODBC) driver because the customer (for some reason) does not want the ODP.NET drivers installed.

Without an abstract interface definition for data access, you will find the task of changing from ODP.NET to ODBC extremely time consuming. You would have to make changes everywhere in your application code to manually change the ODP.NET references to ODBC ones. Let's not forget the long regression testing phase needed to make sure everything still works. For complex systems, the task may even turn out to be technically and financially unfeasible.

If you had defined an interface between the application and the database, this task would have been nothing more than just creating another implementation, as shown in Figure 13-1.

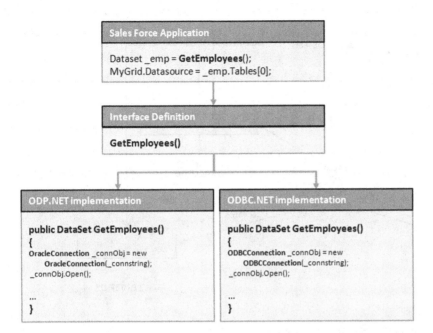

**Figure 13-1.** *An example of how an interface can be used to segregate business logic from the data tier*

# Using the Data Access Object

The data access object (DAO) is a design concept that abstracts and encapsulates access to a data source. The code that calls the DAO is hence shielded from the underlying implementation details of the data source. This is usually achieved by defining an interface between the data and logic tiers.

The DAO also does the plumbing work required to communicate with the underlying data source it represents. Figure 13-2 illustrates how the DAO typically fits into the design architecture of an application.

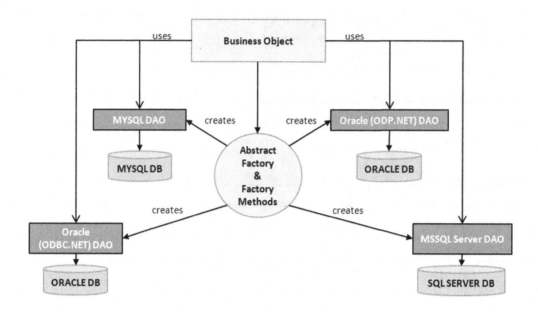

*Figure 13-2. How DAOs are created by the Abstract Factory*

The DAO makes use of two GoF patterns, the Factory Method and Abstract Factory patterns. The Abstract Factory pattern encapsulates a group of similarly themed individual factories. It can be used by calling code to create specific concrete objects. Since the calling code will always work with generic objects, and not the specific objects themselves, it never needs to be aware of the details of their implementation.

For example, an abstract factory might generate specific SQL Server or Oracle DAO objects (via the appropriate factory methods) depending on certain arguments provided, but what is handed back to the calling code is always a generic DAO object. This allows the calling code to access the underlying database (without having to care which type of database it is) through a generic interface.

In the following few sections we take a look at Microsoft's Enterprise library, which implements a Microsoft SQL Server DAO and an Oracle DAO (based on Microsoft's Oracle Provider).

# Using Microsoft's Enterprise Library

Microsoft's huge research and development team comprises a division called the Patterns and Practices group. They've released version 4.1 of the Microsoft Enterprise Library (dated October 2008), which is basically a collection of reusable software components (termed application blocks) based on what they believe to be best practices. These application blocks implement a mixture of GoF design patterns and other design concepts. One of these application blocks is the data access application block (DAAB), which we will look at shortly.

You can download (and install) the library from this location:
`http://www.microsoft.com/downloads/details.aspx?FamilyId=1643758B-2986-47F7-B529-3E41584B6CE5&displaylang=en`.

The DAAB is Microsoft's implementation of the DAO design concept. The DAAB is useful for the following reasons:

- It shields the underlying implementation of database-specific tasks from application code. For instance, instead of calling the **OracleAQQueue** class directly in your application code, you could place it in the DAAB and expose its functionality through a more abstract interface. This way, if Oracle changes or enhances the implementation of **OracleAQQueue**, you wouldn't need to make changes everywhere in your application code. The changes would only be localized to the DAAB.

- It handles all the plumbing required for the configuration and encryption of connection strings, provider types, and so on.

- It is highly reusable and extensible; for example, you can create extensions to the DAAB to support other database types like MySQL or DB2.

- It already conforms to best practices, is well-tested code, and comes with full source code available for you to tweak.

The DAAB comes with three DAOs by default: a SQL Server DAO, an Oracle DAO (based on Microsoft's Oracle Provider) and a generic database DAO. In the sections to follow, you will learn how to extend the DAAB to include the ODP.NET DAO, which we will refer to as Oracle.NET throughout the rest of this chapter.

# Creating Oracle.NET

The Microsoft Enterprise Library fortunately comes with full source code. You can open the source code for the DAAB in Visual Studio by opening the C# project file located in the following folder:

**<Installation Drive>\EntLib41Src\Blocks\Data\Src\Data\**

The SQL Server and Oracle DAO classes are located in the **Sql** and **Oracle** folders of the project respectively. You can copy and paste the code from one of the existing DAOs to create your new ODP.NET DAO. Besides these core classes, you will also need to modify some of the factory classes used by the DAAB to generate DAOs. The full set of steps includes the following:

1. Create the ODP.NET DAO classes.

2. Modify the **DBProviderMapping** class to register the **Oracle.DataAccess.Client** provider name.

3. Modify the **DatabaseConfigurationView** class to create a mapping between the **Oracle.DataAccess.Client** provider name and the ODP.NET DAO object.

## Creating the ODP.NET DAO Class

You first need to add a reference to the ODP.NET libraries in the DAAB project. After doing so, locate the **SqlDatabase.cs** and **SqlDatabaseAssembler.cs** files. You will base your ODP.NET DAO on these SQL Server DAOs. Make a copy of each of these files, and name them **OracleNETDatabase.cs** and

355

OracleNETDatabaseAssembler.cs correspondingly. Open the OracleNETDatabase.cs file, and make the changes highlighted in bold in Listing 13-1.

---

■ **Note** You will notice that the default DAO classes provided by Microsoft come with a number of grayed-out comments that look like XML tags. Those aren't exactly comments; they're directives used to generate documentation. For ease of readability, these comments have been removed from the code shown in Listing 13-1, but I recommend that you keep them in your code for documentation purposes.

---

*Listing 13-1. Modifying the OracleNETDatabase.cs File*

```
using System;
using System.Data;
using System.Data.Common;
using Oracle.DataAccess.Client;
using System.Security.Permissions;
using System.Transactions;
using System.Xml;
using Microsoft.Practices.EnterpriseLibrary.Common.Configuration.Unity;
using Microsoft.Practices.EnterpriseLibrary.Data.Configuration;
using Microsoft.Practices.EnterpriseLibrary.Data.Configuration.Unity;
using Microsoft.Practices.EnterpriseLibrary.Data.Properties;

namespace Microsoft.Practices.EnterpriseLibrary.Data.OracleNET
{

[OraclePermission(SecurityAction.Demand)]
[DatabaseAssembler(typeof(OracleNETDatabaseAssembler))]
[ContainerPolicyCreator(typeof(OracleNETDatabasePolicyCreator))]
public class OracleNETDatabase : Database
{
        public OracleNETDatabase(string connectionString)
                : base(connectionString,  OracleClientFactory.Instance)
        {
        }

        protected char ParameterToken
        {
                get { return '@'; }
        }

        public XmlReader ExecuteXmlReader(OracleCommand command)
        {
                OracleCommand OracleCommand = CheckIfOracleCommand(command);
                ConnectionWrapper wrapper = GetOpenConnection(false);
                PrepareCommand(command, wrapper.Connection);
```

```
                return DoExecuteXmlReader(OracleCommand);
        }

        public XmlReader ExecuteXmlReader(OracleCommand command, OracleTransaction
                transaction)
        {
                OracleCommand OracleCommand = CheckIfOracleCommand(command);
                PrepareCommand(OracleCommand, transaction);
                return DoExecuteXmlReader(OracleCommand);
        }

        private XmlReader DoExecuteXmlReader(OracleCommand OracleCommand)
        {
                try
                {
                        DateTime startTime = DateTime.Now;
                        XmlReader reader = OracleCommand.ExecuteXmlReader();
                        instrumentationProvider.FireCommandExecutedEvent(startTime);
                        return reader;
                }
                catch (Exception e)
                {
                        instrumentationProvider.FireCommandFailedEvent
                                (OracleCommand.CommandText, ConnectionStringNoCredentials,
                                e);
                        throw;
                }
        }

        private static OracleCommand CheckIfOracleCommand(OracleCommand command)
        {
                OracleCommand OracleCommand = command as OracleCommand;
                if (OracleCommand == null) throw new
                        ArgumentException(Resources.ExceptionCommandNotSqlCommand,
                        "command");
                return OracleCommand;
        }

        private void OnSqlRowUpdated(object sender, OracleRowUpdatedEventArgs
                rowThatCouldNotBeWritten)
        {
                if (rowThatCouldNotBeWritten.RecordsAffected == 0)
                {
                        if (rowThatCouldNotBeWritten.Errors != null)
                        {
                                rowThatCouldNotBeWritten.Row.RowError =
                                        Resources.ExceptionMessageUpdateDataSetRowFailure;
                                rowThatCouldNotBeWritten.Status =
                                        UpdateStatus.SkipCurrentRow;
                        }
                }
```

357

```
        }

        protected override void DeriveParameters(DbCommand discoveryCommand)
        {
                OracleCommandBuilder.DeriveParameters((OracleCommand)discoveryCommand);
        }

        protected override int UserParametersStartIndex()
        {
                return 1;
        }

        public override string BuildParameterName(string name)
        {
                if (name[0] != this.ParameterToken)
                {
                        return name.Insert(0, new string(this.ParameterToken, 1));
                }
                return name;
        }

        protected override void SetUpRowUpdatedEvent(DbDataAdapter adapter)
        {
                ((OracleDataAdapter)adapter).RowUpdated += OnSqlRowUpdated;
        }

        protected override bool SameNumberOfParametersAndValues(DbCommand command,
                object[] values)
        {
                int returnParameterCount = 1;
                int numberOfParametersToStoredProcedure = command.Parameters.Count -
                        returnParameterCount;
                int numberOfValuesProvidedForStoredProcedure = values.Length;
                return numberOfParametersToStoredProcedure ==
                        numberOfValuesProvidedForStoredProcedure;
        }

        public virtual void AddParameter(OracleCommand command, string name, OracleDbType
                dbType, int size, ParameterDirection direction, bool nullable, byte
                precision, byte scale, string sourceColumn, DataRowVersion sourceVersion,
                object value)
        {
                OracleParameter parameter = CreateParameter(name, dbType, size, direction,
                        nullable, precision, scale, sourceColumn, sourceVersion, value);
                command.Parameters.Add(parameter);
        }

        public void AddParameter(OracleCommand command, string name, OracleDbType dbType,
                ParameterDirection direction, string sourceColumn, DataRowVersion
                sourceVersion, object value)
        {
```

```
        AddParameter(command, name, dbType, 0, direction, false, 0, 0, sourceColumn,
            sourceVersion, value);
}

public void AddOutParameter(OracleCommand command, string name, OracleDbType dbType,
        int size)
{
        AddParameter(command, name, dbType, size, ParameterDirection.Output, true,
            0, 0, String.Empty, DataRowVersion.Default, DBNull.Value);
}

public void AddInParameter(OracleCommand command, string name, OracleDbType dbType)
{
        AddParameter(command, name, dbType, ParameterDirection.Input, String.Empty,
            DataRowVersion.Default, null);
}

public void AddInParameter(OracleCommand command, string name, OracleDbType dbType,
        object value)
{
        AddParameter(command, name, dbType, ParameterDirection.Input, String.Empty,
            DataRowVersion.Default, value);
}

public void AddInParameter(OracleCommand command, string name, OracleDbType dbType,
        string sourceColumn, DataRowVersion sourceVersion)
{
        AddParameter(command, name, dbType, 0, ParameterDirection.Input, true, 0, 0,
            sourceColumn, sourceVersion, null);
}

protected OracleParameter CreateParameter(string name, OracleDbType dbType, int
        size, ParameterDirection direction, bool nullable, byte precision, byte
        scale, string sourceColumn, DataRowVersion sourceVersion, object value)
{
        OracleParameter param = CreateParameter(name) as OracleParameter;
        ConfigureParameter(param, name, dbType, size, direction, nullable,
            precision, scale, sourceColumn, sourceVersion, value);
        return param;
}

protected virtual void ConfigureParameter(OracleParameter param, string name,
        OracleDbType dbType, int size, ParameterDirection direction, bool nullable,
        byte precision, byte scale, string sourceColumn, DataRowVersion
        sourceVersion, object value)
{
        param.OracleDbType = dbType;
        param.Size = size;
        param.Value = (value == null) ? DBNull.Value : value;
        param.Direction = direction;
        param.IsNullable = nullable;
```

```
                param.SourceColumn = sourceColumn;
                param.SourceVersion = sourceVersion;
        }
    }
}
```

You will also need to have a factory to represent the building of an instance of an **OracleNETDatabase** object. This is the **OracleNETDatabaseAssembler** class. Make the changes highlighted in bold to the **OracleNETDatabaseAssembler.cs** file as shown in Listing 13-2.

*Listing 13-2. Modifying the OracleNETDatabaseAssembler.cs File*

```
using System;
using System.Configuration;
using Microsoft.Practices.EnterpriseLibrary.Common.Configuration;
using Microsoft.Practices.EnterpriseLibrary.Data.Configuration;

namespace Microsoft.Practices.EnterpriseLibrary.Data.OracleNET
{
public class OracleNETDatabaseAssembler : IDatabaseAssembler
{
        public Database Assemble(string name, ConnectionStringSettings
                connectionStringSettings, IConfigurationSource configurationSource)
        {
                return new OracleNETDatabase(connectionStringSettings.ConnectionString);
        }
}
}
```

You will need to create one more file—the **OracleNETDatabasePolicyCreator** class. Add a new class to your project, and name the file **OracleNETDatabasePolicyCreator.cs**. Write the code shown in Listing 13-3 in this file.

*Listing 13-3. The OracleNETDatabasePolicyCreator.cs File*

```
using System.Configuration;
using Microsoft.Practices.EnterpriseLibrary.Common.Configuration;
using Microsoft.Practices.EnterpriseLibrary.Common.Configuration.Unity;
using Microsoft.Practices.EnterpriseLibrary.Data.Sql;
using Microsoft.Practices.ObjectBuilder2;

namespace Microsoft.Practices.EnterpriseLibrary.Data.Configuration.Unity
{
        public class OracleNETDatabasePolicyCreator : IContainerPolicyCreator
        {
                void IContainerPolicyCreator.CreatePolicies(
                        IPolicyList policyList,
                        string instanceName,
                        ConfigurationElement configurationObject,
                        IConfigurationSource configurationSource)
```

```
        {
                ConnectionStringSettings castConfigurationObject =
                        (ConnectionStringSettings)configurationObject;

                new PolicyBuilder<SqlDatabase, ConnectionStringSettings>
                (instanceName, castConfigurationObject, c => new
                SqlDatabase(c.ConnectionString))

                .AddPoliciesToPolicyList(policyList);
        }
    }
}
```

# Modifying the DBProviderMapping Class

The **DBProviderMapping** class in the DAAB holds the full name constants of the ADO.NET providers used in the Microsoft Enterprise Library. You will now need to add a constant for the ODP.NET provider to this class. Locate and open the **DBProviderMapping.cs** file in the DAAB project, and make the changes highlighted in bold in Listing 13-4.

*Listing 13-4. Modifying the DBProviderMapping.cs File*

```
using System;
using System.Collections.Generic;
using System.Text;
using System.Configuration;
using System.ComponentModel;
using Oracle.DataAccess.Client;
using Microsoft.Practices.EnterpriseLibrary.Common.Configuration;

namespace Microsoft.Practices.EnterpriseLibrary.Data.Configuration
{
/// <summary>
/// Represents the mapping from an ADO.NET provider to an Enterprise Library <see
///     cref="Database"/>.
/// </summary>
/// <remarks>
/// <para>
/// The Enterprise Library data access application block leverages the ADO.NET 2.0 provider
/// factories. To determine what type of <see cref="Database"/> matches a given provider
/// factory type, the optional <see cref="DbProviderMapping"/> configuration objects can be
/// defined in the block's configuration section.
/// </para>
/// <para>
/// If a mapping is not present for a given provider type, sensible defaults will be used:
/// <list type="bullet">
/// <item>For provider name "System.Data.SqlClient", or for a provider of type <see
/// cref="System.Data.SqlClient.SqlClientFactory"/>, the
/// <see cref="Microsoft.Practices.EnterpriseLibrary.Data.Sql.SqlDatabase"/> will be
```

```
/// used.</item>
/// <item>For provider name "System.Data.OracleClient", or for a provider of type <see
/// cref="System.Data.OracleClient.OracleClientFactory"/>, the
/// <see cref="Microsoft.Practices.EnterpriseLibrary.Data.Oracle.OracleDatabase"/> will be
/// used.</item>
/// <item>For provider name "Oracle.DataAccess.Client", or for a provider of type <see
/// cref="OracleClientFactory"/>, the <see
/// cref="Microsoft.Practices.EnterpriseLibrary.Data.OracleNET.OracleNETDatabase"/> will be
/// used.</item>
/// <item>In any other case, the <see cref="GenericDatabase"/> will be used.</item>
/// </list>
/// </para>
/// </remarks>
/// <seealso cref="DatabaseConfigurationView.GetProviderMapping(string, string)"/>
/// <seealso cref="System.Data.Common.DbProviderFactory"/>
. . .
```

In the same class, search for the section shown in Listing 13-5. Add a new constant for the ODP.NET assembly name, which is shown in bold here.

*Listing 13-5. Adding a New Constant in the DBProviderMapping.cs File*

```
public class DbProviderMapping : NamedConfigurationElement
{
        private static AssemblyQualifiedTypeNameConverter typeConverter = new
                AssemblyQualifiedTypeNameConverter();

        /// <summary>
        /// Default name for the Sql managed provider.
        /// </summary>
        public const string DefaultSqlProviderName = "System.Data.SqlClient";

        /// <summary>
        /// Default name for the Oracle managed provider.
        /// </summary>
        public const string DefaultOracleProviderName = "System.Data.OracleClient";

        /// <summary>
        /// Default name for the ODP.NET managed provider.
        /// </summary>
        public const string DefaultOracleNETProviderName = "Oracle.DataAccess.Client";
. . .
}
```

## Modifying the DatabaseConfigurationView Class

In the **DatabaseConfigurationView.cs** file, you will need to map the **Oracle.DataAccess.Client** provider name to the Oracle.NET DAO you've created earlier. Make the changes (highlighted in bold) to the file as shown in Listing 13-6. In the same file, add the additional entry highlighted in bold, as shown in Listing 13-7.

*Listing 13-6. Modifying the DatabaseConfigurationView.cs File*

```
using System;
using System.Collections.Generic;
using System.Configuration;
using System.Data.Common;
using System.Data.SqlClient;
using Oracle.DataAccess.Client;
using Microsoft.Practices.EnterpriseLibrary.Common.Configuration;
using Microsoft.Practices.EnterpriseLibrary.Data.Configuration;

//Comment out Microsoft.Practices.EnterpriseLibrary.Data.Oracle since the Oracle
//classes might conflict with the ones in Oracle.DataAccess.Client due to similar
//naming

//COMMENTED OUT : using Microsoft.Practices.EnterpriseLibrary.Data.Oracle;
using Microsoft.Practices.EnterpriseLibrary.Data.Properties;
using Microsoft.Practices.EnterpriseLibrary.Data.Sql;

namespace Microsoft.Practices.EnterpriseLibrary.Data
{
        /// <summary>
        /// <para>Represents a view for navigating the <see cref="DatabaseSettings"/>
        /// configuration data.</para>
        /// </summary>
        public class DatabaseConfigurationView
        {
                private static readonly DbProviderMapping defaultSqlMapping = new
                        DbProviderMapping(DbProviderMapping.DefaultSqlProviderName,
                        typeof(SqlDatabase));
                private static readonly DbProviderMapping defaultOracleMapping = new
                        DbProviderMapping(DbProviderMapping.DefaultOracleProviderName,
                        typeof(Microsoft.Practices.EnterpriseLibrary
                        .Data.Oracle.OracleDatabase));
                private static readonly DbProviderMapping defaultOracleNETMapping = new
                        DbProviderMapping(DbProviderMapping.DefaultOracleNETProviderName,
                        typeof(Microsoft.Practices.EnterpriseLibrary.Data.
                        OracleNET.OracleNETDatabase));
                private static readonly DbProviderMapping defaultGenericMapping = new
                        DbProviderMapping(DbProviderMapping.DefaultGenericProviderName,
                        typeof(GenericDatabase));
                private readonly IConfigurationSource configurationSource;
```

*Listing 13-7. Adding the Entry for the ODP.NET DAO in the DatabaseConfigurationView.cs File*

```
private DbProviderMapping GetDefaultMapping(string name, string dbProviderName)
{
```

```
    // try to short circuit by default name
    if (DbProviderMapping.DefaultSqlProviderName.Equals(dbProviderName))
            return defaultSqlMapping;
    if (DbProviderMapping.DefaultOracleProviderName.Equals(dbProviderName))
            return defaultOracleMapping;
    if (DbProviderMapping.DefaultOracleNETProviderName.Equals(dbProviderName))
            return defaultOracleNETMapping;

    // get the default based on type
    DbProviderFactory providerFactory = DbProviderFactories.GetFactory(dbProviderName);
    ValidateDbProviderFactory(name, providerFactory);

    if (SqlClientFactory.Instance == providerFactory) return defaultSqlMapping;
    if (System.Data.OracleClient.OracleClientFactory.Instance  == providerFactory)
            return defaultOracleMapping;

    if (OracleClientFactory.Instance == providerFactory) return defaultOracleMapping;
    return null;
}
```

## Compiling the New DAAB

Now that you're done, compile the new DAAB. Assuming you've put in the appropriate documentation-generating XML tags, you should be able successfully build the library. This will output the new DAAB library at this location:

<Installation Drive>
\EntLib41Src\Blocks\Data\Src\Data\bin\Release\Microsoft.Practices.EnterpriseLibrary.Data.dll

# Using the ODP.NET DAO

You're now ready to use the ODP.NET DAO in your projects. The first thing you need to do is to create a new Windows Forms Application project. After that, add two references to the project:

- Microsoft.Practices.EnterpriseLibrary.Common
- Microsoft.Practices.EnterpriseLibrary.Data (or browse for the new assembly you've just created)

These references contain the changes you've made earlier. The Microsoft Enterprise Library also uses an application configuration file (app.config) to store the database connection details such as the connection string and provider name. You don't actually have to edit this file by hand; the Microsoft Enterprise Library comes with an Enterprise Library Configuration tool that allows you to generate the entries needed for the DAAB to work.

# Editing the Application Configuration File

First, add an Application Configuration File to the project. Right-click the **app.config** file in Visual Studio, and choose the Edit Enterprise Library Configuration menu item. This will pop open a new frame in the right pane.

---

■ **Note** You can also edit the **app.config** file using the Enterprise Library Configuration tool at Start ➤ All Programs ➤ Microsoft patterns & practices ➤ Enterprise Library 4.1 – October 2008 ➤ Enterprise Library Configuration.

---

You will see your application as a node in the right pane with the Data Access Application Block node directly under it. You need to create a connection string entry so that you can connect to Oracle. Expand your Data Access Application Block node, and right-click the Connection Strings node. Choose the New ➤ Connection String menu item in the ensuing pop-up menu to generate a new connection string entry. In the properties window shown in Figure 13-3, change the Name field to **ProductsDatabase**, choose **Oracle.DataAccess.Client** as the ProviderName, and specify your full ODP.NET connection string. You can use the same connection string you've been using for the earlier chapters of this book.

---

■ **Note** You can also create multiple connection string entries. You will be able to choose which connection you wish to use later on in code. You can also specify the default database in the right pane of the tool window when you highlight the Data Access Application Block node.

---

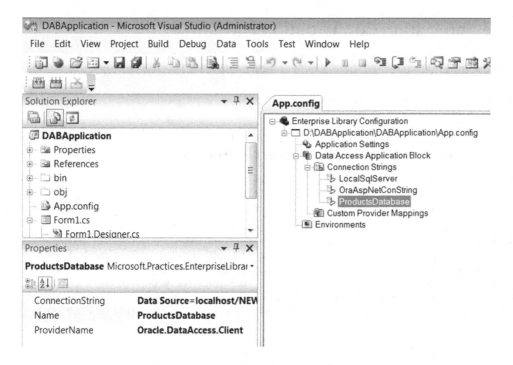

*Figure 13-3. Editing the app.config file using the Enterprise Library Configuration tool*

You can also specify to encrypt the **app.config** file, if you wish, by highlighting the Data Access Application Block node and choosing an encryption provider from the right pane under the ProtectionProvider field. When you've completed all your changes, remember to save them using the File ➤ Save Application menu item. You can open your **app.config** in text mode using Visual Studio to view the changes that have been made to the file. You will notice that your connection strings have been encrypted in this file.

---

■ **Note** Visual Studio might automatically put in `Version` and `PublicKeyToken` entries for `Microsoft.Practices.EnterpriseLibrary.Data` in the `app.config` file every time you make changes via the Edit Enterprise Library Configuration menu. This may raise exceptions in your code later on. It is a good idea to manually remove this information from the `app.config` file by hand.

---

## Accessing Data via the DAAB

When you use the DAAB, you access the database a bit differently than you would under ODP.NET. For instance, you have to use a factory class to hand yourself a connection object instead of instantiating one using the **OracleConnection** object directly. Let's now look at how you can perform common ODP.NET tasks via the DAAB.

First, add a new form to your project. Design the form to look roughly similar to the screenshot in Figure 13-4. Place a **DataGridView** control in the middle of the form and three buttons on the left side.

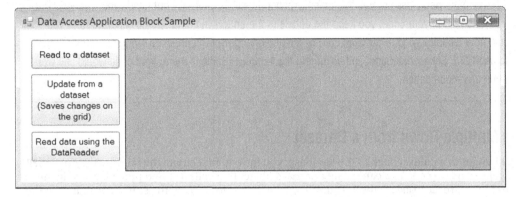

***Figure 13-4.*** *The interface for the data access application block samples*

## Reading Multiple Rows into a Dataset

The first button in this form will use the ODP.NET DAO to read some data from the Oracle database into a dataset and then display it in the grid on the right. When you use the DAAB, you do not need to manually create and open a connection yourself. You simply ask the **DatabaseFactory** class to hand you one. This can be done using the **DatabaseFactory.CreateDatabase** method call. The argument passed in to this method is the name of the connection string entry you've created earlier in the **app.config** file. If you do not pass in any arguments, the default connection string will be used.

To run a query that returns a **DataSet** object, you no longer need to build the **DataAdapter** object manually. The DAAB abstracts these steps by representing them with a single function call, **ExecuteDataSet**. This method takes in a command object and returns a **DataSet** filled with the execution results. The full code to do this is shown in Listing 13-8.

*Listing 13-8. Reading Multiple Rows into a Dataset*

```
private void btnReadDataset_Click(object sender, EventArgs e)
{
        Database _db = DatabaseFactory.CreateDatabase("ProductsDatabase");
        if (_db == null)
        {
                MessageBox.Show("Failed to create the database");
        }
        DbCommand _cmdObj = _db.GetSqlStringCommand("SELECT * FROM Products");
        DataSet _datasetObj = _db.ExecuteDataSet(_cmdObj);
        _datasetObj.Tables[0].TableName = "Products";
        dgProducts.DataSource = _datasetObj.Tables[0];
}
```

---

▓ **Note** You will notice in the code snippet in Listing 13-8 that you are using generic objects such as **Database** and **DbCommand** instead of the **OracleNETDatabase** or **OracleCommand** classes in your code. As you learned earlier, an Abstract Factory patterned class creates the specific (concrete) DAOs internally but hands you a generic DAO. By using the generic DAO in your code, you keep the details of the underlying data source separate from your code. You could now technically go to the **app.config** file and change your connection string and provider type to point to a Microsoft SQL Server database, and assuming the **Products** table is there, your code would still work without requiring any modification.

---

## Updating Multiple Rows from a Dataset

To commit changes in a dataset back to the database, you have to first create the relevant **UPDATE**, **INSERT**, and **DELETE** command objects. You can create a **Command** object that calls a stored procedure using the **Database.GetStoredProcCommand** method. You will need to pass the name of the stored procedure to this method. After defining the relevant **Command** objects, you will need to call the **Database.UpdateDataset** method, passing in the **DataSet** object, **Command** objects and the name of the table to update. The full code to do all this is shown in Listing 13-9.

*Listing 13-9. Updating Multiple Rows from a Dataset*

```
private void btnUpdateFromDataset_Click(object sender, EventArgs e)
{
        Database _db = DatabaseFactory.CreateDatabase("ProductsDatabase");
        if (_db == null)
        {
                MessageBox.Show("Failed to create the database");
        }
        DataTable _dataTableObj = (DataTable)dgProducts.DataSource;
        DataSet _datasetObj = _dataTableObj.DataSet;

        //Create the INSERT command
        DbCommand _insertCommand = _db.GetStoredProcCommand("proc_InsertProduct_DAB");
        _db.AddInParameter(_insertCommand, "Price", DbType.Decimal, "Price",
                DataRowVersion.Current);
        _db.AddInParameter(_insertCommand, "Name", DbType.String, "Name",
                DataRowVersion.Current);
        _db.AddInParameter(_insertCommand, "ID", DbType.String , "ID",
                DataRowVersion.Current);

        //Create the DELETE command
        DbCommand _deleteCommand =
                (DbCommand)_db.GetStoredProcCommand("proc_DeleteProduct_DAB");
        db.AddInParameter(_deleteCommand, "ID", DbType.String, "ID",
                DataRowVersion.Current);

        //Create the UPDATE command
```

```
DbCommand _updateCommand =
        (DbCommand)_db.GetStoredProcCommand("proc_UpdateProduct_DAB");
_db.AddInParameter(_updateCommand, "Price", DbType.Decimal, "Price",
        DataRowVersion.Current);
_db.AddInParameter(_updateCommand, "Name", DbType.String, "Name",
        DataRowVersion.Current);
_db.AddInParameter(_updateCommand, "ID", DbType.String, "ID",
        DataRowVersion.Current);

int _rowsUpdated = _db.UpdateDataSet (_datasetObj,"Products",_insertCommand,
        _updateCommand ,_deleteCommand, UpdateBehavior.Standard );
MessageBox.Show(_rowsUpdated.ToString() + " row(s) updated");
}
```

## Reading Data Using a DataReader

You can also retrieve data using a **DataReader** object with the DAAB. Simply call the **Database.ExecuteReader** method to return a **DataReader** object. You can use the **IDataReader** interface to access the **DataReader** functionality. The full code to do this is shown in Listing 13-10.

*Listing 13-10. Reading Data Using a DataReader*

```
private void btnReadViaDataReader_Click(object sender, EventArgs e)
{
        Database _db = DatabaseFactory.CreateDatabase("ProductsDatabase");
        if (_db == null)
        {
                MessageBox.Show("Failed to create the database");
        }
        DbCommand _cmdObj = _db.GetSqlStringCommand("SELECT * FROM Products");
        IDataReader _rdrObj = _db.ExecuteReader (_cmdObj);
        String _productNames;
        _productNames = "";
        while (_rdrObj.Read())
        {
                _productNames += _rdrObj.GetString(_rdrObj.GetOrdinal("Name"));
        }
        MessageBox.Show(_productNames);
}
```

---

■ **Note** There is, of course, much more that you can do with the DAAB. This section serves merely as a starter to get you up and running with the basics. You can also extend the ODP.NET DAO to include more ODP.NET-specific functionality such as advanced queuing and database notifications.

---

# Considering Best Practices

As I mentioned in Chapter 4, the data layer is one of the most fundamental parts of any application, since it drives all data access between your application and the data source. For example, a data tier that is too rigid would make the introduction of changes difficult. On the other hand, one that implements too many abstraction layers would make the code unreadable and unnecessarily complex. The following sections describe some considerations to keep in mind when designing your data tier.

## Planning for Multiple Data Sources

Your data source may be based on an Oracle database today, but that might change to become a DB2 or MySQL database tomorrow. The nature of business requirements today more often than not requires integration with a multitude of data sources, some of which you cannot foresee during development. By implementing an additional layer of abstraction (via interfaces) between your data layer and the data source, you can make your data layer extensible and allow new data sources to be easily snapped in to your framework.

## Keeping Provider-Specific Code Within the Data Tier

Passing provider-specific classes around in the application tier can be tempting sometimes. For example, you might decide to wrap a live **OracleDataReader** object in a business object and pass that business object around to other functions. This practice is, of course, a bad idea. It makes the life of the object harder to trace. Also, if you had to change the provider to a different one, like ODBC.NET, you would have to go through the entire application looking for these objects.

## Outputting Business Objects, Not Datasets

Many developers are fond of simply getting the data layer to pass back raw datasets into the logic tier. After all, **DataSet**s are pretty versatile objects and can be easily passed around. From a software design perspective, however, this practice is not desirable, since datasets (sometimes) contain raw data that has not been converted into the right types. Take the **System.Guid** .NET data type for example. A developer may decide to store a globally unique identifier (GUID) value in the Oracle database as a **RAW(16)** data type. When this data is retrieved into a dataset, it exists as a byte array, not a readily usable **System.Guid** object.

A better alternative would be to encapsulate each retrieved **DataSet** within a business object and to pass the business object to the logic tier. The business object would handle the mapping of the raw data structures to application-level entities. This way, the logic tier would never need to bother itself with the underlying conversions and formatting necessary before consuming the data.

## Deciding How to Map Data Source Structures to Business Objects

As mentioned in the previous section, raw data structures retrieved from a data source should be mapped to an application entity such as a business object. You should formulate a strategy for each mapping since it may not always be a **1:1** correlation. Tables with master-detail relationships in the database, for instance, must be mapped to the corresponding business objects with this relationship intact.

This mapping must also account for any formatting and type conversions necessary in both directions, when taking in and returning data.

## Deciding How to Manage Data Source Settings

Since the data layer effectively manages all underlying data sources, it must be able to manage data source settings, such as connection strings and provider types. As connection settings are typically stored outside the data layer (for example, in the registry or an external file such as **app.config**), you should also think of a good security model to use to protect this information.

# Summary

In this chapter, you've taken a look at some of the design concepts and patterns you can adopt to write data layers that adapt better to changing business requirements:

- The data access object (DAO) design concept and how it applies to the data layer

- Extending the data access application block in the Microsoft Enterprise Library

- Creating and using an ODP.NET DAO

In the next chapter, you will explore how to use the tools in the Oracle Developer Tools.NET package to improve your productivity.

■ ■ ■

# CHAPTER 14

# ODT.NET Tool Basics

With every major release of the Visual Studio tool, Oracle released a free set of tools, called Oracle Developer Tools.NET (ODT.NET), which integrated tightly with the Visual Studio IDE. These tools greatly enhanced the productivity of .NET developers working on the Oracle database. With ODT.NET, you could, for instance, visually manage your Oracle tables right within the Visual Studio IDE! Or seamlessly jump in and out of PL/SQL stored procedures from your .NET code during debugging. Or even automatically generate entire blocks of code and classes out of an Oracle data source.

ODT.NET is supported on Visual Studio .NET 2003, 2005, and 2008 and will most likely see a new version released for Visual Studio 2010 as well. At the time of this writing, the latest version of ODT.NET is the recently released version 11.1.0.7.20. The last two chapters of this book will aim to cover both the basic and advanced features of ODT.NET, with this chapter focusing on the various tasks that you can perform using ODT.NET and the last chapter focusing on building applications quickly using the code-generation features of ODT.NET.

In this chapter, you will learn how to perform the following tasks within the Visual Studio IDE:

- Browse and manage the Oracle database schema.

- Manage database users, roles, and privileges.

- Edit and debug PL/SQL code.

- Manage Oracle SQL scripts.

- Create and manage AQ queues and queue tables.

- Import tables and data from external data sources into Oracle.

First, let's look at how to install ODT.NET. Then, we'll look at performing the various tasks.

## Installing ODT.NET

You have already installed ODT.NET earlier in Chapter 2. If, for some reason, you did not install ODT.NET earlier, you can still do it later via the Oracle Universal Installer. You can launch the Oracle Universal Installer from the Windows Start menu by selecting Start ➤ All Programs ➤ ORACLE_HOME ➤ Oracle Installation Products ➤ Universal Installer.

When the Oracle Universal Installer launches, click the Next button to follow through the various installation screens in the wizard (as you've done in Chapter 2). The default installation of ODP.NET will automatically install the ODT.NET package.

# Managing the Database Schema

With ODT.NET, you can browse and manage your Oracle database schemas from within the Visual Studio IDE. This ability can increase your productivity since you can create, edit, and delete tables or columns without leaving the Visual Studio IDE.

An Oracle schema can be managed within the Server Explorer window of the Visual Studio IDE. The first thing you need to do is add a new connection to the Oracle database. Open the Server Explorer window by clicking the View ➤ Server Explorer menu item. Right-click the Data Connections node, and choose the Add Connection menu item shown in Figure 14-1.

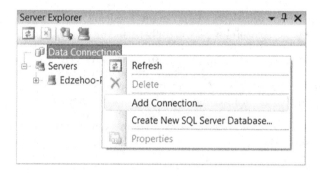

*Figure 14-1. Adding a connection to the server explorer*

The window shown in Figure 14-2 will appear. Select the "Oracle Database (Oracle ODP.NET)" data source, and specify the connection details to your database. You can try logging in using your username and password (in line with the examples in this book, that would be the **EDZEHOO** account). You can also use the Test Connection button to check if you can successfully connect to the database with the specified settings.

*Figure 14-2. Connecting to the Oracle database*

After you click OK, you will be able to see the full list of tables show under the Tables node. You should also be able to see the **Products** table, which you've been using throughout the earlier chapters of the book. If you right-click this table and select the Design menu item, you should be able to view and edit the schema of this table. This step is shown in Figure 14-3.

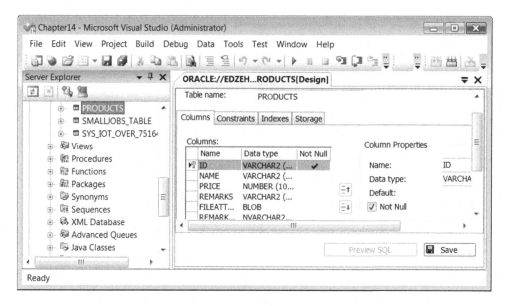

*Figure 14-3. Viewing and editing the schema for the Products table*

You can also run an SQL query against the database within the Visual Studio IDE. Right-click the database node, and choose the Query Window menu item. You can type your SQL in the top-right pane. Click the first icon in the toolbar (the green play button) to run the query. You should be able to see the results show in the bottom pane, as shown in Figure 14-4.

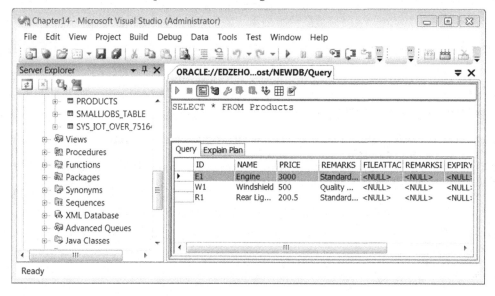

*Figure 14-4. Executing the SQL Query in the Query Window tool*

---

■ **Tip** The number of records retrieved in the query window is limited to a default maximum of 100. You can increase or remove this limit by navigating to Tools ➤ Options in the Visual Studio IDE, clicking the Show All Settings check box, and changing the settings at the Oracle Developer Tools ➤ General page.

---

The following list contains some of the main reasons why you might want to use the ODT.NET database schema feature in your project.

- You can manage your database and run SQL queries without having to leave the Visual Studio IDE.

- You can manage and reuse connection settings across multiple projects in the Server Explorer.

- You can manipulate your database objects without having to type longwinded DDL statements.

# Managing Users, Roles, and Object Privileges

You can also manage your database users, roles, and permissions within the same Server Explorer window. You might first need to grant your user account the ability to create and manage other users. You can do so by logging in as the **SYSTEM** account and executing the following commands in SQL*Plus:

```
GRANT CREATE USER, ALTER USER, DROP USER TO EDZEHOO;
GRANT CREATE ROLE, ALTER ANY ROLE, DROP ANY ROLE TO EDZEHOO;
```

In the Server Explorer, expand the Users node. You should be able to see the list of database users show under this node. Let's try creating a new database user. Right-click the Users node, and choose the New User menu item, shown in Figure 14-5.

*Figure 14-5. Creating a new user*

A new window will pop up in the main frame of your Visual Studio IDE (see Figure 14-6). In this window, you can specify the details of the user account you wish to create. When you are done, click the Save button to create the user.

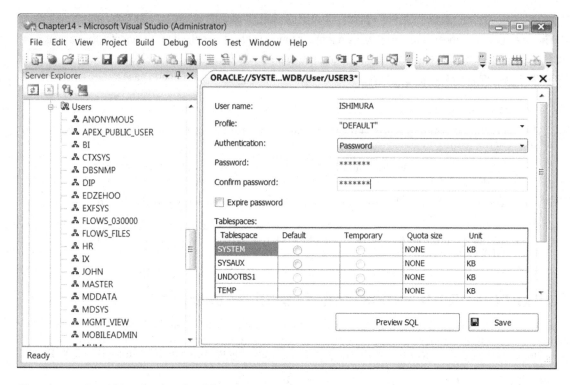

*Figure 14-6. Specifying the details of the new user account*

You can similarly manage and create new roles via the Roles node in the server explorer. Next, we will take a look at how you can set the privileges for a specific table. Right-click the Products table, and choose the Privileges menu item (shown in Figure 14-7).

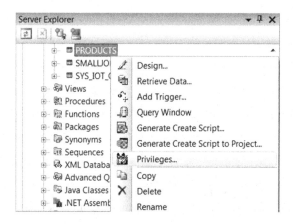

*Figure 14-7. Specifying the details of the account*

Doing so will launch the Grant/Revoke Privileges window shown in Figure 14-8. You can set the privileges for each user shown in the User drop-down list. You can also preview the DDL statements generated from your settings by clicking the Preview SQL button. When you are finished with your changes, click the Apply or OK button. The privileges you've configured will automatically be applied on the selected object.

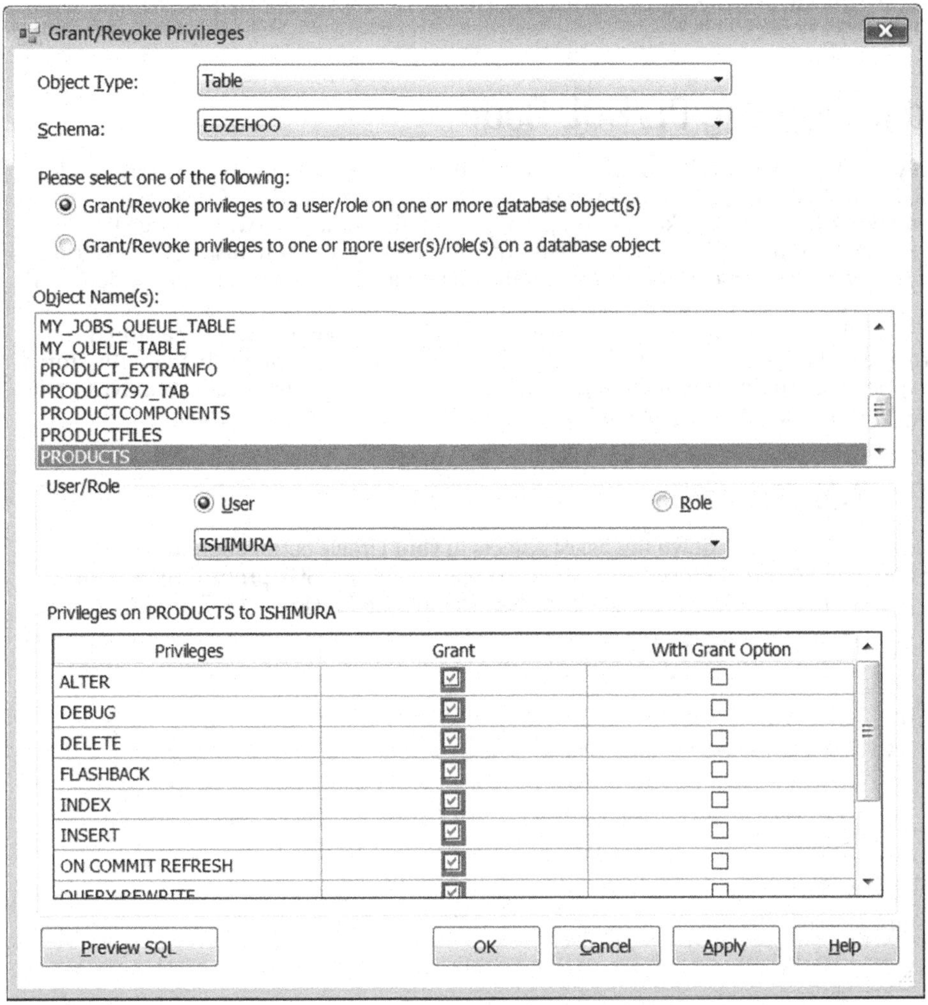

*Figure 14-8. Setting privileges for the Products table*

The following list contains some of the main reasons why you might want to use the ODT.NET roles and privileges feature in your project:

- You can easily create test user accounts easily for sandbox testing and delete them afterward. Being able to see the full list of user accounts visually also allows for better management of your users and roles.

- In SQL*Plus, you had to remember the name of each privilege when attempting to write the DDL to grant or revoke a certain privilege. Having a visual checklist makes this task so much easier.

# Editing and Debugging PL/SQL Code

Over the course of your ODP.NET development, you will definitely find yourself writing PL/SQL code. You can use the SQL*Plus tool, as you've done in the earlier chapters, to create PL/SQL stored procedures and functions, but if you're like me, you probably found it difficult to write a large PL/SQL stored procedure inside a command line window. Without color-coding to distinguish keywords from object names and without proper line formatting, the reduced readability of code can quickly dampen your productivity.

Fortunately, ODT.NET provides a GUI that lets you easily generate skeleton code for a stored procedure and provide a PL/SQL editor built into the Visual Studio IDE to let you further edit the stored procedure. It even provides you the tools to debug your PL/SQL code just as you would your .NET code, allowing the debugger to seamlessly jump from .NET code into a PL/SQL block and back!

## Creating a PL/SQL Procedure

To create a PL/SQL procedure, scroll down the list of objects in your Oracle connection in the server explorer. You will find a node named Procedures. You can create a new PL/SQL procedure by right clicking this node and selecting the New PL/SQL Procedure menu item (as shown in Figure14-9).

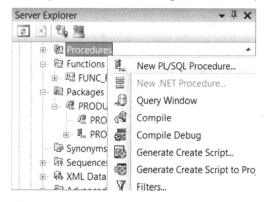

*Figure 14-9. Creating a new PL/SQL Procedure*

When you have done this, you should instantly see the window shown in Figure 14-10. This window allows you to generate the skeleton code for a stored procedure. This skeleton code includes the procedure declaration sections and the procedure arguments. You can also preview the SQL code for this task by clicking the Preview SQL button.

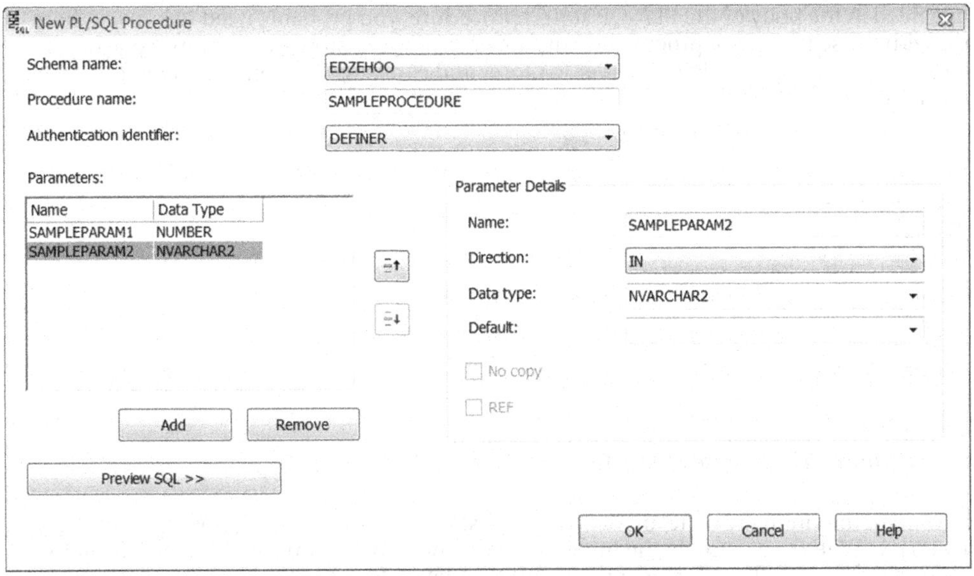

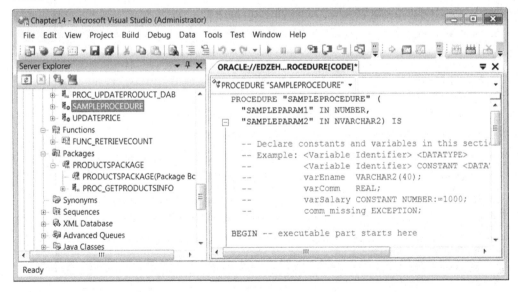

*Figure 14-10. Specifying the details of the new PL/SQL procedure*

When you are finished, click the OK button. This will create an empty stored procedure with the details you've specified and show the skeleton code in the main window pane of the IDE (as shown in Figure 14-11). You can see your stored procedure in the list of stored procedures (in the Server Explorer window).

*Figure 14-11. The generated PL/SQL stored procedure*

After you've filled in the body of the PL/SQL stored procedure, you probably need to know if there is anything wrong with the syntax of the procedure. You can compile your stored procedure by right-clicking the desired stored procedure in the Server Explorer and choosing the Compile menu option (as shown in Figure 14-12).

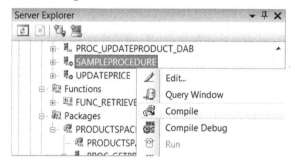

*Figure 14-12. Compiling a PL/SQL stored procedure*

You might want to intentionally write an incorrect SQL statement so that you know the compile feature is doing its job. When you compile the incorrect stored procedure, you should see errors being thrown in the Visual Studio IDE. These errors provide precise detail down to the exact line number where the error occurred. You can see this in Figure 14-13.

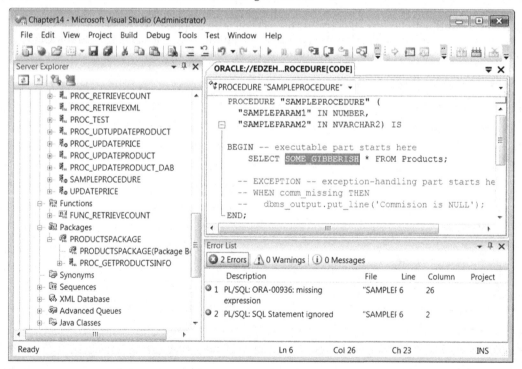

*Figure 14-13. Errors in the PL/SQL stored procedure syntax*

The ODT.NET tool set makes it easier than ever to create PL/SQL stored procedures and functions the same way. In the next section, we will take a look at creating a PL/SQL package.

## Creating a PL/SQL Package

To create a PL/SQL package, look for the Packages node in the Server Explorer, right-click it and choose the New Package menu item (as shown in Figure 14-14).

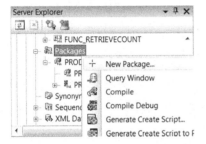

*Figure 14-14. Creating a new package*

You will now see the window shown in Figure 14-15 that lets you specify the details of the package. The concept behind these GUI windows are the same; they are meant to make it as convenient as possible for you to generate the stubs and skeleton code necessary to get going.

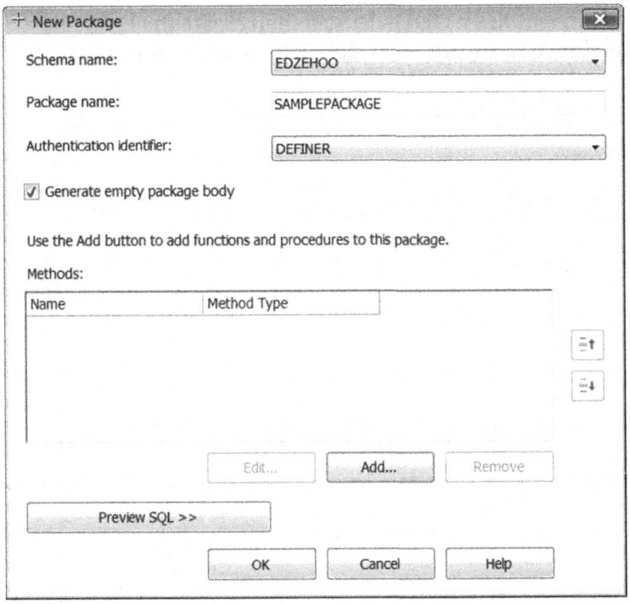

*Figure 14-15. Specifying the details of the PL/SQL package.*

You will notice from this window that there is a table that allows you to define the PL/SQL methods in this package. You can click the Add button to add a new method to the package. When you have done that, the window shown in Figure 14-16 will be displayed. You will be able to specify the list of arguments for the stored procedure or function.

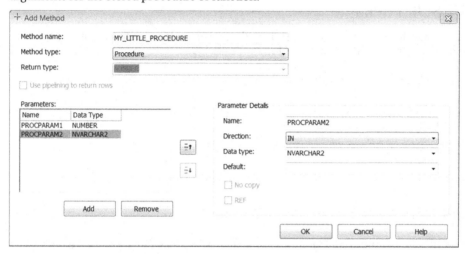

*Figure 14-16. Specifying the details of a PL/SQL package method.*

When this is done, click the OK buttons in both windows. ODT.NET will then create the PL/SQL package according to your specified settings, as shown in Figure 14-17. It will then be up to you to fill in the meat for these stored procedures.

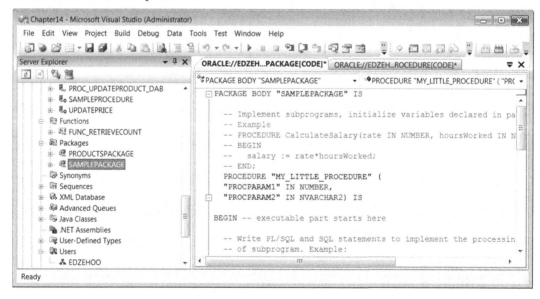

*Figure 14-17. The generated PL/SQL package skeleton code*

In the following section, we will take a look at how you can debug PL/SQL code within the Visual Studio IDE.

## Debugging PL/SQL stored procedures

Before you can debug PL/SQL code within the Visual Studio IDE, you need to do some setup. The first thing you need to do is to prevent the Visual Studio hosting process from getting in the way. You can disable it by navigating to the Project ➤ Project Properties menu item in Visual Studio, clicking the Debug tab, and unselecting the Enable Visual Studio hosting process check box (as shown in Figure 14-18).

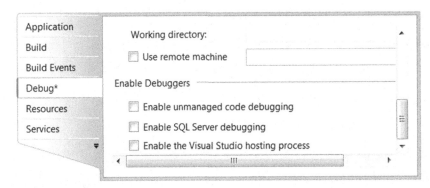

*Figure 14-18. Disabling the Visual Studio hosting process*

After that, you should also grant your user account rights to debug a stored procedure. Log in using the **SYSTEM** account, and run the following statements in SQL*Plus:

```
GRANT DEBUG ANY PROCEDURE TO EDZEHOO;
GRANT DEBUG CONNECT SESSION TO EDZEHOO;
```

Next, you will need to specify an Oracle database connection for the PL/SQL debugger. Navigate to the Tools ➤ Options menu item in Visual Studio. A window similar to the one shown in Figure 14-19 below will be displayed. Select the Oracle Developer Tools ➤ PL/SQL Debugging menu option, and select the Oracle connection you wish to use for the PL/SQL debugger.

---

■ **Tip** If you don't see the Oracle Developer Tools menu item at first, select the "Show all settings" check box at the bottom of the window.

---

385

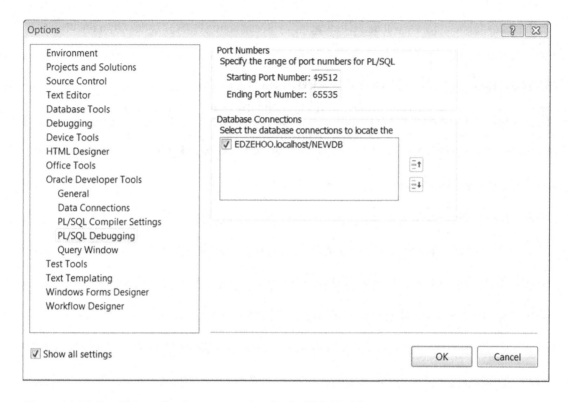

*Figure 14-19. Specifying a database connection for the PL/SQL debugger*

The next step is to enable Oracle Application Debugging itself. You can do this by placing a tick next to the Tools ➤ Oracle Application Debugging menu item. Look closely at Figure 14-20. You'll see the check mark to the left of the second menu item from the bottom.

*Figure 14-20. Enabling Oracle Application Debugging*

You are now all set. Let's create a stored procedure to debug. Using what you learned earlier, create the stored procedure in Listing 14-1. This stored procedure will simply add two numbers together and place the result in a variable named **TotalValue**.

*Listing 14-1. The TestProcedure Stored Procedure*

```
PROCEDURE "TESTPROCEDURE" (Number1 IN NUMBER, Number2 IN NUMBER)
AS
  -- Declare constants and variables in this section.
  -- Example: <Variable Identifier> <DATATYPE>
  --          <Variable Identifier> CONSTANT <DATATYPE>
  --          varEname  VARCHAR2(40);
  --          varComm   REAL;
  --          varSalary CONSTANT NUMBER:=1000;
  --          comm_missing EXCEPTION;

  TotalValue NUMBER(11,2);

BEGIN

  -- executable part starts here
  TotalValue:=Number1 + Number2;
  TotalValue:=TotalValue * 30;
END;
```

Now, add a form to your project, place a button on the form, and write the code shown in Listing 14-2 in the click event of this button.

*Listing 14-2. Calling the TestProcedure PL/SQL Stored Procedure*

```
private void btnAddNumbers(object sender, EventArgs e)
{
        DataSet _datasetObj = new DataSet();
        string _connstring = "Data Source=localhost/NEWDB;User Id=EDZEHOO;Password=PASS123";
        try
        {
                OracleConnection _connObj = new OracleConnection(_connstring);
                _connObj.Open();
                OracleCommand _cmdObj = new OracleCommand("TESTPROCEDURE", _connObj);
                _cmdObj.CommandType = CommandType.StoredProcedure;

                //Pass in two arbitrary numbers to this stored procedure
                _cmdObj.Parameters.Add("Number1", 30);
                _cmdObj.Parameters.Add("Number2", 50);
                _cmdObj.ExecuteNonQuery();
                _connObj.Close();
                MessageBox.Show("Done!");
        }
        catch (Exception ex)
```

```
        {
                MessageBox.Show(ex.ToString());
        }
}
```

Now place breakpoints at the locations in your code shown in Figure 14-21.

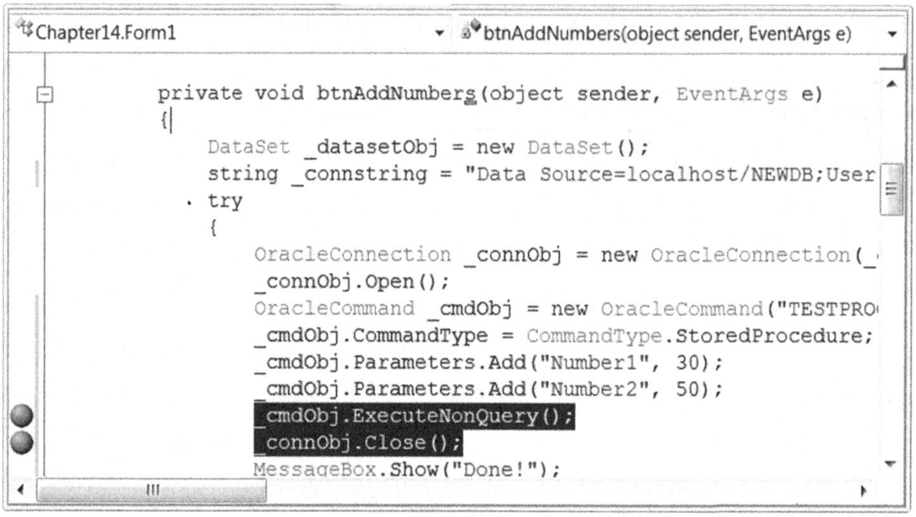

*Figure 14-21. Placing breakpoints in the btnAddNumbers function*

ODT.NET allows you to place breakpoints within your PL/SQL function as well. This allows you to inspect individual variables inside the PL/SQL function as you would any other .NET variable. Place breakpoints inside your PL/SQL function as shown in Figure 14-22.

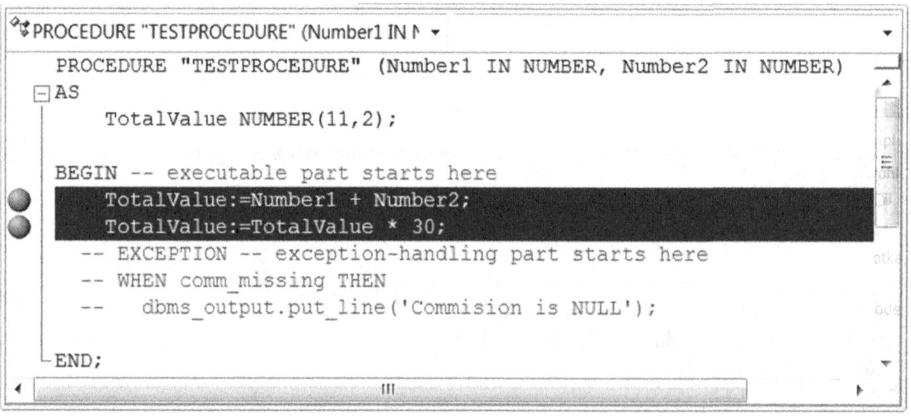

*Figure 14-22. Placing breakpoints in the TESTPROCEDURE stored procedure*

You will next need to place the stored procedure in debug mode. You can do this by right-clicking your stored procedure, and choosing the Compile Debug menu item, as shown in Figure 14-23. The icon for your stored procedure will now change into a slightly different icon (with the DBG tag).

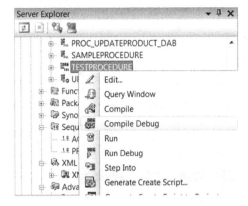

**Figure 14-23.** *Placing your stored procedure in Debug mode*

Now, run your project in debug mode. The execution will halt at the first breakpoint you've defined (at the **ExecuteNonQuery** method). Press the F5 button to proceed. The application will continue to execute until the next breakpoint (which is inside your PL/SQL stored procedure!). If you open the Locals window to inspect the values of the variables, you will see the window shown in Figure 14-24. You can observe that the values held in the **Number1** and **Number2** variables, which are PL/SQL variables are shown in the Locals window.

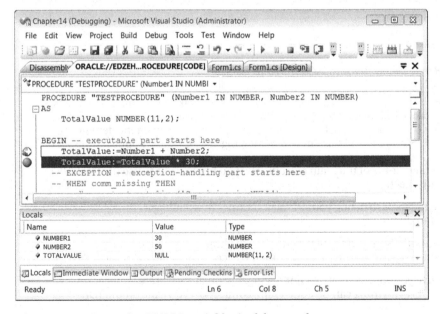

**Figure 14-24.** *Inspecting PL/SQL variables in debug mode*

If you press the F5 button one more time, execution will halt at the next breakpoint. You should see that the **TotalValue** variable now carries a value of 80, which was the sum of the two numbers earlier. Figure 14-25 illustrates this.

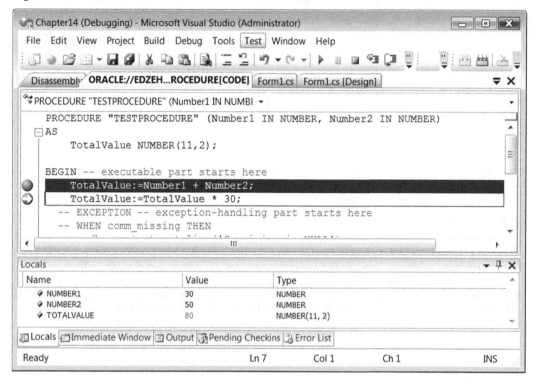

**Figure 14-25.** *The second breakpoint in the PL/SQL stored procedure*

A final press of the F5 button would move execution to the next breakpoint, which is back in your .NET application at the **_connObj.Close()** line. What you have just witnessed is the seamless integration of PL/SQL code debugging together with .NET code debugging. The ease at which the debugger can jump from .NET code to PL/SQL code and back makes debugging your ODP.NET applications an easier and more intuitive task.

The following list contains some of the main reasons why you might want to use the ODT.NET debugging feature in your project:

- You now have the tools to debug your PL/SQL routines in a debugger environment familiar to you.

- You can debug both .NET and PL/SQL code as if they were one, whereas with external tools such as the Oracle Developer tool, you could only debug PL/SQL.

- You can improve your productivity by not having to launch a separate application to debug PL/SQL; everything can be done in the comfort of the Visual Studio IDE.

# Managing Oracle SQL Scripts

When you deploy your application at a customer installation, you might sometimes choose to deploy your database as a series of SQL scripts that you can simply run on the server to rebuild the database objects required.

Some developers start off by hand-coding the DDL statements manually; they then use this to generate the actual database objects used for development and testing. ODT.NET allows you to also do it the other way around.

ODT.NET allows you to generate SQL scripts from existing database objects. This can sometimes be convenient; it frees you from having to manually keep track of your DDL statements every time you make changes to the database. You could visually edit your database as you wish via ODT.NET, and when the time comes for you to deploy your application, you could just generate SQL scripts from each of these database objects.

Let's try to generate the SQL script for the **Products** table. Browse for this table in the Server Explorer window, right-click on it, and choose the Generate Create Script menu item (as shown in Figure 14-26).

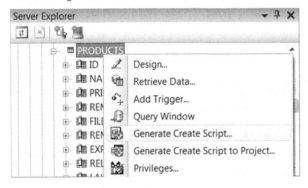

*Figure 14-26. Generating the Create Script for the Products table*

When you have done this, you will be prompted to specify a location to save the generated script file. Specify a location and filename to save your script to. After that is done, you can try opening the script file in a text editor like **notepad.exe**. You should be able to see something similar to Listing 14-3.

*Listing 14-3. The Contents of the Generated Script File for the Products Table*

```
-- ****** Object: Table EDZEHOO.PRODUCTS Script Date: 2/17/2010 1:38:51 AM ******
CREATE TABLE "PRODUCTS" (
  "ID" VARCHAR2(10 BYTE),
  "NAME" VARCHAR2(255 BYTE),
  "PRICE" NUMBER(10,2),
  "REMARKS" VARCHAR2(4000 BYTE),
  "FILEATTACHMENT" BLOB,
  "EXPIRYDATE" DATE,
  "REMARKSINJAPANESE" NVARCHAR2(1000),
  "RELEASEDATE" TIMESTAMP(6) WITH TIME ZONE,
  "LAUNCHDATE" TIMESTAMP(6) WITH TIME ZONE)
  STORAGE (
```

```
      NEXT 1048576 )
/
CREATE UNIQUE INDEX "PRIMKEY"
  ON "PRODUCTS" (
    "ID")
/
ALTER TABLE "PRODUCTS" ADD (
  CONSTRAINT "SYS_C0010349"
    CHECK ( "ID" IS NOT NULL)
    ENABLE
    VALIDATE )
/
ALTER TABLE "PRODUCTS" ADD (
  CONSTRAINT "PRIMKEY"
    PRIMARY KEY ( "ID")
    USING INDEX "PRIMKEY"
    ENABLE
    VALIDATE )
/
```

---

■ **Tip** The Generate Create Script option is available for other database object types as well, such as queues, users, roles, stored procedures, packages, and so on. You can also use the Generate Create Script option at a parent node, such as the Tables node. This will generate a single script file containing the **CREATE** statements for all the tables under that node.

---

You can execute this generated script file within the Visual Studio IDE as well. For example, you might want to restore a table that you have deleted earlier from a generated script file.

To try this out, delete the **Products** table from your database. After that, you will run the generated SQL script to rebuild this table. You can do this by navigating to the Tools ➤ Run SQL*Plus script menu item in Visual Studio. The window shown in Figure 14-27 will appear. Specify the path of the script file you wish to execute, and a database connection to use to execute the script file. When you have done that, click the Run button to execute the script. This will rebuild your **Products** table in the database.

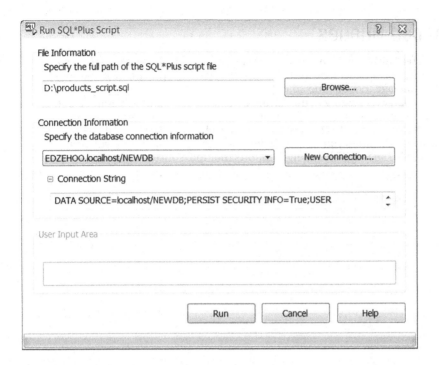

*Figure 14-27. Executing an SQL*Plus script file*

---

■ **Tip** The errors and results from executing an SQL*Plus script file are shown in the Visual Studio Output Window.

---

The following list contains some of the main reasons why you might want to use the ODT.NET SQL scripting feature in your project:

- You can quickly make hot backups of your database objects.

- If you wanted to create a particular type of database object programmatically, you don't need to look up the DDL statement—just generate the SQL script using this feature. This can save you research time.

- You can easily clone database objects among Oracle databases; simply run the generated script on another database to rebuild the database object.

# Managing Advanced Queues

If you recall from Chapter 9, creating a queue consists of two steps—creating the queue table to store queue messages and registering the actual queue itself. ODT.NET makes this process easier as well by providing GUIs to create and manage these queue objects.

You can create a queue table by navigating to the Advanced Queues ➤ Queue Tables node in the Server Explorer, right-clicking it, and choosing the New Queue Table menu item. This will display the window shown in Figure 14-28. The Payload Type box allows you to choose between XML, RAW, and UDT-type payloads. The Storage tab allows you to specify detailed size dynamics for the queue table. Through this window, you can also specify if the queue supports multiple consumers.

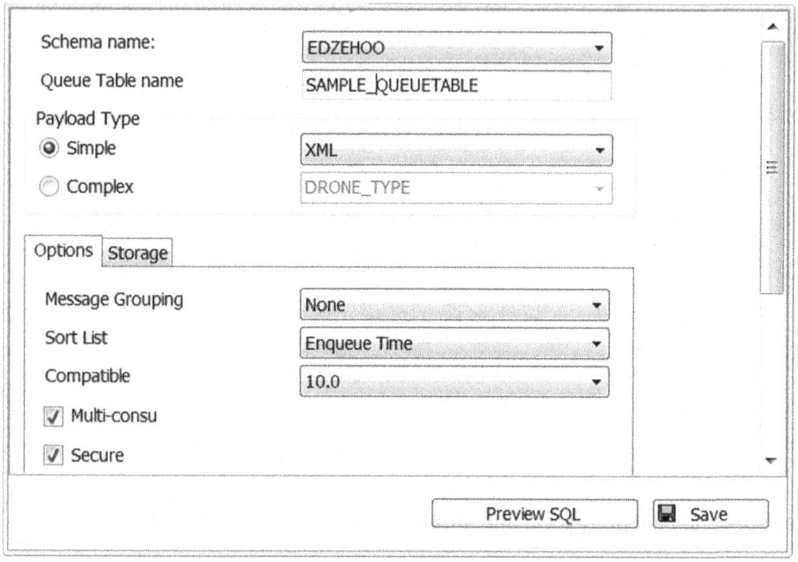

*Figure 14-28. Creating an AQ queue table*

After you have created an AQ queue table, you will need to create and register a queue (and its subscribers). You probably recall doing all this via SQL*Plus in Chapter 9. ODT.NET provides a single window that allows you to do all this visually.

In the Server Explorer window, right-click the Advanced Queues ➤ Queues node, and choose the New Queue menu item to display the window shown in Figure 14-29. You are given the option to create a totally new queue table or to use an existing one. Since you've created one earlier, choose the Existing radio button, and select the queue table you created earlier. Notice that when you do this, certain other options gray out in this screen. The reason is that these options are already defined in your queue table earlier and will be used for the queue.

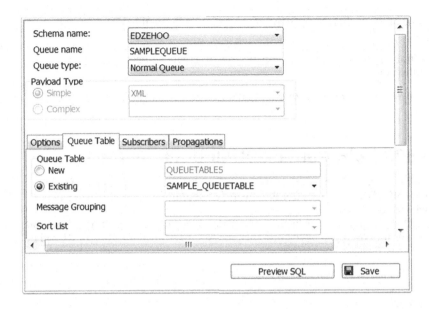

*Figure 14-29. Creating and registering an AQ queue*

You can also specify a list of subscribers for this queue via the Subscribers tab, as shown in Figure 14-30.

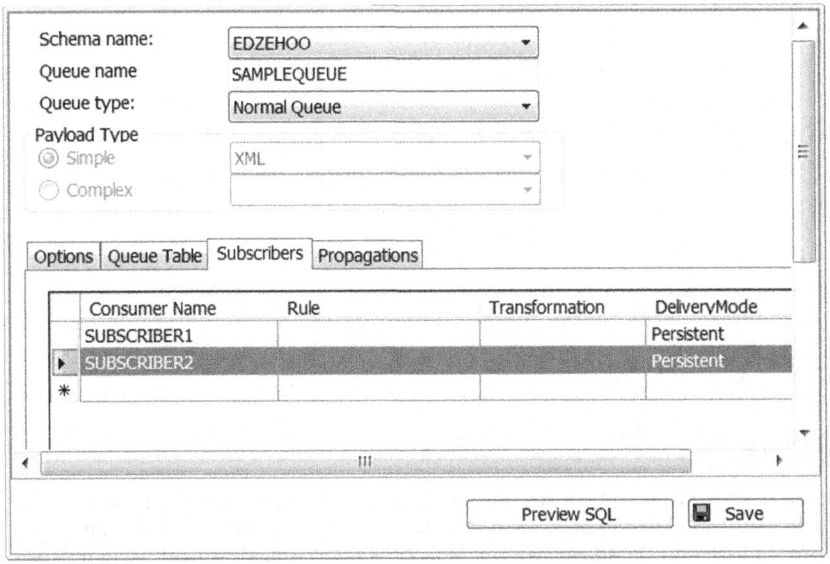

*Figure 14-30. Specifying the list of subscribers for a queue*

The following list contains some of the main reasons why you might want to use the ODT.NET AQ features in your project:

- You can save time not having to manually write the DDL to create a queue, queue table, agent and subscriber.

- You can visually browse and explore the queues you have hosted in your database at any point in time.

# Importing Tables and Data from External Data Sources

ODT.NET also provides the ability for you to import data from external data sources into your Oracle database, all within the Visual Studio IDE. This is better than using any command line tool, since it provides you a step by step wizard to do so.

To begin an import, right-click the master Oracle database node in the Server Explorer window, and choose the Import Table menu item. When you have done this, the wizard shown in Figure 14-31 will be displayed.

*Figure 14-31. The Import Table wizard*

You will next be prompted to select the data source containing the source tables and data to import. If you click the New Connection button, you will be able to specify the connection details for a data source. This can be a Microsoft SQL Server database, Microsoft Access MDB file, Microsoft Excel file, or any other registered database that has a corresponding driver. Choose the desired data source, and click the Next button. In the example here, I use a Microsoft SQL Server database as the data source.

The next step of the wizard shows the list of tables contained in the data source. Tick the tables that you wish to import. You can choose to import data along with the schema by ticking the check box in the Import Data column, which is shown in Figure 14-32.

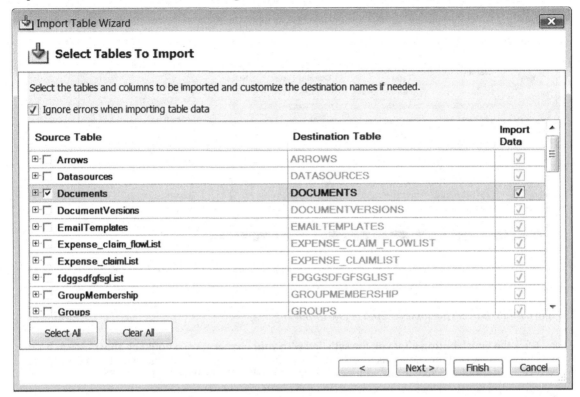

*Figure 14-32. Selecting the list of tables you wish to import*

The next window in the wizard (shown in Figure 14-33) shows a description of the columns in each table. This allows you to modify the table schema before it is created in Oracle. The changes done here will only affect the table in the target database, not the source database.

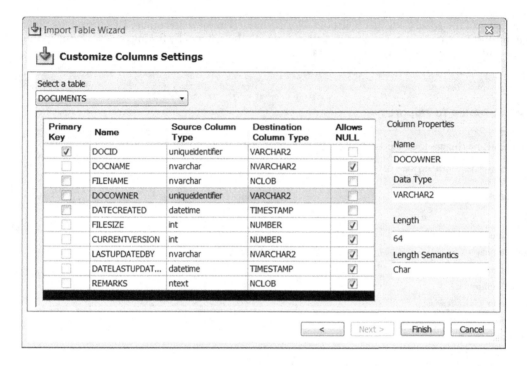

**Figure 14-33.** *Editing the table schema before importing*

Click the Finish button after you are satisfied with your changes. You should be able to see a message showing that the table was imported successfully. If you refresh the list of tables in your Server Explorer, you should be able to see your newly imported table (as shown in Figure 14-34).

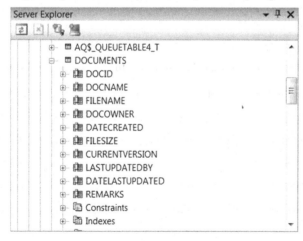

**Figure 14-34.** *The successfully imported Documents table*

The following list contains some of the main reasons why you might want to use the ODT.NET data import features in your project.

- Easily transfer data objects from other non-Oracle databases into your Oracle database. This can save you time, since you don't have to create the fields one by one. The convenience becomes more noticeable when you need to transfer large tables with hundreds of fields.

- You can even define source and target column type mappings visually, allowing you to easily map external data types into Oracle ones.

- You can import objects from a large variety of external OLEDB data sources, including Microsoft Excel sheets and even Microsoft Access (**.mdb**) databases.

## Summary

In this chapter, you've taken a look at some of the basics of the ODT.NET package. You've learned how to do the following:

- Browse Oracle table schema using ODT.NET.

- Create and manage users, roles, and table privileges using ODT.NET.

- Create, debug, and manage PL/SQL stored procedures, packages and functions.

- Create and manage queue tables and queues using ODT.NET.

- Import external tables and data into the Oracle database using the ODT.NET Import Data wizard.

In the next chapter, which is also the last chapter of this book, you will learn how to use the code-generation features of ODT.NET to quickly build Winforms and ASP.NET applications.

# CHAPTER 15

# Building Data-Driven Applications with ODT.NET

Oracle, like any powerful software, has always carried the unfortunate stigma of being complex, unproductive, and generally difficult to use among .NET developers. Although the Oracle database is clearly a superior product, the tightly knit nature of the Microsoft SQL Server database and the .NET Framework easily made SQL Server the database of choice among developers who were given a choice between the two.

ODT.NET is Oracle's answer to this problem. One of the benefits of ODT.NET is that it bridges Oracle's powerful technology with the ease of use that you would expect from Microsoft. Gone are the days when you had to do everything in a tiny command line window. As you've seen in the previous chapter, ODT.NET is effectively an enterprise database manager tool built right into the Visual Studio IDE, with additional code generation features similar to those available for the SQL Server database. When used together with ODP.NET, you will be able to create .NET applications more productively without even leaving the Visual Studio environment.

In this chapter, you will learn a few more features of ODT.NET. You will see how you can achieve better productivity by performing the following tasks within the Visual Studio IDE:

- Visually designing an Oracle database query

- Generating strongly typed **DataSet** objects from Oracle tables

- Generating UI and data access code for .NET Winforms projects quickly

- Generating UI and data access code for ASP.NET projects quickly

- Generating user defined type (UDT) classes from UDT objects and using them directly in your projects

## Designing Queries Visually

You've seen in the previous chapter that you could run an Oracle query from within the Visual Studio IDE. ODT.NET takes this one step further by allowing you to visually design an SQL query via drag and drop.

Visual design is useful in cases where you have large tables with many columns. Sifting through these columns to look for their foreign keys and relationships with other tables without a visual designer can be a messy and troublesome affair. With ODT.NET, you can do that work without leaving the comfort of the Visual Studio IDE. To start designing a query, right-click a connection that you created in the previous chapter. In the pop-up menu, select the New Query menu item, as shown in Figure 15-1.

*Figure 15-1. Launching the visual query designer*

A new window will appear. This window allows you to select the tables that you want to include in the visual query designer. We will attempt to create an **INNER JOIN** query between the **Products** and **ProductComponents** tables using this visual designer.

---

▪ **Note** You can still add tables after you've closed the Add Table window. Do not worry that it represents your one and only chance to include a table in a query. You can add a new table at any time.

---

Select both the **Products** and **ProductsComponents** tables as shown in Figure 15-2, and click the Add button followed by the Close button.

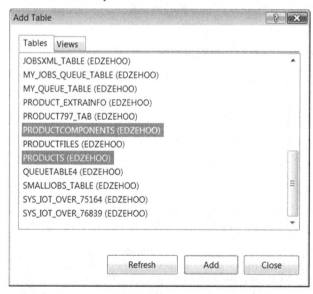

*Figure 15-2. Adding tables to the visual query designer*

Once you've closed the Add Table window, you can see the visual query designer show underneath. The two tables are represented as two small windows in the designer area. You can drag these windows around as you wish. You can also form a relationship between two columns by dragging a column and dropping it on another column in the other table.

In the current example, you need to form an **INNER JOIN** relationship between the **ParentProductID** column of the **ProductComponents** table and the **ID** column of the **Products** table. Drag the **ParentProductID** column, and drop it on the **ID** column in the **Products** table. A link will instantly form between these two fields. This is shown in Figure 15-3. You can also see that the full SQL query is automatically regenerated each time you make any changes in the visual designer area. You can run the generated query by right-clicking the SQL query area and selecting the Execute SQL item (the one with the red exclamation point icon) in the ensuing pop-up menu.

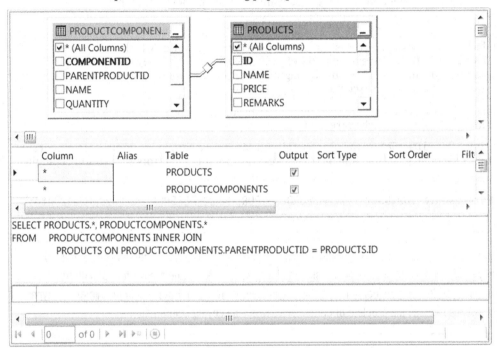

*Figure 15-3. Using the visual query designer*

The following list contains some of the main reasons why you might want to use the ODT.NET visual design feature in your project:

- Create complex SQL queries faster via drag and drop; you no longer have to remember column names when specifying table joins.

- Viewing relationships between multiple tables in a single query is easier.

# Generating Strongly Typed DataSet Objects

A **DataSet** is said to be strongly typed when the data type of its columns are predefined and fixed. In Chapter 4, you dealt mostly with generic **DataSet** objects. Consider the following code that accesses a date column in a **DataSet**:

```
_PODate = _DataSet.Tables[0].Rows[0].Item("PurchaseOrderDate");
```

This type of **DataSet**, a weakly typed **DataSet**, suffers from the following problems:

- You must remember and correctly specify the name of the desired column.

- It lacks IntelliSense support for column and table names.

- It lacks type checking. If you assign the **PurchaseOrderDate** value (which was created as a **DATE** object in the database) to an integer variable, for example, the resulting type mismatch will not be caught during compile time. Instead, your statement will throw an exception during run time.

- It lacks built-in **NULL** checking; you need to write your own code to handle NULL values in the **PurchaseOrderDate** column.

With a strongly typed **DataSet** on the other hand, you can write a simple assignment statement such as the following, and you'll detect any and all of the previously mentioned errors early, during compile time.

```
_PODate = PurchaseOrderDataSet.PURCHASEORDERS.PURCHASEORDERSROW.PurchaseOrderDate;
```

---

■ **Note** One of the biggest advantages of strongly typing **DataSet** objects is that the names and columns of a table are already predefined, and hence appear inside the IntelliSense menus (the menus that pop up frequently in Visual Studio as you type to help you look for a particular function or property). Having column names and types appear in those menus reduces the problem of human error when specifying column names.

---

To create a strongly typed **DataSet**, you must first setup a data source. Click the Data ➤ Add New Data Source menu item in the Visual Studio IDE. You will see the window in Figure 15-4 displayed. Choose to create a database object. Click the Next button to proceed.

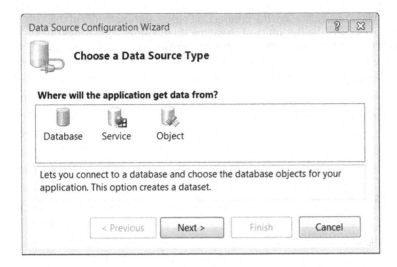

*Figure 15-4. Creating a data source*

In the next window, you will be required to select a data connection to use for the data source. Choose the data connection that you've created in the previous chapter (as shown in Figure 15-5).

*Figure 15-5. Selecting a data connection*

The Data Source Configuration Wizard can also save the connection string automatically in the **app.config** file of your project. This gives users the flexibility of changing their connection strings later from the **app.config** file. Select the "Yes, save the connection as" option, and give the connection string entry a name. In the sample screenshot shown in Figure 15-6, I use the name MyOracleConnection.

*Figure 15-6. Saving the connection to the app.config file*

Next, the wizard will bring you to the screen shown in Figure 15-7. Here, you can choose which database objects to include in the strongly typed dataset.

---

■ **Tip** Do keep in mind that a single **DataSet** object can be composed of multiple table objects.

---

Since your strongly typed **DataSet** will only contain the **Products** table, select the PRODUCTS item. You can also give your **DataSet** object a name. Do take note that this is the name that you will be using to refer to your **DataSet** class from code.

*Figure 15-7. Including the Products table in the strongly typed dataset*

Next, you will be able to see the **Products DataSet** in your Data Sources window. At this point, you might need to edit the generated **DataSet** object. For example, if you proceed to use the **DataSet** you have created up to this point, the **DataAdapter** and **Command** objects that ODT.NET automatically generates for you later on will, by default, retrieve all data from the specified table. Your query is basically equivalent to:

```
SELECT * FROM PRODUCTS
```

However, you might wish for a more specific query. For example, you might wish for only Product IDs that begin with the letter "E", as would be returned by the following statement:

```
SELECT * FROM PRODUCTS WHERE PRODUCTID LIKE 'E%'
```

Fortunately ODT.NET allows you to edit a generated **DataSet** and its accompanying adapter objects. You can do so by right-clicking your **DataSet** in the Data Sources window and choosing the "Edit DataSet with Designer" menu item (as shown in Figure 15-8).

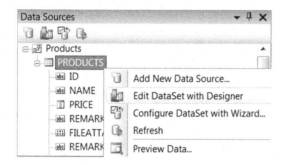

*Figure 15-8. Editing a generated DataSet*

You will be brought to the window shown in Figure 15-9 where you can visually see the details of the **DataSet** object. As you can see, there is already an adapter object created for the **DataSet**. This adapter object retrieves all rows from the table by default. Right-click it, and choose the Configure menu item.

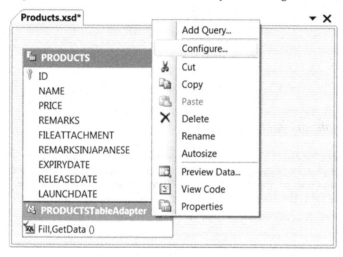

*Figure 15-9. Configuring TableAdapter settings*

When you have done that, a new window will be displayed. You will initially see that the default SQL retrieves all results from the table. Add a filter (a **WHERE** clause) to the SQL statement, as shown in Figure 15-10. When you have done that, click the Finish button. Visual Studio will regenerate the corresponding data access objects.

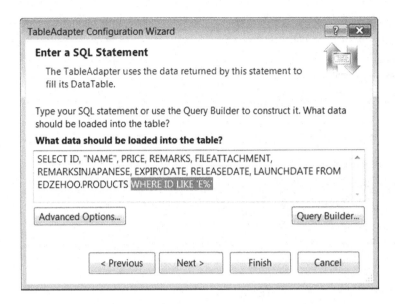

*Figure 15-10. Editing the TableAdapter SQL query*

It's now time to use your strongly typed **DataSet**! Add a new form to your project. Let's say you wanted to display the data in a **DataGridView** control. How do you go about that? Simply drag the **DataSet** from the Data Sources window into the form!

Once you drag the **DataSet** into your form, you will notice that ODT.NET has created a nice **DataGridView** control for you, complete with record navigation controls, a button to insert new data to the table, a button to delete existing data from the table, and even a Save button to save updates made in the grid. This can be seen in Figure 15-11. What is even cooler is that ODT.NET has done all the underlying work of mapping the **DataSet** to the grid! You can in fact run this form as it is without having to write any further line of code.

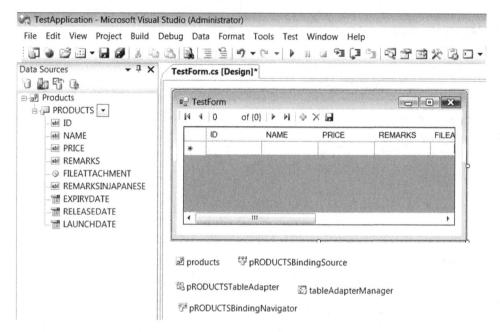

*Figure 15-11. Data access controls automatically generated by ODT.NET*

If you open the code-behind file of this form, you will be able to see the code generated by ODT.NET to power this interface (shown in Figure 15-12). You can still freely edit this code if you wish to tweak the behavior of the form further.

```
TestApplication.TestForm                          TestForm()
        {
            InitializeComponent();
        }

        private void pRODUCTSBindingNavigatorSaveItem_Click(object sender, EventArgs
        {
            this.Validate();
            this.pRODUCTSBindingSource.EndEdit();
            this.tableAdapterManager.UpdateAll(this.products);

        }

        private void TestForm_Load(object sender, EventArgs e)
        {
            // TODO: This line of code loads data into the 'products.PRODUCTS' table
            this.pRODUCTSTableAdapter.Fill(this.products.PRODUCTS);
        }
```

*Figure 15-12. Data access code auto-generated by ODT.NET*

If you try running this form without any changes, you will immediately see your data displayed in the grid control, as shown in Figure 15-13. Take note that only records with Product IDs beginning with the letter "E" are displayed (based on what you specified earlier).

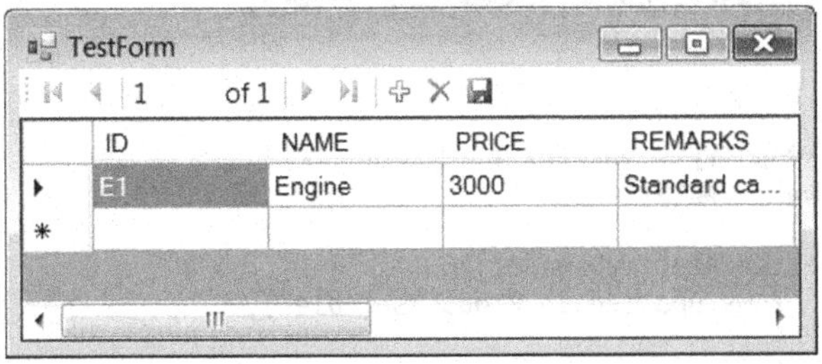

*Figure 15-13. Running the automatically generated UI*

You can even try adding a new record via this automatically generated interface. Click the yellow plus button. A new row will appear in the grid. Specify some dummy data in the various columns. I will use a product named "**Sample record keyed in via UI**" in my example. When you are finished, click the blue disk Save icon. This will prompt the **TableAdapter** object to run an **INSERT** statement against the **Products** table. You can verify that the record was created by running a **SELECT** query against the **Products** table via SQL*Plus, as shown in Figure 15-14.

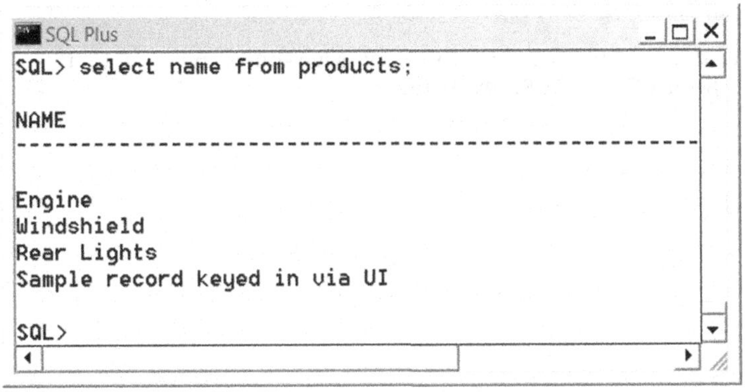

*Figure 15-14. Verifying that the new record was inserted correctly*

At this point, you have yet to use the strongly typed **DataSet** in your code. Now, you will write some code to insert a new product manually via code using the strongly typed **DataSet**. Add a new button to the form, and in the click event of this button, write the code shown in Listing 15-1.

*Listing 15-1. Adding a New Product Programmatically via a Strongly Typed DataSet*

```
private void btnAddNewProduct_Click(object sender, EventArgs e)
{
        Products _myDataSet = new Products();
```

```
this.pRODUCTSTableAdapter.Fill(_myDataSet.PRODUCTS);

//Create and add a new product to the DataSet
Products.PRODUCTSRow _newProduct = _myDataSet.PRODUCTS.NewPRODUCTSRow();
_newProduct.ID = "C5";
_newProduct.NAME = "Cleaner Fluid";
_newProduct.PRICE = 250;
_newProduct.REMARKS = "Added via a strong typed dataset";
_myDataSet.PRODUCTS.AddPRODUCTSRow(_newProduct);

int _Result = this.pRODUCTSTableAdapter.Update(_myDataSet);
MessageBox.Show(_Result.ToString() + " rows updated in Products table");
}
```

When you typed the code in Listing 15-1, you would have realized a few things:

- Column and table names would instantly appear in the IntelliSense pop-up windows. This makes the locating of table columns easier and cuts out human error (for example, specifying the wrong table column name).

- The **NULL** check functions are readily available for each column in the **DataSet**.

- All columns are strongly typed. For instance, you cannot assign a string object to a numerical-based column. This lets you detect data mismatch errors at compile time rather than at run time.

If you run the form and click the button, you will see the pop-up message shown in Figure 15-15, denoting that the row was successfully inserted into the **Products** table.

**Figure 15-15.** *A row successfully inserted into the Products table.*

The following list contains some of the main reasons why you might want to use the ODT.NET strongly typed **DataSet** feature in your project:

- *Easy to code*: Table and column names appear in IntelliSense.

- *Data type checking*: Data mismatch errors are caught at compile time rather than at run time.

- *Less room for human error*: The possibility of column and table names being wrongly spelled or typed is eliminated.

- *Saves time via code generation:* Strongly typed datasets work tightly with the .NET DataAdapter class. Visual Studio automatically generates the `Fill` and `Update` functions in these adapters.

# Generating UDT Classes

As you've seen in Chapter 5, creating a class to represent a UDT object is not particularly difficult, but it can be a rather tedious job. This problem is magnified when you have tables containing large numbers of columns. Human error may also arise if you frequently hand-code such classes, unnecessarily wasting time in debugging these classes later on.

Fortunately, ODT.NET provides you a way to visually define UDT objects *and* to generate the corresponding .NET classes from these UDT objects. In this section, you will create a sample application to display a list of jobs from the database. This list of jobs will utilize an **EMPLOYEE** UDT as the data type for one of its fields. You will learn how to use ODT.NET to create this UDT and also generate the code to read the values of this UDT.

## Designing a UDT Object Visually

To visually create a UDT object, expand the data connection and right-click the User-Defined Types node in the Server Explorer. In the ensuing pop-up menu, select the New Object Type item shown in Figure 15-16.

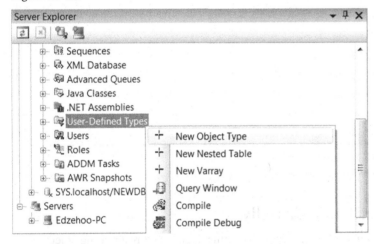

***Figure 15-16.*** *Creating a new UDT visually*

When you have done that, the screen shown in Figure 15-17 will appear. It allows you to visually define the properties and attributes of the UDT. You can specify the name of the UDT under the "Type name" field. Create the attributes of the UDT as shown in Figure 15-17. Try to use a mix of **NVARCHAR2** and **NUMBER** data types.

You can also click the Preview SQL button to look at the corresponding SQL syntax generated to create the UDT. When you have finished designing the UDT, click the OK button to create it. You will be able to see the created UDT in the User-Defined Types node in the Server Explorer.

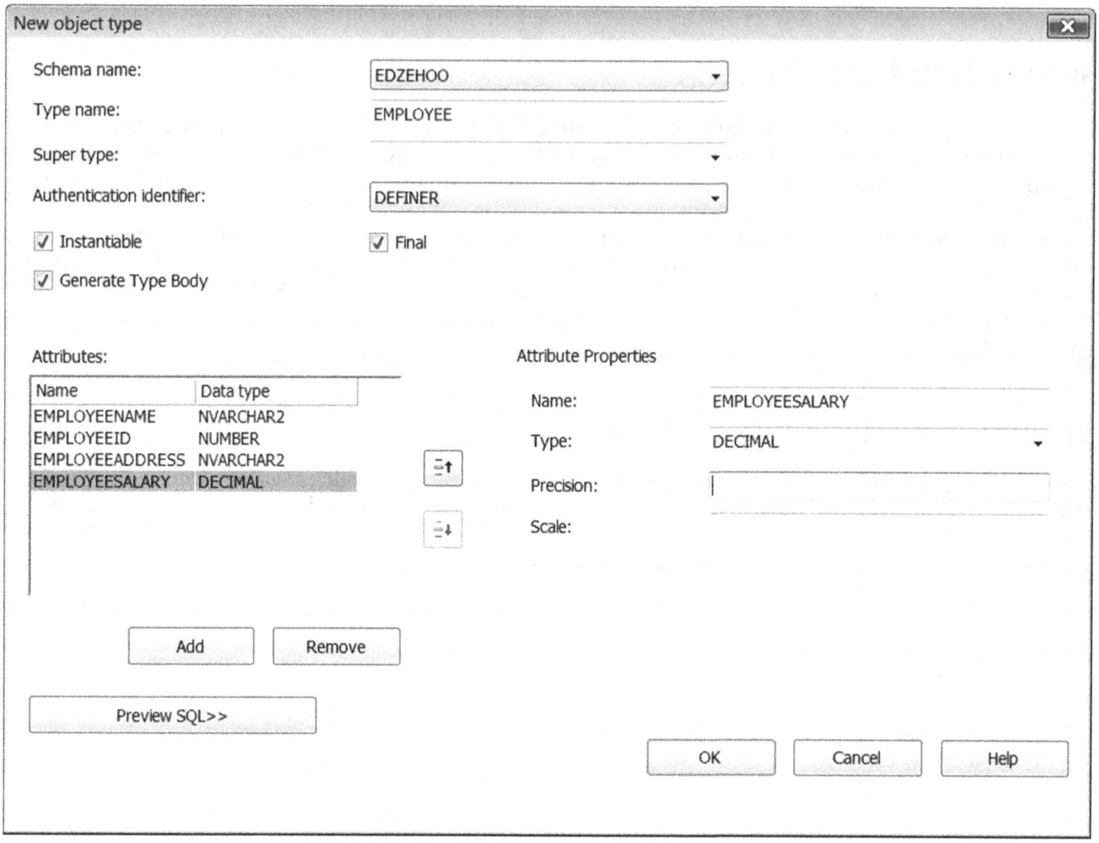

**Figure 15-17.** *Creating a new UDT visually*

## Creating the UDT Object Table Visually

Creating the **Employee** UDT is not enough to begin using it. You must create a corresponding object table to store **Employee** UDT objects.

---

■ **Note** An object table is different from a standard relational table. Object tables are used to store UDT objects instead of relational data. In an object table, each row represents an object, referred to as a row object.

---

To create an object table, right-click the Tables node in the Server Explorer, and choose the New Object Table menu item (as shown in Figure 15-18).

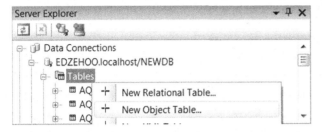

*Figure 15-18. Creating a new object table*

You will now see the object table designer (shown in Figure 15-19), where you can specify the name of the table and the UDT of the objects it will store. In this same window, you will be able to specify other attributes of the table such as constraints, indexes (if any) and storage parameters. Specify **EMPLOYEE_TAB** as the name of the table, and select the **EMPLOYEE** UDT you've created earlier as the object type.

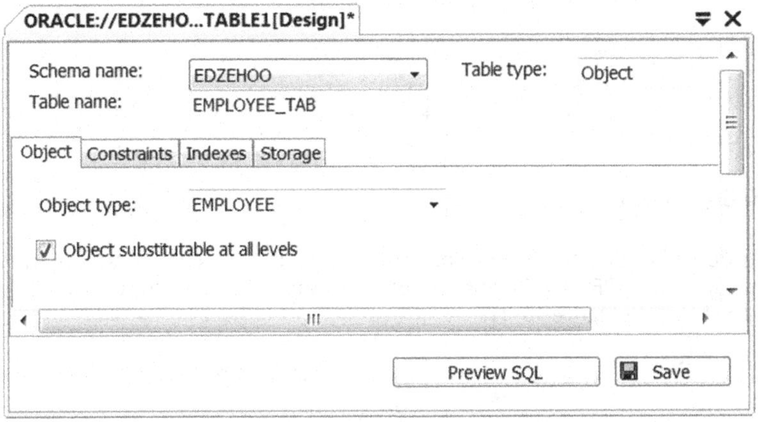

*Figure 15-19. Specifying the details of the object table*

When you are finished, click the Save button to generate the object table. You will be able to see the **EMPLOYEE_TAB** table displayed in the Server Explorer.

## Creating the OVERSEAS_JOBS Table

Our little sample application will try to display a list of jobs in the database. Each job will have a Person in Charge column, and its data type would be the **EMPLOYEE** UDT you've created earlier. You will need to create a new relational table to store the job records.

Right-click the Tables node in the Server Explorer, and choose the New Relational Table menu item to create a new relational table. Specify **OVERSEAS_JOBS** as the name of this table. Create the columns as shown in Figure 15-20 . Take note that the **PERSON_IN_CHARGE** column should be created as an **EMPLOYEE** UDT.

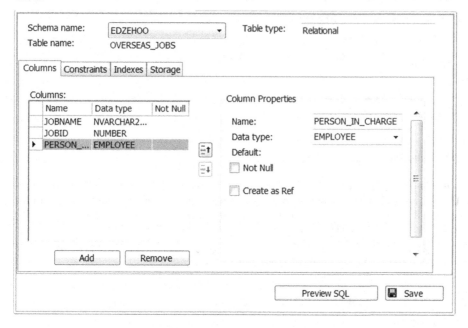

*Figure 15-20. Defining the OVERSEAS_JOBS table*

Click the Save button to continue. This will generate the corresponding table, which you can see in the Server Explorer window. If you expand the **PERSON_IN_CHARGE** column, you will be able to see the details and attributes of the UDT, as shown in Figure 15-21.

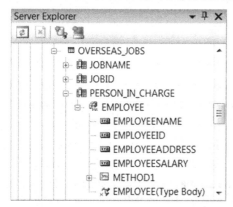

*Figure 15-21. The OVERSEAS_JOBS table*

To run the code samples later on, you will need to key in some data into the **OVERSEAS_JOBS** table. To insert a UDT object, you can specify it in this format:

```
UDT_NAME(<fieldvalue1>, <fieldvalue2>, <fieldvalue3>)
```

Run the following SQL statements either through the ODT.NET query window or through SQL*Plus:

```
INSERT INTO OVERSEAS_JOBS(JOBNAME,JOBID,PERSON_IN_CHARGE)
VALUES ('DELIVERY JOB',1,EMPLOYEE('EDZEHOO',1234,'Fifth Avenue HQ',9000));
INSERT INTO OVERSEAS_JOBS(JOBNAME,JOBID,PERSON_IN_CHARGE)
VALUES ('DELIVERY JOB',2,EMPLOYEE('GREGYAP',5678,'Nanjing Road Shanghai',9000));
INSERT INTO OVERSEAS_JOBS(JOBNAME,JOBID,PERSON_IN_CHARGE)
VALUES ('CLEANING JOB',3,EMPLOYEE('HUISHEN',3338,'Ishimura Doori Tokyo',6000));
```

## Generating the UDT Classes

Now that you have gone through all the preceding setup, you need to be able to access these UDT objects in your .NET code. ODT.NET supports the ability to automatically generate .NET classes from existing UDT objects.

To generate the needed UDT classes, expand the User-Defined Types node in the Server Explorer, and right-click the **EMPLOYEE** UDT object. Select the Generate Custom Class menu item in the ensuing pop-up window, as shown in Figure15-22.

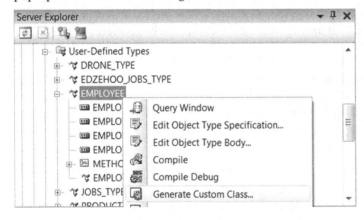

***Figure 15-22.*** *Generating the UDT classes*

Once you have done that, you will be able to see the wizard shown in Figure 15-23. This wizard will generate .NET classes in a variety of languages for Oracle UDTs.

**Figure 15-23.** *The UDT Custom Class Wizard*

Click the Next button to proceed. You should be able to see the screen displayed in Figure 15-24. This screen allows you to specify the name of the class and class files that will be generated by ODT.NET.

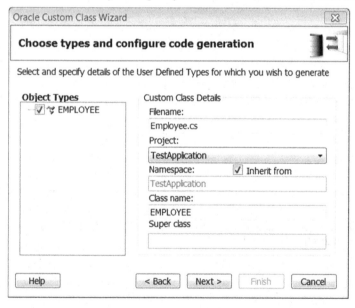

**Figure 15-24.** *Specifying the class details for the UDT*

Click the Next button again to proceed. This time ,the wizard will allow you to map each UDT attribute to the desired .NET data type, as shown in Figure 15-25. This can be useful when you want to pass a string to a property in the UDT class, for example, but have it save and retrieve data to and from the underlying UDT as an integer.

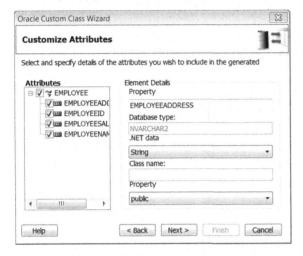

*Figure 15-25. Specifying property details*

After you are finished, click the Next button to complete the wizard. A UDT class file named **Employee.cs** will be generated in your project. If you open this file, you will see something similar to Figure 15-26. Notice that the UDT attributes are represented as properties in this class.

```
TestApplication.EMPLOYEE                      ▼  m_IsNull                              ▼
        public class EMPLOYEE : INullable, IOracleCustomType, IXmlSerializ

            private bool m_IsNull;

            private string m_EMPLOYEEADDRESS;

            private decimal m_EMPLOYEEID;

            private bool m_EMPLOYEEIDIsNull;

            private decimal m_EMPLOYEESALARY;

            private bool m_EMPLOYEESALARYIsNull;

            private string m_EMPLOYEENAME;

            public EMPLOYEE() {
                // TODO : Add code to initialise the object
                this.m_EMPLOYEEIDIsNull = true;
                this.m_EMPLOYEESALARYIsNull = true;
            }
```

*Figure 15-26. Generated UDT class*

419

## Using the UDT in Your Project

Now for the last step—this is where it all comes together. You will list all the jobs from the **OVERSEAS_JOBS** table in a **DataGridView** control. The purpose of doing this is to see if you can retrieve the data from the **PERSON_IN_CHARGE** column (the **EMPLOYEE UDT**) and display it appropriately. If you recall from the earlier sections, you could easily generate the UI for any table using ODT.NET. You will use the same method to generate the Jobs grid.

Add a new data source to your project (like how you've done earlier in this chapter), and include the **OVERSEAS_JOBS** table in the new **DataSet**. Specify **Overseas_Jobs** as the name of the **DataSet**, as shown in Figure 15-27 .

*Figure 15-27. Creating a data source from the OVERSEAS_JOBS table*

Now, add a new form to your project. Drag the **Overseas_Jobs** data source from the Data Sources window into the form (as you've done earlier in this chapter). This will generate the data grid and all the accompanying controls, as shown in Figure 15-28.

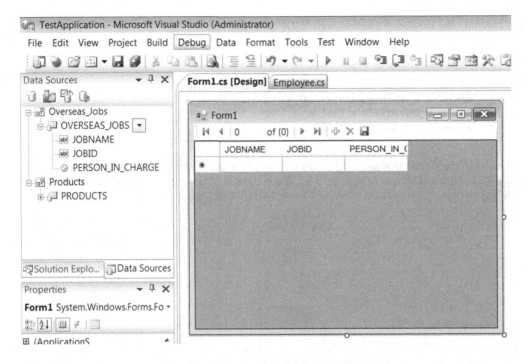

*Figure 15-28. The generated UI for the Overseas_Jobs data source*

Now, if you were to run this form, you can see that it will list the three records you've inserted earlier, as shown in Figure 15-29. Notice however, that the **PERSON_IN_CHARGE** column shows nothing! This is because the generated UDT class does not have a **ToString()** method defined yet, so it is unable to represent the UDT class as a string (which is needed to display an object in a grid).

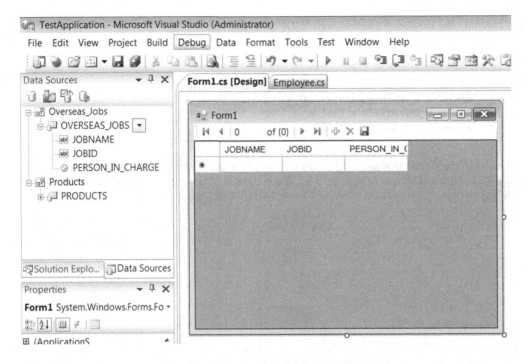

*Figure 15-29. The OVERSEAS_JOBS records displayed in the data grid*

You will now write some code in this **ToString()** method. Open the **Employee.cs** class file, and write the highlighted code shown in Listing 15-2. This will tell the UDT object to represent itself using the **Name**, **ID**, and **Salary** fields of the employee.

*Listing 15-2. Defining the ToString() Method in the UDT Class File*

```
public override string ToString()
{
        // TODO : Return a string that represents the current object
        return  "Name:" + m_EMPLOYEENAME + "\n" +
                "ID:" + m_EMPLOYEEID + "\n" +
                "Salary:" + m_EMPLOYEESALARY;
}
```

Now try running the same form again. This time, you will see some data appear in the
**PERSON_IN_CHARGE** column, as shown in Figure 15-30. If you mouse-over the data, you will be able to see
the individual properties of the UDT (as you've defined via the **ToString()** function).

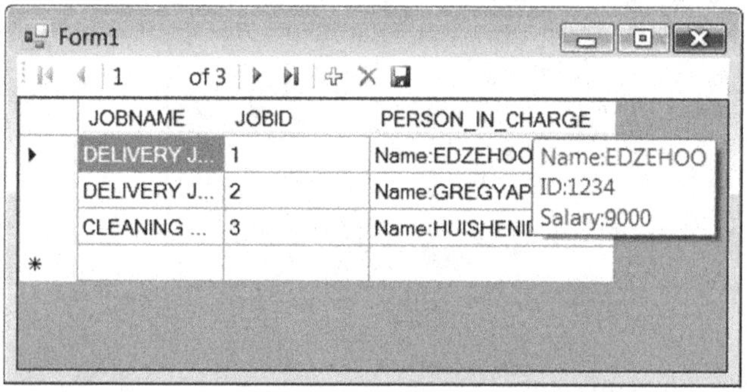

*Figure 15-30. The details of the PERSON_IN_CHARGE column*

What's important to note from this exercise is that you could individually refer to each attribute of
the UDT as a class property in your .NET code. UDT classes have the benefit of strongly-typing UDT
objects in the database—they allow you to pass UDT objects around in your code and to manipulate
them just like any other class.

Attribute names are strongly typed, which reduces human error and improves integration with
IntelliSense. On top of that, ODT.NET now makes it easier than ever to generate .NET classes from large
UDT objects, removing the mundane and tedious parts of your ODP.NET development experience.

The following list contains some of the main reasons why you might want to use the ODT.NET UDT
class generation features in your project:

- *Saves time*: Generating UDT classes is much easier than coding them by hand.

- *Less prone to human error*: Letting ODT.NET generate the code from a UDT object
  reduces potential problems arising from human error.

- *Easier to manage and more flexible*: You can visually map each UDT attribute to a
  .NET data type. This makes it easier to specify how your UDT attributes are
  represented in the generated .NET class.

# Generating ASP.NET Code

If you are an ASP.NET developer working with the SQL Server database, at one point or another you would definitely have come across a feature in Visual Studio that allows you to generate an ASP.NET **GridView** by specifying a SQL Server–based data source. Visual Studio will generate the code to bind your grid to the **DataAdapter** and **Command** objects of the data source.

When you install ODT.NET, this feature will also work together with the ODP.NET provider. What this means is that you will be able to easily generate ASP.NET **GridView** objects (via a few clicks) by specifying an Oracle-based data source. In this section, we will create a simple application to demonstrate this.

Start by creating a new ASP.NET web application. Drag a **GridView** control to the default web page. Click the little arrow in the top-right corner of this control, and choose to create a new data source, as shown in Figure 15-31.

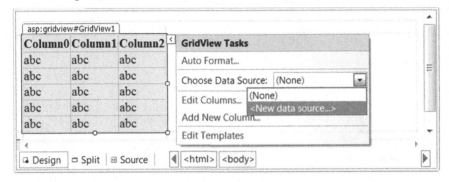

*Figure 15-31. Creating a new data source for the GridView control*

After you have done this, the screen shown in Figure 15-32 will appear. You will be able to choose a data source type. Select the Database icon, and specify an ID for the data source. You can use any name you wish.

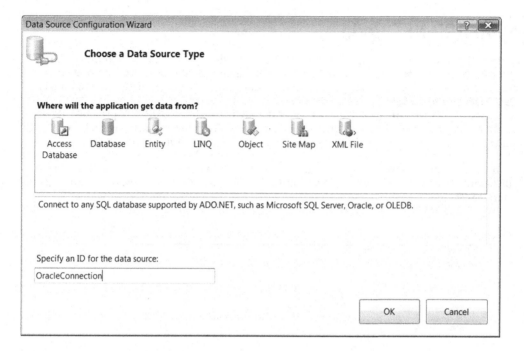

**Figure 15-32.** *Creating the Oracle data source*

After you click the OK button, you will see the window shown in Figure 15-33. This window allows you to pick the database object to use as a data source. Let's try to display the list of products from the **Products** table. You probably don't want to display all the columns, so check only the first four columns. Take note that you can also define the **WHERE** and **ORDER BY** clauses of the SQL statement using the buttons on the right.

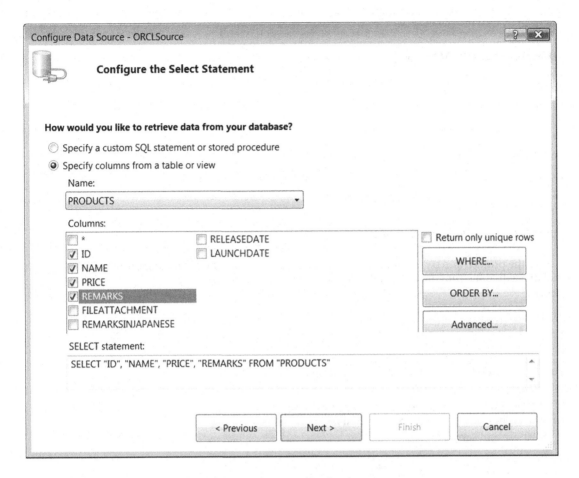

*Figure 15-33. Configuring the SQL SELECT statement for the data source*

After you click the Next button to proceed, you can observe that Visual Studio has done the binding between the data source and the grid. The names of the columns you have selected will appear in the header of the grid, as shown in Figure 15-34.

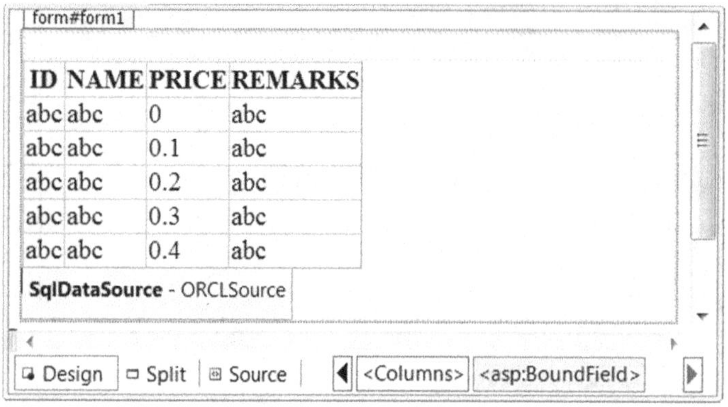
form#form1
ID NAME PRICE REMARKS
abc abc 0 abc
abc abc 0.1 abc
abc abc 0.2 abc
abc abc 0.3 abc
abc abc 0.4 abc
SqlDataSource - ORCLSource
Design
Split
Source
<Columns>
<asp:BoundField>

***Figure 15-34.*** *The data source-bound grid.*

Save the project, and try running the web site. You will see that the data grid is automatically populated with data from the **PRODUCTS** table, as shown in Figure 15-35.

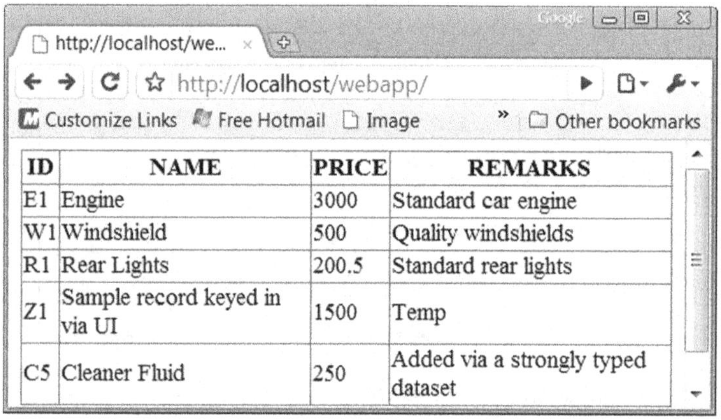
http://localhost/we...
http://localhost/webapp/
Customize Links
Free Hotmail
Image
Other bookmarks
ID NAME PRICE REMARKS
E1 Engine 3000 Standard car engine
W1 Windshield 500 Quality windshields
R1 Rear Lights 200.5 Standard rear lights
Z1 Sample record keyed in via UI 1500 Temp
C5 Cleaner Fluid 250 Added via a strongly typed dataset

***Figure 15-35.*** *The populated data grid displayed in the browser*

The following list contains some of the main reasons why you might want to use the ODT.NET ASP.NET code generation features in your project:

- You can save time by not having to write code to handle simple data entry and row display screens. This feature works great when your SQL queries are straightforward, and you have many tables to display in your website.
- It reduces the learning curve for `SqlConnection` users. If you are familiar with generating ASP.NET interfaces and code using the `SqlConnection` data source model provided by ASP.NET, using `OracleConnection` is no different, since it plugs in to this framework seamlessly.

# Summary

In this final chapter, you've taken a look at the advanced code generation functionality in the ODT.NET package. You've learned how to use ODT.NET to accomplish the following:

- Visually design a query within the Visual Studio IDE

- Generate strongly typed **DataSet** objects

- Visually design a UDT object

- Generate .NET classes from UDT objects

- Generate ASP.NET code from Oracle objects

In conclusion, ODP.NET and ODT.NET make a powerful product combination that harnesses the power of the Oracle database and exposes them to you in the familiar .NET environment. We've now reached the end of this book, and I hope these pages have given you deeper insight into a tool that will help you build compelling Oracle database applications that run faster, more securely, and do much more.

# Index

# O